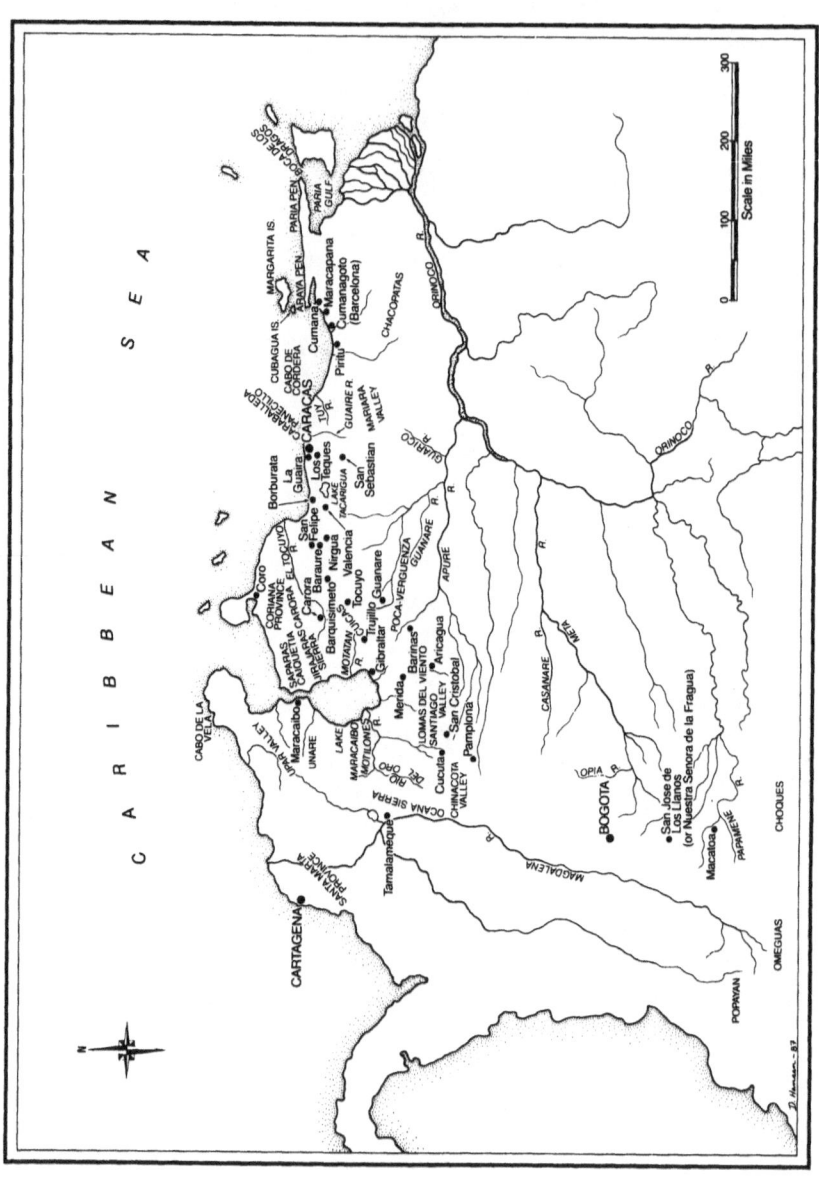

# THE CONQUEST AND SETTLEMENT OF VENEZUELA

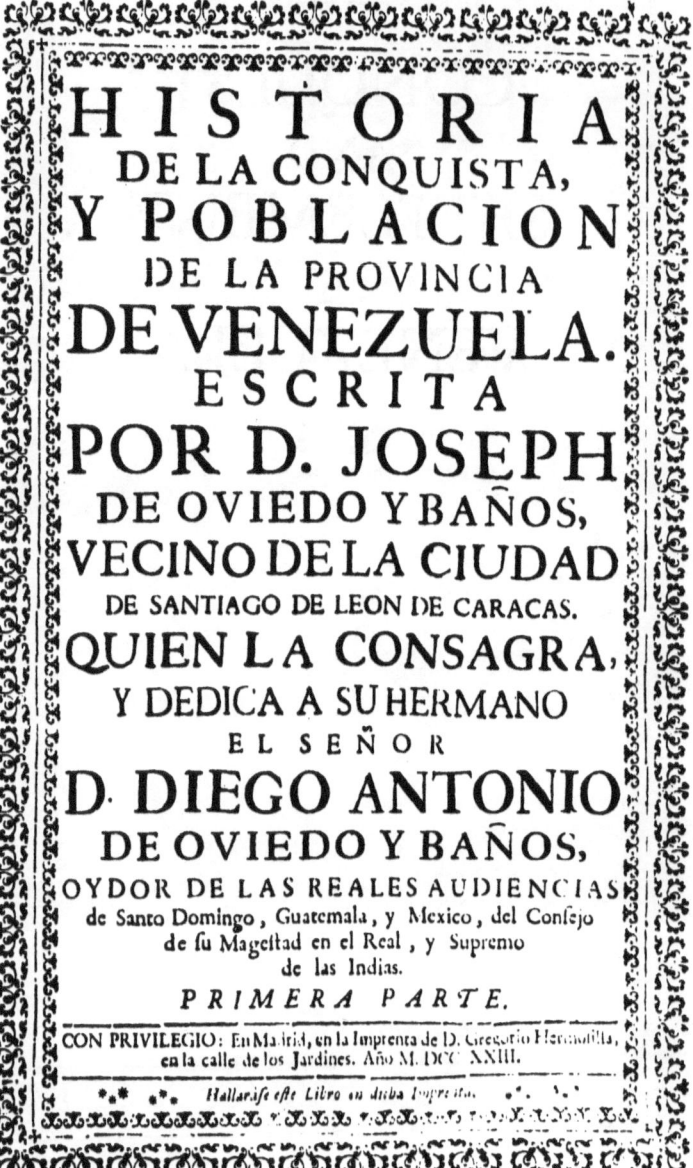

Written by Don José de Oviedo y Baños, resident of the city of Santiago de León de Caracas, who consecrates it to his brother, Sr. Don Diego Antonio de Oviedo y Baños, judge of the Royal Audiencias of Santo Domingo, Guatemala and Mexico of His Majesty's Royal and Supreme Council of the Indies.

Exclusive Rights: In Madrid, The Printing House of Don Gregorio Hermosilla, Calle de los Jardines, where this book may be found, 1723.

# THE CONQUEST AND SETTLEMENT OF VENEZUELA

DON JOSÉ DE OVIEDO Y BAÑOS

Translation, Introduction, and Annotations by
JEANNETTE JOHNSON VARNER

UNIVERSITY OF CALIFORNIA PRESS
Berkeley  Los Angeles  London

The publishers wish to express their gratitude to Joan Palevsky for her generous contribution to the publication of this book.

University of California Press
Berkeley and Los Angeles, California

University of California Press, Ltd.
London, England

Copyright © 1987 by The Regents of the University of California

Library of Congress Cataloging-in-Publication Data

Oviedo y Baños, José de, 1671–1738.
   The conquest and settlement of Venezuela.

   Translation of: Historia de la conquista y población de la provincia de Venezuela.
   Bibliography: p.
   Includes index.
   1. Venezuela—History—To 1810.   I. Varner, Jeannette Johnson, 1909–   .  II. Title.
F2322.09613      1987      987'.02      86–24896

ISBN 978-0-520-30135-1 (pbk. : alk. paper)

To the memory of my husband, John Grier Varner, whose love for Venezuela was exceeded only by his devotion to Texas, land of his birth.

# CONTENTS

| | |
|---|---|
| Foreword | ix |
| Acknowledgments | xiii |
| Introduction | xv |
| THE CONQUEST AND SETTLEMENT OF VENEZUELA | 1 |
| Dedication | 3 |
| Prologue to the Reader | 5 |
| Annotations | 267 |
| Glossary | 279 |
| Select Bibliography | 285 |
| Index | 289 |

# FOREWORD

The Spanish conquest of America was an epic event whose grandeur and scale amazed contemporaries as well as subsequent generations of historians. Thanks to the elegant prose of William H. Prescott's masterpieces of historical narrative, *The Conquest of Mexico* and *The Conquest of Peru,* the bold invasion of Mexico, the heroic struggle for domination of the Inca highlands, and the image of the great Amerindian civilizations have passed into the common knowledge of the English-speaking world. Unfortunately, the vision of Spain's mission in the New World lacks both breadth and depth. While the exploits of Cortés, made forever vivid by the contemporary chronicle of Bernal Díaz del Castillo, rivet our attention to the glamorous, heroic and tragic events of the 1520s, the conquest of Mexico City represents but one glorious moment in what was a several-generation campaign by Spain to dominate the Americas. The less elegant conquest of Peru by the Pizarros became only the second and certainly the last of the heroic conquests.

Where most English-speaking readers leave off studying the conquest of America is precisely where it actually began. It was in the long, tedious, unglamorous, arduous and terribly destructive campaigns of the sixteenth and even into the seventeenth century that America became Spain's territory. Without those efforts, no less heroic than Cortés's or Pizarro's, the Spanish empire in America would never have existed. What Jeannette Johnson Varner brings us in her fine translation of Don José de Oviedo y Baños's *The Conquest and Settlement of Venezuela* is the real thing, the continuing, organic conquest of America. In the same way that Díaz del Castillo brought the gritty reality of conquest to the heroic exaltation of Cortés, Oviedo y Baños offered a clear vision of the process of conquest after the fall of Mexico and Peru. Few texts exist in English that so vividly portray the nature and dynamic of this generation of conquest.

The history of Venezuela's conquest has often been dominated by discussions of the peculiar and anomalous arrangement that delivered the early rights of conquest and exploitation of the Venezuelan mainland to Charles V's bankers, the Welsers. This concession of government and exploration rights to foreigners intrigues the historian because it is different, and in pursuing the Welser connection the main thread of the conquest itself often disappears. Oviedo's remarkable work helps restore the balance, and this excellent translation makes the history available to English-speaking readers.

## FOREWORD

What can be learned from a reading and re-reading of this fascinating chronicle? Experts, of course, must read it in the Spanish original, for the power of language and the nuance of expression will help shape interpretation and verify assertion. But for the rest of us, interested in understanding the flow of the conquest, the motives of the conquistadors and the persistence of exploration, this elegant translation offers a wonderfully accessible view of the Spanish perspective on America. To be sure, Oviedo y Baños wrote from the comfortable prosperity of eighteenth-century Caracas, secure in its sophistication and wealth. He spoke of a distant time, and his sources included documents, tradition and hearsay. Historians have found errors in his text, have established flaws in some of the details of his narrative, but no one has been able to dispute the grand sweep of his story. Oviedo transcended his own time and place to do what all great historians attempt—he brought the past to life in the present.

When reading *The Conquest and Settlement of Venezuela* we first stumble over the archaic style and leisurely rhythms of Oviedo y Baños's prose, carefully preserved in this translation. But as we persist, his story captures our imagination, we become involved with the characters and the conquests, and in the end we vicariously join the conquests to experience a portion of what it must have been like.

The preconceptions of modern scientific thought often blind us to the accomplishments of a prescientific age. Oviedo's story helps refract our myopia, restoring a more complete historical vision. To understand the generations of conquest, we must comprehend their lack of reliable information about the world they explored. Their persistent pursuit of nonexistent geographies and imaginary Amerindian empires becomes understandable in Oviedo's painstaking descriptions of the conquerors' motives and ambitions. Without Oviedo, we tend to recoil at the destructive quality of this American conquest, failing to understand it in our righteous rejection of violence. *The Conquest and Settlement of Venezuela* offers a perspective on the leaders and soldiers in these expeditions. They had short life spans, endured hardships and privations that transcend our understanding, and yet, failure after failure, they continued to pursue their dream until by virtue of trial and error, death, destruction and acquired experience, they dominated the land.

Oviedo's exceptional narrative skill draws much of its credibility and immediacy from his enthusiasm for the heroes and villains of the conquest. Clearly a man of steady judgment and unwavering standards, Oviedo distributes his opinions with a judicious clarity that lends strength to the narrative itself. Oviedo had a perspective, a point of view. He assumed no false neutrality, no unreliable impartiality. Instead, he wrote in order to record the heroic deeds of the Spanish conquerors of Venezuela. The heroes were those Spanish conquistadors, soldiers, generals, clerics and civil servants whose sacrifices and skills made possible Spain's remarkable empire in America. Yet, although the Spanish point of view was clear and paramount, and the justice of the conquest never in doubt, Oviedo y Baños had nothing but respect for heroism, wherever exhibited. No anthropologist or cultural relativist, Oviedo saw the Indian inhabitants as barbarians whose resistance impeded the successful conquest of America. But his enthusiasm for the Spanish enterprise rarely obscured his understanding of Indian or Spanish motives.

Especially revealing is his extended discussion of the long, bloody and difficult conquest of the Valley of Caracas. Each of the Indian chieftains appears in Oviedo's narrative complete with personality and character. Oviedo portrays these Indians not as cardboard villains, but as skillful, creative adversaries, tenaciously holding on to their domains. Oviedo saw the conquest as a conflict not exactly between equals but between respectable and admirable adversaries. He admired the Indian leader Guaicaipuro for his ability to organize a coordinated resistance among many disparate tribes. He provides carefully detailed descriptions of Indian heroism in the face of Spanish arms, heroism that balances equivalent stories of Spanish success. The soldier or leader who died heroically deserves praise and fame. Indians, although clearly the enemy to be dominated, earned Oviedo's respect and consideration. They, too, were heroes of the conquest.

While the preservation of a historical memory of the heroes of the conquest formed an important theme for Oviedo's work, we learn even more about the drive, goals and methods of the sixteenth-century conqueror. The conquistadors depicted in *The Conquest and Settlement of Venezuela* exhibited a remarkable entrepreneurial spirit. They invested their energy, goods and resources in these expeditions in search of greater reward. While they knew little or nothing about the geography and opportunities, they based their chances of success or failure on the quality of leadership provided. Poor leaders, or those with a record of failure, had a hard time putting together reasonable expeditions. But even with the best leaders and the most careful preparation, most expeditions ended in disaster. These enterprises had a truly remarkable failure rate. Two hundred men went out, thirty returned alive after two years of long marches through inhospitable land, attacks by hostile natives and hunger and disease. Yet, the lure of the unknown and therefore incalculable profit, and the afterimage of Mexico and Peru, kept these incurably optimistic entrepreneurs returning time and again to test the harsh, imperfectly understood environment. Of course, accumulated experience eventually provided the knowledge needed for a successful conquest, and the superior arms, tactics and determination of the Spaniards gradually overcame the obstacles of nature and natives.

Among the more famous episodes in this history, the account of the exploits of the Tyrant, Lope de Aguirre, illustrates Oviedo y Baños's narrative and historical powers especially well. Clearly a pathological personality, Aguirre led a band of malcontents on a suicidal mission from Peru, down the Amazon (or Marañón as he called it), to the Venezuelan island of Margarita. From there, Aguirre entered the Venezuelan mainland, eventually meeting superior forces and dying in battle near Valencia. Oviedo tells the incredible story of Lope de Aguirre in the same judicious, careful, but persuasive manner as the rest of the history. For Oviedo, and thus for us, Lope de Aguirre became a symbol of the failure and weakness that characterized so much of the conquest. At the same time, Oviedo's discussion of Aguirre and his description of the men (called Marañones) who followed and cooperated with the Tyrant illustrate the fine line that separated the pathological from the heroic in the conquest of America. Through Oviedo's careful descriptions of the atrocities, heroics and cowardice of the conquistadors, we learn to make the fine distinctions that permit intelligent judgment. When was the massacre of Indian armies inspired by a necessary military strategy and when was it the exercise of unbridled and gratuitous violence? What was the essential difference between the bravery of the Spanish soldier who fought against overwhelming odds and died, and that of the Marañones of Aguirre who also fought against overwhelming odds and died?

Oviedo y Baños's careful distinctions between good and evil, and his ability to distinguish the complex qualities that combined in the Spanish conquistador, make this a landmark work, much more than a mere chronicle. *The Conquest and Settlement of Venezuela* deserves a place among the classic works of Latin American history, and Jeannette Johnson Varner's elegant rendering of Oviedo y Baños's prose style brings this fine history within reach of the English-speaking reader.

JOHN V. LOMBARDI

Bloomington, Indiana
November 1986

# ACKNOWLEDGMENTS

While preparing this translation of José de Oviedo y Baños's *Historia de la conquista y población de la provincia de Venezuela (The Conquest and Settlement of Venezuela)*, I have had the privilege of working in a library whose holdings in Latin American materials are among the broadest of the world. To each member of the staff of the Benson Latin American Collection of the University of Texas at Austin, I gratefully acknowledge my indebtedness.

Special thanks are due to the Fundación La Casa de Bello of Caracas, Venezuela, which, through the gracious mediation of its director, the famed historian Sr. Pedro Grases, granted permission to include a pen and ink sketch of José de Oviedo y Baños by the late, renowned artist, Alejandro Sánchez Felipe.

J. J. V.

Austin, Texas
1987

# INTRODUCTION

The trail of the author of *The Conquest and Settlement of Venezuela*, José Agustín de Oviedo y Baños, leads from the cloud-veiled heights of Bogotá, along the rugged route of the conquistadors to the coastal plains of Lima and back across the Andes to the valleys of Mt. Avila. The future historian was born in Santa Fe de Bogotá in December of 1671.[1] The fifth and last child of Juan Antonio de Oviedo y Baños and Josefa de Baños y Sotomayor, he was baptized there on December 26 by his uncle, Onofre Tomás de Baños y Sotomayor. His father, descendant of a noble family of the ancient province of Asturias in northwestern Spain, came to the Indies as fiscal of the Audiencia de Santa Fe de Bogotá, and later was named an *oidor* of that body. Doña Josefa, whom he married in 1665 or 1666, was a native of Lima, and a member of a family that was especially commendable for its service in the government of that city. After only six years of marriage, Don Juan Antonio died on January 28, 1672, at an early age. Doña Josefa was drawn back to Lima by a deep devotion to her family, and was accompanied by her four sons and one daughter, Doña Rosa, who died soon afterward.

The four brothers, Diego Antonio, Pedro, Juan Antonio, and José Agustín, were affectionately indulged by their maternal grandparents and were nurtured in the literary traditions of their family. While still quite young, José began his studies at the university in Lima, along with his brothers, who all were to pursue laudable careers in Venezuela, Mexico, and Guatemala.

In 1683, their maternal uncle, Diego de Baños y Sotomayor, bishop of Santa Marta, was named bishop of Caracas and invested in his new see on August 12, 1684. Two years after the new bishop's installation, José, still an adolescent, accompanied his twenty-year-old brother, Diego, to Caracas, where they placed themselves under the bishop's care. Based on evidence in his history of firsthand acquaintance with the interior regions of southwestern Venezuela, it can be surmised that the journey from Lima to Caracas was made overland, possibly to avoid the danger of pirate attacks by sea. As Oviedo was known never to have left Caracas after his arrival, except for occasional, brief trips to his nearby farms, this detailed knowledge of the land would have been difficult to acquire otherwise.

The brothers' days in the episcopal palace, a modest mansion of seventeenth-century colonial architecture, were spent in the beauty and elegance compatible with their uncle's station. This house, the center of intellectual and ecclesiastical activity of the city, saw a steady stream of churchmen and scholarly laymen pass through its halls. The atmosphere thus created stimulated Diego and José to excel in their studies in order to emulate their elders.

Since education was of primary concern to the bishop, he had continued the work of his predecessor, Bishop Antonio González de Acuña, by consolidating the founding and development of the College-Seminary of Santa Rosa (precursor of the University of Caracas), where he established chairs of philosophy, the arts, and music. Although both brothers were assiduous and alert in their studies, José attended classes only on an informal basis, perhaps as an auditor. His most productive sessions were with private tutors at the palace, where talk of books and letters was general. His attention was directed toward reading the classics of world literature while studying at the same time grammar, oratory, philosophy, and the rudiments of law.

As a powerful and pleasurable supplement to his education by teachers in classrooms, Don José at first had had access to his grandfather's library in Lima, and later to that in the bishop's palace, replete with the fundamental classics. The young student's favorites were the works of Homer, Plato, Horace, Ovid, Cicero, and Virgil. In addition, he read ceaselessly the works of the most eminent writers of the Spanish Golden Age: Calderón de la Barca, Cervantes, Góngora, Lope de Vega, and San Juan de la Cruz. As he grew older, he developed his own library, which reflected his interest in history, law, literature, philosophy, and the military arts.

As the boy advanced into manhood, he was kept busy with activities typical of the highest cultural and social groups of Caracas. He became known for his patrician courtesy, which inevitably attracted the young ladies of his class. On March 19, 1698, at the age of twenty-six, he was married by the bishop to a wealthy young widow, Doña Francisca Manuela de Tovar. The bride previously had been married to the count of San Javier, Don Juan Jacinto Pacheco, by whom she had had one son, Don Antonio, who succeeded his father as count of San Javier. Besides being based apparently on genuine affection, Don José Agustín's advantageous union brought him a more affluent life than he had previously known, and provided comfortable security conducive to a future dedicated to study and writing.

The young count of San Javier did not long remain an only child. Between 1699 and 1713, he was joined by ten others, three boys and seven girls to whom, from oldest to youngest, the following names were given: Diego José, Rosalía Melchora, Juan Antonio, Melchora Catalina, Melchora Rosalía, Josefa Rosalía, Rosa Rosalía, María Isabel, Francisco Javier, and Francisca Ignacia. Though some of them died young, the household for years did not lack the sounds of childish chatter, shouts, laughter, and sobs. Despite this extensive progeny, the surname did not persist, as the male line died out; but the surviving females married into distinguished families and left numerous descendants.

In addition to the preoccupations that a large family engenders, Don José's hours were allocated in three categories: business affairs, ecclesiastical pursuits, and public service. On his marriage he borrowed money to purchase a house located on the present-day Esquina del Conde, which had previously been owned by the archdeacon of the Diocese of Caracas. Gradually he began to speculate by buying homes for resale, complete with slaves, libraries, furniture, and art objects. He also owned a vast cattle ranch called Las Animas, a maize plantation in La Pascua Valley, and a cacao hacienda on the Tuy River. He personally supervised the operations of all these enterprises while also serving as administrator of property inherited by his wife, stepson, and other dependent relatives, and as guardian of several abandoned orphans. Notarial records of the time provide abundant evidence of such widespread business transactions that he no longer was thought of simply as the bishop's nephew, but as a man of wealth.

His ecclesiastical involvement was natural for one whose personal inclinations toward the Church were augmented by close bonds with his uncle, education by clergymen, and readings of ascetic masterpieces of theological literature. Not given to passive participation in any undertaking, he served as mayordomo of the archconfraternity of Nuestra Señora del Rosario, and as general trustee of the Franciscan convents of Venezuela, and of the Sagrados Lugares y Casa Santa de Jerusalén. At the death of the bishop on May 15, 1706, Don José became patron of the Chapel of Nuestra Señora del Pópulo. His uncle had established and endowed this chapel, and is buried and commemorated there by a statue of the bishop kneeling in prayer. Following instructions in his will, the Cathedral Council awarded the bishop's estate to the Church and halted work on the chapel, whereupon the nephew honored his own obligation by completing the construction and decoration of this shrine.

In keeping with his position as a leader in intellectual, social, financial, and ecclesiastical spheres of Caracas, Don José also participated in public service. On January 1, 1699, he was named *alcalde de segundo voto* (junior judge) of the Cabildo of Caracas, and on May 18, 1703, he bought the position of perpetual regidor. He resigned the latter office on November 26 of the same year, however, which has led to the conjecture that the post was too exacting in its attendance requirements and held possibilities for social complications that he wished to avoid. In 1710 he was elected *alcalde de primer voto* (senior judge), and was reelected in

## INTRODUCTION

1722. In appreciation of his twenty-three years of service in municipal government (1699–1722), he was given a block of royal common lands comprising four plots suitable for raising cattle. Nevertheless, he soon thereafter resigned from public office permanently to devote more attention to his rapidly growing family and fortune. He did continue to allot time and effort to military obligations, however, and on June 21, 1728, in recognition of his services to the king, Don José was promoted from the rank of captain to lieutenant general of arms and militia for Venezuela.

In view of the diversity of his activities, it is not surprising that the future historian at first showed no inclination toward writing. His eventual entry into the field of letters was the outcome of one of his early assignments as a member of the Ayuntamiento, to compile a list of those religious ceremonies which they were expected to attend as a body. The unanimous praise that greeted this modest inventory led him to make a minute search of the Cabildo archives. The result was a manuscript entitled "Treasury of Notices and General Index of the Most Remarkable Items Contained in the Capitular Books of the City of Caracas since its Founding." Thus, the seed was sown for the writing of a manuscript that would be published in Madrid twenty years later (1723) as the first work of note by an American-born resident of Venezuela. Moreover, its second edition, published in 1824, is historically unique as being the first substantial work from Venezuela's recently established printing press, which previously had published only pamphlets, leaflets, and booklets. It is the author's only book, of which only the first part has survived; but it was of sufficiently high quality to assure worldwide acclaim for both the man and his adoptive country. During the more than two hundred years since its initial publication, this book has been read with consuming interest and has been held in great esteem as a literary and historical masterpiece. Until this translation, however, made from the first edition of 1723 and collated with the others, it has not been published in English.

Oviedo's history, dedicated to his eldest brother, Diego Antonio, chronicles events in the region from its discovery until 1600. For the sake of clarity, it is essential to note that the boundaries of the sixteenth-century province of Venezuela differ from those of the present-day country of that name. They correspond roughly to those set in the royal cedula issued in 1528 by Emperor Charles V authorizing the Welsers, a German family of financiers, to explore and settle lands extending westward along the coast of Tierra Firme from Maracapana to Cabo de la Vela, and southward into the interior as far as the Casanare River. In addition to Caracas, the region comprised the provinces of Guayana, Trinidad, Margarita, Cumaná, Mérida, and Maracaibo until 1777. Then,

INTRODUCTION

King Charles III ordered that they be united to form a captaincy general named Venezuela, with its seat of government to be Caracas. Oviedo's history at times extends far beyond the borders indicated by its title to follow events to their logical conclusion, however, as when he relates occurrences on expeditions that originated in the provinces, or of others that terminated there.

Besides archival material, evidence points to Oviedo's having utilized printed sources of the sixteenth and seventeenth centuries in compiling his history, especially Father Pedro Simón's *Noticias historiales de las conquistas de Tierra Firme en las Indias Occidentales* (Cuenca, Spain, 1627). Oviedo also demonstrates familiarity with Bishop Lucas Fernández de Piedrahita's *Historia general de las conquistas del Nuevo Reino de Granada* (Antwerp, 1688), and with Father Pedro de Aguado's *Historia de Santa Marta y Nuevo Reino de Granada*, part 2, subtitled *Historia de Venezuela* (Madrid, 1581). It is probable that he felt the influence of Juan de Castellanos's *Elegías de varones ilustres de Indias* (Madrid, 1589), and some of his accounts bear traces of an unpublished manuscript by a soldier/poet named Ulloa. The last three books of Oviedo's work, however—those dealing essentially with the long and bloody struggle for the conquest of Caracas and its vicinity—constitute a truly original and impartial contribution to the history of Venezuela.

This account is distinguished by its rigorously straightforward and fluent historical narration, enriched by the local vocabulary, used here for the first time as a literary device. The author attained a high level of eminence in Venezuelan letters, and profoundly influenced that country's general culture in both literature and history.

The two qualities most frequently noted by scholars in writing of Oviedo's style—musical and picturesque—are both abundantly displayed in the passage, esteemed as a literary classic, that tells of the wondrous transfiguration of Martín Tinajero (see book two, chapter one). Equally poetic are his delicate descriptions of the gardens of Caracas, the beauty of its plazas and parks, its verdant hills, and sparkling streams. Then, in complete contrast, come scenes in which he writes of Ambrosio de Alfinger's proclivity toward execution by impalement, or the unrestrained brutality of Lope de Aguirre in the murder of his daughter and his confessor.[2] In anthologies of Venezuelan literature, excerpts from Oviedo are included as admirable examples of graceful description and majestic style.

The preliminary materials of Oviedo's work, because essentially routine and mandatory, are summarized in this translation rather than being included in their entirety. The title page is followed by seven pages containing the dedication, censor's report, approbation, license to publish, declaration of exclusive rights, *fee de errata,* or list of errors (all corrected herein), statement of amount of tax (eight maravedies per page) as set by the Council of the Indies, and six laudatory poems by various dignitaries. The author's prologue to the reader follows, in which he professes doubts as to his own writing ability and power to appeal to a wide range of tastes while maintaining authenticity and accuracy. He foresees that some may question his failure to name other authors as sources, but claims that this omission verifies his account, since it is based on so many historical documents that his desire to avoid prolixity does not permit him to cite them.

Since the publication of the first edition there have been six reissues, variously called new editions, reprints, or facsimiles. They vary only slightly as to the text itself, but each has been enriched in some way, by an introduction, notes, documents, commentaries, indexes, or photographs. One contains a map. The first edition was published in Madrid by Gregorio Hermosilla in 1723. In quarto, one volume of approximately three hundred and eighty double-column pages plus four of summary chapter headings, it is extremely rare. Even rarer is the reprint made in Caracas in 1824 by Domingo Navas Spínola. The third printing actually constituted a new edition because of its notes, indexes of personal names, and documents, all the valuable contributions of Cesáreo Fernández Duro. Its two volumes were published in the Biblioteca de los Americanistas series by Luis Navarro in Madrid in 1885. It next appeared as the first of four historical classics of Venezuela in *Analectas de historia patria,* published in Caracas by Parra León Hermanos of the Editorial Sur América in 1935. The unparalleled brilliance and balanced judgments of Caracciola Parra León's exhaustive prologue have placed him in first rank as a source of information on Oviedo. The prologue is especially strong in its well-substantiated biographical details. In 1940, Paul Adams, a longtime resident of Venezuela, as a "Homage of the American Colony to Venezuela," published through Charles Scribner's Sons of New York a deluxe facsimile of the 1824 edition. It features an informative thirty-one-page introduction by Adams, a detailed map, four photographs, and an extensive name and subject index compiled by Rudolf Dolge. The following year, a less elaborate—and less expensive—version was issued to make the book available to a wider readership. In 1965, a reprint was published in Madrid by Ediciones Atlas 19 as the first part of volume 107 in the *Historiadores de Indias* series of the Biblioteca de Autores Españoles. It follows closely the 1885 edition, but for a few minor changes in the spelling of proper names that bring them into accord with modern usage. Guillermo Morón, a prolific and reliable Oviedo scholar, provided its introduction, replete with interesting and valuable new in-

INTRODUCTION

sights. In 1967, another facsimile of the 1824 Navas Spínola edition was published in Caracas as a "Homage to the Four Hundredth Anniversary of the Founding of Caracas," printed by Ediciones Ariel, S.A., of Barcelona, Spain.

Such a variety of editions, reprints, and facsimiles attests to the book's lasting impression on both historians and general readers, and has led curious scholars of the past two hundred and fifty years to speculate on the possible existence of a second volume. Oviedo himself indicated that his history was in two volumes, the first recounting events from the discovery of the province of Venezuela until 1600, and the second continuing with those of the following century, extending into the 1720s. He furthermore announced that the first part was dedicated to his eldest brother, Diego Antonio, and the second to his writer/priest brother, Juan Antonio. In spite of this verification, the most widely accepted judgment is that Oviedo intended to produce a second volume, that he probably made extensive notations for that purpose and may even have written it, but that it was never published and all trace of it is now lost.

The fact that at age fifty-two, Oviedo had reached a comparatively mature age for the publication of a first book is cause for admiration. It is also somewhat surprising that after this highly successful production he did not seek to extend his literary career. Instead, he spent the ensuing fifteen years in his customary activities, centered around family, friends and church, absorbed in social, financial, ecclesiastical, and scholarly pursuits. Then, at the age of sixty-seven, his deteriorating health forced him to his bed with an illness that was to prove fatal. On November 20, 1728, he called for a scribe, before whom he designated his wife and his stepson as administrators of his considerable estate. He made bequests to family members, friends, servants, and the Church. (Although he instructed that all his debts be honored, one loan was repaid only a century and a half later.) After expressing his desire to be buried in the Chapel of Nuestra Señora del Pópulo in the Cathedral of Caracas, he made his final confession, was absolved, and received the sacraments of the Holy Eucharist and Extreme Unction. Following his death two days later, he was buried with impressive ceremonies, for all his wishes were observed. The service was attended by scores of relatives and friends, and subsequently three hundred and forty-four masses were said for his soul. Two hundred years after his death, a commemorative slab was installed in the chapel by the Academia de la Historia, extolling his devotion to the Church.

While no portrait of Oviedo has been located, there is a small, imaginary concept of him by a twentieth-century lithographer, Spanish-born Caracas resident Alejandro Sánchez Felipe, on the cover of a booklet by historian Guillermo Morón. Although we lack a physical representation of the historian, Caracciolo Parra León has deduced certain personality traits from Oviedo's writings and the comments of some of his contemporaries. Parra León envisages Oviedo as generous, steadfast, devoted to his family and friends, of upright character and irreproachable conduct. Oviedo is also universally acclaimed for having made his beloved second homeland known to the entire world.

# THE CONQUEST AND SETTLEMENT OF VENEZUELA

# DEDICATION

*To Señor Don Diego de Oviedo y Baños, judge of the Royal Audiencias of Hispaniola, Guatemala and Mexico of His Majesty's Council of the Royal and Supreme Court of the Indies.*

Under the protection of Your Lordship, this history of Venezuela unabashedly seeks to assure its successful production. To whom, if not to Your Lordship, could I dedicate this work in order to attain this achievement? Cicero said: "If you want much money, choose your patron with great care." The natural gifts with which Your Lordship is endowed in his upper sphere, without flattery, exaggeration or emulation diminishing them, are in every respect extensive. For this reason, the unworthiness of my pen may be excused without the errors brought on by my ignorance drawing attention. "Choose your patron with great care." This is my motive for dedicating this work to Your Lordship, but I omit the most personal expressions of these accolades in order to avoid their being attributed to self-interest.

On the illustrious escutcheon inherited by Your Lordship, symbols of great literature, consummate prudence, singular talent and outstanding valor gleam. In addition, augmented by your many experiences and general comprehension, Your Lordship has expedited the most serious negotiations, which royal confidence has committed to your zeal. You have used the pen of Minerva with the same skill as she on occasion took advantage of the arms of Pallas. By this action, credence is lent to the opinion prevalent that Minerva and Pallas were so similar as to be identifiable with one another. I owe to nature the good fortune of being so close to Your Lordship in blood that critical censorship might attribute to vainglory all that comes from my pen in lauding you, and thus my praise could alienate you.

As related in Chapter XXIII of the Second Book of Kings, when three invincible soldiers presented a glass of water to David, by all logic such an insignificant gift might have been held in scorn by a king. However, that discreet monarch esteemed it so much that, judging it worthy of more sovereign altars, he lifted it to God.* The Sacred Text gives no reason for this demonstrative act other than that it had been taken from the Cistern of Bethlehem with much effort by those three captains. May Your Lordship receive my humble offering as one worthy of his altars,

---

*The incident related here is from 2 Sam. 23:13–17, not Kings.

## DEDICATION

not for what it contains but for the imponderable and constant pains with which I have extracted it from the Cistern of Oblivion in which it was submerged through omission and negligence. The memorable deeds of those valorous Spaniards have provided the material from which I have woven this history so that, coming into being under the aegis of Your Lordship, they will owe to your patronage the acclaim that they deserve. May God keep Your Lordship over the years in his greater eminence compatible with his merits.

Your brother and affectionate servant kisses your hand.
Don José de Oviedo y Baños.

# PROLOGUE TO THE READER

It has always been a tedious mental chore to write as one should for publication and for the pleasure of diverse and exceptional tastes. It required an often unachievable stroke of the pen that, attempted by many, was attained by few. This fact is even more evident in our times, now that the skill with which some writers accomplish this task makes the ineptitude of others even more manifest.

After experiencing this truth, I was led to suspect my own inadequacy in having begun with misgivings and hesitantly continued the development of this history. I felt compelled by gratitude to express my esteem for this province by making known the memorable events of its conquest. Until now it has been concealed by the inexcusable carelessness of its sons without there being among so many superb talents even one to assume this obligation as his own.

The burden of preparing this work has been great. I have had to ransack all the archives of this province seeking material and comparing ancient documents. This special care has been necessary in order to take from their context the substance on which to support the truth with which these events must be narrated. Without giving credence to the platitudinous manner in which some of them are expressed, I have verified the accuracy of what I have written within the authentic assertions that I have found.

May the style for which I have striven prove to be in accord with that generally approved, without its reaching the point of affectation. In this way, it will escape the defect of some modern historians of the Indies who, in order to adorn their writings with embellished locutions, have not eschewed using words incorrectly. These expressions are not acceptable in history, since they introduce in the person of certain Indians, especially caciques, orations as precise and eloquent as Cicero might have used, an eloquence unfitting to the ineptitude of such barbarous tribes. This is a delicate point in formal history. All the authority of Quintus Curtius Rufus could not save him from Father Movne's objection in his *Arte de historia*. Curtius was criticized severely also by Augustino Mascardi and by the erudite Father René Rapin, because of the eloquence which Curtius attributed to the ignorant Sythians when they spoke before Alexander the Great. Their speech seemed inappropriate to these historians.*

*Curtius Rufus, Quintus (Quinto Curcio)—Latin historian of first century A.D., whose principal work is *De rebus gestis Alexandri magni*, a biography of Alexander the Great. Other historians consider this work more story than fact.

## PROLOGUE TO THE READER

If the curious note scant citations of authors whose works I have studied, that lack is the best verification of the truth of what I write because I have been governed in every respect by the ancient manuscripts that I have read. Although their prolixity does not permit me to quote them all, I am assured by their authority of the reliability of the events which I relate. And as in everything, I solicit the benevolence of my readers so that they may tolerate the defects of which I may be accused. Of course, I consider the permission to which I aspire meritorious because I know that they will assist me with my own errors. All mistakes that any censor may uncover in this book, I admit without apology as legitimate children, born of my own ignorance.

VALE.

# BOOK I

## CHAPTER I

*The site and characteristics of the province.*

AMONG the provinces that comprise the vast dominion of America, one that has a place among the best was from its discovery, with fitting allusion, called Venezuela,[1] but later generally was known as Caracas for its metropolis. Its history offers the substance for my pen to save from the ashes of oblivion the memory of those valorous Spaniards who conquered it, but who have had no reward for their labors except scorn and neglect. In this hemisphere, brave deeds commonly have been buried along with the remains of those who performed them, and unfortunately, tradition has preserved nothing more than a few confused notions of the illustrious actions of the conquistadors. This is the motive that compels me to undertake this work, although I am aware that it will be but moderately appreciated by those who should esteem it most.

The province of Venezuela is situated in the region called Tierra Firme de las Indias, and is two hundred leagues in length. It lies between the peak of Unare, which marks its boundary to the east of Cumaná, and Cabo de la Vela, by which it is separated on the west from Santa Marta. It is more than one hundred and twenty leagues in width. The ocean bathes its coast to the north, Nuevo Reino de Granada lies to the southwest,[2] and the mighty currents of the Orinoco River serve as its line of demarcation to the south.[3] Its terrain is varied; within its vast expanse are inaccessible sierras, rugged mountains, high and clean plateaus, fertile plains, and delightful valleys, enticingly cool in perpetual springtime. Its meadows and pastures are well adapted to raising livestock of all kinds, primarily cattle with a prodigious aptitude for multiplying. Goats also are so abundant near Maracaibo, Coro, Carora, and El Tocuyo that the inhabitants of these towns grow rich from trade in tanned hides. They raise thoroughbred horses so excellent that they can compete with Chilean and Andalusian breeds, and enough mules to transport all the inhabitants of the province and their possessions without help from other regions.

Its many waters are clear and salubrious, and there is no mountain gorge or lofty crest that does not spout crystalline streams across the land in fresh torrents to make it productive. There is nothing sown in this land that does not bear fruit amazingly well, for added to its fertility is the wide variety of its temperatures. Within short distances, according to the altitude, either cold, hot, or temperate weather prevails so that what is not felt in one place at all is plentiful elsewhere, and one section will be sterile while another is fertile. The province abounds in wheat, maize, rice, cotton, tobacco, and sugar, from which dainty and exquisite conserves are made. Also there is found cacao, which in trade brings its inhabitants their greatest wealth: fruits, Indian as well as European; vegetables of every kind; and finally anything either required for sustenance or desired as a special treat.

Its forests produce valuable and highly esteemed woods. They consist of tamarind striped in various colors; mahogany; divi-divi; lignum vitae (or *guaiacum*); brazilwood, known for its fine coloration; jacaranda, which resembles tortoise shell in the beauty of its sheen when put to the lathe; and cedar in such abundance that it is used for the most ordinary products. Almost all the trees exude sugar, which nourishes swarms of wild bees that build their hives of golden honeycombs in their trunks. Also raised are vanilla plants, more aromatic than those of Soconusco; and in the vicinity of the city of Carora, wild grain as fine as that of Mixteca which, if the residents devoted themselves to its cultivation, would greatly increase their wealth.[4] Sarsaparilla and indigo are so common that they serve as nuisances rather than assets, and scant attention is given to their production.

Of the large number of animals which the forests shelter, the most abundant are pumas, bears, tapirs, deer, peccaries, rabbits, and jaguars, the most ferocious of which, in America, are those with the smallest spots.[5] The seas and rivers offer a great variety of fishes, some exceedingly common and others prized as unusual and delicious. The coasts provide salt esteemed for both its flavor and the ease with which the beds are set.

The fields are always full of birds, delightful for their beautiful plumage and their melodious songs, as well as their delectable flesh. The most common are the *guachacaraca* or chachalaca, the *paují* or cashew bird, the *uquira* or mountain hen, the dove, the partridge, and many other species that offer diversion to all dedicated to the hunt.

This province produces remarkable simples useful for their medicinal applications: canafistula; tamarind; chinaroot; tacamahac, an efficacious remedy for headache; Carora balsam; and Cumaná or María oil, an antidote for any wound and a highly prized preventive of muscle spasms.

This country has tin mines in different places, and on the site of

## CHAPTER I

Cocorote, Don Alonso de Oviedo, resident of Barquisimeto, discovered copper mines of great opulence and productivity. For a long time, His Majesty profited from the considerable amount of metal that was extracted from them and carried to Spain for casting artillery. After they were leased by the king to Don Francisco Martín, resident of Caracas, for forty thousand pesos, he removed his workers and assigned his slaves and equipment to other foundries of greater advantage to himself.

The province was originally rich in gold, which the sands of the quebradas readily yielded; but today, although traces of that metal are found in some abundance, no use is made of it. This change has come about either because the principal veins have been exhausted and the amounts produced do not compensate for the work required to extract it, or because the colonists are more concerned with the harvest of cacao, which brings them constant riches, than with gold mining, which involves some risk. Blue-veined, transparent crystals, so fine that they rival the aquamarine, and woods for dyes of different colors are also produced. In sum, there is everything that might be desired for the maintenance of human life without any need for the products of neighboring provinces. If the application of its inhabitants were equal to its fertility, and if they knew how to profit from the benefits it offers, it would be the richest province in America.

At the time of its conquest this province was inhabited by a multitude of tribes, each of which, without recognizing one superior monarch as ruler of them all, lived in a village and rendered vassalage to its own cacique. With the continued exportation of Indians for more than twenty years to the Windward Islands (Barlovento) and elsewhere, however, the province has been consumed in such a manner that today, in eighty-two villages, the natives retain only a faint memory of what they once were.

Their pagan customs were those of barbarians, without political organization, government or religion to accredit them as rational human beings. Although all were in accord in being idolatrous and using *piaches* and *mohánes* (*mojánes*) to consult their demons and observe their auguries and superstitions, the cults differed in details. Not having a mutual god for an entire tribe, each Indian attributed divinity to the object which most incited his worship. Thus, almost all animals, vermin, hills and crags had devout adherents who made sacrifices to them on their altars. Their temples ordinarily were in deep quebradas or on lofty mountains, although in some places they used large straw huts called *caneyes* where the mohánes gathered. The concavities of rocky crags or the hollows of trees served as shrines in which their idols, wrought of gold, clay or wood in strange and diverse designs, were placed. To the sound of their harsh *fotutos* (flutes) they invoked the devil, to whom they offered balls of cotton thread and cacao butter that, when set afire in clay braziers, served as burnt offerings. Now, converted to our sacred religion, they live remote from all idolatry, although with some offensive residual observances of auguries and superstitions to which this race is naturally inclined.

Today, the province includes the cities of Santiago de León de Caracas, Santa Ana de Coro, Nueva Zamora de Maracaibo, Trujillo, El Tocuyo, Nueva Segovia de Barquisimeto, Nueva Valencia del Rey, Portillo de Carora, San Sebastián de los Reyes, Guanaguanare (Guanare), Nirgua, and the port of La Guaira. Information on the climate, site, and characteristics of each according to its founding date will be given in this history.

# CHAPTER II

*Alonso de Ojeda discovers Venezuela; later Cristóbal Guerra, following Ojeda's course, sails along the entire coast of the province.*

THIS new world was discovered by Admiral Christopher Columbus in 1492, to the immortal glory of the Spanish nation. In subsequent years he undertook additional voyages and arrived in 1498 to explore Tierra Firme (the Mainland) at a place he named Boca de los Dragos (Mouth of the Dragons), opposite the island of Trinidad. Then, prow set to the west, he sailed on to Araya Point where he headed north and returned to the island of Hispaniola, leaving the exploration incomplete at that time. On this report, their Catholic Majesties commanded Captain Alonso de Ojeda, native of the city of Cuenca, to leave Spain for these shores in 1499. He brought as his pilot the Biscayan cartographer Juan de la Cosa, and ordered him to set a course for Tierra Firme. After a fair voyage of twenty-seven days, they sighted Boca de los Dragos and Maracapana.

Hugging the coast, Ojeda sailed along toward the west. He landed frequently and observed the ports and ebb and flow of the seas for a distance of more than three hundred leagues. When he reached Cabo de la Vela he crossed to Hispaniola, where he basked in the glory of having been the first European to discover the province of Venezuela. Then, because it fell within the bounds of his course, Cristóbal Guerra proceeded with additional information and arrived a short time later at the same destination. Next came Pedro Alonso Niño, resident of Moguer, who obtained license from their Catholic Majesties to make this voyage on condition that he not come nearer than fifty leagues to what had been discovered by the admiral, Columbus. Because of his limited means, Niño formed a company with Luis Guerra, of Seville, and signed a contract that, among other items, stipulated that the latter's brother, Cristóbal Guerra, be captain of the ship used on that voyage. Necessary precautions having been taken, they set sail a few days after Ojeda had departed from the port of San Lúcar de Barrameda, and, steering the same course, arrived soon after him at Paria and Maracapana. There, without paying any heed to the prohibition that they were not to touch on what the admiral had discovered, they cut some brazilwood as the initial act of their official commission.[6] Continuing to navigate toward the west, they stopped at the islands of Margarita and Cubagua, where they bartered trinkets with the Indians for a considerable quantity of pearls, the first ever sent as tribute from this western world to our Spain.

Guerra and his companions, overjoyed at the advantages fortune had offered, continued their navigation. They passed Ancón de Refriegas (Bay of Skirmishes), Araya Point, and the Gulf of Cariaco, after which they arrived at the port of Cumanagoto. When the Indians first saw the ship, they were transported with the novelty of these strange people in their land and, without any mistrust, drew alongside in their pirogues. They wore *chagualas* at their necks, bracelets, and earrings; and they had many pearls, which they bartered freely with the visitors for little bells, knives, and glass beads. These samples of New World opulence left the Spaniards even more intent on pursuing the advantages being unfolded.

With these strong desires, the invaders left Cumanagoto and, rounding the Cabo de Cordera, arrived at the spot where later the city of Coro was to be founded. Bartering with the natives for gold, they passed farther down into the province of Coriana. On the beaches there, they found a crowd of savages who with repeated gestures of friendship urged the strangers to land and trade for the gold jewelry being displayed as lures. The Spaniards then made a rash decision, for even though there were only twenty-three men aboard, they landed and thus turned themselves over to the as yet untested good will of the barbarians. The Indians, however, esteemed the show of confidence and received them with signs of high regard. With grave courtesy they bartered pearls and golden eagle plaques for their visitors' adornment while the Spaniards reciprocated with knives, brooches, and other trifles from Europe whose novelty compensated for their lack of value. Recognizing those people's sincerity and their own need for relief from the hardships of their journey, our men remained there twenty days, enjoying an abundance of rabbits and deer. In accord with this hospitable reception, Guerra and his troops would have tarried even longer were it not for their strong urge to continue the exploration. They followed the coast toward the west, and after a few days discovered a beach on which more than two thousand Indians, armed with bows and arrows, manifested in their own manner scant desire to admit these strange people into their land.

These Indians, judging from the location, were undoubtedly the Cocinas, a cruel, barbarous, and traitorous people who occupy the coast from Maracaibo to the Río de la Hacha, and to this day retain their indomitable ferocity.[7] Our voyagers now had in their possession a considerable quantity of gold and more than one hundred and fifty marks of lustrous pearls, some as large as hazelnuts.[8] Since they were not seeking armed conflict and were not accustomed to such a reception, they decided not to place themselves in jeopardy but to go back up the coast by the same route they had come. They dropped anchor in Araya, where they discovered those celebrated salt marshes whose product is so much desired by nations to the north, and in defense of which Spain has wasted much wealth. Then, leaving those coasts, so filled with amazing riches, they set sail for Spain and, after two months, dropped anchor on February 6, 1500, at a port on the coast of Galicia.

# CHAPTER III

*The Audiencia de Santo Domingo sends the factor Juan de Ampués to the province of Coriana; he establishes friendship with its cacique and initiates the founding of Coro.*

THE men from Cristóbal Guerra's ship spread the news throughout all Spain of the grandeurs that this New World mainland encompassed. It was attested by the riches brought back, and caused such a stir, principally on the coasts of Andalusia, that many merchants equipped ships to augment the returns of their maritime business. Trade continued to increase as time passed, especially after Emperor Charles V gave permission for Indians who resisted Spanish conquest to be enslaved. The traders who proceeded from Hispaniola and other places along the coast

## CHAPTER III

from Paria to Coriana were numerous, and gained much profit from making slaves of Indians without paying any heed to whether or not the circumstances were in accordance with the imperial edict. This proclamation in a short while was regarded as so pernicious that the Audiencia de Santo Domingo was obliged to provide a remedy for the disorders it spawned. For this purpose the Audiencia chose Captain Juan de Ampués, factor of the ministry of finance of that city, as a trustworthy and authoritative person to go to Coriana. He was armed with broad commissions and provisions through which he could restrict the vexatious treatment which traders were inflicting on the miserable Indians, as well as impede their continuous exportation, which reduced them to perpetual slavery.

Ampués, reflecting on the matter with characteristic alertness, readily accepted the assignment. He realized that his own profits would inevitably increase, for he would hold the powerful position of a judge in an abundant land. He quickly prepared a ship and crossed to the coast of Coriana in 1527, accompanied by Virgilio García, Esteban Mateos, and fifty-eight others. He learned that the region was Caiquetía, and that Cacique Manaure, a man rich in treasure and vassals, was its ruler. Using whatever means his prudence indicated, Ampués solicited his friendship until the barbarian, finally overcome by the Spaniard's courtesies, decided to visit him. Displaying his power by his ostentatious retinue, Manaure arrived accompanied by one hundred Indian nobles extravagantly arrayed in panaches of colorful feathers, pearl bracelets and golden earrings. He was carried in an intricately woven hammock on the shoulders of lesser caciques, the adornment of his person corresponding to his distinction and opulence.

Ampués was pleased to see his plan succeed, as it was imperative to strengthen his friendship with the cacique in order to expedite his intentions. He went out to receive his visitor at the door of his lodgings, observing all the laws of courtesy. The barbarian reciprocated by presenting to Ampués several pieces of gold, some marten skins, and other highly prized items whose value, it was generally estimated, reached eleven thousand pesos. Through his liberality, a perpetual alliance by which all of Manaure's Caiquetíos lent vassalage to our king was established between the two. Ampués and Cacique Manaure continued to observe this state with such loyalty that, although the outrageous excesses of our soldiers might reasonably have given the Indians a motive to break the yoke of obedience, they never failed to honor the faith they had pledged. Satisfaction with this continued loyalty resulted in their being always free from tributes, annual taxes, or *demora* in the mines.

Ampués recognized in the cacique's opulence the riches of the land

and the substantial profits that could result for the Crown through its being settled by Spaniards. He therefore, although without authority, was to seek the site which appeared to him most appropriate. On Santa Ana's day of the same year, 1527, he founded a city that, because of its being in the province of Coriana, and as an honor to the saint, he named Santa Ana de Coro. At that time, however, he did not appoint a magistrate or justice for its administration but left it under the jurisdiction that he exercised by virtue of the powers given him by the Audiencia.

This city lies at ten degrees north latitude, in a warm and extremely dry climate, half a league from the seashore. Its terrain is sandy and it lacks water, but the surrounding area is productive and agreeable. Much cattle, many goats and good mules are raised on it, and its salt marshes are abundant. Because of its extensive trade with Cartagena, Santo Domingo, Caracas, and other cities, to which it transports a great quantity of cheeses, mules and tanned hides, it is a rich town, even though small. Its church was elevated to the rank of cathedral in the year 1532 by its first bishop, Señor Don Rodrigo de Bastidas.[9] Then in the year 1636, its bishop, Don Juan López Arbuto de la Mata, fearing an enemy invasion, transferred the episcopate to the city of Caracas. It is served today by two parish priests and a head sacristan; and it maintains a small monastery of the Order of San Francisco and a hermitage dedicated to Saint Nicholas, the bishop.[10]

## CHAPTER IV

*The Welsers contract to conquer and settle this province; Ambrosio de Alfinger is appointed its first governor.*

ENRIQUE de Alfinger and Jerónimo Sailler, German agents of the Welsers, were at that time present at the Court of our Emperor Charles V. The Welsers were esteemed everywhere in Europe as members of a famous company that several merchants had formed in order to trade in large volume and to engage in enterprises throughout the world. Learning of the considerable profits which Coriana and its coasts were enjoying through trade, Alfinger and Sailler surmised that it would be advantageous to their company to acquire the region for its sole benefit. They therefore asked the emperor to lease it to them, but strong opposition was made on behalf of Juan de Ampués who solicited the exclusive right

## CHAPTER IV

to proceed with the conquest and settlement he had already begun. However, inasmuch as the emperor had benefited from the Welsers' money through loans for military purposes, it was not difficult for them to attain their aspirations. There were certain stipulations, nevertheless, on which an accord with the emperor was based, the principal one being that within two years the company would be obligated to found two cities and construct three fortresses in the province conceded to them. This extended from Cabo de la Vela eastward more than three hundred leagues to Maracapana, and its expanse toward the south, on which at that time the limits had not yet been set, was to be whatever might appear suitable to them. The company was to equip four ships to transport three hundred Spaniards and fifty German master miners, who at the Welsers' expense were to be distributed throughout all the Indies to provide greater profit from the metal. In recompense, the emperor granted the title of adelantado to whomever the Welsers might name, and assigned to them 4 percent of all profits set aside as the Crown's Royal Fifth. Furthermore, he ceded twelve square leagues at whatever place they might choose, to be disposed of at their own discretion, and they were authorized to make slaves of Indians who refused to surrender to the yoke of obedience. It also was stipulated that Padre Fray Antonio Montesinos, religious of the Order of Santo Domingo, be designated protector of the Indians and receive one-tenth of the fruits of the venture, to be used in pious works until such time as other disposition might be made.

In 1528, the emperor granted the government of Santa Marta, vacant through the death of Rodrigo de Bastidas, to García de Lerma, his *gentilhombre de boca*, an illustrious native of Burgos. While Lerma was at Court, he and the Welsers came to an agreement specifying that since the areas of their conquest were contiguous, they would always help one another in necessity. In compliance with this decision, Lerma was to go as captain of the three German ships. If he found Santa Marta at peace after the uprisings which had germinated in the treacherous wounds inflicted on his predecessor, Bastidas, by his lieutenant general Villafuerte, he would go, if necessary, to help the people of Coro.

After these terms were accepted by the emperor, the Welsers named as governor Ambrosio de Alfinger and, as his lieutenant general, Bartolomé Sailler. Both Germans, they set sail in 1528, well provided with horses, arms and munitions. Among the four hundred Spaniards who accompanied them there were many hidalgos and noblemen, such as Juan de Villegas, a gentleman of transcendent abilities, native of Segovia, and illustrious progenitor of the Villegas family of Caracas; and Sancho Briceño, from whom the aristocratic families Briceño, Bastidas, Verdugo, and Rosales of Trujillo descended. Also, Juan Cuaresma de

Melo, mayordomo of the dukes of Medina Sidonia, husband of Francisca de Samaniego, came to the Indies at this time and was granted the post of perpetual magistrate of the first city he might settle. Heirs of this cavalier are the Guevaras of Caracas through the marriage of Captain Juan de Guevara and Doña Luisa de Samaniego, granddaughter of Juan Cuaresma de Melo. The captain came with his uncle, the licentiate Iñigo de Guevara, of the habit of Santiago and a judge of Santo Domingo. Also in the company were the accountant Diego Ruiz Vallejo, Gonzalo de los Ríos, Martín de Arteaga, Juan de Frías, Luis de León, Joaquín Ruiz, Antonio Col, Francisco Ortiz, Juan Villarreal, Jerónimo de la Peña, Bartolomé García, the licentiate Hernán Pérez de la Muela, Alonso de Campos, Pedro de San Martín, factor of the royal treasury, and others.

On Alfinger's arrival in Coro, Juan de Ampués examined the German's commissions and, in obedience to the emperor's command, reluctantly turned over the province to the newly appointed governor. Disconsolate at seeing the fruits of his own struggles converted to the profit of another, Ampués spent the rest of his life in retirement on the island of Santo Domingo. His resentment was not lessened even when the emperor appointed him lord of the island of Curaçao.[11]

# CHAPTER V

*Alfinger completes the founding of Coro and goes out with his men to explore Lake Maracaibo.*

ALFINGER took office as governor, but his concerns and those of the Germans who succeeded him were never directed toward the development of the province but rather toward reaping its benefits while the opportunity lasted. Nevertheless, since Coro already had been founded by Juan de Ampués, Alfinger continued the process by instituting the offices needed for prestige and for the ordinary administration of justice. Juan Cuaresma de Melo was named perpetual magistrate and placed in charge of the army. Gonzalo de los Ríos, Martín de Arteaga, and Virgilio García also were appointed to office and they, in turn, selected as first alcaldes Sancho Briceño and Esteban Mateos, the latter a native of Moguer. Cuaresma de Melo spent the remainder of 1528 in making these arrangements; but at the beginning of the following year, he still had ardent ambitions to gain riches as quickly as possible without considering

CHAPTER V

whether the methods used were just or unjust. He consulted persons of experience as to the direction his conquests should take, and was informed that the Lake Maracaibo region was notably productive. Lacking other spoils, he could always profit by making slaves of the Indians captured, since it was the most densely populated area. He decided to put the plan into action, without thought of the evil results of such an unscrupulous scheme, by ordering the construction of several brigantines. This task quickly accomplished, he left his lieutenant, Sailler, in Coro, and dispatched some of his men by sea in the new boats. He ordered them to await him on the lake, after crossing the sand bar, while he and the rest of the army traveled by land over the forty leagues that separated the city of Coro from the lake.

Nature had formed here a beautiful freshwater gulf commonly called Lake Maracaibo, named for a cacique whom the Spaniards had found here. From south to north it measures fifty leagues from the Pamplona River to the sandbar, where it empties into the sea; and, at its broadest point, it is thirty leagues wide and more than eighty in circumference. This monstrous lake is fed by many rivers, the principal ones being the Pamplona (also called the Zulia);[12] the Chama, which originates in the melted snows of the sierra of Mérida;[13] the San Pedro; and the Motatán, which rises on the paramo of Serrada. On the west its flow is fed by the powerful Catatumbo, which gushes down from the sierra of Ocaña and enters the lake by three mouths. This gigantic lake receives also the waters of the Arinas, celebrated for its hidden riches;[14] the Torondoy, noted for its excellent waters; the Sucui, which descends from the cordilleras near the Río de la Hacha; the Astillero, memorable for the abundance of its rich woods; and others that, because they are small, are known by neither name nor place of origin.

Sloops, frigates and other small craft in great number navigate this freshwater gulf; and, because it provides suitable anchorage, seagoing galleons could sail it if the bar at its entrance permitted. However, the sandbanks formed by the undertow at this bar allow passage to medium-sized ships only, and these, consequently, contend for the large trade supported by that port.

When the Spaniards discovered this lake and found large Indian villages built in the water off its shores, they called it Venezuela because of its similarity to the city of Venice.[15] This name later was extended to the entire province, although at present there remain only four of the towns that gave origin to this designation, and they are all so small that the largest, Moporo, had only about thirty houses in the year 1686. Those towns experience a singular transmutation worked by nature that affects the wooden piles of a strong and solid species called vera, on which the houses are built. After several years, the part which is soaked by the lake turns to stone, leaving the rest in the original wood, thus uniting in one shaft two distinct materials.

On arriving at this lake, Alfinger embarked on the brigantines and transported his men to the other side. There, he provisioned a small town, built comfortable houses for the women and children, and assigned a group of soldiers to protect them. Meanwhile, he returned with the brigantines, exploring and devastating everything surrounding the lake. From this ill-conceived plan, perpetuated by the Germans who succeeded him, his own perdition and the total ruin of this province resulted. His soldiers now realized that there was no intention of settling anywhere, that they had nothing to hope for as fruits of their labors, and that they were to have only what they could seize. Undeterred by compassion, they laid waste delightful provinces, destroying the benefits that might have made them secure in the possession of fertile lands for themselves and their descendants if they had settled along the routes they explored. However, the Germans, as foreigners, foresaw that control of the province could not long endure for them, and thus they gave more heed to immediate gains than to future benefits that might be obtained by initial moderation.

# CHAPTER VI

*Alfinger seeks help from Coro; he crosses the sierra above the Upar Valley and arrives at the province of Tamalameque.*

AMBROSIO de Alfinger, after nearly a year of exploring the rivers and coves around the lake without the gold acquired or Indians captured being sufficient to satisfy his greed, returned to camp to embark on new explorations inland toward the west. There were too few men to carry out the expedition, however, because illness, due to bad weather and the humidity of the lake, had consumed them in large number. Also, many soldiers had fled to Coro in discontent, unable to tolerate Alfinger's harsh nature or his strange manner of governing. He punished even minor offenses with the whip and the gallows, and affronted upright men through his cruel and malevolent campmaster, Francisco del Castillo.

To offset this loss, Alfinger dispatched the captured Indians to Coro

CHAPTER VI

to be sold as slaves. Thus his agents, enriched by the vile earnings of this trade, and with gold sent by Alfinger for this purpose, were able to supply the foot soldiers and horsemen, arms and other military supplies needed. Consequently, with his troops, which now comprised one hundred and eighty well-trained men of war, he departed in 1530 and marched toward the west, leaving the sick at camp in the care of Captain Venegas, native of the city of Córdoba. After covering the twenty leagues of level land lying between them and the cordillera, Alfinger crossed the Itotos Mountains and went out into the Upar Valley. There, unmindful of the fact that he was beyond the limits of the area assigned to him, this district being under the jurisdiction of Santa Marta, he devastated the land and robbed its wretched inhabitants. Even the beauty of the landscape was insufficient to temper his rage as he converted towns and fields to ashes. He spread the voracious flames of his anger in extremes so atrocious that in more than thirty leagues of previously populated land, Captain Cardosa did not find a single house standing when he led an expedition there the following year.

Having razed the Upar Valley, Alfinger followed the currents of the Césare River and reached the provinces of the Pocabuces and Alcojolados.[16] Along the way he collected gold from the vast quantity belonging to these tribes and others that he encountered before reaching Tamalameque Lake. Called Zapatosa Lake by the Spaniards, its perimeter was dotted by innumerable towns, but they were all deserted because their inhabitants had had advance notice of the cruelties committed in the Upar Valley and would not expose themselves to the same danger. To avoid the peril which threatened them, they had taken refuge on the islands of the lake, collecting all their canoes so the Spaniards would not have any means of following them. As our men could see from the nearby mainland, the Indians, adorned with golden eagle neck plaques and earrings, felt confident being in the center of the lake and walked about in groups along the shores without precaution. Incited by an immoderate greed for spoils, Juan de Villegas, Virgilio García, Alonso de Campos, Hernán Pérez de la Muela, and twenty-six others, all mounted, hurled their steeds into the lake. Directed by their bits and goaded by Moorish spurs, the horses swam across to the islands with an unexpected resoluteness that terrified the barbarians and left them without courage to raise their bows or set their arrows in place. Some suffered calamitous destruction from lances and others from their own confusion as, trampling over one another in their haste to escape in the canoes, they subsequently sank under the waves, thus meeting death while seeking life.

After routing the Indians, the Spaniards seized immense spoils in gold and, more important at that time, they captured the principal cacique of the lake, Tamalameque, from whom the province took its name. The Indians, afraid that the life of their prince might be endangered, not only did not attempt any armed movement to liberate him but, displaying submission and making signs of surrender, they ransomed him for a large sum of gold. Although some of his captains thought they should press forward in their conquests, Alfinger recognized the essence of this land and would not abandon it until he had reaped all its benefits. He then spent nearly a year moving with various squadrons to different places, during which time he gained a known profit of more than one hundred thousand castellanos of fine gold, not counting what the soldiers hid, an almost equal sum.

# CHAPTER VII

*Alfinger dispatches Captain Bascona (Vascuña) with twenty-five men to seek troops in Coro;[17] they all die of hunger on the way.*

ALFINGER'S wealth was now greatly increased, but his troops were proportionately decreased. He consequently sent Captain Iñigo de Bascona, a valorous native of Arévalo, to Coro to display sixty thousand pesos of gold as an example of the spoils of Alfinger's conquests in an effort to inspire other Spaniards to join in future enterprises. Bascona, accompanied by twenty-five men, was ordered to bring military supplies and the largest possible number of recruits from Coro. Alfinger said that he would try to await them in Tamalameque, but if the captain did not find him there, he should follow the army by its tracks.

Following this arrangement Bascona, his men and several Indians bearing the gold departed for Coro; but guided by his malign destiny, he would not be governed by the course they had taken on coming. He decided that since the site they now occupied was farthest inland from Lake Maracaibo, he could arrive in Coro more easily and in briefer time by following the mountain range on the left, thus leaving the lake to one side without the necessity of keeping it in sight as a landmark. Hardly was he surrounded by mountains, however, than he lost his sense of direction and, turning to the right, entered rugged terrain full of swamps and places subject to floods, so remote from human footsteps that he

## CHAPTER VII

foresaw at once the doom that awaited him. Then, their supplies having been consumed, they began to suffer hunger without any means of ameliorating the situation in that wasteland. Seeing that each day the affliction mounted and that his companions were so weak, thin, and exhausted that they could not even hold their bodies erect, he decided to lighten the load by leaving the gold buried at the foot of a beautiful ceiba tree. There, they would post signs so that if by chance any of them should come out of that labyrinth alive, they could return to retrieve their hearts, which they were burying there with the treasure.

Having rid themselves of the weight of the gold, the wretched Spaniards continued marching with few guides because most of the Indians had died of hunger. Since they had been eating nothing for days except the hearts of vijao (*visao*) plants, their ability to think was so impaired that they could not shed the dark confusion of the forest. With this delay, their necessity increased by the moment and they were in danger of perishing in that last dire moment of distress. To save their lives, they then perpetrated a cruelty so abominable that it can never be exculpated, even in light of the extreme peril facing them. They killed the few remaining Indian servants one by one and, without eschewing the intestines or any other part of the bodies, ate all of them with little revulsion. It happened that when they killed the last Indian, they quartered him and discarded his genitals as things too obscene and loathsome,[18] but one soldier, Francisco Martín, hastily snatched them up and, without waiting to enhance their flavor by cooking, ate them raw. "Why scorn them," he asked, "at a time like this?"

The Indian flesh with which they had staved off hunger for several days having now been consumed, they began to fear and distrust one another. Consequently, in harmonious accord, they separated, each following his own road to whatever fortune might hold. In those harsh surroundings, however, most of them must have perished, as nothing more was ever heard of them with the exception of four who, having the vigor to endure, succeeded at last in reaching the Chama River flowing down from the snow-covered mountains of Mérida. On the banks of that river they soon had evidence that the land was habitable when they sighted a canoe. The four Indians rowing it appeared to be nothing less than angels to those exhausted wanderers as they, on their knees, explained their tribulations by signs and begged for help.

It soon became evident that pity had a place in the brute hearts of those barbarians. Even though at first they did not dare approach the strangers, after seeing them so emaciated and unsightly, they hurriedly rowed upstream; and when they returned, the canoe was loaded with maize, yucca, yams, and other roots. Hardly had they arrived to help, however, than the Spaniards, judging that the supplies were too meager to satisfy their hunger, assailed their benefactors with the intention of killing and eating them. Because of their great weakness, however, the soldiers could not subdue the Indians, and seeing that the natives were about to escape, the Spaniards, so as not to lose them all, released three. By beating the remaining one, all four together were able to kill him, after which they cut his body into quarters and roasted it. They satisfied their hunger momentarily with the liver, lungs, feet and hands, which they ate with as much relish as if they had been from a sheep.

After committing this execrable act they began to fear that the Indians in the canoe might spread news of them in some town and that others might come looking for them to avenge the death of their companion. Thus, not daring to remain there, the three who had most strength loaded onto their shoulders their share of the flesh and other food and turned upstream. They then entered mountainous regions where they must have perished, for they never reappeared. The other, Francisco Martín, was afflicted with such pain from a wound in his leg that he could not follow his companions. He resigned himself to remaining alone, hoping for death to alleviate the tribulations that had pursued him in life. Later, finding by chance beside the river a thick, dry piece of wood that a surge of water had thrown up onto the bank, he fixed all his hope on the slight help it offered. Clasping it in his arms, he floated downstream until, a few hours later, he came upon a town. The docile and compassionate residents removed him from the water and carried him as something strange and singular to their cacique. Amazed at seeing a man with a beard and of a different color, the chieftain appreciated the gift and presented to the white man as a token of esteem some exquisite thing he owned.

Although protected by the cacique, Francisco Martín at first suffered the fears to which a stranger is always exposed. Later, however, he grew so artful in his efforts to conciliate the Indians that he became their absolute lord while imitating their barbarous customs. He renounced clothing, learned to eat malanga (*jayo*), dedicated himself to being a mohán, and devoted himself to sorcery, at which he surpassed everyone. Finally, losing shame before the world and the fear of God, he became a consummate idolater. He acquired such a reputation for his skills that he was selected to be the captain for the wars which they had with their neighbors; and in them he was always so triumphant that in gratitude the cacique gave him one of his daughters as wife, and absolute dominion over his vassals.

# CHAPTER VIII

*Alfinger leaves Tamalameque and, hounded by adversities, arrives at the Valley of Chinácota, where he is killed by Indians.*

A<small>LFINGER</small>, ignorant of Bascona's misfortunes, expected him momentarily to come with help from Coro; but seeing that the year 1531 was already half over and his lieutenant had not arrived, Alfinger decided to leave Tamalameque. He took the road between mountains and flatlands as far as the banks of the Magdalena River, where his progress was hampered by swamps and marshlands. Also, sickness was so prevalent because of bad weather and humidity that he was obliged at the end of a few days to turn back toward the mountains to seek relief in the fresh highland breezes. Thus he avoided floods and swamps, but misfortune continued to pursue him, as the mountains were harsh and the lack of provisions great. The soldiers, faint from constant adversities, remained close to the trees where some became the wretched nourishment of wild beasts.

Alfinger, by persistently struggling to overcome the rugged terrain, came at length to the river which the conquistadors who later went with Gonzalo Jiménez de Quesada to explore the Nuevo Reino de Granada called the Rió del Oro (River of Gold).[19] In this deserted place, however, they did not find anything to alleviate their hunger until some soldiers by chance discovered a lake that, although small, contained enough snails to feed them for several days. They remained at this source of supply because they were too exhausted to go forward without taking time to rest.

Meanwhile, Alfinger dispatched Esteban Martín with sixty men to search for food in nearby Indian villages. After taking several turns around the mountain, Martín came to a site in the province of Guane, near which Martín Galeano would later found the city of Vélez. This land was so abundant and densely populated that Martín easily obtained all the grain needed. He returned after twenty days to the camp and found Alfinger and his men barely subsisting on snails from the lake.

Pleased with the description of the land discovered, the Spaniards lifted camp and set out to examine it. After delaying only long enough to take on the scant provisions available, they turned their route to the paramos of Ceruitá. Later they cursed their fate for not having advanced farther, for thus they might have been the first to enjoy the riches of the opulent provinces of the Nuevo Reino de Granada, whose borders they had reached without realizing the fact. If they had marched ten more leagues to the south, they could have avoided the error, but instead they left the road they had been following and turned northward without noting that they would emerge directly on Lake Maracaibo. On that journey their tribulations were incalculable because of the frigid winds from the paramos and opposition from the Indians of Ravichá, who harassed them unmercifully in skirmishes in which several Spaniards died. After all these afflictions had been overcome, they finally reached the Valley of Chinácota, whose inhabitants, with prior knowledge of Alfinger's cruelties, abandoned their homes and withdrew to the brush without ever having seen his face. They still intended to avenge their grievances, however, and with this objective, they lay in ambush in the thickets surrounding the camp, waiting for the opportunity to put their plan into action.

Alfinger, trusting more than was prudent in the apparent tranquility of the valley, drew apart to communicate with Esteban Martín. As soon as the Indians saw them separate from the others, they came out of ambush and attacked them with such swift vigor that before the two could grasp their swords, Alfinger was already badly wounded. Concealing the injury, he valiantly faced the horde of barbarians and thus avenged the treachery of his near death by taking the lives of many of his attackers. After his comrades came to his aid the Indians withdrew, leaving Alfinger so prostrate from loss of blood that he died within three days. The memory of his atrocities is perpetuated even today in his sepulcher, which lies six or seven leagues from Pamplona, a city that Pedro de Ursúa later founded. Because of its having been the site of the tyrant's death, it retains his name, being commonly known as the Valley of Miser Ambrosio.[20]

# CHAPTER IX

*Pedro de San Martín leads the army to Coro; Juan Alemán, on the death of Alfinger, governs the province; Venegas goes out in search of the money Bascona buried but returns without finding it.*

AFTER Alfinger's death, the desire to command bred dissension in the little army. Although the claimants were many, the choice of the most influential was Factor Pedro de San Martín; but this was a preference that was not so widely accepted as to preclude disorder and tumult. The situation would have brought on insurrection if Captain Juan de Villegas had not been able to calm the troops. The new general, San Martín, ordered the camp at Chinácota lifted at the beginning of 1532, and the Spaniards then crossed the mountains, later named Arévalo. They came out on the high plateau of Cúcuta which, in spite of its unhealthful climate, has fertile pasturage and produces abundant oregano. In addition, the most widely esteemed mules of the Nuevo Reino are bred there.

After a few days at Cúcuta, the Spaniards, suffering serious setbacks and severe hunger, pursued their march until they came upon the province in which Francisco Martín lived. He was now so thoroughly transformed into an Indian and indoctrinated into their crude customs that no trace of the Spaniard remained apparent in him. His father-in-law, the cacique, on receiving the news that intruders were approaching, assembled all his warriors and turned them over to his valorous son-in-law. Martín realized that the strangers could be none other than soldiers from Alfinger's troops, with whom he once had served. Nevertheless, in order to retain a good relationship with his father-in-law and not fail in loyalty to the tribe, he set out with his warriors on the mission. When he felt that they were drawing near to the Spaniards, he left his men waiting in ambush in the neighboring mountains and approached alone. Completely naked, his entire body painted, head crowned with a panache of feathers, a quiver tilted toward his shoulders and a bow in hand, he exhibited strong characteristics of the Indians and in no respect appeared to differ from them.

He approached the Spaniards as they marched, but although he stood directly before them, he was not easily recognizable in such attire. They could not have been persuaded that he was a Spaniard like themselves, had it not been evident from his account of his own lamentable misfortunes and those of Bascona. At length convinced, they embraced him and demonstrated their grief at the death of their companions. After clothing him as adequately as their own scarcity permitted so as to cover the total indecency in which he stood, they walked together to the place where he had left the Indians waiting in ambush. Francisco Martín had acquired such authority over those simple barbarians that they observed as inviolable precepts his slightest wishes. It therefore was sufficient for him to tell them, in their own language, to discard their arms and consider the Spaniards friends for he held them as brothers. He told the Indians to come out of ambush without misgivings and offer submission to General San Martín. With many expressions of friendship they then went to the town, where they were treated cordially by the cacique as brothers of his son-in-law. Several days later the Spaniards departed, taking with them Francisco Martín and several experienced guides who led them along open trails, free of places subject to flooding. They arrived in Coro that same year of 1532, having consumed three years in a useless foray with no result other than having devastated whatever provinces through which they had passed.

On the arrival of the army, Alfinger's death became known in Coro, and a German called Juan Alemán, a close relative of the Welsers, was designated governor of the province. As he was endowed with a quiet nature, there is nothing special to relate about him, primarily because all the time he held office he stayed in Coro, where he avidly sought the profits he could attain with a tranquil tread rather than those he might acquire through conquest.

Captain Venegas had been left in charge of the sick and some others by Alfinger in the camp at Maracaibo, where they waited with remarkable patience during the three years this disastrous expedition lasted. When Venegas learned that the army now had left for Coro, he at once went to that city to see his companions and deal with affairs to his own advantage. Learning there of the sixty thousand gold pesos Bascona had buried on his ill-starred journey, Venegas decided to go with sixty loyal companions to look for them. He took Francisco Martín to indicate where the treasure had been left and they proceeded from Maracaibo to Tamalameque, where they would take up the route Bascona had followed. In the confusion of such dense forests, however, it was not easy to locate the ceiba tree under which the gold had been buried, and Francisco Martín led the men here and there between flooded areas and mangrove swamps. Venegas, equally perplexed, realized that Martín had lost his sense of direction and that if they did not turn back, they would find the same resting place as Bascona had. He ordered the retreat and they followed the short cuts and directional signs which had been left on trees for the return trip to Maracaibo.

Now, to relate at once the ultimate fate of Francisco Martín, he was full of remorse at having left his brutish life among the Indians and ardently longed to see his wife and children again. Blinded by love and violent desire, he fled and returned to the town from which the Spaniards had taken him. He felt such a sense of satisfaction in following familiar barbarous customs that even after a squadron of soldiers had brought him back to Coro, he returned a second time. And he would have committed the same mistake another hundred times if he had not been sent to the Nuevo Reino de Granada. There, distance removed opportunity, and the affection which had made him so completely lose control of himself was subdued. In this remedy consisted his tranquility, for he lived quietly afterward in the city of Santa Fe de Bogotá, penitently confessing the destruction of character to which his appetites had precipitated him.

# CHAPTER X

*The church at Coro is elevated to cathedral; Jorge de Spira (Espira) arrives as governor of the province.[21]*

On being told of the initial promise of the recently founded city of Coro, Emperor Charles V was filled with desire to convert its pagans to the Catholic faith. He therefore asked that it be elevated to a bishopric by the apostolic see. His Holiness Clement II issued a bull from Rome on June 21, 1531, in which he looked with favor on the request and entrusted the act of elevation to whatever person the emperor might present as its first prelate.

Don Rodrigo de Bastidas, dean of the Cathedral of Santo Domingo, had returned to Spain the previous year, 1530, on various negotiations for his church and was still in Madrid. Since the emperor considered him well suited for the position, he was named first bishop of the province. Then, by authority of the apostolic see in Medina del Campo, he elevated the church in Coro to cathedral on June 4, 1532. Although six prebendaries, six canons and eight lesser officials were authorized to serve it, the tithe-rents were not adequate to sustain them all and most of the appointments remained in suspension. For the moment, therefore, it was served by only eight clergymen, although capitulary funds were sufficient to support several more without depriving other churches.

Sr. Bastidas could not proceed at once to take up residence in his newly elevated cathedral because the emperor had entrusted to him a *visita general* in Puerto Rico. He was required to remain there until 1536, when he finally did depart for Coro. In the interim, to take possession in the new bishop's name and to govern the bishopric, in 1534 Bastidas sent as dean Don Juan Rodríguez de Robledo, accompanied by the cantor Don Juan Frutos de Tudela.

Nicolás de Federmann, a man of high ideals and a German by birth, was in Coro when he learned of Alfinger's death. Federmann, who was wealthy, had a close friendship with the Welsers, which encouraged him to seek the position of governor. He therefore embarked for Spain on the first passage available, well provided with money of his own and with some from friends. He presented his position at Court with such skill that the Welsers' agents readily agreed to confer the office on him, and they provided complete and specific stipulations as to how he might ensure the greatest profits for the company.

After the grant had been announced at Court, Federmann began to raise men and stock provisions in order to depart as soon as possible. However, a few who had little affection for him generated enough slander to place him in an unfavorable light with the Welsers. They imputed to him a harsh character, bellicose spirit, haughty nature and arrogant heart. On the contrary, these were the attributes most alien to him, he being endowed with an affable nature, affectionate speech, compassionate heart and calm spirit. Nevertheless the reports were sufficient to bring about the recall of his commission and deprive him of his post. In his stead another German, Jorge de Spira, was sent; but so as not to slight Federmann entirely, the Welsers named him lieutenant general with authority to lead expeditions for himself alone, since the vast expanse of the province provided room for both.

With this arrangement and four hundred men raised in Andalusia and Murcia, Spira's company sailed from San Lúcar de Barrameda on five ships in 1533. After rigorous storms obliged them to return twice to the coast of Spain, almost two hundred of the soldiers, terrified at being forced back to land a second time, decided to remain. At the cost of losing all they had ventured, they succeeded in remaining hidden on land, not daring to pursue a voyage they suspected of being accursed.

Spira, frightened by the sudden desertion of his soldiers, set sail before the rest could abandon him and followed the route to the Canaries. To reinforce his troops, he recruited the first two hundred men he encountered on those islands, disregarding the fact that they were of the rough type generally found in that land. With them and adequate provisions, he pursued his voyage and arrived in Coro at the beginning of February 1534, bringing with him numerous persons of substance who later attested to their aristocratic blood in the conquest and settlement of the province. Among them were Alonso Pacheco, native of Talavera la Vieja, progenitor of the family of this surname in Trujillo and of the Tovars in Caracas; Francisco Infante, native of Toledo, from whom the Blanco Infantes, also of Caracas, descended; Francisco de Madrid, native of Villacastín, whose merits were inherited by the Villegas family; Gonzalo Martel de Ayala, who left descendants in El Tocuyo; Montalvo de Lugo, native of Salamanca, who passed later to the Nuevo Reino de Granada and then, disillusioned, returned to Spain to enjoy a primogeniture he had inherited; Francisco Graterol, trunk of illustrious families; Damián del Barrio, native of the kingdom of Granada, whose services in America equaled those he had previously rendered in Europe with the duke of Borbón at the memorable Battle of Pavia,[22] during the sack of Rome, and from him the Parras and Castillos of Barquisimeto descended; the Silvas of this city of Caracas, and other illustrious families of the province.

# CHAPTER XI

*Spira decides to lead an expedition through the south; he sends some of his men by way of the sierras of Carora; he continues with the rest to Borburata (Burburata), and they all reassemble later at the mouth of the Barquisimeto River.*

WHEN Spira arrived in Coro he found supplies lacking in the entire region because scant rains during the year had left the fields barren. Since he was eager not to lose time in his conquests, he decided to divide his men and send them on different expeditions so that they might provide for themselves more readily in the neighboring provinces. His most practical followers held that the best way to expedite his goals was for the governor himself with four hundred men to take a turn through the plains of Carora, to the east of Coro. They next advised that his lieutenant general, Nicolás de Federmann, cross the cordillera on the west so that the mountain range, thus explored from both sides, would reveal what it encompassed. For this purpose, Federmann went first to the island of Santo Domingo to acquire, on the Welsers' credit, the horses, arms, and other equipment he would need to provide for an additional two hundred men.

When this accord had been reached, Jorge de Spira selected four hundred men and sent three hundred and twenty of them out under command of Captains Juan de Cárdenas, Martín González, and Micer Andrea, another German. He ordered these three to await him on the plains after crossing the mountains of Carora while he, with the eighty remaining troops, all cavalry, went by the coast to the port of Borburata, where they could more easily join the others.

The three captains left Coro and began to climb the steep mountain range with many discomforts because the terrain was severe, the rains continuous, and supplies scant. In addition, they had to carry their weapons constantly in hand because the Indians tried to obstruct their way at every step. The soldiers, most of them recent arrivals from Europe, were surprised by such unaccustomed and painful military tactics, but the obstacles finally were dispelled by persistence. After crossing sixty leagues of harsh and uneven land, they came out at the province of Baraure on the edge of the plains to the east. The natives did not permit them even a brief time for repose but made use of their poison-tipped arrows while the invaders, unable to fire their rain-soaked weapons, offered only weak opposition.

This anxiety and the scarcity of provisions disheartened the soldiers so greatly that, even though the move might jeopardize their reputations, they decided to return to Coro, choosing the route they surmised Governor Spira would take. They abandoned the camp during the darkest hour of the night, maintaining good order so as not to be heard by the Indians or to expose themselves to unforeseen dangers. They hoped not to stop anywhere until they came upon Spira, but the burden of transporting the sick and wounded did not permit them to continue the trip for long. Thus, they were obliged to remain encamped at the mouth of the Barquisimeto for twenty-three days, the same length of time that the governor spent in arriving there. Happy at being together again, they pursued the expedition southward through the plains and, bearing the cordillera always on the right as a lodestar, they started the return to Baraure, from which they previously had retreated.

Self-confident from success attained in past encounters, the Indians, on learning that the Spaniards were entering their province a second time, gathered in great numbers and with their customary shouting and tumult went out to engage the strangers in battle. Attacked promptly by Spira's eighty horsemen, however, they were so frightened by the mounts,

## CHAPTER XI

for they had never seen horses before, that they threw themselves on the ground, stricken equally by fierce lances and dismay at their own cowardice.

The large Indian squadron was easily broken with only three of our soldiers wounded. Then, the barbarians who escaped with their lives quickly gathered their wives and children and withdrew to the familiar protection of the brush. Thus they left their houses free to the disordered will of the Spaniards, who took lodging in them for fifteen days of relief from the heavy rains. During this time many of the soldiers, to assuage their hunger and to seek diversion, engaged in the hunt, enticed by an abundance of deer on the wide plains. One of the most ardent of the hunters, a man named Orejón, went out into some hay fields one afternoon with several companions in pursuit of a deer, but he inadvertently strayed so far that, although he killed the animal with a lance, when he tried to return to the camp, he could not find a way out. His friends, not having missed him, returned after a short while to the camp, but there they realized his absence and the governor ordered several harquebuses fired so that the shots might guide Orejón back to them. He was so frightened and confused, however, that he decided to wait until morning to try to depart. The Indians, who had stealthily followed him, had barely seen him dismount when, seizing him brusquely, they cut off his head with his own sword. The horse, frightened by the tumult, ran furiously through the hay fields and, with better judgment than its master, entered the camp whinnying, from which the soldiers suspected what Orejón's fate had been.

The next morning the governor sent Captain Juan de Villegas with a squadron of soldiers to search for Orejón, but after a turn around the plain without any sign of him, the captain went toward the mountain where at a short distance he saw a sparsely populated town. The natives, trusting in their palisades, tried to defend themselves, but since the superiority of the harquebuses over their feeble arrows was at once apparent, they quickly took flight. This action gave the Spaniards the opportunity to sack the town where they found Orejón's sword and a part of his head, which the Indians had preserved in condiments for a later feast in celebration of their victory. Infuriated by this proof of the disastrous end of their companion, the Spaniards sought to assuage their longing for vengeance by hanging as many Indians as they could find and leaving the town in ashes. They then rejoined Spira who, wanting to improve the location of the camp because of the rigors of the present site, marched for two days to the town of Aricagua which, being closer to high terrain, offered some comfort during the wait for the constant rains to break.[23]

BOOK I

# CHAPTER XII

*Federmann sends his men ahead to Cabo de la Vela and embarks for Hispaniola; Captain Chaves seizes Captain Rivera; Federmann returns to Tierra Firme and initiates its pearl-fishing industry.*

ALTHOUGH Federmann had promised Spira that, on his return from Hispaniola with the supplies he was going to seek, he would go on an expedition across the mountains to the west, it was never his intention to fulfill his word. Instead, as soon as Spira left Coro for Borburata, Federmann revealed to his friends his aspiration to command independently without depending on a superior's whim. He enlisted as many as he could and dispatched them under the command of his lieutenant, Antonio de Chaves, whom he ordered to return to Maracaibo and proceed without delay to Cabo de la Vela. He was to wait there until Federmann returned from Hispaniola, for which he would embark at the same time Chaves left for the lake.

Many days previously, Federmann had secretly communicated his decision to Alonso Martín, who was in charge of the brigantines which Alfinger had left in Maracaibo. Thus, when Chaves arrived at the lake, Martín was awaiting him with these vessels and several canoes, in which all the soldiers then embarked. They crossed to the camp on the other shore, hoping to remain there for an extended period to allow Federmann time to return from Hispaniola. But scarcity of supplies and widespread illness obliged Chaves to divide his men into three squadrons so they could with less difficulty sustain themselves with whatever was found at hand. He then sent them to various places, having ordered them all to reassemble at Cabo de la Vela by a certain date.

In the year 1535, Captain Juan de Rivera was engaged in the conquest of Ramada by order of Doctor Infante, judge of the Audiencia de Santo Domingo who, following García de Lerma's death, became governor of Santa Marta. Pressed by a lack of supplies, Rivera dispatched a troop of twenty men from his camp on the banks of the Macomite River in the direction of Lake Maracaibo to seek help. However, as one of Chaves's squadrons, commanded by Captain Murcia, also took the river road, it was inevitable that the two groups should meet in the mountain pass; but Murcia's men were so skillful that they were able to take Rivera's men prisoner. Chaves, convinced that Rivera had entered

## CHAPTER XII

land within the jurisdiction of Santa Marta, gathered his divided troops and marched to Macomite, where Rivera was quartered. There, he compelled the captain by pleas and threats to continue to Cabo de la Vela with all his able-bodied men, leaving the sick behind to be brought later as time permitted.

After this agreement was reached, they left Macomite together and entered the land of the Guajiros, a haughty and bellicose people. The Spaniards were so tormented by repeated skirmishes with these Indians that at one point Guzmán de Avellaneda and six other soldiers were seized and on the point of being carried off alive. At last, however, without help from their companions, they freed themselves and escaped from that dangerous situation. Chaves then realized the importance of leaving that belligerent nation at once and hastened the pace of his troops until they arrived at the land of the Cocinas. From there he sent three soldiers, Alonso Martín de Quesada, Diego Agudo, and Alonso de Olaya Herrera to Macomite for the sick men he had left behind. Armed with nothing more than swords and shields, they courageously turned back across the land of the Guajiros to Macomite, where they made the sick ready for the journey as soon as the horses sent by Chaves arrived.

The joy those miserable Spaniards felt on seeing the three soldiers was such that, though unable to stand, they slid out of their hammocks to the ground and gave thanks for this help. Hunger and illness had prostrated them and many had died without the few still alive having had the strength even for the merciful act of interring them. Encouraged now, they set out for the land of the Cocinas to join Chaves, and he, delighted at seeing them, left at once for Cabo de la Vela, where he found that Federmann had just arrived from Hispaniola with eighty men and a substantial number of horses.

On learning of the Rivera incident, Federmann tried to convince him to remain in his company and follow him voluntarily; but the captain excused himself, pleading the necessity of returning to Santa Marta. Federmann then allowed him and his men to go freely, and liberally assisted in whatever was needed for the journey.

Federmann next made preparations for his stay in Cabo de la Vela, as he had for some time held secretly acquired information on the vast quantity of pearls which that coast produced. Wishing now to see how fortune would look on the endeavor, he failed to keep the promise he had made to Spira. He instructed his men to wait for him at Cabo de la Vela while he went to Hispaniola to search for experienced men among the many taking part in such activities on the island of Cubagua to help in his efforts. Then he devised a piece of equipment fashioned like a rake to facilitate the pearl fishing. No matter how much he worked with the instrument, however, casting it repeatedly on sandbanks where host bodies were to be found, he could not make a throw that showed promise of succeeding. The same failure plagued many who made this attempt afterward until the better method of diving for pearls, the procedure still in use today, was developed. The profit fell to others, while Federmann's only glory was in having made the discovery. Through his diligence the treasure this sea has rendered in pearls was suggested to those who subsequently cultivated them and enriched the world.

# CHAPTER XIII

*Spira leaves Aricagua and arrives at the province of Barinas; he quarrels with his lieutenant and sends him back as a prisoner to Coro; he crosses the Opia (Upia) River and suffers great hardships.*

AFTER waiting three months in Aricagua for the winter rains to break, Governor Jorge de Spira lifted camp as soon as the dry season set in. Skirting the mountains to the right, he arrived at the province of Coyones whose natives, knowing nothing of Spanish arms but eager to prove their own courage, went out in military order to harass the enemy. They were attacked by our men and for a time held their ground, but eventually withdrew after the loss of their principal leaders. Some of our men were wounded and Captain Montalvo was pricked by arrows after his lance had been snatched from his hands.

Spira lingered there several days seeking food. Then, after two months of confronting continuous obstacles, having crossed over almost impassable mountains, he reached the spot where the city of Barinas later was to be founded. Pursued by hunger, the soldiers, finding no other substance, lived for many days on nothing but hearts of palms and the stalks of vijao plants. They became sick and weak from this diet, lost much weight and even lacked the breath to walk. They were consoled, however, on learning that in the valley there were several towns and fertile fields. The governor accordingly dispatched his lieutenant, Francisco de Velasco, with several foot soldiers and cavalry under orders to stop when they arrived at the towns in the crags of the sierra. He told Velasco to send men to the fields to gather whatever was most abundant, and to make every effort to find salt because the army was totally without it.

## CHAPTER XIII

With these instructions, Velasco departed, and on arriving at the foot of the cordillera he and the cavalrymen stopped as ordered. He sent foot soldiers forward under Nicolás de Palencia, who walked, or rather crawled, through the underbrush until they came upon a large house in a thicket where the Indians had hidden more than one thousand five hundred fanegas of maize. Since Palencia was reluctant to advance farther for fear of losing what fortune had provided, he halted there to guard the grain. He then sent soldiers with all the maize which a considerable band of Indians could carry on their shoulders to Lieutenant Velasco who, pleased and wishing to notify the governor of the bountiful aid, ordered the bearers to bring him another two or three portions like the first. He sent this second load to Spira and told the officer in charge to observe attentively the governor's manner on receiving the supplies. His reaction did not reflect the courtesy and gratitude Velasco had expected; rather, Spira aloofly expressed anger, attributing the delay in sending help to negligence. When he learned of this attitude, Velasco, blind with rage, burst out: "May the body of Christ plague the governor! Why is he not more grateful for what his soldiers do to serve him? By the devil, even though he has a hundred black capes, I have two hundred white ones."[24] Then, gathering together his soldiers and the Indians with all the maize they could carry, he returned to camp.

Velasco's manner of expressing his sentiments seemed inappropriate to all who heard him, among whom many wished to gain favor with their superiors. One of them informed the governor of the outburst, whereupon the enraged Spira imprisoned Velasco at once. After the case had been substantiated and legal action brought, the governor would have beheaded his lieutenant had not Juan de Villegas, Damián del Barrio, Alonso Pacheco, and Juan de Guevara intervened. Their mediation was sufficient to cause the governor to revoke the sentence and remand the offender as a prisoner to Coro. Along with him, Spira sent the sick so as to free himself of the encumbrance they imposed on the march. With an escort to convoy them through the province of Baraure, the sick men in time rejoined the governor who soon lifted camp and entered the immense sea of the open plains, the Llanos. As he was traveling now without excessive hindrance, he could easily, after crossing the Casanare, Sarare and Apure rivers, penetrate to the barrancas of the Opia, where he found several towns with abundant supplies of food. With these provisions it seemed to him that he could sustain his troops without leaving that site during the rainy season and thus avoid the menacing waters of those rivers.

To this end he chose the highest spot, the one least vulnerable to flooding, on the banks of a river close to a mountain; and there he established huts in which to pass the winter. However, that season entered with more vigor than anticipated and the Opia rose in such torrents that it inundated the countryside, converting fields into seas and leaving Spira encompassed by its waters. Also, he still lacked food, and illness constantly plagued him, leading finally to his ruination.

Adding to these afflictions was a horde of jaguars from the nearby mountains which, fleeing the high waters, left only the loftiest peak as a place of refuge for the men. A Portuguese, Manuel de Serpa, lost his life when he and several companions strayed not thirty feet from camp to gather a small fruit called jobo.[25] He was assaulted by a jaguar with such speed that his companions could not prevent his being torn to pieces.

Serpa's tragedy was followed by similar ones, and caused such terror that even the horses dared not graze outside the camp. The Spaniards decided to build a balsa raft in which to cross over to a hamlet on the other bank of the river in search of seeds or roots to make life more bearable. The raft was finished in fifteen days and appeared to be so strong and adequate that the entire army might have embarked on it together.

The Spaniards cast the craft into the water and, with a special oar to steer it and several good swimmers to tow it with ropes, they began the crossing. They navigated with ease until they arrived at some eddies in the stream but there, tossed by the waves, they were forced to yield to the river's violence.

The Indians on the other bank observed the terror of the soldiers and were expecting the latters' death at any moment. The natives sprang hastily into their canoes and set out, rowing at top speed, with hopes of attaining a victory at little or no cost by killing or seizing the men on the raft. It would have happened thus if Francisco de Cáceres, one of the swimmers steering the craft, had not plunged into the waves. While the Indians were diverted by this human target, the raft, pushed by the surge of the river, was able to reach the bank; but after two days the Spaniards began the return to camp with no hope of relief.

After a few days the inclement weather finally relented and the river subsided so that Spira's men were able to ford it at a point above the village. They then entered provinces of such different races and languages that they could not find an interpreter who understood them. The Spaniards did not recognize the Indians at the time but, judging from their location, they were without any doubt the Chiscas and Olanchas, who live along the border of the Nuevo Reino de Granada.

## CHAPTER XIV

*Spira receives information on the province of the Nuevo Reino but does not act upon it; he continues his expedition to the south and arrives at the province of Mal-País.*

An Indian ally understood a few words of the language of one of the barbarians whom Spira had seized, and with difficulty could interpret it in his own clumsy idiom. Responding to various questions, the captive informed him that by traveling several days toward the west he would find rich and fertile lands populated by tribes who wore cotton cloaks and gold jewelry, and who were governed by established laws. Spira heard this account with indifference and such scant attention was paid to guarding the Indian that he was able to flee during the night. Spira was now without a guide but, incited by curiosity and a desire to find these rich countries, he dispatched Juan de Villegas with forty men, among whom were Francisco Infante, Gonzalo Martel de Ayala, Francisco de Madrid, Juan Cuaresma de Melo, Hernán Pérez de la Muela, and Alonso de Campos. Spira ordered Villegas to cross the cordillera to the west to see if the terrain corresponded to the Indian's story. After traveling three days through the sierras, however, Villegas suspended the endeavor and returned to camp, though he had more valid reason to continue, for in several small towns he found portions of cotton mantles and cakes of salt that verified the Indian's report. With the slight effort of advancing ten more leagues, he would have reaped the riches of the Nuevo Reino; but that discovery was forever denied to the Germans. Already, as has been seen, Ambrosio de Alfinger had arrived twice, once in the province of Guane and again on the paramos of Ceruitá, at the threshold of that opulent kingdom, and on both occasions had withdrawn impetuously, changing his route merely to seek better weather. Later, Federmann also turned his back on that conquest even though he was so close to its fulfillment.

After Villegas informed Spira that the sierra was impregnable, the governor did not persist in seeking lands that all now considered to be a mere fantasy. Setting their sights always to the south, they pursued their journey without hopes of finding the riches their imaginations suggested and which the Indians falsely promised to induce the intruders to leave their land. They entered the Llanos, and at the beginning of 1536 arrived at a land so sterile and dusty, so full of ravines and quebradas, that they called it Mal-País (Badland). They held some of its few inhabitants who, responding more by signs than by words, revealed that a short distance to the left there was a sizable town whose inhabitants wore gold jewelry. Spira could not have heard more pleasing news, for he saw this as evidence that his fortune had led him to a place where his greed would be satisfied. Halting at the spot about which he had received the information, he dispatched Damián del Barrio with sixty men and a few Indian guides to lead the Spaniards toward their goal.

After marching a few leagues, they discovered a steep hill covered with luxuriant trees. At its summit on a broad smooth space was a town of up to a hundred houses, so capacious that an entire family with all its relatives could occupy each. Its defense consisted of a wall built of boards and trunks of spiny palms placed close together, but separated at intervals so the Indians could shoot their arrows in safety. This wall was surrounded by a deep moat heavily laced with sharp-pointed, toasted sticks and covered with slender earth-colored rods, so well contrived that the ruse was difficult to recognize.

As soon as Damián del Barrio arrived at the foot of the mountain, he judged that the fortress was unassailable, but he decided to attack so that his gallant spirit would be even more apparent. On signal, Miguel Lorenzo, native of Jaén, dashed out ahead of all, eager to be first in the fray; but he was also first to fall into the trap which the moat hid. Hardly had he stepped on the frail sticks when they crumbled under his weight, but he was lucky enough to fall between their intricately arranged tips and was not wounded, though badly frightened. His companions were able to extricate him just in time, for the Indians started shooting arrows, hurling stones, and throwing spears with toasted tips from the protection of their walls. Most of the soldiers were wounded, without the strength to exact vengeance, and ashamed that they were being compelled to withdraw. They attempted to renew the assault on the village which, because of its similarity to Salsas on the frontier of Catalonia, they called Salsillas. Damián del Barrio, after considering the difficulty of the undertaking, decided that to persist would expose his men to serious risk. Leaving the Indians to glory in their triumph, he turned back in search of Governor Spira with no prize other than an Indian woman whom they had captured. They placed her in fetters but, burdened by the weight of a chain about her neck, she complained bitterly of such inhuman cruelty, saying that the other Spaniards she had had as masters had not treated her so harshly.

These words caused amazement among the soldiers as they pondered on where or how she could have seen other Spaniards when they themselves supposedly were the first to have penetrated these remote provinces. When Spira ordered the woman brought before him so he could determine the origin of this strange story, she explained that ten days' journey downstream, in a province filled with many Indian towns surrounded by palisades, there dwelt white men with beards who used swords for their defense. These men were old, she knew, because it had been many years since they had fled up that river and married Indian women, with whom they had had numerous children. Several moons ago they had come to her town and, seizing her and other women, had carried them off as prisoners; but later the white men had set them free without abusing them.

The soldiers, filled with curiosity by this relation, had an ardent desire to search for those men, for they felt that at the cost of a slight effort, within a few days they might locate them; but Spira did not want to wander from the pursuit of his conquest simply to seek out surprises. He judged the news to be false, and thought it unwise to venture so lightly on an expedition that could end only in disillusionment. Although he succeeded in calming most of the men, there were a few who considered the woman's story to be true. They had no doubt that those Spaniards living on the river were of the group that Commander Don Diego Ordaz had lost when the ship of his lieutenant general Juan Cornejo, battling the waters of the Orinoco, apparently had gone down in its rushing currents since nothing more was ever heard of it. The soldiers now reflected that some could have escaped on small vessels and reached this place in their wanderings. This conjecture took on such substance that His Majesty Philip II, by cedula issued in 1559, ordered the Audiencia de Santa Fe de Bogotá to search out and discover the lost Spaniards. Despite assiduous efforts, however, no explanation was found to lend credence to this supposition. If those who spread this word had compared the circumstances with the time, they would have known how ill-founded was this misconception. It is incredible that even had they escaped the storm with their lives, they could have preserved them while crossing provinces so remote, peopled by hordes of belligerent and barbarous tribes.

# BOOK II

## CHAPTER I

*Federmann leaves Cabo de la Vela and enters the Upar Valley; he meets Captain Rivera and they return together to Maracaibo. From there he dispatches Captain Martínez to the cordillera of Carora with the order to await him in Tacarigua.*

NICOLÁS de Federmann, tired of wasting time on the pearl fishery he had initiated at Cabo de la Vela, consulted his captains on the most advantageous route for new explorations. Most of them favored following the trail which Ambrosio de Alfinger had taken to the banks of the Magdalena River, and from there southward. They felt that the lands discovered upriver gave hopes of rich provinces at the headwaters whose conquest had eluded Alfinger because he had shifted his route to the east. This opinion was contrary to the judgment of several who remembered the hardships of that expedition and were disinclined to experience them again. Federmann, nevertheless, decided to travel the same road in the hope of gaining what Alfinger had missed. He left Cabo de la Vela with four hundred well-armed men at the beginning of 1536 and directed his march toward the Upar Valley. Hardly had he left the coast and entered the warm regions, however, when the change of temperature and lack of water made everyone ill with such violent attacks that the men were prostrated. At each move some died, but even the risk of losing them all was not enough to induce Federmann to delay in order to help anyone. His only aim then was to reach the Upar Valley as quickly as possible in the hope that its benign climate would cure their many ailments, and indeed, from the moment he set foot on its fertile land, improvements did set in. At the same time he had the pleasure of again meeting Captain Rivera who, after having taken leave of Federmann, had departed from Cabo de la Vela to return to Santa Marta. Disappointed at having been unable to reach the city because of swollen rivers and opposition from the Chimila Indians, he returned in search of Federmann, hoping to buy a ship from him since by sea he could travel more safely.

As Federmann's army was severely reduced by his losses en route, it seemed to him a good time to recruit Rivera and his fifty men. With skillful manifestations of esteem, he effected an accord that they would pursue the expedition together. Rivera's men resented this agreement, however, finding it difficult to consider serving under another, especially since they had imputed to Federmann duplicity in dealing with their captain. They consequently attempted a revolt that was averted at the very beginning by the torture death of the two most guilty and the flight of six others seeking to avoid the same fate. They fled by unfrequented paths and did not stop until they reached Santa Marta, where they found the adelantado de Canaria, Don Pedro Fernández de Lugo, serving as governor. On learning of Federmann's intention to continue southward to provinces included within the limits of his own grant, Fernández de Lugo wrote the intruder a courteous letter asking him not to pursue this inimical act. Accompanied by friendly Indians, Fernández de Lugo reached Federmann's territory on the Magdalena River near the sierra of Ocaña. Forewarned by friends of the strength of the adelantado's forces, however, Federmann chose not to place himself in the danger of coming to an open break. Confused by divergent opinions, he elected to heed the most damaging. Thus he repeated the error, so many times committed by Alfinger and Spira, of abandoning the route to the south and returning to the Upar Valley; and thus, like the others, he lost the glory of discovering the Nuevo Reino. As the strong desire to command independently was tugging at him he decided to return to Coro, where he thought the commissions expected from his government would be awaiting him.

Federmann divided his men into two squadrons so that they might more easily provide food for themselves as they proceeded by different routes to Maracaibo, one group under his own command and the other entrusted to Pedro de Limpias. The latter, marching along the sierra which divides the Upar Valley from the lake, arrived in a few days at some towns built on reeds and marshes, and they named these swamplands Brazos de Herina (Arms, or Bay, of Herina). Here Limpias seized a substantial amount of gold jewelry and gold dust from the natives and then passed through in search of Federmann's camp at Maracaibo. From this unexpected incident was born the fame of the Brazos de Herina, whose riches, nevertheless, have remained so well concealed that, although many have sought them, only disappointments have resulted.

When Limpias arrived at Maracaibo, he found Federmann already embroiled in a thousand worries, consisting primarily of a lack of food and difficulties anticipated in crossing the lake. The problems arose from Antonio de Chaves's having burned the brigantines when he left Maracaibo for Cabo de la Vela to await Federmann, thinking there would be no need to return to the lake or use the boats further. Fortunately, however, it happened that while the freeboard of one of the ships had been consumed by fire, the hull itself had remained whole. It had sunk to the bottom of the lake but was recovered by Federmann's soldiers, who succeeded in raising it. The craft, repaired as thoroughly as possible under the circumstances, comfortably transported the entire army to the other side. There Federmann ordered Diego Martínez, native of Valladolid, to march with the greater part of the troops along the side of the Carora Mountains until he came out at the Valley of Tacarigua. He was to await Federmann there while the latter returned to Coro to seek news of the expected government dispatches. Then, with the greatest number of men available, Martínez was to join Federmann in an attempt to discover the riches of the Meta River, which has its source near Boyacá beyond Tunja.

After Federmann departed for Coro, Martínez left for the mountains, where he suffered the usual lack of food. Hernando Montero, whom he sent out with a group of soldiers to look for aid, lost one of his men, Martín Tinajero, who died of an illness that he had concealed. Tinajero, native of Ecija in Andalusia, had never affronted anyone and had conducted himself in an unpretentious manner in the many disorders generated by an army. After his companions had buried him in an excavation that the winter rains had made, they gathered all the grain they could carry and returned to camp. Because they were waiting for Federmann, Montero and his troops traveled slowly, and as a consequence, Martínez, after a few days, was obliged to send another squadron to seek food. Among them, several of those who had buried Tinajero were moved by curiosity, on approaching the ravine, to see whether the Indians had disinterred him. However, before drawing very near, they were assailed by a fragrance so mellow and an odor so singular that they were perplexed as to the source of so wondrous an effect. Looking toward the grave they realized that Tinajero's body was half uncovered and that the delicate scent was emanating from that rigid cadaver. Swarms of impassioned wild bees had invaded the body to blend its aroma with the fragrance of their honey. His companions, not daring to touch the remains, were amazed and, on returning to the camp, related the prodigious occurrence and reminisced about Tinajero's modest habits and quiet discretion. As the conquistadors had their sights fixed more on discovering riches than on verifying miracles, however, they were so little concerned that they did not even bother to give the body a more decent burial nor install a memento of where it lay.[1]

## CHAPTER II

*Martínez fights the Jirajara Indians; he enters the province of Carora and continues to that of El Tocuyo, where some of Governor Ortal's soldiers join him.*

DIEGO Martínez, aided by the food supplies his soldiers were able to pilfer, continued his march until he encountered the bellicose tribe of Jirajara Indians, for many years the scourge of all this province of Venezuela. At the news that strangers were approaching their lands, the natives prepared their weapons, formed squadrons and went out to battle. Their courage was so great that the Spanish vanguard, commanded by Juan Gascón, later a resident of the city of Vélez, was broken and routed. The Indians would have won the victory had not Martínez persistently assailed them until they took flight. Our troops suffered considerable losses and many were wounded, including García Calvete, who was struck by an arrow that entered the lacrimal duct and traversed the nape of his neck. Not only was he healed but his sight afterward was as clear and free of damage as before. All those who knew him later as a resident of Vélez bore witness to this portentous event.

The Jirajaras were deeply angered by the rout, even more so on seeing that the Spaniards, once the skirmish was over, had taken possession of their town. Seeking vengeance but not daring to attempt it openly, it seemed fitting to them to resort to treachery by expressing a false desire for peace. To implement the deception, more than one thousand remained in ambush while four hundred entered the town, carrying their arms hidden in bundles of hay in which they feigned to be bringing gifts of fruit. Their guile was discovered, however, by alert Indian servants who warned Martínez of the ruse. He hurriedly ordered his men to take up arms and fell upon the Indians so suddenly that, leaving most of them dead and up to eighty captured, he obliged the rest to seek safety in flight. On hearing the clamor of their departure, the Indians in ambush, thinking the time to attack our men off guard had come, went out joyously to assault them. Finding the Spaniards with arms in hand, however, and seeing their own four hundred companions dead, captured or routed, they became so perturbed that they sought peace without trickery, ransoming the prisoners with gold and food.

A few days after this event, Martínez and his men left the town and arrived at the site where years before Captain Salamanca had founded the city of Portillo de Carora. Finding in that vicinity a large number of Indians of affable nature, with an abundance of food, he decided to remain several days to restore the men with rest and indulgence. After lingering two months, he pursued the journey to the south through valleys and mountain passes until he reached the province of El Tocuyo, where a city of the same name was later established. Martínez decided to await Federmann there, billeting his troops on the ruins of a town that only a short time before had been sacked and burned by the Gayón Indians who inhabited the immediate sierras and harbored a natural enmity for the Tocuyos.

As Martínez was reposing in his quarters, Captains Jerónimo de Alderete and Martín Nieto arrived at the camp with sixty men. These soldiers had been on expedition with Governor Jerónimo de Ortal, whom the emperor had appointed on the death of Commandant Don Diego de Ordaz to govern Paria and Maracapana. While Ortal was engaged in conquests, Alonso de Escalante, inspector of the Royal Treasury and a man of rebellious nature, was instigated by Machín de Oñate to lead the army in brazen revolt against Ortal. They took him prisoner and, together with his lieutenant, Alvaro de Ordaz, three horsemen, and ten foot soldiers, transported him to the coast. Many of the soldiers, not wishing to become involved in so ugly an operation, returned to the coast with noble resolve to follow their governor in his adverse fortune. The rest, either afraid of punishment or imbued with the hope of finding some rich province in which to settle profitably, named as their leaders Alderete and Nieto. Next they plunged inland and crossed from the banks of the Orinoco to the province of El Tocuyo. Recognizing traces of Spaniards there, they feared that these might be soldiers of Governor Antonio Sedeño, with whom they had had hotly disputed differences in Paria, or they thought perhaps that it was some judge sent by the Audiencia de Santo Domingo to punish the disrespect shown the governor. Learning soon, however, that they were people with whom they had had no prior unpleasant encounters, they approached the camp without misgiving. There they found Martínez, who could not persuade himself that these sixty men had crossed such vast provinces as those lying between El Tocuyo and Maracapana. This reasoning led him to suspect that the squadron might be a group that Governor Ortal was following in an attempt to force them to abandon Federmann and follow him. For this reason, Martínez reassembled his divided troops and took great care in assigning them to their quarters, an attention that did not prevent Nieto and Alderete from distrusting Martínez. Thus, located in separate camps although in the same valley, they remained wary of one another until an unexpected event led them to reconcile their differences.

## CHAPTER II

It happened that from the sierra the Gayones saw smoke coming from the Spaniards' camp and inferred that the Tocuyos had reoccupied the town which the Gayones had burned. The latter considered this daring act a reflection on their reputation and resolved to give the Tocuyos the punishment their disrespect deserved. They began the process by opening new roads through a craggy mountainside until they came upon our men. Although surprised at not finding the ones they sought, they attacked with such courage that the soldiers of both companies desperately needed their companions to repel the four thousand warriors (*gandules*) who composed the enemy army. The defeat of the Indians earned high praise for Alderete, to whom the major part of the success was due. The Alderete and Nieto factions set aside all suspicions and communicated without duplicity everything that had happened on their expeditions and Martínez sent an account of these events to Federmann who, blind with desire to be governor, still remained in Coro hourly expecting the appointment. After receiving Martínez's news, however, he started out immediately, doubling the days' marches until he arrived at El Tocuyo, where he succeeded in incorporating the sixty men into his troops. They followed him voluntarily, although captains Nieto and Alderete, having higher aspirations, excused themselves from accompanying him and asked only for an escort to convoy them to Coro en route to Santo Domingo. There Nieto subsequently died and Alderete traveled on into Peru and later became Adelantado of the provinces of Chile.

Federmann, rejoicing in the reinforcement of his army with those sixty men, revealed to his soldiers his lack of arms, accoutrements and provisions. Since affability in a superior is a pleasant surprise, he used this quality to procure the loan of all the gold his men possessed. With these funds he dispatched Captain Beteta to Coro, and he returned with the supplies needed within a few days. Wishing to take advantage of the little time remaining of the summer of 1537, Federmann then evacuated his camp at El Tocuyo and passed on to the Valley of Barquisimeto.

BOOK II

# CHAPTER III

*Governor Spira fights the Indians of Mal-País and other tribes; he reaches the province of Papamene.*[2]

GOVERNOR Jorge de Spira's soldiers, relying on the Indian woman's relation, were eager to go in search of the lost Spaniards, but Spira was trying to dissuade them. To deprive the men of the leisure to think more about it, he hastened his departure; but before he started out, the Indians decided to use arms to rid themselves of oppression. With this purpose, all tribes in the vicinity of Mal-País came to the camp one morning at daybreak and, finding one of the sentinels asleep, took his life with a blow of a burnt-tipped spear. The other sentinels then quickly apprised the Spaniards that the Indians were attacking from all sides. Facing each other as the first light streaked the sky, the two forces joined battle with such spirit that for several hours the outcome was in doubt. Besides being numerous, tireless and resolute, the barbarians had a strong asset in a group of stonecutters who, with snapping slings and hurling rocks, so frightened the horses that neither bit nor spur could compel them to enter the battle. When the Indians noted this circumstance, they were inspired to even more fury. Spira therefore ordered Alonso Pacheco to go out with fifty foot soldiers and fifteen horsemen to attack the Indians from the rear.

Pacheco, carrying out Spira's orders, caught the Indians off guard and unable to counter the surprise attack. They therefore fled the camp and left the victory to our troops, although at great cost to us. Many of our men were wounded, some so gravely that Spira was obliged to remain there fifteen additional days for them to be treated. Then he pursued his journey without straying from the foothills until he reached a town on the site of which Juan de Avellaneda later was to found the city of San Juan de los Llanos. At that time, however, Spira's soldiers called it Nuestra Señora because in it they celebrated Assumption Day in the year 1537 with a great feast and much rejoicing. Although the Indians' promise of opulent provinces farther on was a ruse to entice the Spaniards to move out of their lands, Spira regarded it as true; and since he was impatient to possess them, he set out the day following the fiesta. After a few hours' march, the Spaniards were attacked by a sizable number of Indians with bows and arrows to impede their passage. However, our men were advancing cautiously with weapons in hand and, at

## CHAPTER III

the first rain of arrows, the horsemen, lancing and trampling, charged with such fury that they quickly defeated the natives. The Indians were so terrified that, observing the horses from a distance, they hurled themselves to the ground without the courage to move and covered their faces to avoid seeing them. This strong preconceived fear allowed Spira to pass on without hindrance to the banks of the Ariare River, where he remained several days because its turbulent waters did not allow fording.

The Indians who lived on the other bank were not surprised by the strangers. Without misgivings they rowed across at once to trade, carrying a quantity of food to exchange for items from Castile, especially the little bells which pleased them most. Before landing they prudently asked the Spaniards by signs to vacate the beach where the Indians would place what they wished to exchange and collect what the soldiers left there as payment for local products.

Without seeking communication other than that cautious contact, Spaniards and Indians continued to trade until the river receded. This delay gave Spira an opportunity to cross to the other bank, after which he led his army through the lands of the Canicamares and Guayupes. He had to open a passage by force of arms because of the tenacious opposition of those tribes, especially the Guayupes, who offered a ferocious battle. Their heads were crowned with feathers and their nude bodies painted with the juice of the genipap, a fruit something like an apple with which they stained their skin in order to appear more formidable to their adversaries. With us, however, they gained scant advantage with such contrivances for, although they valorously resisted our foot soldiers, when attacked later by the horsemen they were easily routed. They abandoned their towns to the soldiers, who knew well how to profit from what was in them. Passing on without delay, they discovered, after a few days' march, the waters of the celebrated Papamene River. It seemed wise to Spira to linger a while here to allow his men to rest; and he also wished to question the guides about the riches which his desires assured him were real.

The unexpected visit of the Spaniards amazed the Indians of Papamene, as their persons, beards and clothing, together with the horses, were all things alien to the natives. Feeling a strong desire to become acquainted with the strangers at closer range, they cautiously approached in their canoes. The soldiers, by signs more than words, assured the Indians that they could with confidence disembark, but they had no faith in the unknown intruders and withdrew to the other side of the river. More than three hundred canoes soon congregated there and about two thousand Indians, reassured by their own great number, were then transported to the bank on which the Spaniards awaited them. The Indians drew close to the beach but a vestige of distrust still kept them from leaving their canoes. Then Spira, to rid them of their suspicions, assured them through interpreters that since he aspired only to their friendship, they might communicate without fear. Adding to the words concrete evidence of esteem, he sent them away with such gifts as knives and little bells, happy with the Spaniards' liberality.

With Spira's affable treatment, the Indians continued to come to the camp almost every day with fruits and grilled fish. Little by little they lost their apprehension to such a degree that they entered the soldiers' quarters as freely as their own houses. With this familiarity the Spaniards acquired information about the provinces and tribes which lay ahead and tried to determine whether they would find in them gold or silver. To each inquiry the Indians responded in accord with the desire revealed by painting the lands as so fertile and abundant that the soldiers felt they already held treasures in their hands. So as not to defer possession of something that might be endangered by delay, they left Papamene, taking four or five Indians to guide them safely to the riches they considered inevitably theirs.

# CHAPTER IV

*The Indians deceive Spira by maliciously leading him to the province of the Choques;[3] he sends Esteban Martín to reconnoiter the territory, but the mission is unsuccessful.*

SPIRA and his troops crossed the Papamene River in canoes and followed the guides with confidence; but they, either through ignorance of the route or out of malice, led them into the province of the Choques. They then fled by night, leaving the Spaniards in that rugged and swampy terrain, which was inhabited by bellicose Indians of deceptive temper, surly behavior, and an intractable disposition. They were skillful and courageous in war, in which they used spears of palm stakes whose blades were edged with human shin bones. Barbaric in their customs, the father was not safe from his own son, nor the wife from her husband, as they killed each other like wild animals solely to satiate their bestial appetite for human flesh.

In this disagreeable land, Spira sought the cleanest and least humid site in which to quarter his men. He ordered his campmaster, Esteban Martín, with fifty foot soldiers and twenty cavalry to explore the condition of the land and estimate the number of its inhabitants. After marching only a few leagues, however, Martín found so many bogs and swamps that neither the foot soldiers nor the horsemen could surmount them. Although the men attempted to pass through many places, they were always submerged in mire up to their horses' girths and were injured by the sharp branches and roots of the mangrove trees. Thus they were obliged to return and report to Spira the difficulties they had encountered, but they were not sufficient to cause him to change his mind. On the contrary, he ordered Martín to leave the horsemen, go back out at once with the fifty foot soldiers and, following another road, complete without excuse the mission entrusted to him.

Esteban Martín, a veteran of several expeditions, was a high-spirited man, well acquainted with the region and Indian war methods. In light of the unfavorable disposition of the land and the ferocity of the Choques, he recognized the danger to which Spira's stubbornness gave rise but he did not dare dissent for fear his prudence might appear to be lack of valor. He nevertheless did say to the governor: "Your Grace has ordered me to explore this province. May it please God that at least one of us may live to bring back an account of the disastrous end to this venture." Then he set forth with his fifty men to carry out the command, plagued by rain that fell both night and day. They passed through the towns near the camp and reached a mountain so overcast and full of ravines that they felt doomed. The unfavorable weather, lack of comforts, and sparse benefits to be expected led them, at the end of five days, to go back over that wretched trail. After four days' march, they came to some maize fields from which a long open path stretched. This they followed without stopping to rest, and during the last quarter of the night they came out at a little town of about thirty houses, built on the top of a hill.

After Martín had explored the village he halted to reorganize his men and to wait for the exhausted Indian servants who had lagged behind. Since they still did not arrive and he wanted to take advantage of the darkness for an assault, he ordered Nicolás de Palencia, later a resident of the city of Pamplona in the Nuevo Reino de Granada, to await the bearers there while he advanced on the town. On hearing this clamor, the Indians awoke, seized their arms and rushed to the scene of action. They attacked so suddenly that the Spaniards, previously divided, now formed one body because the Indians were numerous, handled their spears skillfully and were on familiar terrain. They had a significant advantage over our men who, confused by the heavy downpour and the dark of the night, did not even know where they were and could not parry the repeated thrusts of the barbarians' spears. Martín tried to inspire his soldiers but they, frightened by the catastrophes which had made the skirmish so bloody, took shelter on the steep incline of a barranca that protected them from the rear. Here they stopped to regain strength and to await Nicolás de Palencia's return with the men who had remained behind.

Once all had regathered, in spite of the fact that many of the soldiers were suffering from grievous wounds, Esteban Martín advanced a second time on the town. He acted with such courage that the Indians, although they bravely tried to defend themselves, could not resist the slashing swords and the crossbow shots. They were obliged to abandon their town, leaving our men free to set fire to their houses. Only three, sitting somewhat apart, were spared to serve as shelter for the troops while they remained there.

# CHAPTER V

*Esteban Martín fights the Indians again; he is defeated and quietly retreats by night. In spite of many obstacles, he overtakes Spira, but he dies soon afterward of seven wounds received in the skirmish.*

THE Spaniards went out at sunrise to reconnoiter the place to which the Indians had retreated the previous night. Fear having left the natives with scant strength to flee, they awaited their foes just a few steps outside the town, all standing with their lances in place. The Spaniards were not pleased with this adherence to discipline nor with the fact that the barbarians' distress at their wounds and grief at seeing their houses burned were not sufficient to daunt them. The soldiers tried to dislodge the natives, but no matter what they did the effort was fruitless. Without moving more than a step forward, the Indians awaited the attack, detaining the entire Spanish force with their lances and wounding many without receiving any harm to themselves or being driven out of the stance they had assumed.

Esteban Martín, observing this military discipline and noting that the number of barbarians was increasing, considered it unwise to remain there any longer. Accordingly, the troops, divided into three units, quietly

## CHAPTER V

abandoned the town during the first watch of the night. Moving silently in this manner, they came at dawn to another town whose inhabitants attacked the exhausted soldiers as they arrived. Although the front squadron resisted and the Indians were forced to retreat, so many charged the two following groups that they were unable to withstand the attack. Martín recognized defeat, for he had sustained seven mortal wounds, but he continued to do battle so his soldiers would not be disheartened by realizing his peril.

Nicolás de Palencia, to restore courage in the men, told them that lacking a captain they would be short only one man, for he could fight as no more; but they were not, for want of that one, to display any weakness since all had the same strong motive for defending themselves.

These eloquent words, added to the unexpected arrival of the painfully wounded Esteban Martín, led the Spaniards to cast aside their fear and take shelter in their quarters to have their wounds treated. The invaders, however, could not maintain order because the barbarians had taken their supplies, clothing and equipment, and had stabbed their Indian bearers to death. These disasters, augmented by the grave condition of many of the wounded, made remaining there impossible for the Spaniards. They therefore prepared hammocks in which to carry Martín, Valdespina, and two other soldiers as the ones in most danger, while the rest could only preserve their lives through their own ingenuity.

When night closed in they began their silent march with great caution, leaving a dog tied in a hut so that at the sound of his barking the Indians would be less alert. This stratagem worked so well that the Indians did not become aware of the Spaniards' departure until the day was well advanced. Our men had no choice but to proceed at a slow pace, having to carry the wounded and endure a rain so heavy that all the paths resembled ponds, the quebradas, rivers. In many places they had to swim in water up to their chests so that, after having traveled all night, they found in the morning that they had progressed only a league from the town. Since it had been more than forty hours since they had eaten, they were so exhausted that they longed for death as alleviation. Thus they devised a cruel but essential remedy, to carry only Esteban Martín and Valdespina and leave the others who, besides being severely wounded, were beyond hope since they had been thoroughly chilled by the rain. They placed the two men in the brush so the Indians would not find them and, with tears and sighs, left them there to die abandoned in that solitary spot. Partially relieved by this drastic action, the Spaniards pressed forward to a suitable campsite on the barrancas of a river. They lit a fire to warm themselves and bake the small fruits of a wild palm, from whose stalks they sucked a bitter pith.

The Spaniards were in this state when a soldier named Pedro de la Torre, seeing the dangers which threatened all, asked Martín's permission to go forward alone to advise the governor of their condition so he could send food and men to help carry the wounded. He pledged to reach his destination that day even though it was twenty leagues distant, and he had such a keen sense of direction that he did arrive late that night at Spira's camp. The governor, grieved at hearing Torre's account of the miserable state of his companions, recognized belatedly that his own rashness had led to the disaster. He tried to make amends by sending Torre and several other soldiers to lead the wounded out in some comfort. When the group returned after two days, however, Valdespina was already dead and Martín's wounds were so ulcerated that, despite their haste in transporting him to the camp, he died three days after his arrival to the deep sorrow of all, for he was well loved.

# CHAPTER VI

*Federmann enters the Llanos but, to avoid bad weather, returns to the sierra. He reaches the site of Poca-Vergüenza; Jorge de Spira leaves the land of the Choques.*

DURING the calmest weather of the dry season, Captain Beteta brought all necessary supplies from Coro to Nicolás de Federmann's army, which now included Ortal's sixty men; but Federmann jeopardized this advantage by procrastination. Convinced that at any hour he might receive the official appointment as governor, he would not leave Barquisimeto. The soldiers, annoyed at such inactivity, gave vent to their feelings, and a few even discussed leaving their leader to return to Coro; but some of his closest friends, on hearing of this movement, warned him of the danger.

This distrust finally obliged Federmann to leave Barquisimeto and return to the Llanos, which he entered at a place named Boquerón. The Spaniards traveled divided, with Federmann leading half of the army and Captain Martínez the rest, through the province of the Guero Indians; but after several days, they were forced to leave the Llanos for the mountains to the west. There, with inundations so heavy that the plains looked like lakes, they were to pass the rainy season.

## CHAPTER VI

Federmann could not calm his agitated spirit and found consolation only in the prospect of receiving the long-awaited dispatches from his government. Surmising that they might already have arrived in Coro, he left the army in the mountains in care of Captain Martínez and returned to Barquisimeto. After several days, however, seeing that his hopes were not being realized, he dejectedly returned to his men.

Resuming his march toward the beginning of the year 1538, he crossed various provinces until he arrived at a town whose inhabitants, though they at first gave a show of receiving our men with friendship, later took flight. At this breach of confidence, Federmann regretfully ordered his soldiers to pursue them; but some were more concerned with pillaging the huts than obeying the general's orders. On observing their actions, Federmann, gazing steadily at them, shouted wrathfully: "Oh, soldiers, how little shame you have!" Since in the affable nature of that man his troops had never detected any anger, these words astonished them to such a degree that they named the town Poca-Vergüenza (Little Shame).[4]

Meanwhile, Jorge de Spira was in the province of Los Choques, oppressed because it seemed that fortune had conspired against him, for in addition to a serious lack of supplies, the continual assaults of the Indians left him no peace. And the heavy mists caused so much sickness that most of the servants and many of the soldiers died without any remedy for the distinctive illness they suffered. The horses shared these noxious effects. Some were swollen to bursting due to the poor quality of pasturage; and in others such an abundance of intestinal worms was generated that after spewing them from their mouths the animals fell dead. The greatest distress was that the rain continued night and day, delaying Spira's departure an entire year. At last, although he had very few men left, he decided to retreat and to resume their march, fleeing that land which had served as a miserable sepulcher for several of their companions. The invaders found all the regions through which they passed were now deserted because the Indians, having learned from the hostile behavior of those who had passed that way before, had fled. Unable to bear the lack of food, most of the sick died. Among them were many distinguished persons, such as Juan Cuaresma de Melo, Francisco de Murga, Antonio Ceballos, Pedro de Cárdenas, and Francisco Murcia de Rondón. The latter had served as secretary to Francis I, king of France, while that monarch was imprisoned in Madrid; and it was in fact this soldier who had disclosed to the emperor the king's plot to flee from prison.

Spira next arrived at a small town whose residents had all fled, leaving a considerable supply of yucca and yams, a gift more esteemed by our men than any vast treasure would have been. With this aid, they decided to remain there several days in order to recover their strength. Four soldiers, rummaging around the huts trying to find nourishment, by chance came across a child little more than a year old whose mother, in her haste to flee, evidently had left forgotten. Those men, or rather, beasts, killed the child and put a quarter of the torso, the head, feet and hands in a pot on the fire.

While these parts were cooking, they ate the half-done entrails, liver and lungs, savoring them with broth. Just then, a Christian, Spanish-speaking Indian woman, servant of Francisco Infante, entered the house. Recognizing by sight and odor that the soldiers were cooking human flesh, she soon departed and informed her master of their evil act. When this news reached the governor, he went at once to seize the men, determined that they should pay for so enormous a crime with their lives. Later considering what the loss of four men would mean to his meager forces, however, he commuted the sentences to other punishment which, although grave, did not compare to the one they deserved. Nevertheless, in a few days Heaven took vengeance, for all died from different causes but with equal anguish and pain, confessing their sin and recognizing their death as the penalty for their iniquity.

# CHAPTER VII

*Spira arrives at the Sarare River, and Federmann at the Apure; the latter has news of his governor but, seeking to avoid him, he enters the Llanos; Spira continues his expedition and reaches Coro.*

SPIRA left this town, which had been named Muchacho (Boy) on account of the event related in the preceding chapter, and traveled slowly because of his men's great weakness. He reached the banks of the Sarare River just as Nicolás de Federmann arrived at the Apure, a stream that rises in the province of Mérida in the quebradas called both Aricagua and Bravo. Informed by Indians that Spira was encamped nearby, Federmann suspected that the governor might try to lure men from him if the two should meet. To avoid this risk, he departed from the mountain toward which Spira was advancing and, taking the road to the left, reached the Llanos without coming near the governor. After fifteen days,

## CHAPTER VII

Spira made camp on the banks of the Apure and found indications that Spaniards had been there. At this he was filled with caution, for he was unable to surmise who might be traveling through such remote lands. By questioning the natives persistently he learned of a Spanish-speaking Indian woman among the Caiquetíos who lived near the Apure. She had come from Coro with Federmann, but because she had fallen ill she had been left behind. She gave Spira an extensive relation of all that had happened, with details so explicit that she even named the principal persons accompanying Federmann.

Spira, beset by confusion, vacillated between the varying opinions of his captains without being able to decide whose counsel to accept. Most of his men held that he should pursue Federmann at once and, assuming the command of his lieutenant's troops on his authority as governor, seek new conquests, an outcome Federmann had always feared. Spira did not dare take this advice, however, because he had few men, most of them sick, and Federmann had many, all in good health. To place himself in Federmann's hands with little protection was to expose himself to the discretion of another's courtesy and to run the risk of suffering some incivility to his authority and person.

After several days of irresolution, Spira decided to resort to generosity in order to assure Federmann's obedience, and to obligate him more completely, the governor gave his lieutenant new powers to engage in explorations and conquests in his own name. In addition, he wrote him a cordial letter, informing him in detail of his misfortunes, and warning of several threatening possibilities to guard against. Spira then sent Felipe de Utre, a German of the house of the Welsers, with thirty men to overtake Federmann. Utre found the Apure flooded, however, and during the thirty days he waited for the waters to subside they constantly increased. Despairing of being able to ford it, he went back in search of the governor, whom he found now encamped in the mountains of Coro. He was suffering considerable discomfort from the Indians who, safe from harm on a mountain top, were inflicting substantial damage with their arrows.

Spira prepared an ambush one night, where on the following day many Indians were killed and thirty captured. Then, with excessive violence and in cold blood, he ordered ten of the captives impaled and thus brought his expedition to an end with this act of cruelty. Without further incident he reached Coro in February of 1539, after five years of wandering. During this time he had lost three hundred and ten soldiers of the four hundred he had led out of Coro in 1534. Returning with only ninety, and they naked, sick, and completely broken, he had gained nothing except a knowledge of the extent of suffering men can endure and a lasting memory of his ill-fated expedition into the province of the Choques.

When Spira reached Coro, he found Bishop Don Rodrigo de Bastidas, who in the year 1536, his official visit of inspection to Puerto Rico having been completed, had arrived to preside over his church. Spira also found Doctor Navarro, whom the Audiencia de Santo Domingo had sent with various commissions concerning the mistreatment and sale of Indians. Soon thereafter, Spira embarked for a brief visit to Santo Domingo to settle various business matters with the Welsers' agents.

# CHAPTER VIII

*Federmann returns to the cordillera; he crosses it and enters the Nuevo Reino; next he goes to Spain with Generals Quesada and Benalcázar; and he dies in Madrid.*

A few days later, Federmann, fleeing toward the east from his governor, entered the Llanos. There he was impeded by two vast swamps which, although they contained little water, were difficult to cross because of their size and the bogs into which the horses sank up to their cinches. Finally, however, he came to drier land and, still wishing to avoid a meeting with Spira, traveled so far from the mountain that he lost it from view and wandered out into the Llanos to the banks of a mighty river. Since there were various signs that the region at other times had been densely populated, Federmann wished to ascertain the cause of its present desolation. He learned from several captured Indians that in the river there lived an animal so carnivorous and voracious that it had eaten many of the inhabitants.[5] The rest had abandoned the site and fled to a remoter section to escape the ferocity of so deadly an enemy. Federmann and his soldiers considered this statement true because by night they had heard the formidable bellows of the wild beast. Some even said they had seen it and affirmed that it was a species of serpent of terrifying corpulence.

Since it seemed certain to Federmann that he now ran the risk of encountering Spira, he left the Llanos road and, his troops having been reinforced by fifteen men brought from Coro by Juan Gutiérrez de Aguilón, he again attempted to cross the cordillera. For this purpose he

## CHAPTER VIII

dispatched Pedro de Limpias from the River Pauto, where he had been encamped for several days, to search out the less rugged places, but the terrain was so intractable that the captain soon returned, assuring Federmann that the route was impassable.

Seeing his desires frustrated, Federmann turned south along the right-hand skirt of the range, holding it always as a guide. Then almost by the same steps that Spira had taken, he reached the town of Nuestra Señora, which his soldiers called La Fragua because they established there a forge to repair arms and tools. As Federmann had set his hopes on crossing the cordillera, he sought information on the disposition of the land on the opposite side. Hearing from the Indians that there were rich and heavily populated provinces ahead, he decided to continue on this route. He consequently sent Pedro de Limpias forward with a few soldiers and several local guides to search for a suitable passage for the army.

With this order, Limpias left the camp and on the second day began to scale the top of the sierra, suffering trials that only his insuperable valor could overcome. He crossed frigid paramos and peaks so sharp that in many places picks and bars had to be used to establish a firm footing for the horses. In others, so rough that this recourse was not feasible, the men tied the horses with ropes and suspended them until they could gain a foothold.

After ten days Limpias arrived at a hill that offered only a very narrow path for ascent. On its summit there was a medium-size level space full of much long dry straw, surrounded on all sides by steep precipices and sharp peaks. Some frightened Indians had gathered for protection on the site, but on seeing the Spaniards ascending and recognizing that even there they were not safe, they set fire to the straw. Fanned by a heavy wind, the flames increased with such violence that in a brief time all the summit was transformed into a conflagration. Limpias and his men were in such distress that they had no recourse other than to rush back down the mountain or be burned alive. A soldier named Vivanco, judging it preferable to die quickly than to end in flames, threw himself from a rocky peak and was dashed to pieces. The rest would have suffered the same fate had not Limpias hastily built an opposing fire, but the remedy was not entirely effective as one Spaniard and several Indian bearers were burned to death.

A few days after escaping the conflict and crossing the mountain by exhaustive efforts, Limpias reached the Valley of Fosca on the edge of the *zipa* of Bogotá's dominions.[6] These provinces had been conquered two years previously when Gonzalo Jiménez de Quesada, serving as lieutenant general to the adelantado de Canaria, Pedro Fernández de

Lugo, had come up with his army from Santa Marta. The Indians of the valley told Limpias that other Spaniards were in the land, but he considered this impossible until he reached Pasca, where he found Captain Lázaro Fonte exiled in revenge for some trivial discord with General Quesada. Thus, having been informed that others had already arrived there to enjoy the spoils of that kingdom, Limpias waited for Federmann who, with the rest of the army, was following in his tracks. During this interval Fonte had time to advise Quesada, in Bogotá, of their coming. The latter was quite disturbed by this report as it came when he was already worried by information that Sebastián de Benalcázar, a captain under Francisco Pizarro, was approaching through the Valley of Neiva to Bogotá after having settled Quito and Popayán. Quesada feared that the two generals might unite to his detriment and cast him out of the Nuevo Reino, even though he had discovered it. This apprehension was well-founded, as in fact they did attempt just what Quesada had feared, each claiming that the kingdom of Bogotá was included within the demarcation of his own conquests. This dispute was so far advanced that Quesada felt obliged to defend with arms what he had won with them. The ecclesiastics who ministered to the three generals intervened, however, and held that the matter should remain in suspension until the emperor determined to which of them possession belonged. The prelates suggested that in the interim the three unite to settle the kingdom and enjoy without dispute the honors and profits of conquistadors.

Under these conditions and with a gift of four thousand gold pesos to Federmann, as he was considered poor, the disturbance was quelled. To the enthusiastic acclaim of Quesada's men, Federmann entered Bogotá in mid-1539, after three years on the road from Cabo de la Vela. Although he had started out with four hundred men and added sixty of Alderete's and fifteen of Aguilón's on the way, he brought to the Nuevo Reino only thirty cavalrymen and one hundred and fifty-three foot soldiers, the rest having perished from the rigors of the expedition.

As the three generals had decided to travel together to Spain for the emperor to arbitrate their claims and for each to solicit rewards for his services, they built brigantines to descend the Magdalena River to Cartagena. Embarking there for Spain, they arrived safely at the Court. There, amidst the anxieties of being a contender and having several lawsuits instigated against him by the Welsers, Federmann, who deserves to be remembered among the most laudable heroes of his time, reached the end of his life.[7] Born in the Swabian circle in Upper Germany, the red-haired, fair-skinned general was handsome and affable, and his brave deeds and singular bravery brought him much fame in only a few years. Although the malice of his rivals led them to attribute his generosity of spirit to pride, his military inclination to anxiety, and his courtly conduct to exaggerated caution, there is no doubt that the gifts with which nature endowed him were singular. Had he not allowed himself to be deluded by an excessive desire for independent command, even the most prying could not have found any defect to record of him.

# CHAPTER IX

*Lope Montalvo leaves Coro and seizes Captain Reinoso in Barquisimeto; following Federmann, he enters the Nuevo Reino; the Saparas rebel and discords arise concerning their pacification.*

SHORTLY before Federmann's death, when he had set out from Coro after returning from Cabo de la Vela, he assigned his close friend Lope Montalvo de Lugo, native of Salamanca, to raise the largest number of troops possible and follow him. Montalvo left Coro several months later, and with forty well-armed soldiers crossed the Carora sierra and the Valley of El Tocuyo. He arrived at length at Barquisimeto, where he waited for the winter rains to subside so he could continue his journey through the Llanos.

Since during this period repeated complaints of Governor Antonio Sedeño's continued violence reached the Audiencia de Santo Domingo, that body dispatched Licentiate Frías, its treasurer, to proceed against the governor and send him back as a prisoner to Santo Domingo. However, Sedeño, as the culmination of his crimes, committed yet another outrageous act. Forgetting the obligations of his noble blood, ignoring the respect due to a representative of so exalted a body, and refusing to obey the orders of the Audiencia, he brusquely seized Frías and everything he had brought with him. Then, fearing punishment but continuing to hold the treasurer prisoner, Sedeño went inland on the pretext of pursuing his conquests. There, death overtook him in the district of the Tiznados from poison administered by one of his servants.

On Sedeño's death, his soldiers prepared to proceed on the expedition with the same hope that he had had of stumbling onto the riches of the Meta River. To lead them they named Pedro de Reinoso, son of the lord of Autillo in Castilla la Vieja, and Diego de Losada, son of the lord of Río Negro in the kingdom of Galicia; but later, differences developed and they separated into two squadrons. The one led by Losada returned to Maracapana and thence to Coro, where they provided plentiful material for this history; the other, under the command of Reinoso, went to Barquisimeto where Montalvo received them amicably. Learning later, however, of Sedeño's death and the events of that journey, Montalvo seized Reinoso, absorbed the men he had led and sent him back to Coro. From there he was sent to Santo Domingo, where respect for his noble blood was his best defense against charges that the treasurer of the Audiencia instigated against him. Released from custody, Reinoso married an illustrious lady of that city and, after many years of life together, left a profuse succession.

Lope Montalvo, his company augmented by the soldiers he had taken from Reinoso, left Barquisimeto as soon as the waters subsided. He followed Federmann's tracks and suffered many misfortunes, but finally, at the end of 1539, Montalvo entered the city of Bogotá with eighty men. There, because of his personal qualities and the much-needed help he brought, he was received with singular rejoicing by all, particularly Hernán Pérez de Quesada who, in the absence of his brother, Gonzalo Jiménez de Quesada, was governing these provinces. As Montalvo's talent, prudence and valor made him well liked everywhere, he won such esteem in the kingdom that he later served as governor in the absence of his cousin, the adelantado Alonso Luis de Lugo. The latter's prejudices, added to his violent conduct, had given rise in Bogotá to many discords between the Caiquetíos and Quesada's followers. Montalvo was affected by the difficulties only because he was a relative of the adelantado, whose unreasonable actions obliged Montalvo to return to Spain. There, on the estate in Salamanca that he held through primogeniture, he lived quietly until his death.

As soon as Jorge de Spira arrived in Coro, he left the government of the province to Juan de Villegas and crossed to the island of Santo Domingo, as related in chapter seven. After quickly finishing the business he had gone there to discuss with the Welser agents, Spira returned to Coro. During this time the Sapara Indians, who inhabited the sand bar of Lake Maracaibo, had killed several Spaniards, and, to thwart the movement before it gained force, he decided to perform the task personally. As a result, disturbances broke out in the city because Spira's soldiers considered it unseemly to serve under a foreigner, especially one in whom they had little faith because of the adverse events of the expedition to the province of the Choques. Counseled and supported by the authority of Doctor Navarro, the soldiers declined to follow Spira, explaining that not having been given a Spanish commander, they preferred to lose their lives rather than leave Coro. And although at first Bishop

CHAPTER X

Rodrigo de Bastidas agreed with them, later, at Spira's urgent entreaties, he turned in favor of the governor. The bishop's commitment was clearly manifested in a sermon in which he said it was very disrespectful that, already having a governor, they should seek a governor, and that, having a king, they should seek a king. The soldiers, however, stung by the harsh words of the sermon, closed ranks so that there was no way to shake their resolve. Thus, Doctor Navarro had the support of all, and the governor, seeing that it was he who had aroused the soldiers, did not wish to risk a break in which his authority might be resisted. Thus he prudently assumed the pretext of being ill and entrusted the task to Alonso de Navas, appointing him to punish and subjugate the Saparas. Their insurgence was in this manner restrained, although its unfortunate consequences could not be avoided.

# CHAPTER X

*After the Saparas are punished, Navas and his soldiers plan to return to Cubagua; Doctor Navarro goes out to detain them but Navas's soldiers seize him and take him to Cumaná; Jorge de Spira dies, and Villegas governs the province.*

THE title of captain was bestowed on Alonso de Navas and he started to raise men. Since his appointment was so satisfactory, soldiers clamored to accompany him, but, not wishing to take more than necessary, he chose the hundred he considered most useful. With them he left Coro in search of the Saparas whom he easily routed in two encounters. He then seized the most culpable in the aborted rebellion and sent them under heavy guard to the governor.

The expedition ended after a brief time because the soldiers abhorred German domination. Now at liberty to choose, they fled from this heavy subjugation and, resolved not to return to Coro, took the road to Cumaná. From there they planned to continue to Cubagua where, because of the many pearls to be obtained, people had gathered in greater numbers than in any other place along the coast. They began to travel toward the mountains, leaving the city to the north and proceeding toward El Tocuyo. From there, crossing a portion of the Llanos, they were to have continued to Cumaná, but some of the soldiers regretted so rash a resolution, it seeming to them that so extensive a journey would require extreme effort. Consequently, they fled quietly one night by unfrequented roads and returned to Coro to advise the governor of all that had happened. Spira and the bishop at once burst into immoderate complaints against Doctor Navarro, blaming him for having entrusted the peace effort to Navas. This discord caused the soldiers to leave the city exposed to enemy invasion, an action that drew reprimands from the Welser agents because of possible losses to their company. To calm the public clamor against him, Doctor Navarro offered to go in person to subdue the soldiers and bring them back to the city. He assembled sixty well-armed men, took the coast road to the port of Borburata, and from there went on to Barquisimeto to cut off passage before the rebels could enter the Llanos. Since Navas and his men were traveling on foot through harsh terrain, Navarro arrived first and waited for them in a town of Achagua Indians. The soldiers, however, learned in El Tocuyo where Navarro was and changed their route, entering the Llanos at the mouth of the Baraure, and they did not stop until they reached the banks of the Pao River.

A few days later Navarro learned that Navas had passed that way and, guided by information acquired from Indians, he came upon him and his troops still lingering on the Pao. He reprimanded them for their desertion and for the ingratitude with which they had repaid his kindness even though he had come to their defense, causing all to blame him for Navas's flight.

The soldiers responded that abandoning the province was not disloyalty, for they would give their lives to serve their King. However, they added, their integrity as Spaniards would not permit them to live subject to the will of a foreign dominion. Thus, while affairs at Coro might proceed under the compromise established, efforts to dissuade them would be vain because they were determined not to remain in the province any longer.

Their obstinate reply greatly displeased Navarro and he again angrily ordered them to prepare to return to Coro, for by resisting his command they would oblige him to resort to force. The soldiers pretended that they were ready to follow him, and in this manner allayed his fears. Then the men deprived Navas of his post without explaining to him their motives, and with great secrecy chose as their commander a soldier named Pancorbo. When they found Doctor Navarro that night not observing the vigilance warranted in light of his danger, they seized his arms and horses, repaying his confidence in them with that affront.

Navarro, disarmed and at the mercy of the soldiers, resorted to humility in an attempt to lessen their resistance. He entreated them to

## CHAPTER X

consider the dignity of his person, to spare him such infamous treatment and to restore his arms and horses so he could return to Coro. The soldiers arrogantly responded that they would restore to him a few horses so that he and his men might pass safely through Indian territory. They added that, without wasting more time trying to dissuade them, he should return at once, and they promised not to detain or harass him. But Navarro, not being sufficiently callous to return to Coro to become the target of Spira's rage, decided to proceed with his followers to Cubagua. Some of his men were pleased with the plan, although they now shared the fortune of one whose authority they previously had opposed, but others did not consent to it because they feared some betrayal. Thus, Navarro was allowed only his four most devoted followers while the rest were sent to Coro with three horses and a few weapons. Navarro's little group then entered the Llanos with no more guide than their own knack for following an imaginary line. After a few months of severe hardships, they arrived at Cumaná and from there crossed to the island of Cubagua.

Governor Jorge de Spira died on June 12, 1540, in Coro, and the government of the province passed on to Juan de Villegas, then serving as *alcalde mayor* of the city until the Audiencia should fill the vacancy. On receiving this news in Cubagua, Doctor Navarro, although he had intended never to return to Coro, considered that the scene had changed with Spira's death and that he could without embarrassment fulfill the commissions which had been suspended. He consequently embarked in a pirogue and arrived after a few days in Coro, where he quickly attended to all his obligations. He then retired to the quiet of his home in the city of Santo Domingo, where he had copious holdings and no necessity for missions in order to live in ease.

BOOK II

# CHAPTER XI

*The Audiencia names Bishop Bastidas governor; Pedro de Limpias enters the Lake Maracaibo region; and Felipe de Utre (Urre, Hutten) searches for El Dorado.*[8]

ON Jorge de Spira's death, the Audiencia de Santo Domingo named as interim governor Bishop Rodrigo de Bastidas, and as his lieutenant for war and new explorations, a relative of the Welsers, Felipe de Utre, a prudent young German. The bishop took up his new position on December 7, 1540, and began at once to put the business of the province in order. He paid more heed, however, to his baton of secular power than to his bishop's crozier and allowed himself to be influenced by an atmosphere that led all officials of the Indies to aspire to being conquistadors. As soon as he took possession of his post, he sent to Hispaniola for the men, arms and horses needed for previously planned military operations. Lacking the means to fulfill his financial obligations, he then sent Pedro de Limpias with a squadron to Lake Maracaibo to seize and sell Indians to satisfy debts which the bishop had incurred.

Pedro de Limpias arrived in Maracaibo in 1541 and easily captured five hundred Indians including men, women, and children, whom he led to Coro and turned over to the bishop for sale. The success of this operation, inhuman as well as unworthy of a prelate, encouraged the bishop to send his lieutenant general Felipe de Utre out on new conquests. He was strongly urged to take this action by some who had accompanied Spira because they were convinced that their blunders resulted from Spira's inept leadership. Also, since Limpias assured him that information gained when he accompanied Federmann into the Nuevo Reino of opulent provinces lying to the south was reliable, Utre had no difficulty in inspiring the men to participate in the expedition. After a few days he had completely outfitted one hundred and fifty soldiers, whom he sent out from Coro in June of the same year under the command of Captains Bartolomé Welser, Sebastián de Amescua, and Martín de Arteaga, with Limpias as campmaster. To make the exploration more attractive, Utre began calling the provinces he intended to conquer El Dorado, an ostentatious name initiated in 1536 in Quito by Sebastián de Benalcázar's soldiers. They may have chosen it because of an old Indian's fantastic relation of a powerful kingdom lying to the east of the Llanos. Or possibly it was born of a dream that had spread throughout all America,

## CHAPTER XI

leading the Spaniards to persist in searching for these chimerical lands and their fabled riches.

Utre left Coro and took the coastal road for fifty leagues to Borburata. From there, crossing the short distance to the mountain range, he came out at the site where the city of Valencia was later to be founded. Then, looking for the mouth of the Barquisimeto, he entered the Llanos and followed the route Federmann had taken. At length Utre came to the town which Federmann had named La Fragua, but which Spira had called Nuestra Señora, in the province of Maruachare. It seemed imperative to Utre to camp there until the rainy season was over and to acquire a solid basis of information about the lands he was seeking. Questioning the Indians intently, he learned that a few days before, impelled by the same purpose, Hernán Pérez de Quesada had passed that way with two hundred and fifty men and a considerable number of horses. Also misled by the exaggerated accounts Benalcázar's soldiers had given of the treasures of the mythical El Dorado, he had abandoned the comforts of governing during his brother's absence to follow the uncertainties of a nebulous hope. When, broken and defeated, he came to realize the deception, he left for the city of Pasto in the province of Popayán, with two years having been wasted in excessive hardships with no other fruit than a lesson learned from the experience.

This news of Hernán Pérez upset Utre greatly. If he decided to follow the same route and found some powerful kingdom, he realized that Hernán Pérez would still enjoy the advantages of having been first, and Utre and his men would receive only scant rewards as auxiliaries. On the other hand, for Hernán Pérez to hazard the risk of a doubtful conquest would be unreasonable unless he had positive hope of discovering a kingdom capacious enough to accommodate both. This judgment appeared so sound to his captains that they decided to abide by it, and without waiting longer they began to march, following Hernán Pérez's tracks. Although there were some obstacles on the road, they were hastily surmounted, and in a brief time the province of Papamene, which begins at the edge of Timaná in the jurisdiction of Neiva, was sighted.

In one of the towns, Utre found an Indian of illustrious lineage, mature and serious, from whom he sought to extract information on the benefits to be expected from the journey. Responding with candor, the Indian advised Utre of the error of following his present route and explained that, like other Spaniards, he would meet his doom there, for rugged mountains and severe weather made the region uninhabitable by human life. He suggested, however, that by turning back Utre would find what he desired, and he offered to accompany the Spaniard until he entered rich and heavily populated lands, abundant in gold and silver.

He said that the soldiers should march always toward the rising sun until they reached the city of Macatoa on the banks of the Guayuare River. As proof that he spoke the truth, he showed Utre some little golden apples, or nisperos, which he said one of his brothers had brought back from that land.⁹

Nevertheless, circumstances did not sustain this relation sufficiently for Utre to swerve from his tenacious intent to follow in Hernán Pérez's footsteps. Thus, paying no attention to the Indian's warnings or the opinions of many of his soldiers, Utre lifted camp at the beginning of 1542 and continued the march along the same route. The Indian accompanied him willingly for eight days but then saw that neither intractable mountains, swift rivers, nor quaking bogs and swamps were sufficient to cause Utre to admit his error. After he realized that to pursue that course further would be to meet a painful death, he fled back to his village, exulting over the blindness with which the foreigners were bringing about their own destruction.

# CHAPTER XII

*Utre continues his exploration; Diego de Boiça (Buiza) governs the province and is succeeded by Enrique Remboldt (Rembolt); Villegas proceeds to Maracapana, and the Audiencia names Licentiate Frías governor.*

THE unexpected flight of the guide, added to hardships and illness brought on by difficult terrain and noxious weather, caused the soldiers general distress. They gave strong vent to their feelings and questioned openly their failure to heed the Indian's warnings. Although reports of this disagreeable mood reached Utre's attention, nothing could cause him to swerve from his established route, and it even seemed that he was deliberately seeking his own ruin. Constant trials, sickness, and deaths were mounting by the minute, however, and the repeated warnings of the most prudent finally induced him to shift to the southeast. After a few days of marching along what at first appeared to be a different cordillera from the one they had followed from Barquisimeto, they observed jutting out above the Llanos a pinnacle which they named Pardaos Peak. They hastened their pace to examine it more closely, for one of the clues leading to El Dorado was that it was located at the foot of a sierra separated from the other which had always served as the polestar for expeditions into the Llanos. These hopes withered in the light of truth, however, as they recognized that the peak was but a branch of the same cordillera which had been in view from the outset of the journey.

Since the rains had begun to inundate the countryside, the army decided to climb Pardaos Peak to escape the hardships of that low terrain, but because the district was sparsely inhabited and lacked food as a consequence, they almost starved. The most satisfying sustenance they could find was a ball of corn, which they left at the entrance to an ant hill until the insects covered it. It was then kneaded until it consisted more of ants than of meal, but since this coarse dish was their only food and there was not enough of it for all, there were many who did not reject any vermin, no matter how revolting, but actively sought them out. From this diet some became bloated; others lost their hair, beards, and eyebrows; and finally, full of pestiferous tumors and poisonous ulcers, the entire squadron was overcome by afflictions. After the waters subsided, Utre fled from this desperate situation and returned by a different route to Nuestra Señora, where he arrived at the beginning of 1543, having wasted an entire year in his pursuit.

When Utre departed from Coro in June of 1541, Bishop Bastidas was left there as captain general of the province. He held this post until the beginning of 1542, when His Majesty promoted him to the bishopric of Puerto Rico and sent as his replacement Doctor Miguel Jerónimo de Ballesteros, former dean of the Cathedral of Cartagena.[10] When Bastidas embarked for his new church, he left both the military and political government in the charge of Diego de Boiça, knight commander of the Orden de Cristo, son of Portuguese parents though born in Castile, and a gentleman of remarkable gifts. The Audiencia de Santo Domingo approved the recommendation and confirmed Boiça, but before the year 1542 was out, it dispatched another interim governor, Enrique Remboldt, a German serving in Coro as factor of the Welsers' company. Because of meager advantages for the residents and the inept leadership of the Germans, however, Coro was so impoverished that the few inhabitants who remained considered relocating with their families to neighboring provinces.

Juan de Villegas was steadfastly opposed to this resolution, knowing that by following it he would be relinquishing with discredit what until then he had valiantly maintained. To abandon such a major province would be so irregular a deed that it would be judged reprehensible. Contriving to calm the spirits of those contemplating such action, Villegas decided to go to Cubagua and Cumaná to seek men to come to Coro from among the many who were then engaged there in the inhuman trade of capturing and selling Indians as slaves. Villegas considered it advantageous to make the journey in the company of Diego de Losada, for he was a practical man of recognized authority in those provinces, having served there as supreme leader. Consequently, Remboldt gave equal power to him and Villegas and ordered them, with an escort of twenty men, including the accountant Diego Ruiz Vallejo, to carry out the mission.

It was already March of 1543 when Villegas and Losada left Coro, traveling along the coast to Borburata. They crossed the mountains and entered the Llanos, making an inspiring show of perseverance and courage. They marched more than two hundred leagues through a region to this day considered impassable because it is so densely inhabited by barbarous tribes, and fraught with dangers. After arriving in Cumaná, Villegas discussed with the justices of Cubagua the matter of establishing boundaries for the province from Maracapana to the Cabo de la Vela, which the emperor had conceded to them in his contract with the Welsers. Since these orders indicated that the region was included within the province of Venezuela, Villegas, by authority from Remboldt, took possession before Andrés de Andino, scribe of Cubagua. Immediately thereafter he began to exercise jurisdiction, both civil and criminal, as *justicia mayor,* the title which the governor had given to him.

This matter having been concluded so favorably, Villegas and Losada now discussed activating the principal project entrusted to them. As these coasts were heavily populated and esteem for the two leaders soliciting recruits was strong, it was not difficult to raise ninety-six additional men in a brief time. With them and one hundred and seven cavalry, the two officers turned back toward Coro sharing equal authority, but they could not agree on the command of even so small a squadron without jealousy arising between them. Beginning with secret resentments, they soon developed beyond dissent to openly declared discord of such obstinacy that it lasted all their lives. This state caused highly prejudicial uneasiness as well as turmoil among partisans and friends, for each of the two captains tried by all means to discredit the other.

Similar effects were being experienced at the same time in Coro. After Governor Enrique Remboldt died and the government was left in the hands of the *alcaldes ordinarios,* Bernardino Marcio and Juan de Bonilla, each began to arrange matters in his own fashion with such resultant confusion that what one commanded, the other countermanded. The residents did not know whom to obey, and the city was reduced to such monstrous disorder that there was nothing but injustice.

The province was in that disharmony when Villegas and Losada arrived from Cubagua and Cumaná in September of 1544. Then, either because of misgivings the alcaldes held for the authority of these gentlemen or fear conceived at the news that the Audiencia de Santo Domingo had named Licentiate Frías as governor of the province to inflict the punishment their transgressions merited, they felt endangered. Consequently, they fled one night with such secrecy and precaution that nothing more was ever heard of them. Thus the city remained free of their evil presence but was soon to endure others.

# CHAPTER XIII

*Juan de Carvajal arrives in Coro; he falsifies the provisions of the Audiencia and introduces himself as governor; Felipe de Utre leaves the town of Nuestra Señora and sights Macatoa.*

WHEN news of the alcaldes' flight from Coro reached Santo Domingo, the fiscal Frías had not yet finished preparations to depart. It now seemed to him that with this turn of events his immediate presence there was no longer essential. Since he had been entrusted by the Audiencia with several missions affecting the island of Cubagua, he considered it more urgent to finish them first so that later he could place himself completely at the disposal of his government. He accordingly embarked for Cubagua, sending to Coro Juan (not Francisco, as some have called him) de Carvajal, secretary of the Audiencia, who would govern as his lieutenant general until Frías's arrival.

With these orders and a supply of soldiers, arms and horses, Carvajal set sail at the same time as Frías. Contrary winds overtook him on the crossing, however, and he had to disembark at the beginning of 1545 at the port of Paraguaná, several leagues to the leeward of his destination. Villegas went out at once to receive him, since the former was now committed to open enmity with Losada and was trying to win Carvajal's good graces and ensure his ill will toward Losada. Finding a kindred soul in Carvajal, Villegas emphasized his desire to destroy his rival; and Carvajal, invested with this biased information, took care to observe even the slightest of Losada's movements. From this scrutiny he learned that Losada was well loved in the city and exercised special influence over all. This evaluation caused Carvajal to fear that such a man might pose an obstacle to the treachery he was contriving. Still, not daring to break with Losada without cause, he prepared several moves with which to intervene. Losada, however, learning of his opponent's depraved intention, took advantage of an unexpected opportunity offered elsewhere and left the province so that he might observe from a distance and without risk the effects of the tempest threatening Coro.

Carvajal, freed of anxieties by Losada's absence, began to scheme with iniquity. His plan required that, in an attempt to raise men to follow him willingly and obediently, he falsify the Audiencia's provisions by substituting the title of governor for lieutenant general. He did this so clumsily, however, that many recognized the deception and opposed receiving him; but since the number who took his part was greater, he was accepted as governor. As such he at once named Juan de Villegas as his lieutenant general but was thereby later plagued by many woes.

Carvajal, confirmed in his position, strove even harder to raise men for his explorations, using severity and violence to compel them to follow him. Many of the exasperated residents, particularly those who knew that his government was fraudulent, chose to live among wild beasts rather than be subject to such a tyrant. They fled the city and took shelter in the brush, but Carvajal searched them out and punished them cruelly. This severity caused the others to follow him meekly, and he was able to raise two hundred well-provisioned men. He was careful not to leave any horses or weapons in the city, so that when the fiscal Frías arrived from Cubagua he would be helpless to punish him. With these preparations, Carvajal left Coro and, crossing the Carora Sierra, went out with his troops to the Valley of El Tocuyo where he leisurely made camp.

Felipe de Utre, still in the town of Nuestra Señora, was eager to return to the lands described by the Indian from Papamene. Undaunted by the adversities suffered thus far, he was determined to continue toward his goal. During the time he had to remain in that place for his soldiers to rest and recover from their illnesses, he ceaselessly inquired if there were in nearby towns any Indians to verify the information given him previously. He found many who agreed on details of the statement but varied on the name of the tribe which inhabited those rich provinces, some calling them Ditaguas and others Omeguas (Omaguas).[11] Not allowing this simple difference in name to raise any doubts, however, Utre, with only forty men and the guides needed, set out again in search of Pardaos Peak as soon as the weather permitted, keeping his sight always on the city of Macatoa as his most stable landmark. He did not spare any diligence that might lead to success and tried constantly to learn more of the nature of the Indians, which he would need to know to ensure their defeat.

Since their responses were in accord with Utre's desires, he pro-

## CHAPTER XIII

ceeded toward the conquest of the Omeguas. The Indians, at the same time, reasoned that the occasion had arrived for vengeance by another's hand for the grievances the tribes of the Llanos had suffered from the Spaniards. The number of soldiers composing that squadron being so small and the valor of the Omeguas so widely known, the Indians were convinced that the foreigners would be quickly defeated by the natives' sharp-edged macanas.

The Indians, seeing that their reports greatly comforted Utre and that their malicious plan was rapidly succeeding, conducted him along open roads and well-worn paths to the banks of the Guayuare. The deep currents of this powerful river did not permit the Spaniards to ford it but did allow them to cross in canoes or by swimming. Utre had camped on its banks without knowing on which side the city of Macatoa lay, but he soon was relieved of this uncertainty by an Indian captured while gathering shellfish downstream on the banks of the river. After the Spaniards dispelled the fright that seeing such strange people had caused, the native willingly answered their questions. He revealed that at a short distance from the river upstream they would find the city but that they would need canoes to cross over to it.

Utre gave the Indian some glass beads, bells, and other trifles from Castile and asked him to go to Macatoa to tell the cacique that they were en route to more distant lands. He added that he requested the cacique's alliance and friendship, and he promised that neither lands nor vassals would suffer any hostile act from the Spaniards. The Indian gave a show of accepting the message with pleasure. Then, confident of the power of his oar, he stepped into a wretched little boat that barely accommodated him alone and started upstream to fulfill implicitly the charge entrusted to him.

# BOOK III

## CHAPTER I

*Felipe de Utre enters Macatoa and, with the help of its cacique, discovers the Omeguas; he is wounded in the first encounter, and Diego de Montes treats him in a strange manner.*

THE captive, who lived in a town near Macatoa, was grateful for Utre's pleasant manner and gifts, and wished to reciprocate by performing promptly the task entrusted to him. His cacique, having decided to accept the Spaniards' friendship, sent one of his sons the following day with five large canoes and ninety warriors to conduct Utre to the city. They rowed downstream and a little after dawn came in sight of the Spanish camp. Our men immediately took up arms; but the Indians, without showing surprise at seeing those they had sought in peace assume so warlike an attitude, landed and asked for the leader. Informed that Felipe de Utre was commander, the cacique's son embraced him and said: "Yesterday you sent greetings to my father, the cacique of Macatoa, advising him of your arrival and offering your friendship and peaceful treatment of his vassals. Your intentions, you said, were simply to acquire information on the tribes that inhabit the slopes of a mountain range lying near this river. My father recognized by your courteous words that your deeds differ greatly from what certain persons of bordering regions had given him to expect, for they had stated that you were enemies of peace, instigators of war. He sends me to greet you and to tell you that he is pleased to accept your friendship and to offer not only the information you asked for, but to aid in every way. He will provide safe guides to lead you to the kingdom of the Omeguas, and he begs you to proceed to the city so he may communicate better with you and thank you properly for your friendship. For this purpose, he sends these canoes and vassals to transport you to the other bank of the river."[1]

Utre responded gratefully and prudently to this message, with Pedro de Limpias serving as a fair interpreter. For fear that the cacique's son might bear some hidden treachery, however, Utre decided to reject the offer to cross the river in so few canoes to avoid the risk of being divided.

# CHAPTER I

Making excuses to disguise his prudence, Utre then asked the cacique's son to express to his father the Spaniards' appreciation for the attention shown. At the same time, however, he suggested that the cacique send sufficient boats for all to cross together on another day so that they might in brief time enjoy his hospitality. The youth, who discerned the meaning of the reply, did not accept its implications but rather, remaining in camp with the Spaniards, dispatched a small boat to Macatoa that soon returned with eight additional canoes. Utre could no longer offer any objection to the crossing and embarked his men that afternoon so that the Indians would not attribute to fear what had been simple caution. They swam the horses across, guiding them from the canoes with plowlines, but since it seemed to Utre that the preferred time to enter the city would be during daylight, he camped on the riverbanks until the next day. Disappointed that the Spaniards still delayed, the young man returned to Macatoa to tell his father how close the foreigners now were. Early the following day the cacique sent fifty Indians bearing generous portions of fish, maize, cassava and venison to give the visitors new strength and better spirits for their march to the city.

Located on a pleasant site, this community of up to eight hundred inhabitants had broad, level streets free of grass, stones and other debris. Its houses were well built, and its other buildings, though of rough construction, had attractive designs and were light and airy. When Utre entered the city, he found it empty, for, to offer greater convenience and hospitality, its inhabitants had withdrawn about the radius of a harquebus shot to the very edge of the river; but they left the houses well stocked with food. Their urbanity amazed our men, who previously had thought these courtesies alien to a crude and barbaric race. The Spaniards asked the cacique the motive for vacating the city when four houses would have been sufficient to lodge them all. To this he replied that his vassals, recognizing the superiority of the Spaniards, would have felt disrespectful to have remained with them there.

This cacique, who appeared to be about forty years old, had pleasant manners and held lucid discourse; he was of medium build and had well-proportioned limbs, a thin face, and an aquiline nose. His vassals, the Guayupes, were generally reposed in speech and docile, qualities that led Utre to expect to learn from them all he needed for his purpose. He noted that the information they furnished corresponded to that provided by previous informants; for example, they assured him that in the foothills of a certain mountain range the Omeguas had opulent towns that abounded in gold. Utre consequently formed plans to leave Macatoa to assure a glorious end to his exploration immediately, but the cacique tried to dissuade him, considering the idea rash. He said that since Utre had so few soldiers they would fall prey to their adversaries. However, finding Utre tenacious in his decision, the cacique gave him the guides he asked for and provisions for nine days, a supply that would last until Utre reached another friendly city whose cacique was his present host's confederate. He received the Spaniards cordially and lodged them in comfort, although the novelty of the travelers, their unique weapons, and strange mounts struck him with amazement.

The affection this cacique developed for Utre and his soldiers after several days made him fear the reverses which surely would follow if the visitors passed on to the kingdom of the Omeguas. He tried to divert them from this course because he knew how great a number of bellicose people lived in those provinces. He explained that, thanks to continuous wars and civil disorders, they were expert in battle. He pointed out that, being so few, it was more rashness than bravery in the Spaniards to provoke a vast horde of warriors. He also noted that since there were in these lands animals almost as large as horses, which must have been sheep like those of Peru, it would be easy for the natives to ride them against the few invaders and match their advantage in battle.[2] However, because the cacique at the same time described the great riches in silver and gold to be had, there was no danger that could have deterred the Spaniards.

Since the cacique now perceived that the Spaniards were determined not to take a backward step, he resolved not to trust the outcome of their journey to any guidance other than his own. Thus, attended by some of his vassals, he led the visitors along wide open roads through unpopulated territory. After five days they reached a village of little more than fifty houses, which the cacique explained served as shelter for those who guarded the Omeguas' fields. This must have been true, for several Indians, scattered throughout the fields, had barely caught sight of the strangers when they rushed toward the town.

The Spaniards were now on an elevated site with a clear view in all directions. They saw at a short distance a town so large that they could not conceive how far it extended. Its streets were straight, its buildings close together. Outstanding among them was one of superb construction which, according to their cacique friend, was the palace of that town's cacique, Cuarica. It served as both his habitation and a temple to the many gods of whom he had golden statues.

Since the Spaniards were now in sight of the Omeguas, the cacique took leave of them because he felt that his presence was no longer necessary. On parting, however, he advised Utre to try to capture the Indians who had fled toward the town before they could sound the alarm. Utre and the cavalrymen accordingly spurred their horses and raced

## CHAPTER I

toward the town; but the Indians, with even greater speed, were able to reach safety. Only Utre, riding an exceptionally swift horse, succeeded in overtaking one warrior who, with spear in hand, was trying to escape. Seeing himself in danger of being trampled by the horse, however, he faced Utre and hurled his spear with such force that it penetrated the captain's armored tunic and pierced him between the ribs below the right arm. As the warrior rushed into the town, Utre was able to turn his horse around. Despite his painful wound he at last rejoined his companions, who had been so upset by the attack that they were now undecided as to what to do.

The cacique friend was no less disturbed, for he had remained close enough to see the attack and felt that the disaster was a well-deserved admonishment for the disregard accorded to his counsel. He was afraid now that the entire Omegua race might charge before they had a chance to withdraw. In a brief time confused outcries were heard which, mixed with the uproar of drums and the clamor of flutes, filled the air with horror, making it appear that the entire world was conspiring against that small band of Spaniards. Finally night fell and delayed the Omeguas' pursuit, which afforded a chance for Utre to be placed in a hammock. His men then marched so rapidly that on the following night they arrived at the friendly cacique's town, where they sought treatment for the wound.

This task fell to a soldier named Diego de Montes, a native of Madrid who later accompanied General Diego de Losada in the conquest and settlement of Caracas. He was a singular man and possessed such rare skills that throughout the province he was called venerable. A resident of El Tocuyo, he died there at an advanced age, having garnered such esteem that his words were regarded as oracles.

Although this soldier did not understand surgery, he began Utre's treatment. Since the wound was between the ribs and there were no probes to determine whether it was above or below the membranes of the heart or had damaged them, he devised a method to settle the question that was as rare as it was bold. With the consent of the cacique, he chose the oldest Indian of the town, who must have been a slave, and mounted him on horseback with the same breast tunic that Utre had worn. Then he forced another Indian to wound the first one through the same tear in the material with a spear similar to those the Omeguas used, a test that cost the miserable old man his life. Opening the body then to examine the anatomy of the area, Montes found that the wound had been above the heart and that the membranes had not been damaged. Free of doubt now, he cut Utre open further so that the wound remained clearly revealed. He then washed it with myrtle water and other mixtures that, when stirred from side to side, caused the clotted blood to be expelled. The captain was entirely cured within a few days to the amazement of the cacique and his vassals, who were engrossed in pondering the suffering the patient was able to bear during the agony of this treatment.

## CHAPTER II

*With a powerful army the Omeguas pursue Felipe de Utre; Pedro de Limpias defeats them in battle; the Spaniards withdraw to the town of Nuestra Señora, and from there they return to El Tocuyo.*

EVEN in the dark of night, the Omeguas were aware of the Spaniards' withdrawal, but to allow time for the better organization of their army, they delayed their own departure until daybreak. Then, to the strident sound of horns and flutes, fifteen thousand combatants began to pursue the Spaniards and were perceived only when they arrived within two leagues of the friendly cacique's town. Utre was warned by the cacique of the threat which the proximity of so powerful an enemy represented, but since the pain of his wound was intense, he could not mount his horse or take charge of the situation. He entrusted the operation to his campmaster, Pedro de Limpias, a man of broad experience in war in the Indies. Commanding the men with concord and brevity, he went out to meet the Omeguas who, wearing feathered headdresses and carrying banners, approached across a vast field. Since the terrain was eminently suited to the use of horses, the Spaniards, though so few, initiated the battle and took such advantage of the site that the first ranks of Indians were thrown into disorder by the ferocity of the foot soldiers. Commanded by Bartolomé Welser, this unit made the affray even bloodier as he recognized the need to extricate his men from this difficult situation. He rivaled Limpias in courage and worked marvels that day while the rest of the soldiers, inspired by Welser's example, converted their swords into flashes of lightning. The Indian warriors tried to sustain the combat but were unable to resist the force with which those thirty-nine Spaniards trampled them down. The natives began to withdraw in an orderly manner at first, but they soon realized that their adversaries had taken on a new desire to prove themselves invincible. They then hastily abandoned the field, leaving it strewn with corpses and feathered headdresses, without the invaders' having incurred any damage other than a spear wound suffered by Captain Martín de Arteaga.[3]

This was the celebrated Battle of the Omeguas in which the Spanish race manifested its highest level of bravery and good fortune. It will forever be remembered that an army of fifteen thousand combatants of a bellicose race was routed by so small a number as thirty-nine Spaniards, almost consumed by the adversities they had suffered. The negligent documentation of that century has dimmed the memory of those brave men and made impossible the identification of more than fourteen of them.[4] They were Pedro de Limpias, Bartolomé Welser, Diego de Montes, Martín de Arteaga, Diego de Paradas, Alonso Pacheco, Juan de Guevara, Sancho Briceño, the accountant Antonio Naveros, the treasurer Gonzalo de los Ríos, Luis de León, Juan de Badillo, Damián del Barrio and the cantor Juan Frutos de Tudela. The lack at that time in Coro of friars to minister to the sick and dying motivated Frutos de Tudela to offer to serve as chaplain. Even though he lacked the requisite residence in Coro and the permission of his church to enlist as a soldier, it is certain that he did participate.

Having recovered from his wound, Utre decided a few days after the victory was won to return to Macatoa and continue from there to Nuestra Señora in search of the sick soldiers he had left behind. After a discussion with his men as to what course to follow, it seemed to him ill-advised to become involved in an enterprise of such consequence with so few men. The friendly cacique regretted this decision, for he had hoped to benefit from the association by acquiring the civility and manner of living which he had observed in the visitors. Nevertheless, comforted by the promise of their early return, he was compelled to accept their judgment and gave them the provisions needed and guides to lead them until they reached Macatoa. However, the guides soon fled and left the visitors to travel with little direction. Their only hope was that, by marching always toward the west, they could not miss the Guaviare River, which would lead them to Macatoa. After reconnoitering the waters above the city and observing the demarcation of the site, Utre decided to send Limpias with a few soldiers to Macatoa in search of canoes. This officer hastily carried out the assignment and returned the next day with sufficient boats for all. The troops were transferred to the other bank and continued until they reached Nuestra Señora, three months after having left there.

The sick rejoiced at their companions' reports of the grandeur and treasures of the kingdom of the Omeguas, one and all being persuaded that El Dorado had been discovered. They attributed their having attained the goal which had eluded so many others to the favor of fortune, but had they been asked their reason for saying that the province was El Dorado, they would no doubt have been unable to explain. This being an imaginary place, founded on pure fancy, any conquistador in whatever part of America, on finding such a province, might have asserted that it was El Dorado. Nevertheless, it cannot be denied that Utre's soldiers had reason for taking pride in their discovery. They had had the strength to bear unutterable misfortunes, deprivations and famine for four years, during which they had crossed the extensive provinces between Coro and the Amazon River to reach the seat of the Omegua kingdom. Also, there can be no doubt that this land was the same as that of which Francisco de Orellana had heard reports while navigating this river in 1541. After he was sent out by Gonzalo Pizarro, who was exploring La Canela,[5] he learned in the province of Machífaro that the powerful lord of the Omeguas lived just a few leagues inland. Orellana shunned its exploration, however, because, impelled by principles that breached the kinship and friendship he owed Pizarro, he was trying to reach the Mar del Norte so as to return to Spain. Utre, for his part, missed the opportunity to undertake the exploration and lost his life as a result of discord and partisanship among the soldiers. This disunion originated in differences between Pedro de Limpias and Bartolomé Welser on military procedure for, being open rivals, one a lieutenant general and the other a campmaster, no occasion arose in which the two did not become angered. Limpias strongly resented this situation, for Utre, as a fellow countryman and relative of Welser, favored the latter in every respect. Thus, Limpias sought a means to avenge himself by ruining the two, although at the loss of his own good reputation. He was able to carry out his project in a devious way, as everyone in Nuestra Señora was debating whether the conquest of the Omeguas should be pursued. Although there were adverse opinions, the most feasible plan was to return to Coro to reorganize with more men. To attempt with so few the subjugation of a kingdom so densely populated and so remote that help was considered impossible was to run the risk of failing completely and losing through haste that which would be assured with patience.

Pedro de Limpias found in all this confusion the opportunity he desired to consummate his perfidy. Thus, he approved this decision and offered to go personally to Coro if given twenty men as escort, and to return in the briefest time possible with the troops, arms and horses needed for the conquest almost within their grasp.

The proposal seemed excellent to Utre, for in that manner, without depleting his camp or depriving it of food supplies, he would obtain the assistance needed to pursue his objective. Without suspecting Limpias's malice, Utre dispatched him to Coro. A few days later, however, he realized his error and repented having placed faith in a man whom he had had reason to censure in the past. He began to distrust Limpias when he learned that in Coro not only was the campmaster failing to provide what he had promised but that he was assembling an inferior group of soldiers in order to discredit the expedition. Not having any other means of averting the damage he feared, Utre lifted camp and, with double marches each day, went in pursuit of Limpias. However, the latter, foreseeing what might happen, had increased his pace so greatly that when Utre arrived at Barquisimeto Limpias had already been in El Tocuyo for several days. There, Limpias succeeded in winning the good graces of the fraudulent governor, Juan de Carvajal. Securing in this manner the means of tarnishing all of Utre's actions, Limpias exaggerated Utre's bad judgment in always following Hernán Pérez's route, and stressed his imprudence in abandoning the conquest of the Omeguas. Limpias then sought to incline Carvajal's tumultuous spirit to this enterprise by representing to him the honor and profits which could result from it. Carvajal embraced this proposal willingly and would have implemented it at once had he not been impeded by new conditions that soon developed.

# CHAPTER III

*Utre and Carvajal are in disagreement concerning government; Carvajal seizes Utre and beheads him; later, Carvajal founds the city of El Tocuyo.*

As soon as Felipe de Utre, pursuing Pedro de Limpias, arrived at the mouth of the Barquisimeto, he learned from some Spanish-speaking Indians that in the Valley of El Tocuyo a captain called Carvajal was encamped, accompanied by many other Spaniards. As Utre could not at first determine exactly who they were, he halted in Barquisimeto and worked cautiously to learn as much about them as possible. Because the two camps were so close together, few days passed on which the soldiers did not exchange messages. Thus the intentions of both officers soon became clear, leading each to set double sentinels and observe extra vigilance. Meanwhile, Carvajal was endeavoring to persuade Utre to offer him obedience and give him command over the men whom he, as captain general of the province, had brought with him. Utre, however, aware of the perfidy of his adversary, refused to accept the situation. He was confident that he, sent by the Audiencia in accord with provisions set by His Highness, could withstand an intruder governing by mere dint of arms.

Pedro de Limpias, for his part, stirred the embers as much as possible, and all feared that the flames might gain such strength that they would engulf the entire province in civil unrest. Impelled by ill will conceived through his passion against the Germans, Limpias counseled Carvajal to seize Utre, basing his reasoning on the violent right of arms, for Carvajal had three times as many men as his adversary. The astute Carvajal did not think it wise to risk his position through the uncertainty of confrontation, however, and held it preferable to use sagacious dissimulation to remove Utre from his post. Several of Utre's friends who were with Carvajal, on learning of this design, advised Utre of it immediately and warned him to be careful not to allow the malicious cunning of his rival to succeed. Nevertheless, Carvajal's deceit was so great that he was able to persuade Utre that they should submit the question to impartial arbiters who, seeing the credentials of each, would determine the one to whom the government belonged. To assure Utre of his sincere desire for peace, Carvajal proposed, as an alternative to putting the matter in the hands of a third party, that they govern the province together and unite their men to conquer and settle among the Omeguas.

Utre's nature was so mild and artless that, notwithstanding the warning of his friends, he allowed himself to be swayed by Carvajal's cunning. Without suspecting fraud, Utre assented to the last proposal against the judgment of his most trusted aides and then left his quarters in Barquisimeto to proceed with his men to the camp at El Tocuyo. There, Carvajal, apparently to disguise his intentions, received him with a show of friendship and provided lodgings for him with all the courtesies his duplicity indicated. Utre soon recognized the deception his complaisance had invited, however, for without giving him a role in government as promised, or paying any attention to him, Carvajal sought only an occasion to seize him without tumult. Aware of this situation and repentant of having put himself in the hands of his enemy, Utre was now governed by the advice of his close friends. Then Carvajal, wishing to end this pretense, invited him to dine at his quarters with the idea of effecting during the banquet the capture he had planned. Utre recognized the danger in these attentions but, trusting in his own valor and the large number of his friends in Carvajal's retinue, he went to the feast, placing

## CHAPTER III

Bartolomé Welser and the rest of his faction on the alert to help him at the least disturbance. Carvajal took note of this precaution and did not dare to make any show of what he was trying to accomplish. Then, after the meal was finished, Utre, emboldened by the fear he recognized in his adversary, said that he was aware of the deception with which he had been treated. He had not received anything that he had been promised and had experienced only threats of continued violence. He added that it was imperative to correct the situation because he could expect no benefit with the duplicity surrounding him. He asked only to be allowed to return to Coro with his men, and from there to go to Santo Domingo, where he would give an account to the Royal Audiencia of all that had transpired.

Carvajal became agitated at this proposal and, rising from his chair, with disordered movements and altered voice, he replied that Utre was free to go wherever he wished. He was not to think of taking soldiers with him, however, or of daring to use the title of captain general or even lieutenant, for jurisdiction lay only in himself while decrees from the Audiencia were still pending. At this insolence Utre put his hand on his sword and with labored breath called on each person present to rally to the king. Those partial to each leader came forward at once and, since many of Carvajal's men declared in favor of Utre, his faction held such an advantage that he could without difficulty have put an end to the contest with the death or imprisonment of his enemy. Impelled by his own noble spirit, however, he contented himself simply with taking from Carvajal all his arms and horses. Then, leaving him humiliated, Utre retired with his soldiers to Quibor Valley, six leagues distant from El Tocuyo.

Carvajal, undismayed by such adversity, invented new means to avenge this affront. He dispatched his lieutenant general Juan de Villegas, Melchor Gurbel (Grubel), and his chaplain, Toribio Ruiz, to Utre's quarters. There they undertook to impress upon him the enormity of the offense he had committed in disarming with violence a governor of the province. The mediators then endeavored to reduce the matter to a friendly accord so that Utre and Carvajal might end such dissension at once. They offered such promises that they persuaded Utre to sign a pact restoring the arms and horses he had taken from Carvajal. He furthermore agreed to desist for the time being from pursuing the action he had been planning against the government and to proceed to Coro with those who wished to follow him. From there he would embark for Santo Domingo to report to the Audiencia on the progress of his conquest. Hardly was Carvajal again provided arms and made aware that his adversary's adherents were disorganized, however, than he began to pursue Utre and soon overtook him encamped on a quebrada that runs through the mountains of Coro.

Carvajal, seeing the Germans free of distrust, dismounted and with no difficulty seized Utre, Bartolomé Welser, Captain Palencia, and Romero. He then ordered a black man of his forces to bind their hands and behead them with a machete. Since the blade of this instrument had been blunted by continual use, their lives ended in prolonged agony, more from repetition of the blows than from slashes of the blade, without awakening the slightest pity in Carvajal's heart. On the contrary, he joked with Limpias and Sebastián de Armacea while the executions were taking place and extolled as a pastime the spectacle of those wretched men in torment.

This was the doleful end of General Felipe de Utre, certainly worthy of a better fate. This native of the city of Speyer (Spira), Germany, carried away by youthful ardor, had crossed to America where he constantly manifested his prudence and courage. These qualities, added to his kinship with the Welsers, had provided the Audiencia de Santo Domingo ample motive to name him lieutenant general under Señor Bastidas. Desire for approbation, more than a longing for riches, impelled him to search for El Dorado, where his error in tenaciously following Hernán Pérez's footsteps prevented him from attaining the glory forecast for him by Fortune. No captain of all those who served in the Indies bloodied his sword less, for even though he crossed more provinces than any other in his extended journey of four years, this moderate commander was moved to war only when he found no other means of gaining peace. He doubtless would have discovered the kingdom of the Omeguas, had Pedro de Limpias's infamous revenge and Juan de Carvajal's treacherous cruelty not hastened his death in the flower of his youth. They cut the thread of his life before he had completed his thirty-fourth year, and with him buried the most lucid information on the opulent kingdom of the Omeguas, whose exact location remains undetermined to this day.

After Utre's execution, Carvajal returned at once to the Valley of El Tocuyo, where he unloosed his cruelty. He used the slightest pretext, and the day was rare when he did not hang one or two of those who had been partial to Utre. Even his closest friend, the factor Pedro de San Martín, who dared to warn him of the evil he was committing by executing such bloody punishments, was almost ordered hanged and eventually was censured as a traitor and sent in iron fetters as a prisoner to Coro.

Carvajal occupied himself with these exercises until the end of 1545, when he decided to found and settle a city where his camp was

## CHAPTER III

then situated because of the great advantages the region offered. After laying out the streets he had the surrounding forest cleared, but reserved as an arrogant symbol of his cruelty a beautiful ceiba whose leafy branches, serving as a gibbet, had been the scene of his injustices. He did not reflect that, like another Haman, he was leaving it as the gallows for his own death and the instrument of his dishonor.[6] On the seventh day of December, 1545, he founded the city and named it Nuestra Señora de la Concepción del Tocuyo. Its first settlers were Diego Ruiz Vallejo, Esteban Mateos, Damián del Barrio, Juan de Guevara, Juan de Quincozes de la Llana, Luis de Narváez, Gonzalo de los Ríos, Sancho del Villar, Cristóbal de Aguirre, Licentiate Hernán Pérez de la Muela, Alonso de Campos, Cristóbal López, Juan Sánchez Moreno, Juan de Antillano, Antonio del Barrio, Domingo del Barrio, Tomé de Ledesma, Amador Montero, Cristóbal Ruiz, Diego de Montes, Gonzalo Martel de Ayala, Diego de Morales, Bartolomé García, Francisco Sánchez, Juan de Villegas, Francisco de Villegas, Luis de Castro, Diego de Ortega, Francisco de Vergara, Blas Martín, Alonso Martín, Juan de Salamanca, Melchor Gurbel, his son, Leonardo Gurbel, Diego de Escorcha, Diego de Leiva, Juan Mateos, Bernardo de Madrid, Francisco de Madrid, Bartolomé Suárez, Juan de Cisneros, Juan Cataño, Vasco de Mosquera, Gonzalo Martel, Pedro Hernández, Juan Muñoz, Pedro Alvarez, Luis Tani de Miranda, Juan de Tordesillas, Hernando Alonso, Toribio Ruiz, Francisco Muñoz, Francisco López de Triana, Juan Roldán, Pedro de Limpias, Cristóbal Rodríguez, Sebastián de Almarcha, Alvaro Váez, and Francisco de San Juan. Of these, Carvajal named Damián del Barrio, Juan de Guevara, Alonso de Campos, and Bartolomé García as first councilmen, and Luis de Narváez as chief constable. These officials, in turn, selected Esteban Mateos and Juan de Antillano as alcaldes.

This city is located in a beautiful valley made fertile by the clear waters of El Tocuyo River. Its temperature is mild, its terrain bounteous. It produces fragrant roses, much cotton and sugarcane, wheat, maize and other grains, and many fruits, native as well as foreign, especially delicious apples. Its pasturelands nourish innumerable herds of goats from whose hides excellent skins are prepared, and these pelts serve its residents as merchandise for trade. At present the city is inhabited by one hundred and thirty residents, among them some from illustrious families, descendants of the first settlers as well as of those who came later. In addition to the parochial church it supports two small convents, one of the Order of San Francisco, the other of Santo Domingo.

BOOK III

# CHAPTER IV

*Licentiate Frías arrives in Coro; the emperor divests the Welsers of the administration of the province. Licentiate Juan Pérez de Tolosa comes to govern it; he seizes Carvajal, condemns him to death, and Carvajal is hanged.*

CARVAJAL'S insolent acts were so excessive that reports of them quickly reached Cubagua. There Licentiate Frías was occupied with the mission entrusted to him by the Audiencia but, on learning of his lieutenant general's evil conduct, he named substitutes to administer his duties while he rectified the situation. He crossed to Coro at the beginning of 1546, accompanied by Losada who, having retired to Cubagua after his first difficulties with Carvajal in Coro, had been watching the conflagration from a distance. Since Carvajal had foreseen this development and had carried with him all the arms and horses Coro afforded, Frías found the city so ill provided that he had to remain there several days. During this time he sought provisions for the trip to El Tocuyo, for he did not dare to enter in search of Carvajal without bringing well-armed men.

During this interval Licentiate Juan Pérez de Tolosa, native of Segovia, a prudent and scholarly man whom the emperor had sent as governor and captain general of the province, arrived in Coro.[7] The Welsers had been divested of their administration because of repeated complaints that reached His Majesty of irreparable abuses by the Germans. These grievances were so numerous that Friar Bartolomé de las Casas, in his book *Destrucción de las Indias,* justly described this province as miserable and hapless. If it had not been subject to foreign domination for eighteen years, it would have been one of the most opulent in America. Its vast extent, fertile land, benign climate, abundant waters, convenient port, and multitude of Indian inhabitants assured that it would have had no equal. Still, the Germans looked upon it without love, considering it simply a thing on lease. Nor did they try to preserve or improve it but aimed only at exploitation without reflecting that the measures they were taking might destroy it. Without settling the beautiful country they discovered, they took all with blood and fire; and there was nothing to which they did not lay waste. As the enslavement of the wretched Indians was the principal source of their profit, they captured the natives by the thousands to sell to merchants who flocked to Coro, drawn by the enticement of this enterprise. The result of this trade was that most of the province was depopulated because the Indians deserted their towns for the interior of the Llanos. There they have remained until this day, resulting in the loss to the Crown of many vassals and to the Church, many souls.

News of these and other proceedings induced the emperor to divest the Welsers of their charge and send Licentiate Tolosa as governor. As soon as he arrived in Coro, he was informed by Frías and others of Carvajal's tyrannical conduct, which daily caused more Indians to flee. Tolosa decided to go immediately to El Tocuyo and put a stop to those actions and apply the punishment that such deeds deserved. Taking the same precautions as Frías, Tolosa and some of his men left Coro and arrived early one morning at the huts of the new city. There, he surrounded Carvajal's quarters and took him and his lieutenant general, Juan de Villegas, prisoner.

This done, Tolosa convened all the citizens of the city to calm the spirits of those who were partisans of Carvajal. After showing his credentials as governor and captain general of the province, and personal dispatches from the emperor detrimental to the Welsers, he explained his motives for seizing Carvajal and his lieutenant. Furthermore, he promised that he would hear them and administer justice because of his desire to further peace among the citizens. Everyone felt so relieved at this attitude that they accorded him general acclaim and received him into the exercise of his functions. Nevertheless, he was extremely careful, fearing opposition from Captain Juan de Ocampo, whom Carvajal had sent a few days before with sixty of his most trusted followers to explore the valleys of Umúcaro. To eradicate this misgiving quickly, Tolosa dispatched Diego de Losada with several warriors in search of Ocampo with evidence of the emperor's provisions so that Ocampo would return to the city at once. This assignment required little of Losada, for Ocampo immediately recognized Tolosa as governor without reservation. All rejoiced at being free of the oppression suffered under Carvajal and the violence of the Welsers as they turned once again toward El Tocuyo.

After everything had been arranged to Tolosa's advantage and he felt assured of the peaceful possession of his government, he examined accusations against prisoners. At the end of a lengthy investigation, no charges whatsoever resulted against Captain Juan de Villegas, as it was evident that he had not assisted in Carvajal's excesses. Therefore, on September 25, 1546, Tolosa declared Villegas free, and to compensate for his imprisonment named him lieutenant general.

Carvajal's end was very different, for such were his atrocities that Tolosa felt obliged to condemn him to death.[8] He ordered that, after

Carvajal had been dragged through the most public streets of the city, he was to be hanged on the same ceiba tree which had been the scene of his own injustices. Although this verdict was appealed by the criminal, and several friends interceded on his behalf, Tolosa was firm in his resolution and the sentence was executed. Thus, Carvajal justly paid with his life for the many which he had taken without reason. A spectacular phenomenon was then noted: that from the instant he died on the ceiba, until then covered with heavy foliage, it began to wither so rapidly that its decline evoked as much wonder as had its former beauty.

# CHAPTER V

*Alonso Pérez de Tolosa goes out to explore the Sierras Nevadas; he crosses the Apure River and reaches the Lomas del Viento (Hills of the Wind) and the Valley of Cúcuta.*

THE tragedy of Carvajal now ended, Juan Pérez de Tolosa sought to return to normal, to give new form to his government and permanence to the recently founded city. Since the principal manifestation of its stability lay in encomiendas of Indians, he strove to make certain that no door would remain open for any future governor to deprive the settlers of that reward for their services. Recognizing the invalidity of the distribution made by Carvajal because of his lack of jurisdiction as an intruder governor, Tolosa declared all encomiendas vacant. Then, without making any changes, he returned them to the same persons who had held them previously and issued new titles for their greater security. The grateful citizens then urged him to award to himself the Indians of the Valley of Cubiro, which had been Carvajal's, but he accepted nothing more than a few small families in repartimiento, simply to satisfy their pleas. The rest he gave to Diego de Losada, the only remuneration he received in this province, though his services made him worthy of the greatest recompense.

From these proceedings Governor Tolosa learned that there were many Spaniards in El Tocuyo without any benefits because the encomiendas were too few to compensate all. Seeking a remedy for the situation, he ordered his brother, Alonso Pérez de Tolosa, to go out with one hundred men to explore the Sierras Nevadas, on the foothills of which the city of Mérida was later to be settled. These mountains, considered a landmark on expeditions into the Llanos, were said by some Indians to hold great riches, undoubtedly the principal objective of the present journey. Some, however, claimed that its purpose was to search for a cattle route from El Tocuyo to the Nuevo Reino, a motive held by Cristóbal Rodríguez who, as one who had first come with Federmann, knew the value of this commerce. It was he, in fact, who later succeeded in introducing this trade into Bogotá, for which he was amply rewarded.

Finally, however, whether for one reason or the other, Alonso Pérez took Diego de Losada as his campmaster, and left El Tocuyo at the beginning of February of 1547. His function was, according to the express order of the governor, to follow in every respect whatever lead might be offered. Going upstream along El Tocuyo River after having spent several days on its banks and crossed the mountains which lie to the west, Alonso Pérez came out at the Guanare River, whose course along that span bears the name Zazaribacoa. Entering the Llanos, he traveled to the foothills of the Sierras Nevadas with the intention of crossing their summit to search for treasure on the other side.

As some of the men were set on seeking roads propitious for introducing cattle into the Nuevo Reino, they opposed Alonso Pérez. They gave as their reason that crossing the mountain was impractical and carried the risk of death. Consideration of these circumstances caused them to follow the road through the Llanos until they arrived at the banks of the Apure, where Tolosa stopped for several days. During this time the Indians of the region, encouraged at seeing the small number of Spaniards in comparison to those which had passed through there on other occasions, decided to test fate by forcefully expelling them from the land. Accordingly, one morning at daybreak they rushed in well-formed battalions on our men, who were deep in carefree slumber. Awakened by the uproar, they remained calm, hastily rounded up the horses and, seizing their arms, broke through the barbarians' squadrons. The Indians were thrown into disorder on the first encounter and, after losing their most valiant warriors, left the victory to the Spaniards, who nevertheless paid at a cost of one soldier dead and more than twenty wounded.

Alonso Pérez delayed only long enough to treat the wounded and to allow Captain Romero with forty men to search for food. He then resumed the march toward the mountains, entering at the source of the Apure River, for he reasoned that that spot, apparently less rugged, would offer easier passage. At a break in the cordillera, he found a medium-size town whose inhabitants, on guard but with only a modest defense, obstructed the Spaniards' entry. The natives seriously wounded

Captain Romero and four other soldiers, and offered valiant resistance, but they could not avoid defeat. Almost all were captured and the town was sacked, robbed, and destroyed at the whim of the invaders.

After the seizure of the natives, their maize, cotton robes and edible roots, the Spaniards followed the same river and, on marching a few leagues, came across a little town of Tovoro Indians on the opposite bank. At first the natives made a show of defending themselves but, on observing the horses as they hurled themselves into the current in their pursuit, they fled the site. They left the town to be pillaged, but two soldiers, not content with what they found, went out onto the mountain to see if a more diligent search might reveal anything that had been hidden. Happening on an ambush, one of them immediately lost his life and the other would have suffered the same fate had not his terror inspired in him exceptional speed. He ran until he reached the protection of the village, where Alonso Pérez would have had him garroted if several captains had not pled that his punishment be commuted to a lesser penalty.

From this Tovoro village Tolosa continued his march along the Apure River until he arrived at the mouth of another stream, no less abundant, which joined it.[9] Then, leaving the Apure, he resumed his journey in search of the valley which today is called Santiago and in which San Cristóbal was afterward founded between Pamplona and Mérida. At the news that foreigners were arriving at its outskirts, its inhabitants went one day's journey downriver to take advantage of a narrow passage that the valley formed between two hills, hoping to halt the invasion. Captivated by the novelty of the attire and organization of the Spanish army and the speed and vigor of the horses, however, they were too astonished to use their bows and arrows for offense or their feet for flight. Attacked by our men, with some warriors by now dead and others wounded, the natives were forced to retreat, abandoning the entire valley to the discretion of our soldiers, who sacked the first town they encountered. After having lodged there for the night, they learned the following day that farther up the valley there was another densely populated town, later called Aviamas by those who settled San Cristóbal. Departing hastily, Tolosa soon found it, and though the Indians offered no opposition, he executed several of them.

Having collected the pillage afforded by this town and then crossed the San Cristóbal River, Alonso Pérez went on to the next town, where the shrine of the miraculous image of Nuestra Señora de Táriba was later to be built. In fearful anticipation its natives had gathered with their families and belongings at the summit of a towering mountain, thinking to find security there; but the Spaniards were able to follow their tracks.

Placed on the defensive, however, the Indians offered such resistance that the Spaniards' victory was costly. Six horses were killed, and Alonso Pérez as well as several other soldiers were badly wounded with no profit other than four worthless ornaments. Disconsolate at these niggardly spoils, they abandoned the Valley of Santiago, hoping to have better fortune elsewhere. Then, after crossing the Lomas del Viento through the town of Capacho, they came out into the great Valley of Cúcuta, today the celebrated breeding place of the best mules produced in the Nuevo Reino. There, the woods are filled with oregano, and hardly any other plant is seen in all the vast expanse of this warm and fertile terrain.

# CHAPTER VI

*Juan de Villegas begins the exploration of Tacarigua; he takes possession of its lake and returns to El Tocuyo; on Governor Tolosa's death, Alonso Pérez continues the expedition.*

AFTER Alonso Pérez left El Tocuyo to explore the Sierras Nevadas, Governor Tolosa was inspired to bring renown to his term in office with new towns and conquests. With the hope of discovering gold mines from which samples had been found, he thus ordered his lieutenant general, Juan de Villegas, to lead eighty men of his own selection across the Valley of Barquisimeto and along the side of the mountains toward the east. In addition, when Villegas reached the province and lake of Tacarigua (now Lake Valencia), he was to found a town at any place that seemed to be the most suitable point of control for the district. To fulfill this order, Villegas left El Tocuyo in September of 1547 accompanied by Luis de Narváez, Pedro Alvarez, inspector of the Royal Treasury; Pablo Suárez, chief constable of the camp; Juan Domínguez, Gonzalo de los Ríos, Sancho Briceño, Hernando del Río, Juan Jiménez, Cristóbal López, Esteban Martínez, Juan de Zamora, Miguel Muñoz, Pedro González, Antonio Sarmiento, Juan Sánchez Choque, Luis González de Rivera, Bartolomé Núñez, Juan Sánchez Moreno, Pedro de Gámez, Alvaro Váez, Juan de Escalante, Diego de Escorcha, Antonio Cortés, Pedro Suárez, Alonso Vela León, Rodrigo Castaño, Juan Díaz Marillán, Jorge Turpi, Vicente Díaz, Francisco de San Juan, and others, up to the number of eighty. Skirting the mountains to the east, they arrived at the shores of Lake

Tacarigua which, in a valley sixty leagues from El Tocuyo, twenty from Caracas, and seven inland from the sea, occupies fourteen leagues from east to west and six from north to south. It is so deep that even at a short distance within its shores no plumb line can sound its depths. Its banks are delightful, covered with fresh trees sheltering a variety of birds. Several islands add to its beauty, among them two that measure more than a league and a half, and they all abound in peccaries, cashew birds, chachalacas, ducks, and other varieties prized by hunters.

This massive lake is formed by fourteen rivers, which continually empty into it. A layer of broad leaves on its surface, fallen onto intertwining roots and added to driftwood and silt, takes on substance and little by little forms a cover two or three varas thick and more than thirty or forty long. This foundation is so firm that it supports small trees and at times rather large ones, according to the disposition of the material. When blown from all sides by the wind, these deposits appear to be mobile islands or hanging sea gardens until that connection is broken by the constant motion of the waves and strong tug of the undertow. Pliny describes similar formations in the North Sea; and Botero speaks of them in the ancient French province of Artois.[10]

With the intention of settling the Valley of Tacarigua, Villegas took legal possession before a public scribe, Francisco de San Juan, on December 24, 1547. Not a trace of gold mines was found, however, even though the entire district was thoroughly searched by Hernando Alonso, Juan Jiménez, and Juan Sánchez Moreno, miners whom Villegas had brought for this purpose. Thus disappointed, he abandoned the lake and valley that had pleased him so much, crossed a mountain range only seven leagues long, and went down to Borburata, on the seacoast. It seemed more fitting to settle in this beautiful port because of its comfortable capacity for accommodating more than a hundred ships, its safety from winds and its favorable anchorage, which permitted them to unload with planks directly onto land. Another reason for the choice was that they had found in the surrounding quebradas particles of gold so fine that they exceeded twenty-three carats in assay. With this promise of vast riches, all agreed to settle in that port, and Villegas, after taking legal possession before the scribe, founded the city which he named Nuestra Señora de la Concepción de la Borburata.

While Villegas was occupied with these things, the emperor granted Tolosa an extension of three years on his assignment. Inspired by this honor, Tolosa arranged affairs in El Tocuyo and left for Cabo de la Vela to investigate certain frauds perpetrated with regard to the King's Fifth of pearls, and to conduct an official inspection of the ministers of that town. Even as Tolosa was most favored by Fortune, however, his hopes

## CHAPTER VI

were cut short by his untimely death. Traveling toward Cabo de la Vela across a desolate stretch of land he died of an acute fever, and all memory of him was buried there with his body in that solitary place. Even today, the location of his final resting place is not known, a lamentable end for so venerable a man whose literary gifts, unselfishness, and singular prudence were special attributes that deserved a better fate.

The news of Tolosa's death brought the colonization of Borburata to a standstill for a time. Juan de Villegas, who had been appointed head of government for the entire province during Tolosa's absence in Cabo de la Vela, now considered the desirability of going immediately to El Tocuyo to prevent any movement prejudicial to his continuing in that role. Thus, spending no more effort on settling the city, he abandoned Borburata and traveled so rapidly that on March 19 he and his army entered El Tocuyo. There, the alcaldes of that city and of Coro raised questions, alleging that each of them in his own jurisdiction was affected by the vacancy because the title on which Villegas based his claim was insufficient. Nevertheless, since his following was large and the partisanship of his friends strong, the two Cabildos ordained that he remain in charge.

Very remote from these things was Alonso Pérez in the Valley of Cúcuta where the natives, as soon as they heard of his coming, abandoned their huts and retired to a stronghold. It was protected by a double palisade, broken at intervals by embrasures from which they could shoot their arrows, and it served as a refuge in their wars on one another. In it they now resisted so vigorously that, although Alonso Pérez attacked them, he was compelled to desist after three of his soldiers and several horses were killed. He passed on without delay to the Zulia (or Pamplona) River, forded it, and entered the territory of the Motilones, penetrating as far as the mountains in which the Carates live on the north edge of the city of Ocaña. On this march, in addition to the harshness and desolation of the land, he suffered such lack of food that he was obliged, after traveling seven days, to turn back to the Valley of Cúcuta. There, restored by the abundance of supplies and several days' rest, he followed a new route down the valley in search of Lake Maracaibo and came out where three rivers join to empty into the lake. Keeping it always in sight on the left, he continued marching toward the east until, after several encounters with inhabitants on its banks, he reached the plains of San Pedro, not far from where the city of Gibraltar later was to be founded. This was the seat of the Babur Indians, an affable and only mildly bellicose tribe, their sole instruments of war being blowguns for their little poison-tipped arrows. This poison had such singular powers that a person injected with it appeared to be dead for two or three hours, the time needed by the archer to reach safety; but after that, the wounded man regained consciousness without suffering any other damage. Thus, with little hindrance from this tribe, Alonso Pérez pursued his march through the Llanos, skirting the lake to return to El Tocuyo. But no matter how persistently he followed this route, he found himself thwarted by a marsh that, mingling its waters with those of the lake, penetrated the mountain area for more than a league at the narrowest point. It was so swampy that, in spite of his strong effort to ford it, he did not succeed, even though he delayed six months on the lake's shores to see if at the height of the dry season its waters would recede. Since they remained always at high levels, he lost all hope of being able to cross it and decided to return by the road on which he had come, to seek help in Cúcuta, the valley where fortune seemed to bring him refuge from affliction.

# CHAPTER VII

*On Villegas's order, Pedro Alvarez founds the city of Borburata; Alonso Pérez pursues his journey and then returns to El Tocuyo.*

As soon as the alcaldes settled the question of succession, Villegas began his duties. To make certain that the hard-won fruits of his exploration of Tacarigua would not be lost, he turned his attention to the settlement of Borburata, which had been interrupted the preceding year by his haste to return to El Tocuyo. For this purpose, at the beginning of 1549 he sent as captain the inspector Pedro Alvarez with sixty men, among them Alonso Pacheco, Alonso Díaz Moreno, Vicente Díaz, Sebastián Ruiz, Francisco de Madrid, Andrés Hernández, Pablo Suárez, Juan de Escalante, Luis González de Rivera, Alonso Vela León, Pedro de Gámez, Juan de Zamora, Francisco de San Juan, Antonio Sarmiento, and others who, wishing to enjoy the benefits that the new city promised, decided to settle there. Without difficulty they arrived at Borburata, where on May 26, 1549, they started their town. Named as regidors were Francisco de Madrid, Alonso Pacheco, Juan de Escalante, and Alonso Vela León who, in turn, selected as alcaldes ordinarios Vicente Díaz and Alonso Díaz Moreno. In the beginning this city anticipated growth because of the wealth expected from port trade and the gold that the quebradas offered. Its site at the edge of the water with no means of

## CHAPTER VII

defense, however, led to continuous attacks by pirates. These raids caused its inhabitants to abandon it a few at a time until the year 1568, when they deserted it entirely in spite of Governor Pedro Ponce de León's efforts to prevent its dissolution.

Threatening conditions also existed in Alonso Pérez's camp which made him so disconsolate that he decided to return to Cúcuta. From there he sent Captain Pedro de Limpias with twenty-four companions to report to Governor Juan Pérez de Tolosa, his brother, that he was returning defeated and without profit from his expedition. Although on the third day after Limpias departed, five of his men were killed in a skirmish with Indians, he and those remaining finally reached El Tocuyo.

Alonso Pérez suffered no less on his retreat than Limpias and his men had experienced. He was forced to march at a slow pace because of the large number of sick men, and there was such a lack of food that within a distance of ten leagues twenty-four soldiers died of hunger. Pérez was so distressed at this loss that he left the road to search for fields of food-bearing plants. On this detour he discovered mountains to the left never before seen by Spaniards. Finally, he found a little town of six or seven houses which his men searched, but the few inhabitants put up such resistance that the greatly weakened Spaniards could not sustain combat for long. They consequently declined the challenge and pressed forward to sack a hut which, to judge from its provision of maize, roasted meat, and roots, must have been the common storehouse for that village. The Indians, encouraged by the favorable outcome of their first offensive, charged the Spaniards who, in disarray, tried to seize whatever food they could. In this first encounter, the Indians killed two and wounded six, and the damage would have been even greater if the Spaniards' debility had not changed to strength at their awareness of grave danger. They attacked with such courage that the barbarians fled, leaving their homes and storehouse unprotected. The exhausted invaders were invigorated to march on from this town until they came for the third time to Cúcuta.

After convalescing with an abundance of food in that beautiful valley, they turned back toward the Lomas del Viento. They passed through the Valley of Santiago and the narrows of its river to the banks of the Apure. They followed this stream until they arrived at the space between it and the Sarare, close to another small one called the Río del Oro. Here thirty of Alonso Pérez's soldiers, dissatisfied with scant profits from El Tocuyo, asked leave to pass on to the Nuevo Reino. He granted this request because the situation now required only a small escort. These thirty named Pedro Alonso de los Hoyos as their leader and took the path skirting the cordillera until they arrived at the Casanare River, which rises in the land of the Chitas or Cocuyes. They followed its currents, led on by the cakes of salt and the cotton garments found, since they were known to be products of the land they were seeking. At length they reached the towns of the Lache Indians, in the jurisdiction of Tunja. Since Pedro de Ursúa was at that time raising men for the conquest of the Chitarero Indians, these thirty men enlisted under his banner. Thus, they were among those who, under command of that celebrated leader, subjugated this warlike nation and settled the city of Pamplona. Here their leader, Pedro Alonso de los Hoyos, remained as a resident and encomendero. In this way they discovered a convenient road from El Tocuyo to Bogotá over which, to the great advantage of the Nuevo Reino, they introduced a large number of cattle. These animals, thanks to the fertile pasturage available, multiplied then in the same abundance as they do today.

A few days after Pedro Alonso and his thirty men had departed, Alonso Pérez lifted camp from the banks of the Río del Oro. He traveled down the Apure to flat land where some peaceful Caiquetíos gave them food, enabling them to proceed to the Barinas River. There, during a rest from the difficult journey, he gathered new strength to finish the expedition and entered El Tocuyo by January of 1550, after two and a half years spent in fruitless exploration and inauspicious attempts at conquest.

# CHAPTER VIII

*The mines of San Felipe are discovered; Villegas founds the city of Barquisimeto; the black Miguel leads a rebellion and is crowned king; Diego de Losada goes out in search of him, then defeats and kills him in battle.*

THERE was in El Tocuyo at this time a large number of men, those who had been defeated with Alonso Pérez de Tolosa as well as many who had drifted in from various places. Several persons were working diligently toward organizing a new expedition against the Omeguas to conclude Felipe de Utre's execrable exploration of that kingdom. Broad experience, however, had taught Governor Juan de Villegas that such military activities were the reason for the wretched state of that province, since men, arms and horses were consumed in those pursuits with no result other than wasted time. He did not agree with the pernicious claim that the opportunity to settle that region had been lost, but it appeared

## CHAPTER VIII

to him more suitable to remain in cities where the stability of the area was assured. Nevertheless, an inducement to settlers to become permanent was provided at that time by news of the discovery of gold mines, verified by samples of both gold dust and jewelry found among the Indians. At the beginning of 1551, Damián del Barrio was dispatched by Villegas with a suitable escort to the province of Nirgua, east of El Tocuyo between Barquisimeto and Tacarigua, where it was commonly believed the principal lodes lay. Although specimens from various places were at first unrewarding, after several days a productive vein was found on the banks of the Buría from which Damián del Barrio at once sent samples to Villegas. News of this find was received with such delight that the governor went to examine the quality of the mine without delay. He named it the Real de Minas de San Felipe de Buría and, feeling that it would be unwise to disregard it until others of greater substance were found, decided to work it in proper form.

Villegas was encouraged by the success of his mission, and aware of the advantage of having a sufficiently large number of Indians in the region of El Tocuyo and the mine to support a town of Spaniards. He therefore established in mid-1552 a settlement in the Valley of Barquisimeto that he named Nueva Segovia de Barquisimeto in homage to his home city in Spain.[11] Its first citizens were Diego de Losada, Esteban Mateos, from whom in that city as well as throughout the province there is illustrious descendance; Diego García de Paredes, valiant son of the hero of that same name whose brave deeds were the amazement of Italy;[12] Damián del Barrio, progenitor of extremely noble families; Pedro del Barrio, his son; Luis de Narváez, Gonzalo Martel de Ayala, Juan de Quincozes de la Llana, Francisco de Villegas, Melchor Gurbel, a German; Cristóbal de Antillano, Francisco López de Triana, Diego García, Hernando de Madrid, Francisco Sánchez de Santa Olaya, Pedro Suárez del Castillo, Vasco de Mosquera, Gonzalo de los Ríos, Bartolomé de Hermosilla, Pedro Hernández, Pedro Suárez, Cristóbal López, Diego de Ortega, Esteban Martín, Juan de Zamora, Juan Hidalgo, Pedro González, Juan García, Sebastián González de Arévalo, Francisco Sánchez de Utrera, Cristóbal Gómez, Diego Bravo, Diego de la Fuente, Francisco Tomás, Pedro Viltre, a German; Sancho Briceño, Jorge de Paz, Diego Mateos, Pedro Mateos, Jorge Lans, Francisco Graterol, and others, of whom Villegas appointed as regidors Gonzalo Martel de Ayala, Francisco López de Triana, Cristóbal de Antillano, Diego García de Paredes, Hernando de Madrid, and Francisco Sánchez de Santa Olaya; and as scribe of the Cabildo, Juan de Quincozes de la Llana. These men then selected as first judicial magistrates Diego de Losada and Damián del Barrio; and as general solicitor, Pedro Suárez del Castillo.

Villegas founded the city at the site of present-day El Tejar, but when the residents of Barquisimeto experienced certain misfortunes during the time of Governor Manzanedo, it was moved to its present location. Twelve leagues to the east of El Tocuyo, on high and barren plains, it has a healthful and pleasant climate, although somewhat warm; but its waters are murky and unsavory. It has somewhat more than one hundred and fifty Spanish residents, among them, gentlemen of illustrious lineage; and its natives are affable and courtly in manner. The colonists could be very rich if they knew how to make the most of the vast cacao plantations in the valley. Though many merchants from neighboring provinces come to trade for this product, the Spaniards' continual irresponsibility keeps them always under financial stress. This city enjoys the title of Very Noble and Loyal, with which His Majesty Philip II honored it in 1592, a favor that King Charles II reaffirmed in 1687. Also, it rightfully takes pride in counting among its sons the illustrious Friar Gaspar de Villarroel, archbishop of Las Charcas. Besides its parochial church, to which two curates minister, it maintains a convent of the Order of San Francisco with four to six clergymen, and a shelter where charity is dispensed to the sick.

Profits from the San Felipe mines were so great that the settlers of Barquisimeto realized a marked increase in their wealth. Thus encouraged, they sent more than eighty black slaves and a number of Indians from the encomiendas to extract the metal under the supervision of Spanish miners with the title of mayordomo. One day in 1553, one of these miners was preparing to punish a black man named Miguel, slave of Pedro del Barrio, and skilled in the Castilian language. On being bound for a lashing, he snatched up a sword close at hand and created such a disturbance that he was able to reach the door. He retreated into the brush but came out by night and, communicating secretly with other blacks who worked in the mines, tried to persuade them that they could shake off the yoke of servitude. Although most shunned such counsel and persisted in their work, Miguel succeeded in inducing twenty to flee with him. These he led on the town, where they killed some of the miners and seized the rest so that their martyrdom might be more prolonged. With the cruelest torture, he took the lives of all those who had either beaten or abused him and his companions in other ways, and then freed the others. He arrogantly ordered them to warn the residents of the city to be expecting him, for he planned in a short while to crown his victory by slaying them all, and wished the event to be even more laudable because of his having advised them in advance.

Miguel continued to urge the blacks and Spanish-speaking Indians to follow him, and they did come a few at a time to join his forces until they soon numbered one hundred and eighty. With them he retired to the remotest part of the mountain, and at the place that seemed most suitable, he built a fair-sized town surrounded by strong palisades and ditches. There, feared and respected by his men, he changed subjugation to vassalage as he had himself acclaimed king, and a black woman named Guiomar, with whom he had had a son, crowned queen. And, so that the child might also enter into that fantastic monarchy and become a character in the farce, his father proclaimed him crown prince. Miguel then created a royal household, including all officials he had heard of as serving in the palaces of kings. In order that his jurisdiction should not be restricted to temporal dominion, he appointed a bishop, choosing a black man who in reality had a right to aspire to the rank for, because of his pompous speeches, he had already been designated canon by everyone while still working in the mines. As soon as he was selected, he raised a church in which he celebrated pontifical mass every day and preached to his flock the nonsense that his incapacity dictated and his ignorance spawned.

Miguel provided bows and arrows for the Indians and spears made from small rakes and hoes for the blacks, as well as a few swords that he had collected from the Spaniards. In order not to waste time solely in the delights of his court, he then led his men toward Barquisimeto with the fixed hope of destroying it. His sole military plan was to trust to the terrors of the dark night, in whose shadows he arrived at the city without being heard. Setting fire to several houses, he attacked from both sides at the same time and, in the confusion, a priest named Toribio Ruiz and two or three other residents were killed. The rest, however, hurriedly grasped their arms and in a group of about forty assailed the blacks with such resolution that they killed several and wounded many. The Indians then retreated to a nearby mountain and the Spaniards did not advance further in order not to risk losing the victory.

The residents of Barquisimeto had not been convinced that Miguel would attack the city, although he had promised it, and by failing to heed his threat, they had been taken off guard. Discouraged now, they recognized that it would be necessary in time to resort to punishment to extinguish the rebellion before it became unmanageable. Not daring to move alone, however, they sent word to El Tocuyo at dawn of what had happened during the night. They asked for help so that they might go out in pursuit of the blacks, and the people of El Tocuyo responded by sending troops out under command of Diego de Losada, a leader of great military experience and recognized valor. Gathering all his forces, he set out so hurriedly that before Miguel heard of the foray, Losada was already at the palisades of the town.

Following their king, the blacks gained a temporary advantage, but finally Miguel, exhausted by two wounds, sank into death. At this, his soldiers lost courage and began a retreat at which the Spaniards brought an end to the revolt, which had been so greatly feared because in the beginning it had been disparaged. As the farce concluded in tragedy, Queen Guiomar and her son, the crown prince, who had played royal roles, were forced to return to their former slavery where they found themselves once again beaten down and enchained after having ascended to a throne.

# CHAPTER IX

*The Jirajara Indians rise in rebellion; Licentiate Alonso Arias de Villacinda, who comes as governor, tries to subdue them but does not succeed; Alonso Díaz enters Tacarigua and founds the city of Valencia.*

SINCE the blacks' rebellion had ended on the death of their king, Miguel, the residents of Barquisimeto thought there would be no further interference with the mines. No sooner had that fire been extinguished, however, than another broke out which for seventy-four years burned with an intensity that made labor impossible. In time, even the location of the vein was erased from memory, and the settlers were deprived of its metals until this day. The Jirajara Indians, a valiant but haughty race who inhabited the province of Nirgua close to the mine site, became disturbed by this situation. Incited either by the example of the blacks or afraid that the riches the Spaniards sought were to be obtained only through slave labor, the natives sought to inhibit the reason for their servitude by repeated assaults on the mines. Consequently those in charge, not daring to operate the mines any longer, abandoned them and returned to the city, although certain that poverty would be the inevitable result for all.

Licentiate Alonso Arias de Villacinda was named governor and arrived in Coro in 1554, but he tarried there only a few days before passing on to El Tocuyo and Barquisimeto. Informed by the citizens of what had happened in the Miguel affair, he decided that for prompt relief from such danger and in order that the mines might be worked in safety, a Spanish town should be established. The governor, considering this

## CHAPTER IX

decision to be appropriate, named to execute it Captain Diego de Montes, a man celebrated for both his vast military experience and his rare knowledge of curative herbs. He used them to treat wounds from poisoned arrows, applying antidotes in accord with his identification of the properties of the poisons.

Accompanied by forty men, Montes started toward the Buría River, hanging and impaling along the way every rebel Indian he could capture to avenge the deaths they had inflicted on Spaniards, and to terrorize the country. After exploring the district and examining the terrain, he chose a site on the banks of a river that ran through a lovely palm grove near the mines, and there he founded a town that he named Las Palmas. Convinced that the Jirajara Indians would not be so rash as to attempt a surprise move, Montes left it in charge of the alcaldes and returned to El Tocuyo to procure necessities for the new settlement. At the same time, several residents of Barquisimeto who had accompanied him as far as Las Palmas returned to their homes. This left so few on the site that they, learning a little later that the Indians were contemplating an attack, did not dare await them but withdrew to Barquisimeto.

Governor Villacinda was distressed by this setback, for he had believed that the Indians would become subservient with the founding of the town and that production from the mines would return to normal. Without these benefits, the settlers had no means of support and consequently, in the following year of 1555, they mounted another expedition for the pacification of the rebels. Thirty-five well-armed men left Barquisimeto under the command of Diego de Paradas, a native of Almendralejo in Estremadura and one of the thirty-nine Spaniards who had fought under Felipe de Utre in his battle with the Omeguas. Crossing through enemy territory, he inflicted punishment on the Indians, convinced that the demonstration would be sufficiently frightening to persuade the rebels not to attempt to take up arms again. Settling the town a second time, he called it Nirgua because it lay on the banks of the Nirgua River, from which the entire province takes its name. It did not become more stable, however, and its inhabitants could remain in it only during the relatively pleasant dry season. The Indians were favored by the continual deluges during the rainy season, which kept the Spaniards from exploring the land and seeking food supplies. The natives blockaded the town and attacked it without cease, forcing its residents to abandon it as they recognized that the lack of food and the obstinacy of the enemy made its defense impossible.

Governor Villacinda was next inspired with the hope that, once finally subdued, the region might serve to facilitate the conquest of the Caracas Indians. Thus, he gathered all the soldiers available in the three cities of Coro, El Tocuyo and Barquisimeto, and naming Alonso Díaz Moreno, resident of Borburata, as commander, he dispatched him with the order to found a city near the lake. He took such pains with this assignment that, although the Indians struggled to stop him, they were soon defeated. The Spaniards founded Nueva Valencia del Rey that same year of 1555 on a beautiful plain, seven leagues from the port of Borburata and a little more than half a league from Lake Tacarigua, where it still stands today. It has a parochial church whose gross income is nine and one-half percent of the tithes collected, and a convent of the Order of San Francisco with limited accommodations for two or three clergymen. It could have been an opulent city if it had not been burned and sacked in 1667 by French corsairs, and if the proximity of the city of Caracas had not drained it of a large part of its most illustrious citizenry. These drawbacks, added to its inhabitants' idleness, are fundamental causes for its drastic decline.

# CHAPTER X

*Francisco Fajardo undertakes the exploration of the province of Caracas; Diego García de Paredes enters the land of the Cuicas and settles the city of Trujillo.*

AT this time, Francisco Fajardo, son of a Spanish nobleman of the same name and of Doña Isabel, cacica of the Guaiquerí Indians, lived on the island of Margarita, of which he was a native. Doña Isabel was a granddaughter of Charaima, cacique of the Valley of Maya in the province of Caracas, named for the tribe which inhabited part of its coast. She was widely known from the time of the discovery of that land by the Spaniards. It lies within the province of Venezuela and measures twenty leagues from north to south and forty leagues from Borburata to the east. It was inhabited then by a multitude of barbarians of the Caracas, Tarmas, Taramainas, Chagaragatos, Teques, Meregotos, Mariches, Arbacos, and Quiriquires, scattered throughout its beautiful extent. Francisco Fajardo often conversed with Doña Isabel on these tribes, the fertile lands, mild climate, peaceful aspect of nature, rich quebradas, and other singular qualities of this province. He reflected that the situation would allow much opportunity for improving his fortune if he should succeed in discovering and settling it. Although Doña Isabel recognized the

## CHAPTER X

difficulties that so bold a resolution entailed, she nevertheless not only concurred in the idea but also urged him to implement it as soon as possible.

Fajardo was determined to strive to attain through skill that which, because of scant resources, could not be accomplished through force. Reassured by the ease with which he spoke all the languages of the coast, and trusting the outcome to fate, he left Margarita in April of 1555. Alonso and Juan Carreño, his half brothers on their mother's side, and Pedro Fernández, along with twenty other vassals of Doña Isabel, accompanied Fajardo on the short crossing from Margarita to Tierra Firme in two pirogues, in which they carried a few items for barter. They sailed along the coast of the province of Cumaná and, after rounding the Cabo de Codera, made port in the Chuspa River, the first stop on the land they were attempting to explore.

On hearing the news of Fajardo's arrival, Caciques Sacama and Niscoto went down at once to the shore, accompanied by one hundred Indians. Fajardo, speaking to them in their own language, explained that the motive for his voyage was nothing more than to seek their friendship and establish trade agreements with them. The caciques were pleased at the affection with which Fajardo spoke and granted him uncontested disembarkation privileges. He landed with the precaution that the occasion warranted and bartered jewelry, golden eagle neck plaques, hammocks and other provisions. His hosts were attentive to him for three days, after which he departed with progress in friendly communication assured. Applying the same treatment to Cacique Guaimacuare, who lived two leagues farther south, Fajardo passed on in search of the most powerful lord of that coast, Cacique Naiguatá, who, as the son of a brother of Doña Isabel's grandfather Charaima, was her uncle. Fajardo found with him the same hospitality he had received from the others, and after several days of conversing, a familiarity developed between the two. Fajardo, recognizing that what he had discovered in this land corresponded to information given him in advance, felt it time to put into practice the ideas on which he had founded his hopes of winning the land. When he revealed to Naiguatá who he was, the cacique and his vassals developed much love for him because of kinship, and soon the entire area was subject to his will and judgment. Profiting by the occasion, he also effected a cordial relationship with the caciques who lived in the land on the other side of the mountain range. In this manner, he gained complete familiarity with all the province so that he felt that he had already attained on this journey all he needed for certain success. Then, much to the regret of the Indians, he returned to Margarita, having spent in this exploration the rest of the year 1555.

At the beginning of 1556, Governor Villacinda died in Barquisimeto, leaving the government of the cities to the alcaldes ordinarios, each within his own jurisdiction. After the governor's death, the people of El Tocuyo learned of the province of the Cuicas, which lies to the west of the city and extends for more than thirty leagues, running north to south from the sierras of Mérida, also called the paramos of Serrada, to the city of Carora. They applied all means possible to subject it, motivated by profits they hoped to acquire with its conquest. The accountant Diego Ruiz Vallejo,[13] who had come there in 1549 to search for gold mines in the Valley of Boconó, had recognized it as a bountiful province, fertile in all kinds of fruits and especially abundant in cotton. This was the product most esteemed by the people of El Tocuyo, where the natives had developed skill in exquisite weavings of this material that had high retail value as merchandise for trade.

The decision to undertake this conquest was approved by the alcaldes, who then entrusted it to Diego García de Paredes. Fleeing the rebellion in Peru, he had come to Venezuela, preferring to lose his reward for services in the other kingdom than to place himself in jeopardy in the upheavals of his fellow countryman and kinsman, Gonzalo Pizarro. With seventy foot soldiers, a dozen horsemen and a large number of *yanaconas*,[14] he left El Tocuyo and, without encountering any opposition, marched westward to the province of the Cuicas, seeking a site suitable for settlement. He arrived next at the populous town of Escuque on the steep sloping banks of the Motatán River, which, born in the paramos of Mérida, runs into Lake Maracaibo.[15] Since this spot appeared propitious, Paredes founded there in that same year of 1556 the city of Trujillo, honoring with this new town his birthplace in Estremadura. After appointing a justice and body of councilmen for the ordinary administration of government, he distributed the Indians in encomiendas among the inhabitants, and then returned to El Tocuyo to give an account of what he had done.

In Paredes's absence, some youths who had remained in the new city, lacking both supervision and respect, imposed on the pacific nature of the Indians by running around wildly, following the senseless appetite of their evil desires. Not content with stealing the Indians' meager treasures, they proceeded to abuse the natives' wives and daughters, and they did not hesitate to perform these ugly acts even in view of the very ones offended. As these inane affronts became more distressing, the Indians changed from complaisance to barbaric fury. In revenge they killed all Spaniards found engaged in this lascivious diversion, and, with warriors from the entire province, placed the city under close siege. Its inhabitants, enclosed in a strong palisade, were reduced to such straits that if Diego García de Paredes had not rushed to their aid with fresh troops, the Indians undoubtedly would not have left a single Spaniard alive. The barbarians were obliged to lift the siege, but this setback did not diminish their rancor. Instead, supported by reinforcements, they repeated their assaults with such persistence that Paredes, now with ten foot soldiers dead and many wounded, considered resistance to be impossible. Moreover, every measure he proposed for peace gave the Indians a new incentive to continue the war. He then resorted to the old trick of leaving lights burning and dogs on leash so that the Indians, hearing them bark, would not suspect a retreat. Abandoning the city and a large number of cattle, which the Spaniards had brought for their own sustenance and for breeding, Paredes set out at a rapid march and reached El Tocuyo during the first days of 1557.

# CHAPTER XI

*The Audiencia names Gutiérrez de la Peña governor;*
*Diego Romero enters the territory of the Jirajaras;*
*Fajardo returns to Caracas; he founds but later*
*abandons the town of Rosario.*

WHEN news of Licentiate Villacinda's death reached Santo Domingo, the Audiencia named Gutiérrez de la Peña as interim governor. He reached Coro early in 1557 and, after being invested in office, passed on to El Tocuyo. On his arrival, the people of Barquisimeto solicited the restoration of the San Felipe de Buría mines, without whose profits they were unable to support themselves. In response he dispatched Diego Romero with fifty men to terrorize the Jirajaras so that the town might be resettled, and work in the mines resumed.

The province was thrown into disorder by Romero's incredible cruelties against the Indians as he followed these instructions. He reestablished the mining town on its original site and changed its name to Villa Rica; but, since several disadvantages had been recognized in the location, it was soon moved to the banks of the Nirgua River and its name changed to Nueva Jerez. It was to remain there only until 1568, when its inhabitants, harassed relentlessly by the Indians, were obliged to abandon it. The following year, by order of Governor Pedro Ponce de León, Juan de Mota rebuilt it, but in its short duration it experienced the same reverses. In 1628, as related in the second part of this history,[16] with the general extermination of the Jirajara race, Governor Juan de Meneses y Padilla relocated the town on the site it occupies today and renamed it Nuestra Señora de la Victoria del Prado de Talavera.

Francisco Fajardo was still on the island of Margarita after his first voyage to the coast of Caracas. Encouraged by his successful beginning, he wished to return immediately to pursue the conquest but, since his forces were insufficient for so arduous an undertaking, he had to delay until 1557, when he set out again from Margarita accompanied by Doña Isabel. Also with him were his two half brothers, Juan and Alonso Carreño, Pedro Fernández, Martín de Jaén, Francisco de Cáceres, and Cortés Richo, all natives of Margarita except the latter, a Portuguese, and one hundred Guaiquerí vassals of his mother. With a few weapons and articles for barter, he crossed to Tierra Firme but, because the number of his men was too limited for establishing a colony, he remained in the port of Píritu instead of continuing at that time to the coast of Caracas. This territory had two caciques, now christianized and baptized under the names of Alonso Coyegua and Juan Caballo.[17] Engaged in the pearl trade on the island of Cubagua, they were both esteemed by the Spaniards and had a close relationship with Fajardo. He had stopped at that port for several days to enjoy festivities offered in his honor, and there he acquired five more companions: Juan de San Juan, a Biscayan; Abrahán de Ese, Flemish; Francisco de Robles, Juan de Burgos, and Gaspar Tomás. They had been driven off course from Maracapana through mishaps at sea and had just arrived by pirogue on the coast of Cubagua.

Fajardo, now with eleven dedicated Spaniards, gained new impetus to pursue the conquest as planned. Without further delay, he left Píritu, taking with him Cacique Juan Caballo with one hundred of his vassals. After rounding the Cabo de Codera, Fajardo reached land a little to the leeward of the port of Chuspa at El Panecillo, where news of his arrival caused Caciques Paisana and Guaimacuare, as well as other close neighbors, to gather at once. Fajardo had acquired dominion over them partially because of his charm and his flawless use of their languages, but the principal influence was their respect for his mother as a cacica of their race. This time he had brought Doña Isabel with him, thus increasing their love so much that the caciques insisted that she remain with them. They offered as inducement the entire valley of El Panecillo, extensive farmlands and their aid; and since this was the outcome Fajardo had hoped for, he willingly accepted their offers in her name.

Fajardo had entered this exploration on his own authority, but he now was in a situation which required that he establish a town to

CHAPTER XI

strengthen the progress of his conquest, for he dared not go farther without sanction from the governor of the province. To obtain this permission, he left his men in El Panecillo engaged in building straw huts while he rushed downstream in a pirogue with only two companions and some Indian rowers. He traveled the forty leagues to Borburata, which, as the most populous city to the windward of this province, had jurisdiction over the entire coast. There, he gave an account to its cabildo of what he had accomplished and then sought out Governor Gutiérrez de la Peña in El Tocuyo. After communicating his aspirations to the governor, he was authorized to govern in Peña's name all the coast from Borburata to Maracapana, with permission to establish the towns necessary to ensure his conquest.

Satisfied with these negotiations, Fajardo returned to Borburata and from there went to El Panecillo in search of his men. Finding now completed the houses they had just begun at the time of his departure, he named that collection of huts Rosario. At first, the Indians had been pleased with this town because of their affection for the Spaniards, but there now was growing dissension due to the soldiers' violent conduct. Annoyances increased with the passage of time, but the Indians feigned tolerance, even as they regretted having sought the recent arrivals' friendship. Thus, they resolved to remedy this error with arms, but Guaimacuare held that before arriving at an open break, they should try to free themselves from oppression without unnecessary violence. This plan provided that Fajardo leave the city in friendship and return safely to Margarita with his men, for otherwise he might complain that he was attacked without cause. Nevertheless, Cacique Paisana was determined to exact vengeance without delay, at which Guaimacuare and Paisana grasped their macanas and might have challenged the protesters if the cacique of the town of Caruao had not intervened.

Fajardo was aware of the meeting of the caciques, for Guaimacuare had advised Fajardo at once of his threatened expulsion. To avoid this situation, Fajardo withdrew toward the seashore so as to have his rear guard protected by the ebb and flow of the tide. He fortified his camp, surrounded it with double stakes and set up a trustworthy sentry. There he awaited the attack of the Indians as they, led by the proud Paisana, arrived in the early morning. The natives attacked with customary tumult by attempting to tear down the palisades. Though few, Fajardo's soldiers were well distributed, and both the Guaiquerí Indians whom he had brought from Margarita and the Píritus whom Juan Caballo had provided were protected by the stockade.[18] Using the wooden joints as embrasures, they inflicted with spears and arrows such slaughter on the troops that Paisana was obliged to desist. As the hatred conceived against the Spaniards burned implacably in that barbarian's heart, however, the damage done to his forces did not diminish his violence; on the contrary, he attacked more savagely to force the town to surrender. In addition, he poisoned the well water so that Fajardo and his men would not have that indispensable resource for survival.

Fajardo might well have wished to abandon the city, but since that move would have had to take place by sea, he could not withdraw because his pirogues were in need of a complete careen before again being seaworthy. In the interim, he decided to break the enemy by attacking them on their own ground, risking his fate on this one encounter. He left only twenty Indians on guard at the fort for its security and Doña Isabel's protection, and he divided the rest of his men into two squadrons. He commanded the one composed of his eleven companions and the Píritu Indians provided by Juan Caballo. The other, consisting solely of the Guaiquerís from Margarita, was led by a valiant and daring Indian named Diego Guerra. They left the palisade in the silence of a dark night and, finding all asleep in Paisana's camp, the two squadrons joined to rout the enemy army. After recovering from the first onslaught, however, the natives fought so bravely that Fajardo was obliged to retreat to the town. Nevertheless, the Indians were so crushed by the deaths of their bravest warriors that Paisana did not dare to wait for a second attack but lifted the siege that night and led the remainder of his broken army to safety.

Fajardo at once started preparing the pirogues for his return to Margarita, to allow time for the Indians' fury to pass. He also was very concerned that pollution of the water had caused widespread illness in his ranks and several deaths among the Guaiquerís and Píritus, most painful being that of his mother Doña Isabel. All these motives obliged him to hasten his departure but, when just ready to embark, he received a message from Paisana. The cacique expressed remorse for what he had done and asked permission to visit him, to which Fajardo freely consented with no assurance other than his confidence in the cacique's word. Paisana entered the town accompanied by sixty warriors, and at the same time, Cacique Guaimacuare sent Fajardo a warning not to trust Paisana, for his subterfuges were aimed solely at finding an opportunity to kill him. This information angered Fajardo so much that he seized Paisana and all his companions. With no justification other than what his wrath dictated, he then publicly renounced his promise and hanged the cacique and ten of his principal vassals from a roof beam. This action tarnished Fajardo's reputation, and he could never plausibly excuse himself for so cruel a violence. Considering that punishment sufficient requital for his anger, he set the other Indians at liberty and, gathering his men together in the pirogues, set sail for Margarita toward the end of 1558. Almost at the same time, on the death in Coro of Bishop Jerónimo Ballesteros, His Majesty presented as his replacement Friar Pedro de Agreda, Dominican clergyman and professor in the Colegio de San Gregorio de Valladolid, although his coming to the province was delayed until 1560.[19]

# CHAPTER XII

*Francisco Ruiz settles Miravel in the land of the Cuicas;[20] Pablo Collado comes as governor; the conquest is restored to Diego de Paredes, and he rebuilds the city of Trujillo.*

GOVERNOR Gutiérrez de la Peña was informed of what had happened in the province of the Cuicas and of the causes for distress in the newly founded Trujillo. At the same time, he was told of the fertility of the region, the abundance of native inhabitants and the profit that might be extracted from so bountiful a land. Although the people of El Tocuyo strongly urged him to desist in its conquest, he considered inaction unwise in view of the wealth implicit in the export trade of cotton. He decided to send out a second expedition but, inasmuch as there had been some enmity between him and Diego García de Paredes, he declined to entrust it to that officer, naming Francisco Ruiz, resident of El Tocuyo, as commander instead. Ruiz was accompanied by Alonso Pacheco; Francisco Graterol; Bartolomé Escoto; Alonso Andrea de Ledesma; Tomé de Ledesma, his brother; Sancho Briceño; Gonzalo Osario; Francisco Infante; Francisco de la Bastida; Jerónimo de Carmona; Gaspar Cornieles; Diego de la Peña; Juan de Segovia; Lucas Mejía; Agustín de la Peña; Pedro Gómez Carrillo; Luis de Villegas; Juan de Aguirre; Francisco Ruiz; Juan de Baena; Francisco Moreno; Gaspar de Lizana; Lope de Encira; Luis de Castro; Juan Benítez; Francisco Terán; Andrés de San Juan; Vicente Riveros; Juan de Miranda; Rodrigo Castaño; Francisco Jarana; Pedro García Carrasco; Luis Quebradas; Juan de Bonilla; Hernán Velázquez; Francisco Palacios; Pedro González de Santacruz; Juan de Miranda; Esteban de Viana; Gregorio García; and others, up to the number of eighty, most of whom had come in with Paredes. Ruiz took an exploratory turn around the region of the Cuicas, penetrating as far as the Valley of Boconó. There he halted to put his arms in order and have *escaupiles* made, because he recognized the unrest his entrance had caused among the Indians.

At the same time as Francisco Ruiz left El Tocuyo, Juan Maldonado, encomendero of the Cuicas, set out from a city recently settled by Juan Suárez. After crossing the Sierras Nevadas with all the discomforts of freezing weather, he arrived at a valley occupied by the Timotes. There, he quartered his troops in comfort and then continued with only twenty men to explore the lands to the north. By this route at the beginning of 1559 he reached the Valley of Boconó, where Francisco Ruiz was encamped with his army. Coming across two of Ruiz's soldiers hunting, he ordered them to tell their captain to seek another place in which to settle because the right to conquer that one belonged to him. This message intimidated Ruiz so slightly that he sent out his own message threatening vengeance. Their angry words soon mounted to the point of challenge but, after considering the matter more maturely, they ended the disturbance. Maldonado retired to the valley where he had left his army encamped, and Ruiz and his men went on to Escuque. Earlier, Paredes had founded Trujillo on this site, but had had no intention of resettling it. Piqued by Maldonado's discourteous words, however, he now decided to rebuild the city which, in order not to duplicate the first founding, he called Miravel instead of Trujillo. He then appointed alcaldes and regidores, and distributed Indians among the settlers, actions which affronted Maldonado, who interpreted them as scorn for his valor and point of view. He therefore went a second time to wrangle with Ruiz, and on both sides such insulting messages transpired that the two would have brought ruin on each other had not the persons of best intentions in both camps composed them. It was agreed that Maldonado would return to Mérida, setting the land of the Timotes as the limits of his conquest; and Ruiz would remain in Miravel, holding as his possession the province of the Cuicas. In this manner the spheres of the two Audiencias of Santo Domingo and Santa Fe de Bogotá remained divided in a way that up until then had been ill defined. Ruiz was relieved at this disposition, without reflecting that it might offer harmful consequences to his quiet possesssion of Miravel.

In that same year of 1559, Licentiate Pablo Collado arrived in El Tocuyo to serve as governor and captain general of the province in place of Licentiate Villacinda. Since Diego de Paredes had been keenly wounded by the disdain Gutiérrez de la Peña had shown him in depriving him of the conquest of the Cuicas, he proceeded at once to express his grievances to the new governor. After hearing his claims, Pablo Collado revoked the rights granted to Francisco Ruiz and issued new authority

## CHAPTER XII

to Paredes. He ordered him to rebuild or resettle the place he considered most desirable, and to make a new selection of regidores and judges.

With this authorization, Paredes left El Tocuyo with a few of his soldiers and, on arrival at Miravel, showed his commission to the Cabildo, which accepted him promptly into the exercise of his duties. His first act was to restore to the city its original name of Trujillo, but the settlement lasted only a brief time longer. Excessive humidity, continuous rains, and constant thunder and lightning led him to ask permission of the governor to better the location. The town was moved to the head of one of the valleys that run alongside the Boconó River, because there in the center of the Cuicas territory he could more easily go forward in his conquest; but for many years the settlement was unstable and shifted location frequently. Several days after the town was refounded, certain disagreements between Governor Pablo Collado and Diego de Paredes caused the latter to decline jurisdiction and leave the province to live in Mérida. This action brought about the complete ruin of Trujillo, for hardly had its citizens lost Paredes than they divided into factions and were consumed by discord. Since those who wanted the city to be relocated were more powerful, it was moved to a broad and barren plain called Los Truenos, after a storm that Juan Maldonado had once experienced there on the banks of the Motatán River. Here a great plague of ants hampered them in farming, and much cattle was devoured by jaguars. Consequently, they changed without asking the consent of the governor to an even more unsuitable place four leagues downstream on the same river. Located in the center of a mountainous region, it was so harsh, humid, and full of jaguars, as well as mosquitoes, ants and other insects, that they cursed their dissensions for having brought them these afflictions. Most regrettable was their having settled in a place where the climate was so noxious that it made them sick, pallid and exhausted, so that the community had more the aspect of a hospital than a town.

Although the settlers disclosed their miseries to Pedro Ponce de León, who succeeded Licentiate Pablo Bernáldez as governor, he would not grant them license to relocate. At last, however, after Don Pedro's death, they went eastward six leagues to the Valley of Pampán, but could not remain there because of the extreme heat and humidity. Finally, in 1570, tired of so much wandering, they chose Nuestra Señora de la Paz as patron saint of the city and made their last move to the present site. In a valley of temperate climate, it runs from north to south for almost a league, and from east to west it is so narrow that it accommodates only two streets up to the center of the city with just one running the rest of the way. Also, it appears that the saint they chose provides the protection they sought and serves them well, for there is such general peace and quiet among the inhabitants that they do not know what litigation is. They owe these qualities to the benign influence of their sky, and it is sufficient to know that a person was born in Trujillo for him to be judged free of malice, of affable nature and exemplary conduct.

Having decided to keep the city in that valley, they built costly homes, some of ashlar, others of brick or adobe. Then, transported by that vanity which leads men to attempt to make themselves immortal, they adorned the portals with shields bearing their coats of arms, thus giving body and luster to their nobility. Also, they nurtured the growth of their new town so carefully that in a brief time it became an opulent city because of its extensive trade, primarily in cacao. The residents planted vast groves in the Valley of Pocó, from which the cacao, taken across Lake Maracaibo for sale in Gibraltar, brought them large sums of money. The city's good fortune later turned to bad, however, and it experienced such recessions that it preserves today hardly the shadow of its former self. The cacao trees were ruined by floods and, without this trade, it lacked the mainstay that had brought it riches. This vicissitude was followed in 1668 by its being sacked by the French pirate Monsieur Gramon with such inhumanity that, not moved to compassion even by the sumptuous buildings, he burned them and reduced their beauty to ashes. Nevertheless, it is inhabited at present by more than three hundred residents, many of them of quality and nobility, and includes a primogeniture estate of the family of the knights of Covarrubias, descendants of Gaspar Cornieles, one of the first settlers.

It sustains a parochial church served by two rector-curates and two monasteries, one of the Order of Santo Domingo and the other of San Francisco. It has a temple of ornate and elegant architecture; a hermitage of Nuestra Señora de Chiquinquirá, site of a hospital; and a convent for Dominican nuns who make beautiful items, especially their pita products and other needlework. It is a delectable and opulent land because of its fertility and the many Indian workers in the district. The fields produce wheat, barley, maize, cotton, chick-peas and other grains in abundance, and sugar from which exquisite conserves are made. Beautiful cabbages, lettuce, and other vegetables are grown throughout the entire year; and all the fruits of America and many from Europe, such as apples, quince, pomegranates, figs, and grapes, are plentiful. In its pastures excellent sheep, swine, chickens, turkeys and other fowl are raised, and no special delicacies are lacking. In the midst of such plenty, however, this city suffers one great disadvantage, which some attribute to its waters. On the throats of many of its inhabitants, primarily women, swellings or goiters grow so generally that the person without one is rare, and some are so large and malformed that the mere sight of them is horrifying.

## CHAPTER XIII

*Fajardo returns to the coast of Caracas and with the governor's aid founds El Collado; he discovers the mines of Los Teques; he is seized by Pedro de Miranda, and returns after being released.*

FAJARDO did not remain idle in Margarita, his constant aim being the conquest of Caracas, and neither the scant means at his disposal nor any other obstacles were sufficient to deter him. Since his wealth was so limited, he succeeded in equipping only two hundred of his mother's vassals and recruiting eleven Spaniards. They were Lázaro Vázquez de Rojas, native of Salamanca, from whom there is today illustrious descendance; Juan Jorge de Quiñones, native of Margarita; Cortés Richo, a Portuguese; Gaspar Tomás, Martín de Jaén, Juan de San Juan, Hernando Martín, Andrés González, Luis de Seijas, Juan Hernández Trujillo, and Alonso Fajardo, native of Coro, son of Captain Juan de Guevara, the elder. With beads and other items for barter, Fajardo crossed for the third time to Tierra Firme but, with the fear of not being well received by the Indians because of past unpleasant encounters, he went down the coast in search of Guaimacuare without entering the ports of El Panecillo or Chuspa. He found the cacique in Caruao to be as constant a friend as ever but, as Fajardo had learned how little he could trust the volatile will of those barbarians, he did not want to stop in that valley while he was without sufficient men. Rather, to make himself more secure at once and to embark on the conquest on a firmer basis, he boldly resolved to cross the mountain range with only five of his companions and to march overland the forty leagues to Valencia. His aims were to learn what the province contained, to become self-sufficient, and to urge Governor Collado to give him men with whom he could start settling.

Guaimacuare was extremely sorry to see Fajardo insistent on this reckless course and tried to dissuade him, but as Fajardo trusted his natural gift for languages to win the goodwill of the Indians, he scorned the cacique's fears. Accompanied only by Juan Jorge de Quiñones, Lázaro

Vázquez, Cortés Richo, Martín de Jaén, and Juan Hernández Trujillo, he left the rest of his men under the protection of Guaimacuare and traveled from Caruao to Valencia without any difficulties. He then arrived at Las Lagunetas highlands, where the Arbacos, a proud and warlike tribe, roamed the hills and quebradas leading down to the Tuy River. Their cacique, Terepaima, regarding the entry of those few Spaniards into his land as rash impertinence, went out with several archers to take their lives. So vehement were Fajardo's motives, however, and so strong the power of his words over the Indians that nothing more was needed than for him to speak to Terepaima in the local language and tell him whose son he was for the cacique's fury to fade. He then accompanied Fajardo down a difficult road to the savannas of Guaracarima and left him free to enter Valencia.

Fajardo went immediately to El Tocuyo to advise Governor Collado of his desire to pursue his conquest. Since his enterprise was taking place in a district under Collado's jurisdiction and its success would bring both glory and profit to the administration, the governor needed little persuasion to concur. He immediately sent Fajardo the thirty men he was able to assemble in El Tocuyo and gave him the title of lieutenant general with broad powers to conquer, to settle and to distribute encomiendas.

Having obtained powers so favorable with such ease, Fajardo did not need to spend more time in Valencia. At the beginning of 1560 he acquired a supply of beef and other items needed for an efficient expedition and returned to Caracas with the firm intention of going forward. Assured of Terepaima's support and friendship, Fajardo planned to make this bond even stronger so that the door would always remain open to whatever might come to him from Valencia. When the cacique went out to meet him on Cucuizas Hill, Fajardo presented him a cow, a gift for which the barbarian was so grateful that Fajardo could proceed without apprehension. He penetrated the Guaire Valley, which the Indians named for the beautiful river that flows through it from west to east and makes the land fertile.[21] Fajardo renamed it the Valley of San Francisco, present site of the city of Caracas; and there, because of its many pastures, he left herds of cattle and several servants to care for them. Having established peace with the Teques, Taramainas and Chagaragatos, who all lived in the valley, he went down to the coast to seek the companions he had left with Cacique Guaimacuare. With them and the others whom he had brought from Valencia, he founded a city at the port of Caraballeda, two leagues to the windward of present-day La Guaira and, as a compliment to the governor, he named it El Collado.[22]

After appointing Lázaro Vázquez regidor and Martín de Jaén alcalde, Fajardo returned to the Valley of San Francisco to look for gold

## CHAPTER XIII

mines, for he had seen samples of that metal among the Indians. Although he did not find the mines in the beginning, he was so persistent that he finally came across them. In the area of Los Teques, six leagues southwest of the Valley of San Francisco and fourteen from El Collado in the same direction, he discovered several veins of fine gold, highly esteemed for its weight and the relative ease with which it could be extracted.

It was far from Fajardo's intention to implement his own ruin by seeking approbation, but he immediately sent samples of the metal, which incited jealousy and awakened greed in Collado's soul. Then some of the citizens of El Tocuyo, envious of Fajardo's good fortune, urged the governor to take the conquest from him, suggesting that it would be preferable to appoint someone who held the governor's confidence to put the mines into operation. They advised him not to trust Fajardo since the veneration and love which the Indians bore for him and the general domination he held over them made him suspect.

These misgivings, reinforced by concern for his own profit, made such an impression on the governor that he revoked Fajardo's powers and named Pedro de Miranda, citizen of El Tocuyo, to continue the conquest of Caracas. As soon as Miranda arrived at El Collado, he seized Fajardo and sent him back under guard to Borburata; but Fajardo's innocence was innate and no charge against him developed other than the obvious fiction his rivals had concocted. In order to continue the productivity of the mines, Fajardo went to El Tocuyo to express his grievances to the governor who, convinced of the validity of Fajardo's stand, was obliged to declare him free. Moreover, since his just complaint required satisfaction, the governor, wishing to placate him, named him chief justice of El Collado, leaving the rest of the province under the authority of Pedro de Miranda.

With these favors, Fajardo returned to El Collado at the same time that Miranda with twenty-five soldiers and several black slaves left for Los Teques to examine the mines. Finding them to be of even greater consequences and more productive than Fajardo had indicated, Miranda remained there and set the blacks to work. He sent Luis de Seijas and the twenty-five soldiers to travel through the province, whose numerous towns from the edge of the Valley of San Francisco for ten leagues running eastward were inhabited by the Mariches. Seijas had hardly set foot on the outskirts of the first town than he was attacked by Cacique Sunaguto, whose squadrons of archers encircled the Spaniards on all sides. This action placed Seijas in such danger that his men needed all their strength to reach some barrancas where, protected from the rear, they could defend themselves until nightfall. The Indians then suspended the fight and Seijas was able to prepare a small culverin (*verso*) which, loaded to capacity with balls and small stones, he aimed toward the spot where he judged the enemy would return to the attack. At the first light of day, with barbarous confusion and bustle, the Indians drew near to renew the skirmish.

Seijas engaged them in battle and, when the time seemed opportune, ordered the culverin fired. It reached a large number of targets in that turbulent multitude, and that one blow killed Cacique Sunaguto and many others. As the Indians threw themselves to the ground, breathing with difficulty and trembling in cowardly terror, the Spaniards easily put them to flight, as those who did not meet death deemed it safer to flee.

Seijas well knew, however, that the Mariches were brave enough to offer opposition and that he himself, having so few men, would be imprudent to persist in going farther inland. This consideration obliged him to return to the mines, where he found Pedro de Miranda upset because the Teques, persuaded by their arrogant cacique Guaicaipuro, had given clear indications of aspiring to rebellion. Miranda, not daring to await it, abandoned the mines as soon as Seijas arrived, and returned to El Collado with a considerable portion of gold dust. There he left the province entrusted to Fajardo and embarked for Borburata on the pretext of going to El Tocuyo to give an account to the governor of all that had happened.

# CHAPTER XIV

*At the governor's order, Juan Rodríguez enters Caracas and settles the town of San Francisco; Guaicaipuro attacks and kills everyone in the mines; and Julián de Mendoza conquers the Taramainas in battle.*

GOVERNOR Pablo Collado, informed by Pedro de Miranda of the riches of the mines Fajardo had discovered, the vast number of native inhabitants and other circumstances that made the province of Caracas enticing, decided to negotiate more persistently for its conquest and settlement. The governor was fortunate in having brought to his attention the presence in El Tocuyo at that time of a person of experience and valor, Juan Rodríguez Suárez, native of Estremadura, resident of Pamplona in the Nuevo Reino de Granada, and founder of the city of Mérida. Assailed by envious rivals, however, he was imprisoned in Bogotá and

## CHAPTER XIV

sentenced by its Royal Audiencia to be hanged. With the aid of friends, he was able to escape a biased tribunal and flee to this province.[23] From here, protected by Diego de Paredes, an old comrade whom he had met in the Boconó Valley when he was settling the city of Trujillo, he proceeded to El Tocuyo with letters of recommendation. In this superior gentleman, Collado found the person he needed and, with his selection as leader, assured the success of the project.

Juan Rodríguez left El Tocuyo with thirty-five men whom the governor had sent to him and, without anything unusual occurring on the way, he crossed the hill of Arbacos and entered Los Teques. From there he advised Fajardo, in El Collado, of his arrival and of the powers that he bore so that they might direct their actions toward one common goal. Fajardo matched this courtesy by sending reinforcements at once because he had had news of Cacique Guaicaipuro's movements and expected some openly declared break from him soon. This supposition was accurate, for the barbarian, vain for having forced Miranda to abandon the mines, anticipated that it would not be difficult to terrorize Juan Rodríguez into following the same course. But Guaicaipuro did not yet know the man whom he was opposing, although experience soon enlightened him, for Juan Rodríguez, unable to pacify the cacique's unrest, was forced to resort to arms. In the ensuing battle the cacique attacked five times to evacuate the mines but was routed on all occasions with the loss of his most valiant warriors. Guaicaipuro was so humiliated that he sought peace and Juan Rodríguez gladly conceded it, glorying in the knowledge that his name would forever be feared among the Indians.

After subduing the rebellion of the Teques, Juan Rodríguez, trusting Guaicaipuro's feigned submission more than he should have, filled the mines with Indians to extract the ore. Leaving with them three small sons whom he had brought from the Nuevo Reino,[24] he led his soldiers toward the coast to meet Fajardo. He entered the land of the Quiriquires on the banks of the Tácata and continued without opposition along the Tuy in Mariche territory as the Indians bowed their heads in admiration mixed with fear.

As soon as Guaicaipuro saw that Juan Rodríguez had left the mines filled with unarmed men, he assembled five hundred of his outstanding warriors and fell on the camp in the silence of the night. He put all its inhabitants to the knife including Juan Rodríguez's sons, without showing those innocent children any pity. One of the Spaniards' Indian allies escaped to a thicket and fled along unfrequented paths until at the end of twelve days he came upon Juan Rodríguez just as he was leaving the land of the Mariches to enter the Valley of San Francisco. From the distortion of the Indian's face, Rodríguez had a presentiment that some catastrophe had occurred. He stopped his horse and asked: "Son, what has happened in Los Teques?" The Indian, bursting into sobs, responded: "Sir, your sons and all those you left in the mines are dead. It was Guaicaipuro who committed this evil deed, and only I escaped to bring you this sad news." At this information Juan Rodríguez's heart struggled between grief at the death of his two sons and a desire for vengeance. As flames of anger burst forth, he fingered his beard and in pain and sorrow exclaimed: "Ah, Guaicaipuro, you have taken vengeance, but as surely as I am Juan Rodríguez, you will pay for it!" Urging his soldiers to a faster pace, he marched up the valley to the ranch Fajardo had established for the cows he had brought from El Tocuyo. Halting there, he found new cause for distress, for he saw the houses reduced to ashes, the servants all dead, their mangled bodies scattered across the fields, and the greater part of the cattle shot through with arrows. Paramaconi, cacique of the Taramaina Indians, incited by Guaicaipuro to help in expelling the Spaniards, had gone down to the Valley of San Francisco as soon as he had had news of the destruction of Los Teques. Then, catching the invaders off guard, he had initiated the revolt against them.

Since the Indians considered such daring a certain sign of some general conspiracy among the tribes, Juan Rodríguez at once deduced the approach of all-out war. The Spaniards thus felt it essential to attack without delay before the natives joined into one body so that the punishment of a few would serve as a lesson for the others. Wishing to discuss the matter with Fajardo before becoming more involved, however, Juan Rodríguez left his men in the valley under the command of Julián de Mendoza. Accompanied by only two foot soldiers, he departed for El Collado, but not half an hour later, Cacique Paramaconi with six hundred archers could be seen coming down through the pass at Catia toward the ranch.

The Spaniards at the time were rounding up the cattle that were still alive to drive them back into the pens. They recognized that the enemy was near and took up arms to defend themselves, using the corrals as protection for the rear guard. Julián de Mendoza, Antón de Albornoz, Fraga, Pallarés, and Castillo rode roughshod over the enemy, breaking through the ranks with their lances. Since they made their move at the very time that the Indians began the battle, the cavalry would have run the risk of being routed except for the help of the foot soldiers. The Indians, skillfully dodging lance blows, hit Antón de Albornoz's hands twice with their arrows, leaving him unable to handle his weapon. Next, seizing Pallarés's lance, they pierced the breast of Fraga's horse, an injury from which it died instantly. Then Julián de Mendoza, gravely wounded by the blow of a macana, fell unconscious to the ground. Thus the battle

## CHAPTER XIV

raged on both sides as Alonso Fajardo and Juan Ramírez, seeing Don Julián in danger, left the protection of the corrals and entered with swords in hand through the enemy lines to aid him. The other Spaniards engaged in skirmish; but just as replacements reached Paramaconi, Don Julián was rescued, and our men once again sought rear-guard protection at the corrals. The Indians next charged the Spaniards so suddenly that the cattle, pressed from all directions and unable to stand, broke the palisade on one side and, rushing out in a wild stampede, trampled the Indians, wounding some and knocking others to the ground. The Spaniards, taking heart from the enemy's confusion, attacked with a fury so frightful that in a brief time Paramaconi recognized the devastation of his forces. He then ordered his routed troops recalled with conch trumpets for the retreat to Catia.

During the last tragic moments of this encounter, Juan Ramírez retrieved the lance the Indians had taken from Pallares and with this weapon pierced the breast of the warrior who had made such skillful use of it. Wishing to see if among the dead on the field he could recognize the cadaver of that Indian, he went out with other soldiers, as soon as Paramaconi withdrew, to reconnoiter the battle site. As the Spaniards were engaged in this pursuit, an Indian sat up from among the dead and, unable to stand because both his legs had been broken, he called for them to come to where he was seated. Juan Ramírez drew near and asked what he wanted. The barbarian, with more desperation than strength, responded: "Only to kill you; but since my wounds prevented me from seeking you out and since you made so bold as to approach me, I, a mere Indian, challenge you." He then fitted an arrow into his bow and shot with such expert aim that it lodged in the forehead of one of the soldiers and left him badly wounded. Juan Ramírez ordered two Indian allies, vassals of Guaimacuare, to kill the barbarian but he fired two arrows so quickly that he pierced both thighs of one and the chest of the other, splitting his heart in two. This daring act so infuriated a soldier named Castillo that he threw an armored cloak over what he already was wearing and attacked with a sword. Before he was able to accomplish his purpose, however, the Indian, steadying his body with his bow, shot so many arrows at the Spaniard that if he had not worn the double armor, his wish to avenge the agony of the others would have cost him dearly. Finally Castillo placed his sword against the native's chest, ready to take his life, but the barbarian seized the edge of the blade and tried to clasp his attacker in his arms to avenge his own impending death by first choking the Spaniard.

After the battle Don Julián remained a while with his wounded and exhausted men but, fearing that Paramaconi might return, he dared not stay longer. Consequently, he ordered the wounded placed in hammocks, and lifted camp. A short distance down the road toward El Collado, he met Juan Rodríguez, who had been informed of the Taramainas' assault. Without having had an opportunity even to talk with Fajardo, Rodríguez returned to help Mendoza in any emergency. Holding retreat to be unwise because of the vainglory it would create in the Indians, the Spaniards turned back to the Valley of San Francisco. Then, so that the Indians might know how little fear he had of remaining there permanently, Rodríguez founded a town that he called San Francisco from the name of its valley, on the original site of the cattle ranch (today the city of Caracas). Then, after distributing the land to its citizens and naming alcaldes and regidores, he tried persistently to subjugate the rebellious caciques of the vicinity.

. Several days passed without his being able to come to grips with the Indians, because after they withdrew to the quebradas not one of them was to be seen in the entire valley. This development caused Rodríguez to be so extremely careful that he mounted his horse and, accompanied by the expert rider, Juan Jorge de Quiñones, and eight foot soldiers, he ascended the hill on the other bank of the Caroata arroyo. When they arrived at its highest point, Cacique Paramaconi could see them from his retreat and, choosing an Indian named Toconai to accompany him, he set out to meet them. These two Indians had quivers at their shoulders and bows in one hand, while in the other they held sturdy palm spears whose shafts contained two of the half swords which Guaicaipuro had come upon in the mines. From the multicolored feathered panaches which adorned their heads, jaguar skins hung across their shoulders, either to suggest greater ferocity or to make their gala dress more ostentatious.

On reaching the summit of the hill, they went out to meet Juan Rodríguez and Juan Jorge who, since they were on horseback, had traveled considerably faster than the foot soldiers. Now only a short distance from the two officers, Paramaconi audaciously proclaimed: "You cowards have the advantage of fighting on horseback, but I am Paramaconi and am sufficient to punish your arrogance. Since we are now alone on the field, it is time for each to prove his valor at arms." The two Spaniards, unable to bear more of the barbarian's insolence, spurred their horses to attack. Meanwhile the Indians hastily knelt and fixed the tips of their weapons firmly on the ground to receive the enemy as one awaits a bull. When this structure was noted by the horsemen, they, to keep their mounts from being wounded, shifted their course to one side and passed without stopping or touching the Indians. They hurled their spears at the same time and shot their arrows so rapidly that

## CHAPTER XIV

before the Spaniards finished the run the Indians had shot an arrow through the shoulder of each above his armored cloak. Nevertheless, even though Juan Rodríguez and Juan Jorge were pricked, for a second and third time they persisted in turning on the Indians at half speed, bearing their lances extended over the left arm for greater safety from the blows. But the Indians were so swift in handling their weapons and skilled in foot movements that, using almost simultaneously their spears and bows and arrows, they completely frustrated the two horsemen. Meanwhile, the eight foot soldiers had arrived and the Indians, not daring to prolong the combat against so many, retreated one by one; but Paramaconi, before withdrawing, released all the arrows remaining in his quiver. Toconai went down the slope to the quebrada but, seeing that Juan Jorge was pursuing him at a rapid rate, he halted and faced him. At the moment the Spaniard was about to strike, Toconai snatched his lance from his hand with such force that Juan Jorge had to hurl himself from his horse to retrieve his weapon. As he and the barbarian fell with arms intertwined, Juan Jorge drew a dagger from his waistband and stabbed Toconai, leaving him dead at his feet. Juan Rodríguez, with an intense desire to complete the victory, entered the mountain region in pursuit of Paramaconi to kill him also. He was too exhausted from the wound of an arrow that had passed through his armored cloak and pierced one of his nipples to complete the task, however. At the insistence of his companions, he returned to the town and was treated for his wound. In the interim, other events were taking place throughout the province.

# BOOK IV

## CHAPTER I

*Bishop Pedro de Agreda arrives in Coro; Sancho Briceño goes to Spain as procurator for the province; the tyrant Lope de Aguirre arrives at Margarita.*

ON Bishop Ballesteros's death, His Majesty appointed Friar Pedro de Agreda of the Order of Preachers to succeed him. He arrived in Coro in 1560 and found his bishopric so lacking in ministers that if there had not been some natives who had already been baptized, others would have remained pagans for lack of officiants. To obviate this disadvantage, the zealous prelate left Coro and traveled through all the towns of the region as far as the Carora mountains. He preached, catechized and baptized like a parish priest and sowed seed whose fruit has been incalculable. Having in this manner satisfied to some extent the obligations of his pastoral office, he returned to the city, recognizing that some sons of the province who aspired to the ecclesiastical state could never attain this joy because of their total ignorance. As there was no one else to teach them even the first rudiments of grammar, he organized studies and read Latin with all who wished to learn it. He hoped by this means to find some with special aptitude whom he might ordain to relieve the lack of priests. This dearth was so great that when Trujillo's priest died, the bishop asked the priest at Mérida to come to Trujillo during Lent so that its residents might fulfill this annual obligation.

This urgent need, along with a desire to solicit measures for added protection, led the Cabildos of the province to send a representative to the Court to ask for items judged most essential to the common good. As the choice of all, Sancho Briceño, a man of authority and talent, and a resident of Trujillo at that time, was named for this mission. He embarked at Coro for Spain, where he obtained favorable disposition of most of the petitions entrusted to him. At his request, His Majesty granted permission for a registered merchant ship to come once a year to the port of Borburata, the colonists to pay only half the customs duties

## CHAPTER I

on its cargo at entrance as well as exit. The province enjoyed this favor for several years, even after Borburata was abandoned and the ships docked at the port of La Guaira, but because of disuse this permission eventually was rescinded.

Briceño also obtained unrestricted authorization to introduce without taxation two hundred slaves who would work in the mines and cultivate the fields. To remedy the lack of priests, royal documents charged the provincials of Santo Domingo and San Francisco of the island of Hispaniola with sending clergymen of their orders. They were to take as their responsibility the conversion of the Indians; but it seems that some of them never came, although the bishop had requested them most urgently.

One of the principal instructions given to Sancho Briceño was that he seek clarification on the form of government a province should take when a governor died. In this way his successor could avoid such competition and disturbances as took place when Juan Pérez de Tolosa and Villacinda vacated their posts and the lieutenant general and alcaldes all attempted to adjudicate power. In this respect, His Majesty provided by cedula that whenever a governor in Venezuela died, the alcaldes ordinarios should govern until another governor was provided by the king. This cedula was issued in Toledo on December 8, 1560, by order of His Majesty before the scribe Francisco de Eraso.

This order was the origin of the privilege the city of Caracas still enjoys today, whereby its alcaldes govern the entire province when, through the death or absence of the officeholder, the post is vacant. Another royal cedula, issued on September 18, 1676, ordered that whenever the post of governor fell vacant, the alcaldes of the city of Caracas should govern the entire province without the president or Audiencia de Santo Domingo having authority to name an interim governor. This is a unique honor and privilege, without equal in America, which came about because Sancho Briceño's concern one hundred and sixteen years earlier had laid the foundation on which the decree was based.

The torture of his wound now eased, Juan Rodríguez took his men out on campaign in an attempt to drown in vengeance his sorrow at his sons' deaths. Entering the territory of Los Teques in search of Guaicaipuro, he was consistently victorious in skirmishes but could never learn where his enemy the cacique was hiding. Terrified and cautious, the Indian avoided risking his person and awaited only the opportunity to bring about Juan Rodríguez's death.

In 1559 Don Andrés Hurtado de Mendoza, the marquis of Cañete, viceroy of Peru, had been informed by Brazilian Indians of the existence of the powerful province of the Omeguas, undoubtedly those that Felipe de Utre had discovered. This report caused the marquis to use the pretext of a new conquest to purge the troops of the many idle soldiers who had remained from the uprisings of Gonzalo Pizarro, Francisco Hernández Girón and Sebastián de Castilla. An additional incentive for the marquis to explore and conquer those opulent provinces was the rumor of their abundant riches.

General Pedro de Ursúa, a native of Navarre who through heroic deeds during his youth had acquired esteem for his name throughout America, was in Lima at that time. In the conquest of the Nuevo Reino, having subdued the Chitarero Indians, he had founded in their territory the city of Pamplona;[1] and he had commemorated the conquest of the Muzos by founding Tudela in the province of Santa Marta. With only twelve companions to follow him in the celebrated battle of the Pasos de Rodrigo, he had trampled the Tairona tribe, reputed until then to be invincible. In Panama after the runaway blacks of Los Palenques had been defeated and King Bayano captured,[2] they admitted that the valor of such a man was not to be tested twice. The excellent qualities of this gentleman being evident to the marquis, he named Ursúa general of the projected exploration and governor of the land of the Omeguas and of El Dorado, including all that he might conquer.

Ursúa assembled four hundred men and provided them well with firearms, forty horses, and a large number of servants. They departed toward the end of September of 1560, on brigantines built for this expedition on the Motilones River. Among his soldiers there were many, however, who had been expelled from Peru by the viceroy, and Ursúa feared their reckless and volatile nature. Outstanding among them were Lope de Aguirre, Lorenzo de Salduendo, Juan Alonso de la Valdera, Cristóbal de Chaves, Alonso de Villena, Alonso de Montoya and others. Accustomed to riots and tumult, they began at once to mount conspiracies, trying to undermine Ursúa's operations with gossip and rumors. They proceeded so cunningly that they attracted others to their side, among them Fernando de Guzmán, son of an alderman of Seville, who became an accomplice on being promised the post of commander of the army. After navigating seven hundred leagues on the Marañón River, they reached a little town in the province of Machífero, where they stabbed Governor Pedro de Ursúa and his lieutenant general Juan de Vargas to death. Supreme command of the army was then turned over to Fernando de Guzmán, and Lope de Aguirre affixed his signature to a report written to justify this action, followed by the word "Traitor" as title. He then persuaded the others with ugly exhortations to change the destination of the expedition and return to Peru to take possession of

## CHAPTER I

that kingdom. All agreed to this infamy, some of their own free will, others through fear of Aguirre. Then, foreswearing allegiance to the kingdom of Castile, they invested Fernando de Guzmán as Prince of Peru; but it was not in Aguirre's nature to render homage to another but rather to establish his own tyranny. Backed by a following of more than eighty men devoted to him because they were of like character, in a few days he had Lorenzo de Salduendo, Doña Inés de Atienza, Gonzalo Duarte, Alonso de Montoya, Miguel Bodebo, Miguel Serrana, Baltasar Cortés, and Licentiate Alonso de Henao, chaplain of the army, all stabbed to death. He ended this tragedy by murdering their prince, Don Fernando, who for three and a half months, deceived by Aguirre's counsel and impelled by his own ambition, had played his majestic role in the farce.

The monster Aguirre, now free of all opposition to his designs, declared himself commander of that frightened and confused army, as Supreme Leader of the Marañones.[3] Because of its entanglements and snares, the river, previously called the Orellana or Amazon, was renamed the Marañón, and Aguirre's soldiers were called the Marañones. He then decided to go forward with his plans to return to Peru, hoping that many of his companions who had remained there would join him in terrorizing that kingdom. He continued down the river until, during a furious storm, he came upon the Caribbean Sea after having committed atrocious cruelties.

Aguirre headed straight for the island of Margarita and sighted land on the seventeenth day of navigation after a voyage made more trying by lack of food than by storms. Since the brigantines were separated by a tempest that struck them on reaching port, Aguirre dropped anchor in a cove called Paraguache. It is known today as Puerto del Traidor (Port of the Traitor), and is four leagues distant from Mompatare, the principal anchorage of the island. His campmaster, Martín Pérez, anchored two leagues farther north. Before landing, in order not to neglect his barbarous habit of shedding human blood, Lope de Aguirre had Diego de Alcaraz and Gonzalo Giral de Fuentes garroted without even allowing them to confess. As a consequence of these atrocities, in 1561 a call to arms was sounded in all ports along the coast of Venezuela, warning that the tyrant Lope de Aguirre had arrived with his armada at the island of Margarita.[4]

BOOK IV

# CHAPTER II

*Aguirre seizes the governor of Margarita; he robs the royal treasury, sacks the city, and with great cruelty kills several of his own soldiers.*

AGUIRRE, proud of his brutality, landed at Margarita on Monday afternoon, July 20, 1561, with a few of his closest friends standing beside him on deck and the rest of his soldiers hidden below. He dispatched one Rodríguez to the port with orders for his campmaster, Martín Pérez, who had already anchored, to come that same night to join him. He also ordered Rodríguez on the way to garrote Sancho Pizarro, of whom Aguirre was suspicious and for whom he had little liking. In addition, he sent Diego Tirado at the same time to notify Governor Juan de Villandro that they were exhausted after their voyage from Peru and in urgent need of food.

At this unexpected news a group of residents of the city went at once to see the strangers. Aguirre related various events of his long meandering voyage and told them that, after stocking supplies on that island, he planned to return to Peru without stopping in Nombre de Dios. Inclined to sympathy by the good light in which he painted himself, the colonists had two cows killed for him and sent to nearby farms for cassava and additional meat. Aguirre showed his gratitude not only in copious words but even in deeds, by presenting a large gilded silver cup and a scarlet cape decorated with gold beads to a citizen named Gaspar Hernández.

This spurious generosity was the bait the tyrant had devised to make the catch. Pleased with these tokens of esteem, Hernández informed the governor of the many riches Aguirre and his men had brought from Peru and explained that they wanted nothing more than to buy ship's stores and then to continue their voyage. When the governor received this news, greed instantly worked its customary effect, making this seem a good chance to assure whatever part of the treasure that might be due him. Indiscreetly and imprudently, accompanied only by the alcalde Manuel Rodríguez, the regidor Andrés de Salamanca and four other leading citizens, he rode out of the city a little after midnight toward the port where Aguirre was quartered. Arriving there at dawn, he was received with such sham respect and servility that the tyrant even held his stirrup when he dismounted. At this, the governor responded with urban-

## CHAPTER II

ity, promising Aguirre his protection, his house and his person in whatever way he might serve him on that island. They spent a while in these courtesies, but then it seemed to Aguirre that it was time to disclose his treacherous intent. Mixing gallantry with subservience, he said: "Sir, the soldiers from Peru gave preference to stocking good weapons rather than fine attire, but they did bring some clothing for appearances' sake. They beg Your Grace's permission to disembark with their harquebuses and other possessions to trade with the settlers here."

The unsuspecting governor willingly ordered that they be allowed to come ashore safely and said that it would be a pleasure to have them. This request granted, Aguirre returned to the brigantine and called out to the soldiers hidden below deck: "Well, Marañones, sharpen your weapons and clean your harquebuses. You have license from the governor to land, but even had he not granted it, we would have done so anyway." With this they came on deck, firing their harquebuses as a salvo to the governor; but he, suspicious at seeing so many armed men, drew apart to communicate his distrust to his followers. Aguirre, after landing and placing his men on guard along the route, approached the governor and in a style quite different from that he had used up until then, said: "Sir, we are on our way to Peru, but since you seem to think that we will not be going with the idea of serving the king, you are an obstacle to us. Kindly lay down your arms, for otherwise it would appear that you are not so hospitable as we might wish and we would have to take you and your men prisoner."

The governor, amazed at such disrespect and disturbed by the risk at which his imprudence had placed him, murmured: "What is this? What is this?" He then dropped back a few steps and put hand to sword in an attempt to defend himself; but when the traitors placed halberds and harquebuses at his chest, he prudently submitted to being taken prisoner. He then turned over his arms to the tyrant, who immediately mounted the governor's horse and, more through mockery than consideration, forced his prisoner to mount the animal's croup. Marching his troops to the city in battle formation, at a short distance from the road he met his campmaster, Martín Pérez, who, with the men from the other brigantine, had come to join him after having garroted Sancho Pizarro as Aguirre had ordered. The traitors, reunited and joyously celebrating the ease with which they were accomplishing their evil deeds, soon arrived at the city. Ignorant of the storm soon to be unleashed, its inhabitants were relaxing when Aguirre's soldiers, shouting: "Liberty! Liberty! Long live Aguirre!" ran through the streets to occupy the fortress.

After imprisoning the governor and other citizens, the tyrant displayed his insolence in his first official act. He went to the building that served as treasury and, without asking for keys, knocked the doors down, ripped books to pieces, and broke open chests from which he extracted a considerable amount of gold and pearls from the King's Fifth of the Cubaguan fisheries. In imitation of their leader, the soldiers, having divided into teams, sacked the city and committed the insolent acts that might be expected of such a depraved lot. So no one would fail to experience their violence, Aguirre issued an edict that all residents of the island were to gather at once in the city under penalty of death and make a declaration of their arms and wealth. They were so extremely upset by this decree that some tried to escape, but none succeeded. Some disreputable men who lived on the island, admiring Aguirre's soldiers for the ease with which they fearlessly committed robberies and lawless excesses, enlisted under the tyrant's banner. As they were completely familiar with the island and were thieves of the same ilk, they joined with the traitors to form a gang of ruffians. There was no hiding place to which they did not lead the marauders, disclosing everything that the wretched colonists had been able to hide, and they caused the most diabolical affliction that that city had ever suffered.

Father Francisco Montesinos, provincial of the Order of Santo Domingo of the island of Hispaniola, was at that time working on the coast of Maracapana to convert the Indians. When the tyrant learned that the provincial had a well-provisioned and armed, medium-sized ship, he equipped a brigantine, manned it with eighteen soldiers under the command of Pedro de Monguía, and ordered that the provincial's ship be seized and taken to Margarita. Taking the occasion to free themselves from subjugation to the tyrant, however, Monguía and his companions remained in Maracapana with the provincial father. They gave a true account of all that had happened and of the cruelties of Aguirre in Margarita. The provincial father received them kindly but, suspecting some hidden betrayal in their sudden change of loyalty, relieved them of their arms. Embarking all the men he had, as well as the Marañones, he set sail to alert the ports of Borburata and Santo Domingo that the tyrant might appear. On the way, he took the opportunity to pass by Margarita on the chance that he might be of assistance to its residents.

As soon as Aguirre had dispatched Monguía, he ordered supplies prepared so that he could embark without delay, for he was eager to reach Nombre de Dios as soon as possible en route to Peru. In the interim, on no other basis than a bit of gossip, he had Enríquez de Orellana, captain of munitions, hanged without allowing him to confess. This act caused some of his soldiers to decide to abandon him, although it meant risking their own lives. Those who made this choice were Francisco Vázquez, Gonzalo de Zúñiga, Juan de Villatoro, and Luis Sánchez del Castillo, who in the quietest moment of the night fled the city, choosing to seek protection among wild animals rather than to contend with a monster. When Aguirre learned of their flight, he became so infuriated that he bellowed with rage and frothed at the mouth. So that their desertion would not serve as an example, he ordered the fugitives brought in even though they might be dead, and made it clear that if those four soldiers were not returned, everyone would pay with his life. Since he knew how to realize his threats, their fear caused the citizens, as well as the governor, although a prisoner himself, to search the island thoroughly. Two of the fugitives, Juan de Villatoro and Luis Sánchez del Castillo, were in fact discovered and brought into Aguirre's presence. Without delay he had them hanged on the public pillar in the plaza, shouting a thousand opprobriums during the execution to augment their anguish. So hardened and shameless was he that after they were dead he had placards placed on them which read: "These men, loyal servants of the king of Castile, were hanged, a fate which Francisco Vázquez and Gonzalo de Zúñiga escaped by hiding, thus evading the cruel threats and diligent efforts of the tyrant."

# CHAPTER III

*Aguirre orders Captain Turriaga killed, garrotes the governor, and takes his campmaster's life; the provincial arrives at Margarita by ship but withdraws without accomplishing anything there.*

WHILE Aguirre was occupied with these evil deeds, he became concerned by the fact that one of his captains, the affable Juan de Turriaga, had a following among poor soldiers because he freely offered his table to all. This action aroused doubts in Aguirre and he succumbed to the suspicion that the only purpose of Turriaga's geniality was to garner friends to oppose the tyrant. On no other basis than this, Aguirre decided to kill Turriaga and entrusted the execution to his campmaster, Martín Pérez. He went with several soldiers one night to Turriaga's home at an hour when the captain, dining with many of his constant guests, was far from suspecting the treachery that Aguirre had planned. Seeing Martín

Pérez enter, he arose from the table to receive him with all courtesy as his campmaster. Hardly had he removed his hat, however, than the late arrivals wounded him and trampled him in his own blood so repeatedly that he died instantly. Since in every way the tyrant's actions were abnormal, the following day he displayed great sorrow at Turriaga's death, even though he had had him killed. As he ordered the captain buried with all funereal pomp and ceremony, the troops bore the cadaver with lowered flag to the sound of strident drums while Aguirre himself observed the interment.

Aguirre was involved in this extravaganza when the provincial sailed from Maracapana. He warned the people of Cumaná, El Collado, and Borburata of Aguirre's proximity and then continued toward Margarita. The tyrant, assuming that Monguía was bringing the provincial as prisoner, was pleased at the prospect, since he was preparing for his own departure. In a brief time, however, his joy changed to fury as a black man from Maracapana told him of the defection of Monguía and his companions to the provincial. Aguirre, erupting into blasphemies against God and threats against the residents, angrily swore that he would put everyone on the island to the knife and inundate the city with blood without leaving stone on stone so that the memory of his anger would endure in its ruins.

It was now clear that the ship was coming in to anchor at a site called Punta de Piedras, the island's principal anchorage, lying five leagues from the port of Mompatare. The tyrant, suspecting the provincial and his men would attempt to land, began to prepare his troops to go out to meet them. Before starting this action, though, he ordered his Alguacil Francisco de Carrión to go to the fort and garrote the prisoners, Governor Juan de Villandrando, Alcalde Manuel Rodríguez, Chief Alguacil Cosme de León, Regidor Cáceres, and Juan Rodríguez, the governor's servant. Carrión took with him several blacks with thin ropes as instruments of torture, descended to a subterranean room of the castle and announced to the inmates the bitter sentence of death. Although at first they could not believe the reality of such tyranny, they soon recognized that it was irremediable. Consequently, making good use of the little time those cruel agents permitted them, they asked God for mercy, then bared their throats to the noose and handed their lives over to the executioners.

Juan de Villandrando had not yet reached forty years of age when he came to this lamentable end. His body, covered with a straw mat, along with others in the same room, remained until a little past midnight when Aguirre summoned his soldiers and, outlining his motives for committing this infamy, showed them by torchlight the already decomposing cadavers. He was trying to persuade them with the very atrocity of the crime, in addition to those they themselves had committed, to relinquish all hope of pardon from the king. Thus, obdurate with fear of punishment, his Marañones would intensify the rebellion already begun, and since they would not dare to desert him, he could persist in his tyranny.

This spectacle of horror now over, Aguirre ordered two graves opened in the same room, and there the bodies were buried. So that the other settlers should also participate in the frightful ceremony, he forced them at that hour, about two o'clock in the morning, to gather with their wives and children inside the fortress. There, ignorant of the governor's demise because Aguirre had taken great pains to conceal it, they expected their own death momentarily during the remainder of the night. At dawn Aguirre, with eighty harquebusiers, left the fort and prisoners to his campmaster, Martín Pérez, and started the march to Punta de Piedras where the provincial had anchored. A short time before Aguirre arrived at the port, however, having been informed that the provincial's ship had lifted anchor and was headed toward Mompatare, he hastily returned to the city, afraid that his absence might cause some irreparable turn of events.

One of Aguirre's captains, Cristóbal García, formerly a crafty thief, warned Aguirre secretly to be careful because his campmaster and other soldiers had decided to kill him at the first opportunity. During the tyrant's absence in Punta de Piedras, they had met to celebrate an agreement to revolt and then retire to France. The conspirators had held a banquet with toasts and fanfare, and since it had been public it was not difficult for Aguirre to verify the event, if not the motive. He learned that on that same day some soldiers in the plaza had been discussing who might have command in case of Aguirre's incapacity or absence. Martín Pérez had offered: "Well, gentlemen, here I am; I will serve you and do whatever is necessary in case we should be without the old man." This incriminating circumstance, together with others, appeared to be sufficient reason for the tyrant to take his campmaster's life. Consequently, he sent for a youth named Chaves and several others, just boys in age but crafty in habits, to stab Martín Pérez as soon as he entered the fortress. They were so prompt in carrying out the order that hardly had he set foot in the building when they stabbed him several times from behind and from the sides. Badly wounded and exuding intestines and brains, Pérez fell dead, begging in vain for confession. Since the hapless man had dashed from side to side and the murderers had run after him furiously, the confusion in the fortress was so great that the distressed occupants had considered this their last hour. Seeking some means of escape, Domingo López, Pedro de Angulo, and María de Trujillo, wife of Francisco de Rivera, had thrown themselves from the parapet of the fortress but, despite the long fall, they were not harmed and assured their freedom and their lives by hiding among some cactus plants.

One of the principal accomplices in Martín Pérez's conspiracy was Antón Llamoso, whom Aguirre had named in place of Enríquez de Orellana as captain of munitions. The tyrant, seeing him pass that way shortly after the death of the campmaster, said: "They tell me, my son, that you were involved in the plot against me. Why, now; was that friendly?" Llamoso protested with oaths and blasphemies that this was false testimony by his rivals to show him in a bad light. When Llamoso saw that Aguirre was giving scant credence to his words, he threw himself on Martín Pérez's cadaver, tore it to pieces and spread it out on the floor. The crazed man then started drinking the victim's blood and sucking his brains out through a wound in his head in a rage comparable to that of a mastiff sucking on a dead cow. With this inhuman behavior, Aguirre was assured of Llamoso's fidelity, but all others present were appalled at the barbarous impiety of that demon.

The provincial's ship, decorated with pennants, flags and streamers, continued to sail from Punta de Piedras for Mompatare. Although the distance was short, the ship was delayed by currents and adverse winds so that it did not reach land for two days; but finally, early one morning, it anchored, far out to sea for fear of damage from artillery. Aguirre, advised of its approach, left the fortress, taking with him five bronze falcons and a supply of well-loaded guns. Then, with what appeared to him to be a sufficient number of men, he marched to shore just as those from the ship were approaching land. Recognizing the unfavorable reception awaiting them, however, they stopped rowing and remained at a distance at which they could still hear each other's voices. They hurled a thousand insults at the traitors, to which the response was an equal number of obscenities; and when all had vented their rage without risk, the provincial's men returned to their ship and Aguirre's to the city. The tyrant was so gratified by the success of the encounter that as soon as he reached the fortress, he wrote a letter to the provincial that read as if its writer's only occupation in life had been breaking colts and mules, which, in fact, was how he had spent his time in Peru. Somewhat prolix, its tenor is as follows:

> Very magnificent and reverend Sir: I should have preferred to receive Your Paternity with branches and flowers rather than harquebuses and artillery fire as I have been told by many that you are more than magnanimous in every way and certainly, to judge by

## CHAPTER III

what we have seen today, this is true. We are as fond of military exercise as is Your Paternity, and our men act honorably with sword in hand. We left Peru by the Marañón River to explore and populate, some of us healthy, some crippled, others with only one arm or leg. Because of our sufferings in Peru, we had hoped to find land in which to take refuge and settle. Failing in this, however, we have lived by grace alone, the river, the sea, and hunger all having threatened us with death. Your Paternity should punish your soldiers who call us traitors, for to attack King Philip of Castile is both splendid and brave. If we held some wretched little office, we would lead ordered lives; but it is our fate to know nothing except to make bullets and sharpen lances, which is what counts here. If there is any need for more details, we will provide them; but I believe it impossible to explain how much Peru owes us and the reason we have for our actions. I therefore shall say nothing further about it; but tomorrow I shall send Your Paternity a report of all that has transpired, each act recorded frankly as it happened. I say this while wondering what excuse will be given by those who swore fidelity to Fernando de Guzmán as their king and renounced allegiance to Spain, mutinied, rebelled, usurped justice, disarmed colonists and plundered their estates. Among them were Alonso Arias, Don Fernando's sergeant, and Rodrigo Gutiérrez, his gentleman-in-waiting. There is no need, though, to take any note of others because they are worthless scoundrels, or even of Arias if he were not so consummate a rigger and Gutiérrez, an honorable man except that he always looks at the ground, the sign of a traitor. If by chance you have with you one Gonzalo de Zúñiga,[5] a bushy-browed priest of Seville, consider him a vulgar clown whose offenses are many. He was with Alvaro de Hoyón at Popayán in his rebellion against His Majesty, but just when they were going out to fight, he deserted his captain and fled. After this escape, he went to Peru and took part in a revolt in Piura with Silva during which he robbed the king's strongbox, killed the magistrate, and then fled again. Though he is a man who, while there is enough to eat, is diligent, in time of battle, he always flees; but his record remains behind. There is only one man whose absence I regret, and that is Salguero, who is needed to take care of the cattle. I send greetings to my good friends Martín Bruno, Antón Pérez and Andrés Díaz. May God pardon Monguía and Arteaga. I ask Your Paternity to inform me as to whether they are alive or dead, for if they are alive I would find it impossible to restrain myself. We all wish Your Paternity were our patriarch. Please do not go to Santo Domingo, for we regard it as almost certain that you would be deposed. I beg Your Paternity to reply; let us treat each other well. May the war go forward. God will punish traitors and the king will restore the faithful, although until now we have not seen him resuscitate anyone, nor has he healed any wounds or saved any lives. May Our Lord protect Your Paternity, and may you prosper. From the fortress at Margarita, your servant kisses Your Paternity's hand.

Lope de Aguirre

This was the tyrant's discreet letter. In spite of the meager results the provincial could hope for from that perfidious man, in his reply he made an effort to persuade him to surrender to his king. He added, though, that in case Aguirre would not follow so just a course, he should at least honor women, attend church services, and cease bathing his sword in so much innocent blood. As soon as he had sent this reply by the same Indians who had brought him Aguirre's letter, he lifted anchor and raised sail for Santo Domingo, where he reported on the tyrant's operations. The provincial's actions are considered imprudent even today, for just the sight of his ship on its arrival at Margarita was enough to cause Aguirre to take the life of the governor and other colonists. These crimes perhaps would not have occurred if he had not feared the favor these officials might have given the provincial had they remained alive.

# CHAPTER IV

*Pedro Alonso Galeas flees from Margarita; the tyrant hangs Ana de Rojas and, after perpetrating other cruelties, abandons the island.*

THE provincial's persuasions had so little effect on Aguirre that his malice converted the prelate's sound advice into poison. As if the flood of his ire had been released from its dam, the same day that he received the letter he had two of his soldiers hanged on the public pillar in the plaza. Their crime consisted of lying on the beach in the shade of some thistles, but Aguirre's distrust made him surmise that they were waiting for an opportunity to flee. This injustice was accompanied by an even greater one when he ordered garroted one of Governor Pedro de Ursúa's cousins, Martín Díaz de Armendáriz, whom Aguirre had brought, disarmed and a prisoner, from the Marañón. The tyrant had given him license to remain on a rural estate on that island, where he had lived from the time that Aguirre had arrived at Margarita. Repentant now of this compassion, he sent the executioners to Díaz's house to garrote him. They, seeking to please the tyrant by making the cruelty more horrible, executed Martín Díaz without allowing him to confess, although a priest was present.

Having lost hope of seizing the provincial's ship, on which he had

## CHAPTER IV

planned to make his departure, Aguirre arranged for a vessel that Governor Juan de Villandrando had had under construction to be finished with all haste. With this and two medium-sized ships he had sacked from the Marañón, he could easily accommodate all his men. While it was being completed, he ordered banners made of black taffeta adorned with red swords, and he exhibited as his escutcheon this symbol of death and destruction. Then he shamelessly had them blessed on the day of the Assumption of Our Lady with the celebration of a solemn mass, as if those infamous standards could bring any glory to the Church. After they had been blessed, he turned them over to his captains, charging them to persevere in the rebellion he had begun against the king and giving them permission to commit any atrocities the occasion might demand. In spite of this broad leeway, however, there were some soldiers who, made violent by fear, maintained their own group and never ceased searching for an opportunity to escape.

Pedro Alonso Galeas, native of Almendralejo in Estremadura, who had been a captain of infantry under General Pedro de Ursúa, was one of those now seeking a way to cross to Tierra Firme before the tyrant left the island. In secrecy he made a bargain with two Guaiquerí Indians, natives of Margarita, to build a pirogue and hide it in a cove a little more than half a league from the city. This arrangement constituted the first step of his flight; but in order to escape without being missed, he devised a shrewd ruse.

Aguirre had reserved for himself from the spoils of Juan de Villandrando a chestnut horse characterized by its high spirits, handsome mien, graceful pace, and violence on the course. The tyrant enjoyed watching Pedro Alonso, one of the best horsemen of his time, ride the animal, and took pleasure in the beauty they displayed in action. One afternoon, as the rider purposely held the reins more tightly than usual, the horse's rage was boundless by the time it arrived at the plaza. Seeing it in such a fury, Aguirre ordered Pedro Alonso to start the course. Lashing the animal's flanks, he loosened the reins and applied the spurs so that it would not stop for more than a mile. He would thereby have cause to attribute to the horse what was actually a part of his own scheme. Continuing to ride in this manner every afternoon, he extended the course a bit each day. Many came to watch the race, and Pedro Alonso delayed so long on the run that he did not return for an hour. When it seemed time for him to carry out his flight, he told the two Guaiqueríes to await him on the shore. He then mounted the horse as usual, applied the spurs firmly and did not stop until he arrived at the cove where the pirogue was hidden. Seating himself beside the Indians, he started rowing at full speed toward Tierra Firme, grasping at time to reach safety while the deception lasted. Aguirre, thinking the procedure would be the same as on previous days, did not begin to worry about the horseman's delay until three hours had passed. Fearing some misfortune, Aguirre sent several soldiers to look for him; and they, following the horse's tracks, found it tied to a tree at the cove, along with other evidence of flight.

Having astutely thwarted the tyrant's malice, the fugitive could now cross without fear to Tierra Firme. Continuing down the coast to Cumanagoto he found Francisco Fajardo, who had left El Collado to try to overthrow the tyrant. He was thwarted, however, by the old rivalry, with which Alonso Cobos, official in charge at Cumaná, always tried to discredit Fajardo's actions. Using the pretext that he was taking Indians without permission, Cobos sent a corporal with armed men to seize him just as he was preparing to embark the five hundred Indians given to him for the expedition by two cacique friends, Alonso Coyegua and Juan Caballo. Next, an Indian who had just arrived from Cumaná advised him of what Cobos had done, and Fajardo sent Pedro Alonso on his way to Borburata. Then, without waiting for the other Indians, he set sail for Margarita with only the sixty who had already embarked.

Aguirre's effusions when he learned of the cruel trick Pedro Alonso had played on him were phenomenal. The next day another soldier, Alonso de Villena, one of Aguirre's accomplices in major delinquencies, also fled, giving further proof that his closest friends were deserting him. Unable to avenge himself because the object of his wrath had not been apprehended, Aguirre ordered Francisco Domínguez and Diego de Loaísa killed simply because they were comrades of Villena. Next, he ordered Doña Ana de Rojas, one of the leading ladies of the city, executed at the public pillar in the plaza on the pretext that she had had prior knowledge of Villena's flight. Turning that act into a festival, one of Aguirre's squadrons made her, already half dead, the target of their shots. They fired their harquebuses at her from a parapet in sight of their infamous general, who was eager to applaud the skill of anyone who might decapitate that lady or strike her in the heart.

Doña Ana's husband, Diego Gómez de Ampuero,[6] a noble gentleman from Santander, was old, crippled and ill; and at that time he, accompanied by a priest of the Order of Santo Domingo, was living in retirement on one of his country estates. Aguirre, surmising that the husband might also have had a part in Villena's flight, ordered Pedro de Paniagua, the camp alguacil, to garrote him. The alguacil not only promptly took the poor old man's life but also that of the clergyman, without any authority other than his own. He reasoned that the more severity he showed, the more pleased Aguirre would be; and this was

## CHAPTER IV

true, for the perpetration of that sacrilege gave the traitor an incentive to commit one that was even more appalling.

There in the city, another Dominican ecclesiastic who, though I have not been able to ascertain his name,[7] was known as a man of commendable behavior and boundless life. Aguirre, more as a formality than a devotion, asked to confess to him, but the holy man was familiar with the tyrant's evil inclinations. Fearlessly intent on fulfilling the obligations of his office, he denied him absolution and reprehended him for his iniquities, thus filling Aguirre with such mortal hatred that he determined to kill the priest. Since the tyrant still had such respect for that venerable man of the Church that he deemed it expedient to delegate his vengeance to another, he said to Paniagua: "You have hands made for killing priests. Kill this one for me and next time you will have no scruples." The alguacil needed no further urging, but left immediately to carry out the order. As the priest came out of the church, Paniagua seized his hand, led him into the entryway of a house and notified him of his death sentence. The holy man heard the pronouncement stoically; then falling to his knees, he began to recite the *Miserere mei Deus*. Before he had finished, however, his executioner, unable to bear the delay, placed thin ropes around the priest's mouth and pulled them from behind until his mouth was torn to pieces. Seeing that he did not die from that torture, Paniagua lowered the ropes to the priest's neck and held them so taut that he expired, thus becoming a martyr as reward for having protected his obligation as a confessor.

After having had Simón de Sumorostro and Ana de Chaves hanged, Aguirre ordered that ships be provisioned and made ready to sail. He was on the point of departure when Francisco Fajardo made port at Margarita, landing with the sixty Indian archers he had acquired in Cumanagoto. He took cover in a little forest near the city to determine if, with the aid of residents, it would be possible to defeat the tyrant. This scheme could not be carried out, however, because Aguirre, not trusting his soldiers and fearing that some might desert him for Fajardo, confined them behind closed doors in the fortress. His departure now imminent, Aguirre hastened the embarkation as much as possible, although with considerable precaution. He ordered a small door broken in the wall which rose above the sea and a ladder placed in it by which the other soldiers lowered themselves one by one. Alonso Rodríguez, his admiral and close friend, advised him to stand back from the shore a bit to avoid being sprayed by the surf. As if this warning were some sort of insult, the tyrant burned with ire and, grasping his sword, cut off one of Rodríguez's arms with a single slash. His anger still not satisfied, he ordered his victim stabbed to death so that one more example would remain on the beach as a token of his cruelty. Finally, after all were aboard, he and the licentiate Pedro de Contreras, curate and vicar of Margarita, embarked and the three small lateen-rigged ships set sail. Fajardo arrived on the scene too late to save the island from Aguirre's wrath. With the pearl fisheries then at their most opulent, the tyrant's operations during his forty-day stay left the island so ravaged that it did not recover from the devastation for many years.

# CHAPTER V

*Aguirre arrives at Borburata; he sacks the city and continues toward Valencia; the governor asks for help from Mérida and prepares for defense.*

IT had been Aguirre's intention to go to Nombre de Dios on the way from Panama to Peru,[8] but as soon as he set out he had cause to reconsider, for the provincial's warning along the coast of the tyrant's arrival at Margarita could have impeded his progress. Changing his course, he ordered the prow set for Borburata, with the idea of going by way of the Nuevo Reino through Popayán to Peru. He next attempted a foolish act which was to cause him to pay with his life for the many that his cruelty had claimed.

He started his voyage toward Borburata with such enormous hindrances as his pilot's inexperience and the countless calms endured on the short crossing. Resultant delays inspired him to erupt into a thousand blasphemies against God, Jesus Christ and His Blessed Mother. At times he shifted his eyes to Heaven and exclaimed: "God, if you have any good in store for me, give it to me now and keep the glory for your saints." At others, with diabolic rage he would say that God was fickle for, having favored him up until then, he now was abandoning him to aid his adversaries. In this vein he reeled off a sea of wild nonsense so sacrilegious that his soldiers, even though heartless themselves, were scandalized by it. Finally, after eight days of navigation, on the seventh of September he made port in Borburata, where his ships were recognized as those of the tyrant by the inhabitants. Since they did not have sufficient forces to resist, however, they retired to the brush with their families and posses-

## CHAPTER V

sions and hastily dispatched word to Governor Pablo Collado, who at that time was in El Tocuyo.

Having this information, the governor tried to prepare for the defense; but his timid spirit could not cope with these matters or persist in military functions to which he, an academician, was little accustomed. He therefore named as general his predecessor, Gutiérrez de la Peña, who had taken up residence in El Tocuyo, and gave him control of armaments and the duty of supervising preparations for war. He then called upon all inhabitants of the province to come promptly to Barquisimeto, where the army was to form. Next he sent to Mérida to ask Pedro Bravo de Molina, chief justice of that city, to come to his aid because the enemy was already in sight. At the same time he wrote to Diego García de Paredes, who, because of some dissension between the two after the founding of Trujillo, had retired to Mérida. Collado begged Paredes not to desert him in so crucial a matter but to put service to the king before his own feelings, and he added that Paredes would soon receive the compensation he desired.

Paredes did not need this urging to fulfill his obligations. As soon as he received the letter from the governor, while Pedro Bravo was preparing troops to take with him, Paredes departed with fourteen comrades for El Tocuyo. There, Collado begged his pardon for past unpleasantness and asked him to accept the office of campmaster. He explained that the urgency of the situation had obliged him to name Gutiérrez de la Peña general already, but that he would not have been chosen had Paredes been present. As Paredes's intention was to serve his king, he accepted without hesitation.

Aguirre landed with his men a half-league from Borburata and, without permitting any of them to leave the beach, he camped there that night, persuaded that he could, as in Margarita, captivate the residents through deception. As the next day began, however, and no one came out to receive him, he was in so foul a humor that he had a Portuguese named Antonio de Faria killed simply because he had asked if they were on an island or the mainland. He then dispatched a squadron composed of his closest friends to the city with orders to study the situation and determine the intentions of the residents. On reaching the town, however, they found that everyone had withdrawn, seeking safety in the mountains. Only Francisco Martín, one of those who, with Captain Monguía, had remained with the provincial in Maracapana, was to be found. Now Martín wished to return to Aguirre, seeking the licentious life of his soldiers. The tyrant was grateful for this manifestation of Martín's friendship, as well as for the information he brought of other companions in the vicinity. Aguirre, wishing to lure them back to his command, wrote a letter full of offers and gave it to Martín, along with good clothing and other valuable gifts, and ordered him to search diligently for the troops. Forewarned of evident risk to their lives, however, they had hidden so well that Martín had to return to Borburata without finding them.

Since the hope that Aguirre had had of reuniting his Marañones was now destroyed, he burned his three ships, and one belonging to some merchants that was anchored there. He then prepared to proceed to Valencia by sending two or three troops of soldiers to search the neighboring country estates for draft horses, but they returned with only twenty or thirty mountain mares. Even those were acquired at the cost of most of his soldiers' being badly wounded by poisoned stakes which the Indians, in cooperation with Spanish residents, had planted along all paths and roads. This action angered the tyrant so much that he shouted his customary blasphemies against God; and to give further vent to his rage, he ordered the proclamation of cruel war by blood and fire against the king of Castile and his vassals. This madman's diminished assets now consisted of only one hundred and fifty unskilled men, six rounds of gunshot, a mule and three horses, all the equipment with which he in his delusion thought to subject the Indies.

As the city was now depopulated and Aguirre's soldiers did not wish to pass on without some profit, they separated into teams and avidly sought spoils. They also greedily scoured the woods for whatever might have been hidden and did not leave a quebrada or thicket unsearched. One of these groups, climbing somewhat higher than the others over badly worn paths, stopped at some huts four leagues from the town. There they found Benito Chaves, alcalde of Borburata, with his wife, a daughter and her husband, Julián de Mendoza, who had returned from the Valley of San Francisco where he had served in the troops of Juan Rodríguez. After stealing all at hand, but without harming the women, the tyrant's soldiers returned to the city.

They took with them only Benito Chaves, for whatever use the tyrant might have of him; Amador Montero, who was treated kindly because of his resemblance to the tyrant's father; and a merchant, Pedro Núñez, who, when asked why the residents had withdrawn, answered that they were terrified of the tyrant. When Aguirre asked him to tell truthfully what was said of him and his companions, Núñez tried to avoid responding. So great was the tyrant's insistence, however, that the wretched man finally blurted out: "Sir, all consider Your Grace and your companions cruel Lutherans."[9] These words set Aguirre into such fiery wrath that he removed his helmet and, on the point of hurling it at Núñez, shouted: "Barbarian, stupid! Is that as obnoxious as you can

## CHAPTER V

be?" and, although his anger for the moment did not pass beyond this point, he was not slow to take vengeance. One of the soldiers, like the others seeking something to steal, came by chance on an olive jar containing some gold disks which Pedro Núñez had buried. With news of the theft, Núñez came before Aguirre asking for restitution, but because the delinquent denied the charge, the tyrant ordered Núñez hanged so that all might know that their leader was concerned for the good of his followers.

On another occasion, a soldier named Juan Pérez went out to enjoy the countryside. There Aguirre, finding him seated at ease on the banks of an arroyo, asked: "What are you doing here, Pérez?" He answered: "Sir, I do not feel well; to seek some relief, I am passing the time watching the river flow by." Aguirre responded: "Well, in view of that, you can just stay here, for I have nothing to do with sick people." "As Your Grace commands," the soldier replied. Then Aguirre, passing by without a glance or another word, went to his quarters and sent his agents to take Pérez prisoner at once. As the mediation and pleas of friends did not suffice to save him, he was ordered executed on the grounds that Aguirre would not spare the life of one lukewarm to war.

Since the time had come to leave Borburata for Valencia, seven leagues away, Pedro Arias de Almesta and Diego de Alarcón considered that in the confusion of the journey little effort would be made to look for them if they tried to escape. They fled from the city by night, but the tyrant, learning of their plan, at once seized Alcalde Benito de Chaves's wife and daughter and called Chaves to his presence. "You as alcalde are familiar with this region," he said, "and should have knowledge of my soldiers wherever they may be. Go search for these two and bring them back to me; if you do not, I shall take your wife and daughter to Peru." Leaving Chaves to obey his command, the tyrant began his journey to Valencia, taking the women with him; but after a short march he saw some Spaniards in a pirogue hastening toward the port. Rushing everyone to the other side of a hill so they would not be seen from the sea, he halted, leaving them in charge of Juan de Aguirre, his trusted friend. With twenty-five harquebusiers the tyrant then went back down to Borburata to seize those in the pirogue and ascertain their intentions. However, on arriving in the city, he and most of his soldiers drank so freely from a skin of wine which they had found that all were inebriated except Juan de Rosales, Pedro de Acosta and Jorge de Rodas. They purposely drank nothing and thus could take advantage of the disorder to hide in the brush and later flee the presence of the tyrant.

While Aguirre and his group were diverted by the wine, the rest of the soldiers were burning on the hillside for lack of water. To allay their thirst, a few went back up the mountain and came upon some huts hidden in the woods. Among clothing found there was a cape which all immediately recognized as belonging to Rodrigo Gutiérrez, one of those who had remained with Monguía in Maracapana. In its cowl was an affidavit executed before the justice of Borburata, to which one of the witnesses had been Francisco Martín. In spite of his having severely criticized Lope de Aguirre's actions, he had nevertheless returned to the tyrant's company on his arrival in Borburata. Juan de Aguirre, blind with rage on reading what had been said about the tyrant, lunged forward and stabbed Martín and then ordered that other soldiers be shot to death. Among them was one named Arana, who either by accident or on purpose struck Antón García with a harquebus shot from which he fell dead. At this, such a disturbance broke out among friends and foes on each side that Arana tried to calm them by saying that García had been killed on purpose because he had wanted to flee that night and that the general would consider the killing well done. Seeing that nothing was sufficient to calm the dead man's friends, however, Arana thought it wise to go down to Borburata, where he informed Aguirre of the upheaval in the camp. At this news, the tyrant went with all haste to settle the differences before the outbreak grew worse.

All now quiet with Aguirre's presence, the march to Valencia was continued the next day over a difficult road. Even the beasts of burden, unaccustomed to such loads, could barely make the ascent; nor could the soldiers, exhausted by the weight of arms and equipment, tolerate such prolonged fatigue, for in many places they had to carry even the artillery. Although Aguirre tried to encourage them by his example, always lending a hand with the heaviest loads, six days of march still were needed for the short distance of seven leagues. This exertion, augmented by the heat of the sun and his burning anger, debilitated Aguirre to the extent that he could not walk but had to be carried in a hammock. Thus, worn-out and despondent from his illness, he asked his Marañones to take his life; but finally, after a period in which his indisposition became more aggravated, he began to improve. As he entered Valencia he learned that its inhabitants had abandoned the city and gathered with their families on the islands of Lake Tacarigua where the soldiers, lacking canoes, were unable to reach them. This precaution so enraged the tyrant that he jeered that neither Indians nor Spaniards would engage his noble army in war, even though it had been practiced since the beginning of time by the most celebrated men of the world and among the very angels of heaven. In this vein he uttered such terrifying absurdities that the ears of his companions were tortured, even though they were so like him.

## CHAPTER VI

*Juan Rodríguez Suárez leaves the city of San Francisco to oppose the tyrant and dies fighting the Indians; Aguirre kills some of his soldiers and prepares to depart from Valencia.*

AFTER Juan Rodríguez Suárez learned that Lope de Aguirre had arrived at Borburata, he set aside his own thoughts of vengeance for Guaicaipuro's treason and resolved to risk his own life to bring death to the tyrant. He consequently left the new city of San Francisco with only six companions, but they were trustworthy, well provided with arms, and trained to achieve their mission. When Guaicaipuro was informed by his spies of his adversary's actions, he envisioned Juan Rodríguez lying decapitated on the edge of an arroyo. In order to fulfill this desire to have done with his enemy, he called on Cacique Terepaima to go out with his troops of Arbacos and Teques across Terepaima Hill to attack the Spaniards from the rear.

Although Terepaima, constant in his friendship with Fajardo, at first refused to place any faith in the plot, he finally was persuaded by Guaicaipuro to take part in it. Juan Rodríguez, ignorant of this agreement, passed the night on the San Pedro River, and the following day crossed to the other side of Las Lagunetas Mountain. There he found the entire hill covered with Terepaima's warriors in feathered headdresses; and Guaicaipuro, proceeding by river, covered him from the rear. Seeing himself attacked on all sides but recognizing in his companions the resolve and strength to conquer or die, Juan Rodríguez broke through the Indian forces, dealing out death at each blow. Because the natives were many and never ceased shooting their arrows, however, the Spaniards could not sustain the combat for long, especially as the Indians' shields and *escaupiles* did not leave any part of them exposed to Spanish fire. The invaders, forced to retreat to the shelter of a high peak as protection for their rearguard, were attacked again; but they easily defended themselves and fought valiantly until night brought a truce. The barbarians considered victory now assured, but to prevent the Spaniards from escaping, they girded the peak with bonfires. With shouts, drums and flutes they obliged the intruders to pass the night standing without daring to lie down even for a short time.

When morning came the Indians renewed the attack, but so many were lost that they at last afforded the seven Spaniards some relief by moderating the conflict. Early that afternoon Juan Rodríguez mounted his horse and, leaving four of his companions to guard the peak, went out with the other two in an attempt to take Guacaipuro's life. He did not find the cacique, however, although he broke through the enemy line in various places. He killed nine or ten Indians with his lance and would have accomplished even more had his horse not been bleeding copiously from several wounds. Since Terepaima and his troops were coming up the hillside at the same time to close off the pass, the Spaniards were obliged to seek refuge on the peak. Remaining there did nothing more than delay death briefly, however, for even had they eluded the Indians, they would have perished from hunger. They consequently decided that one of the seven, in the silence of the night, would go to Valencia to report their desperate straits while the others, at the break of day, would continue to open a path with their swords in an attempt to escape.

Selected for the journey by vote of his companions, Alonso Fajardo, son of the elder Juan de Guevara by his first marriage in Coro, silently left the peak and traveled by night. He went into hiding at dawn in a little thicket, not noticing that he had been followed by a dog he had raised. This animal's loyalty was now the cause of Fajardo's destruction, for by barking at some passing natives, he revealed his master's hiding place and made it possible for them to kill him.

Rodríguez and his five companions abandoned the peak at daybreak and attacked, wounding and ripping to pieces all who opposed them; but, surrounded by that infidel rabble, all their efforts could lead them only to the certainty of death. They had not eaten for two days and their weary bodies were so debilitated by hunger and thirst that their arms could not carry out their wishes. The five, gradually growing weaker because pierced by many arrows, gave up their lives one by one until finally there remained only the invincibly courageous Juan Rodríguez. He continued the fight with such gallant resolve that after more than fifty Indians had died by his hand, the others begged for mercy, but he merely sought a fresh opportunity to quench his anger. Too weak to remain any longer on horseback, he dismounted and sat on the ground to regain strength; and there, gasping with rage and choking from fatigue and thirst, he died without sustaining a single wound to his body. The Indians' fear of him was so great that, even though they saw his inert cadaver, they did not dare approach him for fear that he was still alive. Finally, though, convinced of his death, they stripped him of his clothing and cut his body into pieces which they then distributed for each to carry off his own part as a trophy of victory.

## CHAPTER VI

Thus ended the life of Juan Rodríguez Suárez, who will always be remembered by the Indians with respect for his valiant sword. Born in the city of Mérida in Estremadura, impelled by ardor and bravery, he sailed to America where, among the conquistadors of the Nuevo Reino de Granada, he inspired esteem by his fabulous deeds. He settled the city of Pamplona and received one of the best encomiendas of that district; and later, assigned by the Cabildo to explore the Sierras Nevadas and undertake the conquest of the Timotes, he ably carried out that mission as well. To honor his homeland, he named the city he founded Mérida de los Caballeros, and there he gained such glory that his rivals, incited by envy, denounced even his most heroic actions. Since he was sentenced to be beheaded by the Audiencia de Santa Fe de Bogotá, he was obliged, with the aid of friends, to break out of prison and flee to this province to save his life from a prejudiced judge and a conspiracy of his rivals. Here he came to be so feared by the Indians that, during the time he participated in the conquest of Caracas, one needed only to borrow his red cape to pass freely from one place to another. The Indians learned to recognize this symbol and to respect it so much that there was no safer conduct, a situation that led him to rash acts that eventually cost him his life.

At about the time of Juan Rodríguez's death, Lope de Aguirre's men were busy providing steeds for his carriage and destroying the cattle of the residents of Valencia. So as not to leave any place without the memory of his cruelties, the tyrant had one of his soldiers, Gonzalo de Torres, killed simply because he went out from the city, something like a stone's throw, to gather papayas. At the same time, Alcalde Chaves, after much searching, found the two soldiers who had fled from Aguirre in Borburata. He had them placed in irons and turned them over to Julián de Mendoza, his son-in-law, so that his wife and mother-in-law would be returned to him. Before reaching the city, one of them, Pedro Arias, his courage failing in view of the doleful end that awaited him, threw himself to the ground and begged to be slain. Don Julián answered without shame or ceremony: "For me it is all the same; by bringing in your head, my obligation will be fulfilled"; and mercilessly unsheathing his sword, he started slashing at the prisoner's head. It now appeared to Arias too grave a decision, however, and since he would be reaping certain death immediately to avoid a fate that was still in doubt, he promised to force himself to proceed. Mendoza was persuaded to suspend the execution but, even so, Arias was left with a sizable wound. And, on arrival at Valencia, the prisoner was in fact pardoned because he was a good scribe and Aguirre was in need of his services. His companion, Diego de Alarcón, did not receive the same indulgence but was instantly ordered quartered and dragged through the streets with a public proclamation that read: "This is the penalty which Lope de Aguirre, mighty leader of the noble men of Marañón, ordered for this man for being a loyal servant of the king of Castile." After the execution, the victim's head was placed on the public pillar in the plaza, where the tyrant laughed loudly as he facetiously asked: "Here you are, friend Alarcón; why does not the king of Castile come to your rescue now?"

Rodrigo Gutiérrez, in the cowl of whose cape the information was found that had cost Francisco Martín so dearly, was saved from a similar fate by his own persistence. When Alcalde Chaves learned of the cape, he advised Aguirre to send for Gutiérrez, but the latter understood the implication and skillfully avoided the crafty tactic by removing his fetters and fleeing once again. Aguirre sent Francisco de Carrión to bring Gutiérrez back, but he could not find him and the alcalde's intention was circumvented. Chaves attempted to ingratiate himself with the tyrant by giving extensive information on the precautions the governor had taken to resist Aguirre and the aid he was expecting momentarily from Mérida and Bogotá. Although Aguirre was not pleased with the report, he expressed gratitude for the warning. Then, in order that his delay should not give his enemies the opportunity to make more elaborate preparations to thwart him, he hastily planned to leave Valencia. Next, he granted the curate of Margarita, Pedro de Contreras, permission to return home on condition that he promise to deliver to King Philip II a letter that Aguirre would give him. The priest at first resisted the commission but later was forced to accept, overcoming his own objections in order to be free of the tyrant's oppression.

# CHAPTER VII

*After writing a letter to the king,[10] Aguirre leaves Valencia and goes to Barquisimeto.*

THE letter that Lope de Aguirre gave Father Contreras to deliver to the king does not really deserve to be mentioned. Written as it was by a former mule breaker, it offers proof of that man's absurdity and madness, and a bit of entertainment for the reader. Aguirre wrote:

KING PHILIP: native of Spain, son of the invincible Charles: I, Lope de Aguirre, least of your vassals, am a longtime Christian of

## CHAPTER VII

untainted blood, born of ordinary parents, and in my prosperous days an hidalgo. I am a native of the Basque country of Spain and am a citizen of the town of Oñate. As a youth I crossed the ocean sea to Peru with lance in hand to fulfill the debt that every good man owes. During the following twenty-four years I have rendered many services in Peru in the conquest of the Indians and in settling towns, always without importuning your officials for pay or aid, as will be evident from your royal account books. I believe that you are not grateful to my companions and me for services rendered because those who report to you deceive you. Although you yourself have justly compensated your vassals in this land, my companions and I, no longer able to suffer the cruelties of your judges, viceroys and governors, have left your service and severed allegiance to Spain. We plan now to make cruel war on you as your representatives have disregarded us and given preference to their sons and adherents. My right leg was ripped off by two harquebus shots in the Valley of Coquimbo where I had gone with Marshal Alonso de Alvarado in response to your call to arms against Francisco Hernández Girón, rebel against your service as my companions and I now are and will be until death. In this land your pardon is considered more worthless than the books of Martin Luther. Your viceroy, the marquis de Cañete, evil, lascivious, ambitious and tyrannical, hanged Martín de Robles, who had been outstanding in your service; Tomás Vázquez, a brave conquistador of Peru; the hapless Alonso Díaz, who worked diligently in the discovery of that kingdom; and Juan de Piedrahita, a captain who initiated many battles in your service. And even in Pucará they gave you the victory,[11] for if they had not passed over to the other side, Francisco Hernández Girón today would be lord of Peru. Do not overesteem the services your judges wrote they had performed because they are telling a big lie, unless they call a service having spent eight thousand pesos from the royal strongbox for their vices and iniquities. Punish them for what they are.

King of Spain, do not be ungrateful to your subjects; for you, bearing the blood of your father, the emperor of Castile, were given the kingdoms of these lands without any problems. And remember, my lord, that you, in justice cannot accept any profits from these regions, where you have ventured nothing, without first rewarding those who have labored in them. I hold as certain that few kings go to heaven, for I believe that you are worse than Lucifer [Luzbel] because of your ambition and insatiable thirst for human blood. Still, I am not surprised at this fact since you always call to your service frivolous and inexperienced youths, all of them mad. My two hundred hidalgo Marañón harquebusiers and I make a solemn vow to God not to leave any of your representatives alive, because I know now the extent of their power. We are the luckiest men alive today because of being in this part of the Indies. We hold faith in God's commandments as entirely just and uncorrupted and support all that the Roman Church preaches; and, although sinners in life, we yearn to attain martyrdom through the commandments of God.

After we left the Amazon River, also called the Marañón, we came to the island of Margarita and were filled with horror at the strength of the Lutherans there. I ordered one of them in our company, Monteverde, cut to pieces;[12] for wherever else we may be, we all will comply with the commandment to live in the faith of Christ. The dissolute nature of the friars of this country is so great that punishment should come to the land, for all of them aspire to rule as governor. My king, do not believe what they tell you, for they shed tears there before your royal person only in order to come back here in command. If you want to know what kind of life they lead here, it is as ambitious enemies of the poor, engaged in trading to acquire temporal goods and in selling the sacraments, for no matter how insignificant a friar may be, he has pretentions to rule. Remedy the situation, king and lord, for with these bad examples, the faith is not implanted in the natives. If this corruption in the friars is not eliminated, there will be grave disturbances since my companions and I are ready to die for our just cause. For this and other things that have happened, you, king, bear the blame, as you do not feel compassion for your vassals or consider what you owe them. If you neglect them and are complacent about your judges, the government will never succeed. The only reason to present witnesses is to tell you that at the end of three years each of your judges has seventy thousand pesos in savings, land and other possessions. If they were content to serve as men, it would not be so bad; but they want us to adore them like Nebuchadnezzar, an insufferable situation. It is not because I, who lost a leg, or my companions, grown old and exhausted in your service, have failed to warn you never to trust these learned men; but in being lenient toward them, you do not fulfill your obligations, while they spend all their time marrying off their children to advantage.

Although these friars have received the best allotments of land, they will not preach to the poor Indians. The life they lead is very hard, for each of them has in his kitchen only a dozen or so girls and a like number of boys to fish and hunt partridges for him and bring him fruit. If you do not remedy these evils, a scourge from Heaven will come upon you. What a pity that the emperor, your father, in conquering the German Empire spent so much money, brought from these lands discovered by us, and that now you are not enough by our old age and exhaustion moved even to placate our hunger.

Let wars go on as they will. By man they were made, but at no time nor under any adversity will we cease to be obedient subjects of the Holy Church of Rome. We cannot believe, king and lord, that you would be so cruel to such good vassals as we, but rather that your wicked judges and ministers must act without your knowledge. Near the city of Los Reyes [Lima] a little lake in which fish spawn was discovered two leagues from the sea.[13] Now your depraved judges, to take advantage of the fish for their own enjoyment, lease it in your name, implying to us that it is with your consent. If this is true, let us keep whatever fish we may catch. The king of Castile

## CHAPTER VII

does not need the four hundred pesos for which it is said to be leased, since it is not in Córdoba nor Valladolid that we ask this patrimony. Have the compassion, sire, to feed the poor and the weary with the fruits and profits of this land; and consider that in God's sight all deserve equal justice and rewards, paradise along with hell.

In the year 1559, the marquis de Cañete gave Pedro de Ursúa, a Navarrese, or rather, a Frenchman, permission to explore the Amazon. He delayed in the province of the Motilones until 1560 building ships; but these vessels, because constructed in a damp region, on being set afloat, broke into pieces. Next we made rafts and launched them downstream, leaving our horses and other possessions behind, and we navigated the most powerful rivers of Peru as if we were on a freshwater gulf. After we had traveled three hundred leagues, we killed this perverse and ambitious governor and invested a young cavalier of Seville, Fernando de Guzmán, as our king, and all present signed a pledge of allegiance to him. I was named his campmaster and, because I did not consent to his insults and iniquities, an attempt was made to kill me. Instead, I killed the new king, the captain of the guard, a priest, a woman, a commander of the Knights of Rhodes, an admiral, two standard-bearers, and five or six servants with the intention of advancing the war. Again I named captains and sergeants and they too attempted to kill me, but I hanged them all. We spent nearly twelve months in reaching the mouth of the river after more than one hundred days of travel during which we covered more than five hundred leagues. This fresh water exceeds a thousand leagues in length and its banks are unpopulated in many parts, as Your Majesty will see by an exact report that we have made. God knows how we escaped from that frightful stream; and I advise you, my king, not to give your consent for any armada from Spain to come to this accursed river. May God protect you, excellent king, for many years.

The context of this letter is the most obvious proof of Aguirre's rustic and gross nature and of the disrespect to which his shameless insolence extended. His operations seemed bolder every day as he prepared to leave Valencia after having spent fifteen days there. The night before he was to set out, he ordered Benito Díaz, Francisco de Lora and Antonio Zigarra garroted, one because he said he had a relative in the Nuevo Reino and the other two for appearing to Aguirre to be lukewarm toward war. These cruelties were followed by another, even more appalling. On the morning of departure, seeing a soldier named Sahagún with a rosary in his hand, he stabbed him to death on the grounds that his soldiers should be alien to all devotion and of such quality that, if necessary, they would risk their souls at dice with the devil. They should not waste time in prayers or idle talk which, he claimed, only served to create cowards, rendering them useless for the noble exercise of arms. With this benevolent farewell, he departed for Barquisimeto by the straight road which cuts across the Nirgua sierras, inhabited at that time by the Jirajara Indians.

When Aguirre reached Borburata, Pedro Alonso Galeas, who had so cleverly executed the runaway horse deception and fled from Margarita, was in Valencia. Now, because he feared he might fall into Aguirre's hands, he left for Barquisimeto with Gómez de Silva, a Portuguese gentleman who had been armor-bearer for Francisco Cautino, count of Redondo, when the Portuguese provided aid in Arcila, Morocco. Afterward he was a page of King Juan III of Portugal, but later, fleeing the vengeance of relatives of a gentleman whom he had killed in a duel in Lisbon, he had come to the Indies.

At the same time, Governor Pablo Collado, informed by the residents of Borburata that Lope de Aguirre was already in port, dispatched Francisco Infante from El Tocuyo to learn what designs the tyrant had and the exact number of men in his camp. Infante was to have returned promptly to give the governor a full report, but was delayed unexpectedly on the road for an extended account from Pedro Alonso and Gómez de Silva. Giving as his excuse the urgency of pushing forward in anticipation of the effect of this news, he returned with them to El Tocuyo. There the governor, after hearing their tale, realized that it was now necessary to consider their defense more realistically, for there was no doubt that Aguirre intended to pass through the province en route to the Nuevo Reino. Confused and afraid, Collado turned over the government completely to Gutiérrez de la Peña, whom he had previously named captain general, and authorized him to attend to matters as seemed most appropriate.

One hundred and fifty men who had gathered at the governor's summons were now in El Tocuyo, but there were only two harquebusiers among them, Jerónimo Alemán and Francisco Maldonado de Almendáriz. Nevertheless, Gutiérrez de la Peña was assured of victory by virtue of his large number of valiant horsemen and foot soldiers, all with military experience and well armed with lances and daggers of uncured leather. While he delayed in El Tocuyo making a few necessary preparations, Aguirre was marching through the Nirgua sierras, hindered by rough terrain and persistent rains. These obstacles unleashed his impatience and sacrilegious blasphemies: "What is God thinking: that because it is raining I will not go to Peru? Well, He is very much mistaken. I must go, though it may not be His will. And since I cannot save myself, for even in life, I am burning in Hell, I am compelled to commit such cruelties that my name will resound throughout the land." At other times he told his soldiers that they should not out of fear of

## CHAPTER VII

Hell fail to do whatever their appetites might indicate, for simply believing in God was sufficient for salvation.

While Aguirre was thus engrossed in marching through the sierras, ten of his soldiers, without communicating their intention to one another, succeeded in leaving that infamous company to take cover in the underbrush. This affront infuriated the tyrant greatly and he was amazed at the perfidy of the Marañones who had abandoned him in the gravest moment of his struggle. Finally he came to the Yaracuy River and the Valley of the Damas,[14] where sentinels heard him and departed for Barquisimeto to sound the alarm. Since the residents were unable to defend themselves because Gutiérrez de la Peña still had not arrived with the men he had raised in El Tocuyo, they abandoned the city, sending word to the governor of the tyrant's proximity. At this call to arms, Gutiérrez de la Peña dispatched his campmaster, Diego García de Paredes, with fifteen horsemen to observe more closely Aguirre's movements, while he, Peña, with the rest of the soldiers, pursued the tyrant toward Barquisimeto. On the way there, Aguirre traveled a harsh mountain trail that was so narrow it hardly had space for the soldiers to march in single file, and on this road he met Diego García de Paredes with his fifteen horsemen struggling up the other side. Thus they came upon one another, and our men, filled with fright and hampered by heavy foliage, hastily withdrew, leaving on the road two or three lances and an equal number of pointed hoods made of quilted cotton covered with the local linen. Aguirre jeered at the king's followers for their absurd and preposterous appearance, and ridiculed them for wearing such gaudy and unseemly garments.

The campmaster Paredes did not stop in his rapid withdrawal until he came out on a barren plateau close to the mountain, where he intended to form an ambush. Aguirre, meanwhile, favored by the moon, marched all night with no delay and met Paredes on the plain before the ambush had been set up. He forced the campmaster to rush back the following day to Barquisimeto, where he learned that General Gutiérrez de la Peña had already arrived. The two conferred as to what they should do and decided that it would be preferable not to wait for the tyrant in the city. They reasoned that because they were without firearms and all their strength lay in their horses and lances, Aguirre's offensive advantage would be great since, protected by a ring of horses, he could fire his muskets from the parapet. Consequently, they all left the city and withdrew to the camp on the barrancas of the river.

In the interim, Aguirre arrived within sight of the city and assigned his most trusted men to the vanguard with orders that any foot soldier who separated even three paces from the rest be killed at once. Marching in this manner, banners unfurled and standards flying, to the thunder of repeated salvos from the musketry, he entered Barquisimeto on October 22, 1561. He chose as his quarters Damián del Barrio's lodgings, which occupied an entire square, because of the security of being enclosed by an adobe wall topped by merlons.

# CHAPTER VIII

*Pedro Bravo arrives with help from Mérida; Aguirre writes the governor a letter; the two camps study each other from a distance and, after a few skirmishes, all withdraw.*

JUST as Gutiérrez de la Peña abandoned the city and retired to the barrancas of the river, Diego García de Paredes departed on horseback by an unfrequented road. Then, turning back, he attacked Aguirre's rear guard and seized four beasts loaded with clothing, powder and other munitions without receiving any harm. Paredes's soldiers were so pleased with this beginning that they remained on the barrancas to have a better view of Aguirre's operations. The tyrant, however, did not attempt any new development until the following day, when he allowed his Marañones to sack the city late in the afternoon. Their search yielded only some cedulas which had been left scattered about by Gutiérrez de la Peña at the time of his withdrawal, offering pardon to all who would abandon the tyrant, and a letter for Aguirre, exhorting him to return to the service of the king. The governor offered to serve as intermediary for Aguirre with the king, but in case an accord could not be reached, he suggested that they meet in hand-to-hand combat so that a victory might be declared between the two without excessive bloodshed.

The finding of these cedulas was a heavy blow to Aguirre, who always feared that his soldiers might desert him when it was most advantageous to themselves. Dissembling as best he could, he summoned them to his quarters to reveal the content of the cedulas and to remind them that their thefts and murders exceeded in quantity and quality those previously committed in either Spain or the Indies by any other traitors. He considered that a governor whose men wore pointed hoods would be a fragile guarantee, for even if the king should disregard the crimes

## CHAPTER VIII

of the Marañones, the sentiment of relatives and friends of the dead would ensure that his men would always be pursued. Moreover, the continued stigma of the appellation traitors would make them offensive everywhere. They would suffer the same fate as Tomás Vázquez and Juan de Piedrahita, whom Licentiate Gasca had decapitated in Peru without their previous services availing them in any way.

Having concluded this discourse, which appeared later to have had little effect on his soldiers, Aguirre ordered several houses burned so that they might not serve as shelter for his adversaries. The straw church was included in the conflagration and offered little resistance to the flames; but Aguirre, to give some show of being a Christian, had its images and ornaments removed so they would not be damaged.

While this was taking place in Barquisimeto, Governor Pablo Collado was in El Tocuyo. He was tormented by fear, which Captain Pedro Bravo de Molina, on his arrival from Mérida with twenty horsemen as reinforcements, realized rendered the governor incapable of facing the tyrant. Bravo pointed out to Collado that he would be failing in his obligations if he did not appear personally to lend inspiration to the soldiers on so urgent an occasion. But, although the governor claimed to be indisposed in an attempt to avoid conflict, toward which his pacific nature did not lean, at Bravo's insistence he reluctantly agreed to go to the camp. Thanking the captain for his prompt aid, Collado named him his lieutenant general, a post he accepted against the common judgment of his soldiers. They felt that since he was chief justice of the city of Mérida, he should not submit to the authority of another governor, but should serve independently as auxiliary commander from another district.

Since Pablo Collado had consented, although unwillingly, to take part in all preparations for war, he left El Tocuyo that same afternoon with Pedro Bravo and more than sixty men. After they had been traveling all night toward Barquisimeto to join Gutiérrez de la Peña, they were approached at about dawn by a messenger with a letter for the governor from Aguirre in which he said:

> Very magnificent Señor: Among other papers from you found in this town, there is a letter to me with more offerings and preambles than there are stars in heaven. There was no need for you to have taken this trouble, for I already know the extent of your power. As for favors that you might do for me before the king, your offer is meaningless as I am well aware that your influence at Court goes no farther than the first big crowded room. If the king wanted matters to come to open combat between you and me, I would accept his judgment and even allow you the most advantageous weapons. I consider this idea a trick, however, that he is using on us, his subjects

who won and settled this land, so that you and your appointees may rob us of the fruits of our labors. You claim that you come to do justice and that this justice consists of investigating how we conquered the land. The only favor I ask is that we not have to resort to groping for our cuirasses, for you know how little will be gained in this way. My companions have rightfully given only scant credence to your offer of pardon, and intend to sell their lives dearly. I do not aspire to anything here other than buying horses and additional necessities. Besides being well-paid for them, the towns under your jurisdiction will be spared the serious harm my companions and I would inflict if you should take any other course. By the pointed hoods and lances that some of your fleeing soldiers dropped on the road, we have seen that they are numerous; and, inspired by other observations we have made of this land, we have donned wings and spurs to avoid lingering in it. Now, to return to the letter, you have no right to say that we have left the service of the king. For my companions and me to aspire to do by arms exactly what our ancestors did is not to go against the king. He who acts in our favor, we consider as master, and he who does not, we do not recognize. Consequently, some time ago we renounced allegiance to Spain and its king and created our own king. As vassals of another lord, we can make war against those we have sworn to fight without paying any heed to those who oppose us. In conclusion, I recognize that you and your followers were our fellow settlers, and you will be treated as such. If you look for us here, you will find us ready for action, and the sooner you sell us the provisions I request, the more quickly we will leave this land. I do not place myself at your service because you would consider it an insincere offer. May Our Lord protect your magnificent person. Your servant,

Lope de Aguirre.

When the governor had finished reading the letter publicly, he lamented: "Would to God that this conflict had remained between Aguirre and me for I perhaps would have won; but since He wills it otherwise, let us give Him thanks, for our sins must be the reason the sparks from Peru have reached thus far." He spoke in such dismal tones that his pusillanimous soul was exposed. All present mocked his cowardice and persisted in their biting comments until shortly after midday, when they arrived at the barrancas of the river. There, Gutiérrez de la Peña was encamped with the royal forces and, in light of such effective assistance, he considered the victory assured. He and his soldiers were encouraged by news from Pedro Bravo that he brought with him two hundred men in addition to five hundred from Bogotá, who had remained in Mérida under the command of a judge of that Audiencia. This rumor was brought to the tyrant's attention and confirmed that same night by a black man who had fled from the royal camp and crossed over to Aguirre's side. He verified the arrival of the governor and of the two

## CHAPTER VIII

hundred men whom Pedro Bravo had brought to help. The Marañones were so disconcerted by this report that they held their downfall as inevitable in view of so superior a power, and many decided not to miss this opportunity to pass over to the royal camp to enjoy the amnesty that the governor was offering.

First to act on this decision were Juan Rangel and Francisco Guerrero, who found a means of going over secretly to Gutiérrez de la Peña. They assured him that, with no effort other than coming into view, the governor's forces would in a short time rout the tyrant, for now there were not fifty men who would willingly follow him. Pedro Alonso Galeas, who had searched the hearts of Aguirre's soldiers, substantiated this statement; and that same day Pedro Bravo and the campmaster Paredes went out with forty horsemen, including Hernando Serrada, Pedro Gavilla, García Valero, Francisco Infante and Gómez de Silva, to evaluate the situation. They stationed themselves where they could be heard by the Marañones and shouted assurances of pardon if they would desert the tyrant before battle broke out. Then Paredes and Pedro Bravo, noticing some of Aguirre's women servants washing clothes in the river, went down with twenty companions in single file, seized the women and the clothing, and returned to the barranca.

Aguirre deduced from this episode the unfavorable aspect his position was assuming, and since his soldiers had had opportunity to consider the advisability of seeking the security which the governor had promised, he decided to resort to arms. He consequently ordered Cristóbal García and Roberto de Susaya, after wreaking all the havoc possible, to withdraw at daybreak. The Marañones, however, while wandering along the road without being able to find the camp of the royal troops, were met by Captain Romero who, with some residents of the town of Nirgua, was coming to the aid of the governor. Recognizing that they were from the tyrant's forces, he rushed toward the royal camp and sounded the alarm. In turmoil, Gutiérrez de la Peña prepared his troops and held them in battle formation until the first rays of dawn, when he began to march. The Marañones, learning of his plan, were withdrawing in good order toward their camp when, protected by a dense thicket where horses could not enter because of the barrancas, they halted and turned to defend themselves.

Mounted on his chestnut horse, Lope de Aguirre noted the men's dangerous situation and started forward with his soldiers to attack our camp. Gutiérrez de la Peña, however, recognized that the enemy enjoyed an acknowledged advantage while sheltered in that place, and began to retreat. Since Aguirre was following Peña, a unit of our cavalry was able to occupy the thicket to offset the retreat by placing fifty expert harquebusiers in attack position. Although they fired repeatedly from a rock ledge at only a short distance, the bullets were ineffective against the armored tunics and the horses' thick hides. The royal troops, though ill-provided with only five harquebuses, wounded several Marañones at the first shots and killed the tyrant's chestnut horse. He was so grieved at this loss that he sputtered insults at his soldiers and told them they should be ashamed that a few cowhands in sheepskin jackets could have killed his horse and wounded his men without the Marañones' having been able to bring any of them down.

Diego Tirado, the tyrant's captain of cavalry and one of his closest friends, crossed over to the royal camp on his mare after participating in the skirmish, but Francisco Caballero, spurring his horse to follow Tirado, cut the animal so deeply that he could not force it to take a step. Aguirre took him back into his troops but, having thus learned how little he could trust his soldiers, he hastily retired to his quarters. One of the Marañones, a Portuguese named Gaspar Díaz, entered there, wishing to make a show of his loyalty to Aguirre, and wounded Francisco Caballero with his halberd for having attempted to cross over to the royal camp. As he struck the blow, he shouted: "Death to this traitor." The tyrant, not in a position now to lose any man, however, no matter what he might be, not only prevented the killing but, showing regret at Gaspar Díaz's actions, ordered that Caballero's wound be treated with much care.

# CHAPTER IX

*Aguirre prepares to return to Borburata; his Marañones desert him, passing over to the royal camp; Paredes orders Aguirre executed; he is decapitated and quartered.*

As soon as Aguirre was safely entrenched in the little fort which served as his quarters, he again reprehended his soldiers for their lack of resolve, calling them cowards and weak-willed women. He said that they had failed to take the offensive or carry out any operation of importance. Then, passing from one extreme to another, he decided to garrote those who seemed to be lukewarm in his service. When he revealed his intention to some of his friends and indicated that those to be executed exceeded fifty, they were appalled and tried to dissuade him. They pointed out that through error he might take the lives of some most devoted to him and spare the worst ingrates, as in the recent incident with Diego Tirado, whom he had considered one of his closest friends. It was conceivable that those whom he judged remiss might be promptest to die in his defense. This advice caused him to rescind the death sentence but did not prevent him from disarming the intended victims. Considering the difficulties now facing him, he felt it impossible to pursue his journey to Peru by that road and consequently decided to return to Borburata, where he would set out as soon as he could in search of another route.

Gutiérrez de la Peña was kept informed of these plans by his spies, and constantly kept forty cavalrymen stationed at the tyrant's quarters to impede delivery of food supplies to him. This vigilance reduced the Marañones to the extremity of eating all their dogs and horses as they began to disband little by little and started passing over to the royal camp, one by one and two by two. Aguirre tried to prevent this rejection, which wounded him keenly, by sending out a squadron composed of the soldiers in whom he had greatest confidence. They had orders to disperse with their harquebuses the forty cavalrymen whom Gutiérrez de la Peña had placed in siege of Aguirre's quarters, since their persistent presence caused him extreme anxiety.

Protected by the wall of a hermitage from the impact of the horsemen, the Marañones began to fire their harquebuses, and Captain Bravo was busy reproving his soldiers for insulting their adversaries by calling them traitors. Juan de Lezcano, a mestizo Marañón, noted his lack of attention and took such exact aim that he hit Bravo's horse in the forehead, from which it fell dead. Aguirre's men, pleased because the shot had hit its mark, cheered the deed while Pedro Bravo, provided another horse, stopped the debacle at the first indication of fear. Having learned a lesson, he drew a little apart with his troops, but he did not go so far as to lose the tyrant's quarters from sight so he would be close enough to prevent Aguirre's sudden departure for Borburata. Aguirre started implementing his decision to flee after taking away the arms of those whom he distrusted, but, on the twenty-seventh of October, the disarmed men, resenting Aguirre's insults, refused to follow him, explaining that to lead them out thus without defenses was to sacrifice them to their enemies. Moreover, they said it was disgraceful for one who prided himself on being a valorous leader to turn his back on the challenge because he lacked the courage to face danger. These words persuaded Aguirre to return their arms and ask their pardon for the error he had committed. As some, still offended by the rebuff, refused to accept the weapons, however, his vile cowardice reached so low a plane that he condescended to beg them to do him the favor of receiving them.

Diego García de Paredes and Pedro Bravo, having been informed of the disorder that the tyrant's anger had occasioned and of his impending departure, came to his camp with a large group of horsemen. In an attempt to prevent their carrying off any of the Marañones' servants, who at that time were in the river, Aguirre dispatched Juan Jerónimo de Espínola with fifteen harquebusiers to protect them. Instead, Espínola and his companions, as soon as they were free, hastened their pace and, shouting "Long live the king," passed over to the royal camp to be incorporated into Paredes's troops. This unexpected turn of events brought on the total ruination of the tyrant, as the other Marañones, heartened by Espínola's example, chose not to be last in departing. In sight of Aguirre himself, they all crossed over to the other side and cried out: "Long live the king, whom we came here to serve." This left the tyrant with only Antón Llamoso, who had sworn many times that he would be faithful in life and in death.

The campmaster García de Paredes sent word to governor Pablo Collado to march with his men to reap the rewards of the royal troops' efforts. Aguirre, meanwhile, wavered in fear of the disastrous end into which his rebellious tyranny had plunged him. Observing that only Antón Llamoso remained with him, the tyrant asked: "And why did you not also go to enjoy the king's pardon?" to which Llamoso responded that he wished, by dying at his leader's side, to fulfill what he had promised. Then, without uttering a word of explanation, the tyrant entered a room where a daughter whom he had brought from Peru was seated with a companion, La Torralva, native of Molina de Aragón. Eager to culminate his cruelties with one too heinous to characterize even a beast, he set the cord in his harquebus and told his daughter to commend herself to God, for he was going to kill her to save her from the affront of ever thereafter hearing herself called the daughter of a tyrant. La Torralva grasped the weapon and pleaded to dissuade him from so execrable an evil; but, inflexible in his resolution, he released the harquebus and, drawing a dagger from his belt, stabbed his daughter to death.[15]

After committing this atrocity, he left the room just as men from the royal camp entered. At this sight he slumped onto a cot in a corner, at which one Ledesma, a swordmaker from El Tocuyo, said to the campmaster: "Sir, we now hold the tyrant subjected." To this Aguirre responded: "I do not submit to scoundrels such as you." Then, recognizing Paredes by his insignia but too weak to articulate well, he said: "Campmaster, sir, I beg you as a gentleman to hear me because I wish

## CHAPTER IX

to communicate a matter of much importance to the service of the king." Paredes suspended the death sentence until the arrival of the governor and leaned forward to comply with the request. The Marañones, however, fearing the danger that threatened them if Aguirre should disclose the evil deeds that all together had committed, urged Paredes not to delay when he could assure the victory at once with the tyrant's death. As this counsel seemed reasonable to the campmaster, he gave permission for the Marañones themselves to kill the tyrant immediately.

Juan de Chaves and Cristóbal Galindo took aim and fired their harquebuses at his chest, but Chaves caught him at a slant so that the shot only grazed his arm. Aguirre, observing his form and realizing the defect as soon as Chaves set the cord, said: "Bad shot"; but Galindo, firing one that split his heart open, said: "This is a good one." Aguirre fell dead to the floor, where another of the Marañones, Custodio Hernández, cut off his head and, seizing its very long hair, took it out to receive the governor. The campmaster Paredes, waving the banners of the vanquished tyrant over the parapets, jubilantly announced the triumph; but Governor Collado, resentful that Aguirre had been killed without his order, received the acclamation with gruff coolness. Hiding his feelings as best he could, he ordered the cadaver quartered, and the pieces placed along the roads. The head he presented as a souvenir to the men from El Tocuyo, where it remained on public display for many years in an iron cage in the plaza; the left hand fell to the residents of Valencia; and the right he gave to Captain Pedro Bravo to take to Mérida. Later, however, first some and then others, in light of the inefficacy of such infamous adornments, gave them to the dogs to rid themselves of the obnoxious odor.

General Gutiérrez de la Peña claimed the tyrant's flags as spoils intrinsic to his position according to military law. He held them in such esteem that he obtained authority from Philip II to incorporate them into his coat of arms, where his descendants retain them today. This favor, together with the titles of marshal of the province and perpetual regidor of all the cities that compose it, was a just reward for his services.

Thus ended the grim tyranny of Lope de Aguirre, who held all the provinces of America in terror. Though he was brought down more by trickery than by strength, Venezuela was credited in other countries with the triumph of his death. Aguirre's unworthy birth took place in Oñate in the province of Guipúzcoa, his deeds subsequently to tarnish the name of this noble city; and, although the son of ordinary parents, he was an *hijo de algo* (hidalgo—son of something, someone). His appearance was despicable because of his hideous features and small, thin body. He was an incessant talker and a boisterous charlatan; in company no one was more terrifying, nor more cowardly when alone. Although during his more than twenty years in Peru his assigned function was to tame ponies and exercise horses, he was always restless, a consort of seditions and revolts, and there was no uprising or mutiny in which he did not take part. In the revolt of Sebastián de Castilla, when General Pedro Alfonso de Hinojosa was killed in Las Charcas, he was among the most guilty and thus was condemned to death by Marshal Alonso de Alvarado; but his skill in hiding prevented the execution of this punishment. Later, to obtain pardon for this crime, he enlisted in the royal troops which the Audiencia de Lima had formed against Francisco Hernández Girón. It was in the Valley of Cochabamba that he received the wound from which he always remained crippled. Known everywhere as Aguirre the Mad, he was so insurgent and terrifying that he was rightfully exiled from most cities of Peru, and in Cuzco he was almost hanged. When he went out with Ursúa on the conquest of the Omeguas, he led his own rebellion so that, at the cost of much blood inhumanly shed, the memory of his barbarous impiety remained eternal and he was distinguished as a beast among men.

# CHAPTER X

*Fajardo asks the governor for help; the latter sends Luis de Narváez with one hundred men; they are all killed on the way by the Arbacos.*

CACIQUE Guaicaipuro, vain at having caused Juan Rodríguez's death, and Cacique Terepaima were striving to incite the tribes of the province of Caracas to take up arms against the towns of San Francisco and El Collado in an attempt to regain their liberty. Since the appeal was so widespread, it was no secret to Francisco Fajardo, who had just returned to San Francisco from Margarita. Displaying his natural affability, he tried to quiet the caciques' rebellion, but seeing that nothing could calm them, he decided to advise Governor Collado so he would send help. For this task he dispatched Juan Alonso, resident of El Collado, to inform the governor that Fajardo was hourly expecting a general uprising of the Indians.

Pablo Collado was in Barquisimeto when Juan Alonso arrived a few days after the tyrant's death. On learning of the danger that

## CHAPTER X

threatened Fajardo, Collado quickly raised a hundred men,[16] most of them Marañones who, following the death of Aguirre, had scattered. So that the task would be better performed, he wanted to entrust it to an experienced leader, the campmaster Diego García de Paredes. That gentleman's prior services in other matters, however, for some time had been impelling him to request a reward from the king. Since he wanted to go to the Court to seek it in person, he embarked for Castile with Gutiérrez de la Peña without accepting the governor's offer. Collado then named Luis de Narváez, native of Antequerra in Andalusia, at that time chief alguacil of El Tocuyo, as commander of the expedition. Provided with all necessities, he led an entourage out of Barquisimeto in early January of 1562, and proceeded in disorder toward the top of Terepaima Hill, where Juan Rodríguez had died. Although this was a region which, as the center of the Arbacos, called for the greatest vigilance, the Spaniards marched through it with such overconfidence that they even strapped their firearms onto the pack animals in order to be free of that weight. The Meregotos, natives of the plains of Guaracarima on the banks of the Aragua River, called by the Arbacos to cooperate in their defense, had climbed the sierra and occupied the heights today called the Mostazas. Adorned with emblems and feathered headdresses, they awaited Narváez's arrival, but he, seeing the pass occupied by that multitude, was filled with circumspection when the occasion actually begged for intrepid resolve. Thus, as he began slowly to try to entice the Indians with peace and pointed out the dangers that war would occasion, they shouted ridicule at the invaders and clarified their reply with arms. Using arrows and macanas, the Indians threw the ill-prepared Spaniards into such confusion that their attempt to protect themselves proved ineffectual. Mortally wounded by arrows at the first encounter, Narváez fell from his horse to the ground where, trampled by the Indians, he lost his life as a consequence of his inadequate preventive measures.

The Arbacos, observing the actions of their allies, the Meregotos, on seeing their enemy's desperate situation, marched out and attacked in order to have a claim to victory also. Meanwhile, the Spaniards could not resist the force of the barbarians, and in dismay allowed that enraged rabble to strike with pitiless fury. The Indians wrought havoc as, without sparing anyone, even the servants, they slashed with their macanas; and only Juan Serrano, Pedro García Camacho, and Francisco Freire escaped by hiding in the brush. At the end of five days the first two arrived at San Francisco, where Fajardo had completely lost hope of being able to sustain an assault against the victorious enemy. Realizing that to divide his few soldiers between San Francisco and El Collado was to expose each town to evident destruction, he held it more logical to abandon one voluntarily rather than lose both. Consequently, before the Indians could lay siege to it, he abandoned San Francisco and retreated with all his men to fortify themselves in El Collado.

The other soldier, Francisco Freire, found the road they had come by and fled back toward Valencia. Since a short while later he met some Indian warriors occupying the pass through which he was trying to escape, however, he threw himself from a steep precipice. The memory of this desperate act is retained in the name of the place, properly called Freire's Leap, but corrupted by popular usage to Friar's Leap. He was so fortunate that, even though the distance from the summit to the valley is great, he was unharmed except for being unconscious for a while. When he regained consciousness, he walked haltingly down a quebrada and came out on banks of the Tuy, where he encountered some Meregotos walking along the sierra. Since he could think of no way out, he submitted and on his knees begged them not to kill him. They paid little attention to his pleas, however, and struck him several blows with their macanas. As it now seemed to him better to change tactics, he struck the Indians with a little sword that he carried. With only a few thrusts, he wounded three or four of those harassing him most, while the others held it safest to withdraw and allow him free passage. Without other incident, he arrived in Barquisimeto after a few days with the news of Narváez's death. All sorrowfully attributed the misfortunes of that expedition to the punishment of Divine Justice for the Marañones' evil deeds and considered that their disastrous defeat would serve as a lesson.

# CHAPTER XI

*The Audiencia sends Licentiate Bernáldez to investigate the excesses of Collado; Bernáldez sends him prisoner to Spain and remains as governor in his place; Guaicaipuro besieges the city of El Collado, and Fajardo abandons it.*

ON Aguirre's death, Governor Pablo Collado was free of his cowardly distress. Either because this relief infused in him some ill-placed arrogance, or he wished to take revenge for the scorn with which the settlers were treating him, he began to abuse them harshly. They were amazed

## CHAPTER XI

at this change in his usually affable nature and felt compelled to resort to the Audiencia de Santo Domingo to present their grievances. Their charges and stipulations had little substance and were completely unproven, but they were sufficient for the Audiencia to send a lawyer, Licentiate Bernáldez, to investigate them. Generally called Ojo de Plata (Silver Eye),[17] for the one he wore to fill the socket of the one he had lost, he arrived in El Tocuyo in August of 1562. As his commission bore the usual clause that the defendant, if found guilty, should be sent as a prisoner to Spain, it was urgent that Bernáldez conduct the inquiry quickly so that the stipulation should not become invalid. With little effort on the part of the negotiators, the crimes imputed to Collado were conceded as proven; thus, he was suspended and sent as a prisoner to Spain, leaving the office of governor to Bernáldez.

While this was happening in El Tocuyo, Fajardo was in El Collado, where he never put down his arms because of the Indians' constant attacks. They, glorying in the rout of Narváez and the abandonment of San Francisco, had made a strong effort, at Guaicaipuro's urging, not to leave a single Spaniard in the province. Fajardo was able to withstand this general assault for several days with the aid of Guaicamacuto and the other caciques of the coastal areas, who had refused to become involved in the conspiracy. Guaicaipuro, however, was so astute that he succeeded in bringing about Fajardo's perdition by perverting Cacique Guaicamacuto with nagging persuasions. The Spaniards had built a wooden fort in the town, in which they valorously resisted and did not allow the Indians to gain any advantage in the assaults. Guaicaipuro, now considering some way in which to force them to fight outside the shelter, withdrew his troops and let it be understood erroneously that he no longer wanted war with Fajardo. Allowing several days to pass, Guaicaipuro and his men arrived early one morning in sight of the town of Guaicamacuto (present-day Macuto) and, following a plan the two had evolved with great secrecy, feigned that he had come to make war on Guaicamacuto because of his professed friendship for Fajardo.

Guaicamacuto, simulating great fear, went out from the town, more or less one league distant from El Collado, to meet Fajardo after establishing an ambush on the road. With malicious deception the cacique said: "Because I have been your friend, the Teques have come to destroy me by razing my fields and setting fire to my houses. Since I helped you and your men defend yourselves against them, help me now to avoid the danger which through friendship for you has come to me." It seemed to Fajardo that the cacique was justified in what he asked, and he resolved to favor him strongly. He told Guaicamacuto to hold his men in readiness and promised that when Juan Jorge de Quiñones arrived with his thirty soldiers and three horsemen, he would send them at once to their aid.

The barbarian wanted nothing more. Hurriedly returning to his town, he reinforced the ambush and named the valiant Pararián to command it. Then, with a considerable number of warriors, he lay in ambush farther along the road, and Guaicaipuro served as auxiliary commander to attack with his Teques if the occasion should arise. Not expecting such treachery, Juan Jorge went out with his men from El Collado; but, on approaching the mountains, he instantly recognized the hidden deception. His alertness, however, served only to prevent his being taken unawares as, having time for no more than to order the harquebuses loaded with two shots, he was attacked on all sides. To this his soldiers responded with such spirit that the battle intensified and the mountain was filled with horror and blood; but since the Indian combatants exceeded five thousand, our men had to discard their firearms and take their swords in hand. They converted them into bolts of lightning and rammed them down the throats of the heathen rabble, while Juan Jorge with his three companions on horseback made prodigious efforts to ride roughshod over the enemy. But for each Indian who died, one hundred filled his place, while our men, after more than three hours of fighting, now required all their courage to survive.

Juan Jorge, his strength and spirits restored, returned with his thirty-three Spaniards to see if they might now reach the shore, where they could use the surf to protect their flanks. This supreme effort served only as greater torment, however, for Guaicaipuro, on seeing our men escaping, charged anew and the skirmish raged more desperately than before. In the most ardent fervor of combat, Juan Jorge, after observing Pararián with a *guaica* spear in hand, decided to attack with his lance. When he spurred his horse, however, the animal stumbled on some stones and fell with him to the ground where, unable to escape, Juan Jorge was killed when Pararián pierced him through the abdomen with the *guaica*. This misfortune would have meant the ruin of the others if Fajardo and the rest of his troops, in response to news of his men's predicament, had not come out just at this time from El Collado to help. Under this protection they succeeded in retreating to the fort, but only at the cost of eleven soldiers killed and the rest badly wounded.

Guaicaipuro was not appeased by the outcome of the action in which he had involved Guaicamacuto, and, because he had lost more than seven hundred warriors, he made a new levy to raise men among his own vassals and from the other tribes of the league. He increased his combatants to seven thousand and resolved not to desist until victory was completely won. Consequently, he placed a steady siege on El Collado, with such a rigorous blockade that Fajardo, desperate from lack of provisions, decided to abandon the town. After obliging his soldiers to swear to return whenever he might again attempt to conquer the province, he embarked his men in pirogues and canoes, sending some to Borburata and withdrawing with those remaining to Margarita.

# CHAPTER XII

*The Indians of Caracas kill Diego de Paredes; Don Alonso Manzanedo comes as governor; on his death, Licentiate Bernáldez resumes the post.*

GENERAL Gutiérrez de la Peña and his campmaster Diego García de Paredes, on arriving at Court, needed little additional influence to be amply attended and rewarded, since their outstanding services were well known. His Majesty named Diego García de Paredes governor and captain general of the province of Popayán, and made Gutiérrez de la Peña marshal of that province and perpetual regidor of all its cities. Other special favors granted, though not so patently lucrative, were of more value in substance.

After obtaining these appointments, the general and his campmaster left Spain for Borburata at the beginning of 1563, and sighted land above the port of Catia three leagues to the leeward of El Collado. Paredes remembered that at the time of his departure for Spain, Luis de Narváez had come out from El Tocuyo with help for Francisco Fajardo. Since Paredes had always felt close to Narváez, but was still uninformed of his death and all that had happened in the general uprising of the Indians, he ordered the ship anchored so that he might seek news of his friend.

The cacique of that valley was Guarauguta, who, as a staunch enemy of the Spanish nation, was among those who had helped Guaicaipuro to eject Fajardo. Seeing the vessel anchored in his own port, he placed two hundred of his most valorous men in ambush, waved a white flag in the air and called out from the shore to those on the ship. At these manifestations, Paredes erroneously presumed that Guarauguta was Narváez or one of his soldiers, and ordered a sloop launched. Accompanied by only four Estremadurans and six mariners to row, he landed and was received by the cacique. Paredes at once asked about

Narváez, to which the barbarian falsely replied that he was in San Francisco, but that a vassal would be sent to ask him to visit Paredes. The cacique invited his guest to wait in the town in the meantime, for the reply would be delayed only a brief while, as the distance was short.

Paredes trustfully accepted the invitation, but hardly had he reached the cacique's lodgings than amidst the splendors of a sumptuous banquet he recognized from the servants' agitation the evil aspects of the festivity. Communicating his suspicions to his companions, he wanted to return to the shore to reembark; but they attributed his distrust to temerity and imprudently persuaded him to disregard the risks as imaginary. Then, while all were enjoying the occasion, the Indians came out and attacked them. Although caught off guard, Paredes urged his companions to the defense and killed more than eighty warriors with his own hands.[18] The enemy was so numerous, though, that nothing could prevent most of the Spaniards from paying with their lives for their imprudent confidence. Only one mariner escaped, and, even though wounded by several arrows, he was able to reach the shore and swim to the boat. On board he gave an eyewitness account of that event, which became even more tragic when, a short time later, they saw the Indians on the beach impaling those cadavers, suspending them on high, and filling them with arrows. Unable to retaliate at the time, the Spaniards hurriedly set sail to escape seeing those grievous actions with their own eyes.

Thus ended the life of Governor Diego García de Paredes. His deeds in the Indies were illustrious, for he took pride on all occasions in being son of that celebrated Spaniard of the same name whose bold ventures were the amazement of Italy.[19] Born in Trujillo, Estremadura, he was inclined from a tender age toward the military life, but left Europe, where he could have augmented his fortune, to follow his relatives and friends, the Pizarros, in the conquest of America. Then, in order not to place his loyalty in question, he relinquished the advantages won in Peru; for, seeing Gonzalo Pizarro popularly acclaimed as the defender of that country, Paredes feared that his own reputation might be at risk while his fellow countryman was in turmoil. Without regard to the rewards that his services deserved, he proceeded to the Nuevo Reino, and from there to this province, where, after conquering the Cuica Indians, he founded a new Trujillo, named in honor of his homeland. In the rout of the tyrant Aguirre, his participation was highly significant, but just when the royal hand had begun to bestow favors on him, death from a tragic cause cut short his path.[20]

A few days after Diego García de Paredes's death, Alonso de Manzanedo, appointed governor and captain general of the province by the king to succeed Licentiate Pablo Collado, arrived in Coro. There, he instituted a residencia of Licentiate Bernáldez, his interim predecessor. Since Bernáldez's courteous nature had made him well liked during his short term, little testimony was needed to establish his honesty, leaving his reputation intact. After this judgment, he returned to Hispaniola, where for a short while he quietly enjoyed his retirement as a landowner, but his experience had been so extensive that his talents were soon needed again. Alonso de Manzanedo, now advanced in age and in broken health, was soon prostrate with the change of climate and increasing worries. He died in February of 1564, leaving the government to the alcaldes, as required by the edict expressed in the cedula procured by Sancho Briceño. The Audiencia, informed of Manzanedo's death, renamed Licentiate Bernáldez as interim governor at the request of all the cities of the province. Gratified by the goodwill of the citizens, he promptly embarked for Coro, where his reception attested to the approval of his record.

# CHAPTER XIII

*Fajardo again undertakes the conquest of Caracas; Alonso Cobos seizes him by trickery and takes his life; Governor Bernáldez penetrates the province as far as Guaracarima but then withdraws.*

NEITHER Fajardo's repeated reverses nor his having been twice obliged to abandon the province of Caracas were sufficient to dissuade him from his plan to conquer it. Thus, from the instant he arrived in Margarita after abandoning El Collado, he began more urgently than ever to raise troops in an effort to restore what had been lost and to exact satisfaction for offenses prompted by Guaicaipuro's indomitable pride. Since he had already acquired fame and esteem with the previous expeditions, he quickly prepared for his third campaign. At the beginning of 1564, with one hundred and thirty men, several horses, a large herd of beef cattle, and a significant quantity of arms and munitions, he sent his soldiers, equipment, and supplies to Tierra Firme. They were ordered to await him at the Bordones River, a little more than a league to the leeward of Cumaná, where he planned to assemble his army. Then, finally, when all had been attended to, he and his men began the march.

Alonso Cobos, then chief justice of Cumaná and declared enemy of Fajardo, with no motive other than envy, yearned to rid himself of his rival. Learning that Fajardo was on the Bordones, it seemed to Cobos that he could easily take all of Fajardo's supply of armaments and, after conquering the province of Caracas, garner the praise that he so much resented hearing for his adversary. Consequently, he instigated plans to kill Fajardo by whatever means possible. He feigned a reconciliation to hide the betrayal by sending him courteous messages of welcome and arranging through Marcos Gómez, one of Fajardo's friends, to meet in Cumaná to reaffirm the friendship. Fajardo at first, perhaps because his heart warned him not to trust this conciliatory gesture, tried to excuse himself on the pretext of his early departure. But so great were the urgings and promises with which Cobos assured him of his sincerity that Fajardo eventually went. There, Cobos, to accomplish the predevised malevolence, received him with a display of pleasure and kept him entertained in conversation until night, when Fajardo felt it time to return to Bordones. He tried to take his leave, but several of Cobos's servants and friends, provided with iron shackles for the visitor's feet, approached him from another room. As Fajardo defended himself, Cobos said: "Do not be upset; all this is no more than a formality to quiet disparaging tongues. I do not want anyone to think that because we are friends I would obstruct justice. Allow yourself to be taken and within an hour you will be free."

Fajardo, deceived by those treacherous words, consented to the capture, whereupon Cobos's men at once clamped the shackles on him and seized his weapons. Cobos had Fajardo placed in the stocks, where he was forced to confess before a scribe, Hernando López. That same night, Cobos revealed the charges against him to Fajardo, branding as crimes acts which generally are judged merits; and he imputed as faults Fajardo's singular services in the conquest of Caracas. At the end of the half hour allowed Fajardo to prepare his defense, Cobos sentenced him to death by hanging, ordering that he be dragged to the scene of execution from the tail of a horse.

Fajardo was amazed to learn of the sentence, for cruelty could not have devised a greater violence or tyranny a more hideous injustice. Since he was not allowed to appeal the verdict, he tried to find a way to inform the soldiers he had left in Bordones, for he no longer had any hope of being freed other than by arms. Cobos, suspecting what Fajardo was thinking, decreed a hasty execution and, before his evil act could be known in the town, ordered that Fajardo be garroted. The prisoner defended himself furiously with his hands, however, and would not allow the cords to be put around his neck. Finally Cobos arose in fury from his chair, shouting: "What a lot of fuss just to kill a chicken; let us finish

## CHAPTER XIII

with it!" He himself then seized a rope and fashioned a sliding noose. As if lassoing a bull, he threw it once and then again until he roped Fajardo by the neck and overpowered him. The others finished killing him by beating his head with a board until the wood shattered into splinters. Since Cobos's rancor was still not satisfied, the next morning he had the cadaver dragged from the tail of a horse and hanged by the feet from a scaffold. This spectacle left the people of Cumaná astounded, and all abominated his depravity.

Thus ended the arduous life of Captain Francisco Fajardo, in whom valor and misfortune vied persistently. His lofty ideals, in spite of his being a mestizo without wealth, though of noble birth, were sufficient to place him among the illustrious conquistadors of the Indies. He tenaciously undertook alone and without means the laborious task of the conquest of the Caracas Indians. At last King Philip II honored him with the title of Don and named him perpetual governor of all that he might settle; but these favors came only after his death. His soldiers in Bordones, on learning of the tragedy, were at first moved to proceed to Cumaná to take vengeance; but as they were without a leader, and disorganized, their anger cooled. After the armaments were divided among them, each hastened on his way to seek his own advancement.

The residents of Margarita felt a general grievance at his unjust death and longed to avenge it. In order that Cobos's evil deed should not remain unpunished, they crossed in pirogues to Tierra Firme under the command of Pedro de Viedma, chief justice of that island. On entering Cumaná quietly in the silence of the night, they seized Alonso Cobos and took him to Margarita.[21] There, legal action having been instituted and the crime proven, Cobos was dragged through the streets, hanged and quartered as an example of punishment suitable for that infamous offense.

The hope of recovering what had been lost in the province of Caracas now doomed, Governor Bernáldez undertook that conquest on his own account. After equipping one hundred men recruited from the cities of the district, he departed from El Tocuyo with Marshal Gutiérrez de la Peña, whom he named to take charge of all preparations for the expedition. As the governor was present and final authority still rested in him, however, the marshal at once began to recognize the inconvenience of not being able to administer affairs as he thought best. The governor, though inexperienced, attempted to make plans for the conquest to which the marshal did not assent. At this impasse, all generally foresaw that scant results could be expected from the expedition. Supporting this prediction was the fact that, having arrived on the plains of Guaracarima, the soldiers found the natives up in arms. They were disturbed because the Arbacos and Meregotos, at the news that the governor was entering their lands with armed men, called to their aid their neighbors and friends, the Quiriquire Indians. These warriors approached along the banks of the Tuy as far as the Tiquire River, and were so numerous that on all the heights there was not a space that their feathered headdresses did not fill. At this sight our men began to lose courage, but, urged on by the marshal, they made an effort to enter through a narrow valley which they called the Valley of Miedo (Fear), formed by two sierras with the Tuy running down the center. This move, however, served only to make them recognize more clearly the Indians' opposition and increase their fear. Thus, they decided to retire to the plains of Guaracarima and wait there until they were joined by a larger number of men, because they were too few to succeed in the conquest they were undertaking.

Since the governor wished to reinforce his troops as soon as possible, he turned back toward El Tocuyo, accompanied by the marshal, and left the rest of the soldiers in Guaracarima under the command of Francisco de Madrid for the duration of his own absence. Even though the marshal and the governor went individually to all the cities of the province and urged prospective recruits to accompany them, the attempt to conquer Caracas was so discredited that they could not find a single man who was willing to expose himself to the risk. Since help was delayed more than anticipated, Francisco de Madrid felt obliged to leave Antonio Rodríguez Galán in his place and go personally to El Tocuyo to investigate the feasibility of pursuing the conquest. Quickly disappointed by the unfavorable conditions everywhere, however, he returned to Guaracarima with orders from the governor to disperse the soldiers and postpone the expedition until a more favorable time.

# BOOK V

## CHAPTER I

*Pedro Ponce de León arrives to govern the province; he decides to pursue the conquest of Caracas and names Diego de Losada commander of the venture; the latter leaves El Tocuyo and with his army reaches the Valley of Mariara.*

A little more than a year had passed since Governor Pablo Bernáldez's withdrawal with his army to the Valley of Guaracarima. Now, in El Tocuyo at the end of 1565, he decided to make a second foray into the province of Caracas to see if fortune might look upon him with more favor. He announced the expedition and named as commander Diego de Losada, resident of El Tocuyo, a person of valor and experience acquired from participation in many military operations. He had been camp-master for Governor Sedeño, as well as commanding officer on different conquests. Losada tried to excuse himself on the grounds of failing health, fearing to damage his reputation if he sought to follow such experienced captains as Juan Rodríguez, Luis de Narváez and Diego García de Paredes. The governor, however, convinced that his aspirations would be fulfilled through this selection, persuaded Losada to accept the assignment.

At this time, Pedro Ponce de León, illustrious scion of the house of Arcos, a gentleman of experience and talent, arrived from Spain as governor of the province. He had been commanding officer of the fortresses of Conil and Las Almadranas, had served in other posts and now had orders from the king to make every effort to conquer the province of Caracas. He confirmed Losada's appointment of Sedeño as commander and gave him new powers to settle and allot encomiendas. To obligate Losada even more, the new governor assigned three of his own sons, Don Francisco, Don Rodrigo and Don Pedro, to serve under Losada, which led outstanding colonists from all parts of the province to enlist as Losada's soldiers.

Captain Juan de Salas, an intimate friend of Losada, in El Tocuyo at that time although a resident of Margarita, on seeing him pressed into so monumental an enterprise, offered to accompany him. Salas explained that he first had to return to Margarita to reassemble one hundred Guaiquerí Indians of those who had initially come with Fajardo, for they already were familiar with the province and could greatly facilitate his activities. The two then agreed on a time for a meeting in Borburata, and Salas departed to carry out his promise.

Losada spent all of 1566 seeking arms, military stores, and other munitions necessary to equip his army. Then, at the beginning of January 1567, he left El Tocuyo with his men, adding on the way those whom he had provisioned in Barquisimeto. He continued to Villa Rica (later Nirgua), and there, with bulls, cane games, tourneys, and other military plays, he and the men of his camp celebrated on January 20, the feast of San Sebastián, whom they chose as patron and advocate against the Indians' arrows. From this observance originated the custom still followed in Caracas of commemorating his feast day each year in the cathedral.

Next, Losada ordered his troops to march to Valencia under the command of Francisco Maldonado, and then to await him in the Valley of Guacara. He, meanwhile, accompanied by Pedro Alonso Galeas and Francisco Infante, would go to Borburata in search of Juan de Salas, since the time allotted for him to return with the hundred Guaiqueríes had already elapsed. Not finding him in the port, however, or hearing any news of his arrival, although he waited fifteen days, Losada decided to rejoin his men; but they, concerned at his delay, had gone on to the Valley of Mariara. To replenish his supply of military tunics and other needed items, Losada stopped for eight days while he reviewed his army. It consisted of one hundred and fifty men, twenty of them cavalry under the command of Captain Francisco Ponce, son of the governor; fifty harquebusiers and eighty buckler bearers, as well as eight hundred servants. In addition, there were two hundred beasts of burden, a drift of hogs, and four thousand sheep, of which Alonso Díaz Moreno, lieutenant governor, then a resident of the city of Valencia, had given one thousand five hundred at his own cost.

Losada was pleased with preparations going forward for implementing his conquest, but since he considered that to wait for Juan de Salas was to lose the opportunity offered by favorable weather, he lifted camp and began the march. The conquistadors on the expedition with Losada were: Don Francisco, Don Rodrigo, and Don Pedro Ponce, sons of the governor; Gonzalo Osorio, nephew of Losada; Gabriel de Avila, chief ensign of the camp; Francisco Maldonado de Almendáriz, native of Navarra; Francisco Infante, native of Toledo; Sebastián Díaz de Alfaro, of San Lúcar de Barrameda; Diego de Paradas, of Almendralejo;

CHAPTER I

Augustín de Ancona, servant of the Church, native of La Marca; Pedro Alonso Galeas, of Almendralejo; Francisco Gudiel, of Santa Olaya, in the archbishopric of Toledo; Alonso Andrea de Ledesma; Tomé de Ledesma, his brother; Francisco de Madrid, of Villa-Castín; Bartolomé de Almao, Sancho del Villar, Cristóbal Gómez, Miguel de Santacruz, Juan de Gámez, Martín Fernández de Antequera, Marcos Gómez de Cascajales, Cristóbal Cobos, son of Alonso Cobos who killed Fajardo; Diego de Montes, native of Madrid; Francisco Sánchez de Córdova, Martín de Gámez, Pedro de Montemayor, Julián de Mendoza, Miguel Díaz, of Ronda; Andrés Pérez, Rodrigo del Río, Rodrigo Alonso, Francisco Ruiz, Pedro Rafael, Juan Gallegos, Pedro Cabrera, Cristóbal Gil, Alonso Ortiz, scribe of the army; Alonso de Salcedo, Juan Alvarez, Vicente Díaz, Pedro Mateos, Antonio Rodríguez, Francisco Román Coscorrilla, Martín Alfonso, Alonso de León, Alonso Ruiz Vallejo, native of Coro; Melchor Gallegos, Juan Cataño, Gonzalo Rodríguez, Bartolomé Rodríguez, Cristóbal de Losada, native of Lugo; Francisco de Vides, Esteban Martín, Diego de Antillano, Pedro García Camacho, Domingo Baltasar, Gonzalo Clavijo, Miguel Fernández, Baltasar Fernández, his brother; Gregorio Ruiz, Juan Serrano, Diego de Henares, Juan Ramos Barriga, Simón Jiraldo, Lope de Benavides, Juan Fernández de León, Alonso Gil, Juan de San Juan, Duarte de Acosta, Damián del Barrio, native of Coro; Gaspar Tomás, Andrés de San Juan, Juan Fernández Trujillo, Pedro García de Avila, Melchor Hernández, Alonso de Valenzuela, Domingo Jiral, Pedro Serrata, Juan García Casado, Juan Sánchez, Fernando de la Cerda, Pablo Bernáldez, Pedro Alvarez Franco, Antonio de Acosta, Juan Bautista Melgar, Sebastián Romo, Juan de Burgos, Francisco Márquez, Alonso Viñas, Andrés Hernández, Francisco Agorreta, Antonio Pérez, an African, native of Orán; Gaspar Pinto, Diego Méndez, Juan Catalán, Alonso Quintano, Jerónimo de Tovar, Juan García Calado, Francisco Guerrero, Francisco Román, Gonzalo Pérez, Pedro Hernaldos, Andrés González, Gregorio Gil, Francisco Rodríguez, Manuel López, Francisco Pérez, Francisco de Saucedo, Juan de Angulo, Francisco de Antequera, Antonio Pérez Rodríguez, Gregorio Rodríguez, Maese Francisco, a Genoese; Francisco Tirado, Antonio Olias, Melchor de Losada, Jerónimo de la Parra, Juan de la Parra, his brother; Justo de Zea, Pedro Maldonado, Abrahán de Zea, Francisco de Neira, Francisco Romero, Manuel Gómez, Jerónimo de Ochoa, Bernabé Castaldo, Maese Bernal, an Italian; and Juan Suárez, whom they called the Clown. These are the ones whom my research has brought to light, without time having left any memory of the remaining ones.[1]

BOOK V

# CHAPTER II

*A ship from Spain arrives on the coast of Caracas and the Indians kill all aboard; Losada continues his march and reaches Márquez's Site.*

WHILE Losada was reviewing his troops in the Valley of Mariara, a ship from Spain with forty men and merchandise aboard for Cartagena was sailing along the coast of Caracas. As it was being pursued by French corsairs, the captain tried to reach safety but ran into an unforeseen danger. Fleeing to avoid capture, he took refuge in the port of Guaicamacuto, where, deceived by the Indians' false display of friendship, he disembarked without suspecting treason. He quickly deplored his decision, however, for they were suddenly attacked on every side and all perished through his indiscretion. The Indians, glorying in their triumph, seized all they could handle of the cargo and set fire to the ship, reducing it to ashes. They carried off valuable treasures, which Losada later found, among them several miters, a chalice, and other pontifical accoutrements that were being brought to Friar Domingo de Santo Tomás, then bishop of Las Charcas.

Losada then lifted his camp and continued his expedition. After three days of marching, he arrived at the entrance to the Valley of Miedo on the edge of the land he was seeking, and there the troops found themselves in grave danger. Preparing for all contingencies, the men, as Christians, confessed to two priests, one named Blas de la Puente and the other Baltasar García, friars of the Order of San Juan. Then Losada sent Pedro García Camacho, one of the three who had escaped from the rout of Narváez, with thirty men to seize Indians from whom they might gain information on their position and the condition of the province. Fear made them so cautious, however, that García Camacho was not able to accomplish his aim and was forced to return at the end of three days without having fulfilled his mission.

He had hardly arrived at the camp, however, when squadrons of Indians appeared on all sides, and although they did not reach the point of shooting, with their customary uproar they ferociously threatened our men from a distance. This situation obliged Losada to pass the night on the alert, dependent on the first-ranking sentinels of his army for protection. The following day, he took charge, along with his ensign Gabriel de Avila and Francisco Infante, of the vanguard, and entrusted the rear

## CHAPTER II

guard to Francisco Ponce, Pedro Alonso Galeas, and Diego de Paradas. Then he began the climb up Terepaima Hill, now called Cucuizas Hill, his men carrying their arms in their hands because of the enemy's proximity. This was an essential precaution, for on the Spaniards' arrival at an ambuscade, conch horns and flutes inciting to battle resounded throughout the neighboring mountains. At this clamor the swine accompanying the army rushed through the brush, bringing disorder to the march as efforts were made to recapture them. The Indians filled the air with a flood of arrows, and combat, bloody on both sides, ensued until, recognizing the devastation they were receiving from our harquebusiers, the natives sounded the call to regroup. The ambush was now abandoned, leaving passage free for our troops to emerge on the barren flatlands at the summit of the hill. There, because it was already late and the men exhausted, Losada decided to make camp in order to take advantage of a watering place discovered to one side of the little mountain crest.

That night, without the general's knowledge, Francisco Maldonado, Pedro García Camacho, Juan de Burgos, Francisco Márquez, and a black man called Juan Portugués left their quarters to catch some chickens and ducks which they had seen in huts near the camp in a little valley at the foot of the mountain. The Indians had carefully placed the poultry there and were waiting in ambush for the opportunity to test their plan. On arrival at the houses, Francisco Maldonado, musket in hand, was protecting his companions from the rear by occupying a little height that dominated the valley while the others were busy catching the fowl. The Indians, however, seeing their trick succeed, came out of ambush with such a sudden assault that, before resistance could begin, Francisco Márquez had fallen dead, his head split by the blow of a macana. Burgos, wounded in the face, and Pedro García Camacho, pierced through the loins by an arrow, considered it wise to flee so that all would not lose their lives, for although Francisco Maldonado fired his musket repeatedly, it served only as a warning. Losada, not knowing what had happened, on hearing the musket shots ordered the cavalrymen, Francisco Infante, Esteban Martín and Francisco Sánchez de Córdoba, with ten foot soldiers, to determine the cause of the disturbance. Walking toward the spot from which the uproar had emanated, they met those attempting to flee and, on being informed that Márquez was dead, they felt it a point of honor not to leave his body in the possession of the barbarians. They consequently proceeded toward the valley and, renewing the battle, though at the cost of some blood, with the death of Francisco Infante's horse, they succeeded in retrieving the cadaver. They carried it on their shoulders to the camp where they buried it, his name remaining memorialized at that place, still called Márquez's Site.

BOOK V

# CHAPTER III

*Losada continues his march; he defeats Guaicaipuro in battle and arrives with his troops at the Valley of La Pascua.*

THE following day, Losada set out with the rear guard under the command of Diego de Paradas, and ordered Pedro Alonso Galeas, as deputy commander of the army, to lead twelve foot soldiers to the place where help might be needed most. In this manner, although some Indians were sighted, he marched without obstruction until he arrived at the site of Márquez's rout. There, the Spaniards' grief was revived at seeing the unburied bones of those who had accompanied Narváez in that tragic moment, spread out on the field. The Indians either trusted the advantage offered by the narrow place for safe attack or were inspired by the hope that the destruction of the invaders would surely be accomplished on a site that had previously been unlucky for them. The natives consequently attacked the rear guard and set fire to the plain so that death by both knife and fire would triumph. At the same time, Losada felt himself on the brink of ruin for, assaulted on all sides by the horrors of the fire and the severity of the precipices, he could turn his face nowhere without looking on danger. Diego de Paradas and a group of companions fired their harquebuses at the enemy for a space of two hours, however, valiantly resisting the barbarians, who repeatedly hurled their swift arrows. With this diversion, Losada had an opportunity to come out on open ground and order Paradas to withdraw in the best manner the circumstances permitted. This command was executed with all the wisdom and skill that experience had taught Paradas, by his setting up an ambush for use in case the Indians persisted in hindering the march. This stratagem developed as anticipated, for the Indians, observing the withdrawal, rushed forward without misgivings; but on arriving at the ambush, they halted, apprehensive of the harm it foreboded. Three warriors approached alone, faced the ambush and aimed at the brush that concealed it. Our men, recognizing from the Indians' actions that they had been seen, came out attacking so resolutely that Alonso Ruiz Vallejo, with one backhanded stroke, slashed the bow, arrow, and arm of one, and then stabbed him to death. Then, when Juan de la Parra did the same to another, the rest were so terrified that they withdrew and filed down the hill.

## CHAPTER III

At this, Juan Serrano sharply spurred his quarter horse, an open-browed chestnut, responsive to the rein, and fiery. He went out after the barbarians and eliminated with a lance blow the first one he reached, using all his skill as a horseman and depending on the horse's obedience to the bit not to hurtle forward into a tumble. The beast, lashed by the reins, ran downhill, tottering between halting and falling, while its master stiffened his arms to break the violent descent.

After the Indians had withdrawn, Losada, to afford rest to his exhausted men, remained that night at the entrance to the Lagunillas Mountains. His own repose was disturbed by some Indians who left the quebradas and employed a ridiculous stratagem that consisted of covering themselves with the same dry straw as that found in the plain. Thus concealed, they reached the camp and shot their arrows, with severe damage to the servants who, since they were the least protected, were most vulnerable. They were wounded constantly without being able to detect the origin of the damage until Diego de Henares, upon climbing a tree and carefully searching in all directions, noted those bundles of straw. Fitting a cord to his harquebus and taking aim at one of them, he struck the Indian down, at which the rest retreated.

Losada had until then found opposition only from the inhabitants of those mountains, the Arbacos, because his haste in carrying out his mission had given no chance for the other tribes of the province to unite to obstruct his passage. On Incarnation Day, the twenty-fifth of March, however, which fell that year on Holy Monday, he went down to the San Pedro River, in the jurisdiction of the Teques, and viewed the most beautiful sight that Mars ever could have beheld. For there, on all the surrounding heights, crowned with flags and panaches, he gazed upon more than ten thousand Indians, commanded by Cacique Guaicaipuro who, to the beat of drums and echo of flutes, was arrogantly presenting battle.

Considering the risk to his men, Losada halted to determine what he should do. There were some, even the most decorated, among his officers who chose to retreat rather than risk annihilation; but Losada scorned their lack of confidence and resolved to open a way through the enemy squadrons with his sword, preferring to venture his life rather than retreat. Thus, inspiring his men more by example than words, he raised his voice to call on Santiago, and began the battle. In this saint's name, the cavalry spurred their armored horses with restored courage, and broke through the vanguard where the most valiant warriors, crowned with feathered headdresses and carrying large shields, displayed their strength. Even as they felt themselves invincible, however, they were trampled down by the furious impact of the cavalry's attack and, without using their arms for defense, took advantage of the confusion to flee.

The Indians' vanguard now broken, both foot soldiers and horsemen could use their swords safely on the naked bodies as the warriors ran around the field. All was devastation, blood and fury as the Spaniards spared no lives. The Teques, who had been fighting in the vanguard, could not withstand the force of the horses, but the Tarmas and Mariches were able to reorganize their disordered ranks. At the same time, they discharged so many arrows, darts and stones that the sky was cluttered, and they hurled so many to the ground that movement was hampered.

The Spaniards fought victoriously, the Indians rashly. The outcome was in doubt when Francisco Ponce, followed by Pedro Alonso Galeas, Francisco Infante, Sebastián Díaz, Alonso Andrea de Ledesma, Francisco Sánchez de Córdova, Juan Serrano, Pedro García Camacho, Juan de Gámez, and Diego de Paradas ascended through a defile and came upon the Indians from the rear. The skirmish was renewed with even greater fury as the barbarians exposed themselves to Spanish swords and lances. The rain of stones and arrows was so heavy that the Spaniards, their shields broken and their bodies twisted, could barely sustain the combat, their exhaustion showing in the manner in which they handled their weapons. Nevertheless, Losada inspired his men by saying: "Now, brave Spaniards, is the hour of victory, the time to avenge the oft-shed blood of our nation." At these words, they renewed the battle, bringing such destruction to their adversaries that all across the battlefield, mangled cadavers floated in streams of blood.

Guaicaipuro, recognizing defeat and fearing total destruction, ordered conch horns sounded to regroup as he withdrew from the site strewn with bodies and feathered headdresses. Outstanding that day for their brave deeds were Francisco de Vides, Martín Fernández, Juan de la Parra, Pedro Alonso Galeas, Francisco Infante, and the invisible Diego de Paradas. Francisco Infante, however, came close to losing his life when his horse stumbled and fell into a hole. The rider was trapped beneath the animal and would have died had not Francisco Ponce and Alonso Viñas freed him. Even so, one of his legs was so badly injured that he suffered for days afterward.

After Guaicaipuro withdrew with his defeated army, Losada would not remain there although his men needed rest, for experience had taught him the advantage the Indians held in attacking in their own sierras. Thus, marching to reach level land as soon as possible, he went forward two leagues farther and then halted at Cacique Macarao's town. It is located where the San Pedro River joins the Guaire, in the Valley of Juan Jorge, given this name because Fajardo, on his first expedition, had allotted it to that celebrated cacique, his close companion in conquest as well as in misfortune.

When Losada arrived, Macarao's Indians, ready to harvest the fields and afraid that the Spaniards might raze them, would not leave their town, considering submission safer. As a matter of self-interest, therefore, they received our men with as much docility as artifice could contrive. Losada was aware of the aim toward which this sudden peace was directed, but, taking advantage of the Indians' dissimulation, he let them understand that by laying aside their arms they would enjoy the Spaniards' friendship. It was not his purpose to harm anyone who did not provoke his wrath, and he did not allow any hostility toward the barbarians in their homes or fields, in an effort to garner friends through benevolence.

Losada would not accept more than one night of hospitality in the town, but continued his march the following day at dawn toward the Valley of San Francisco, where he had his sight fixed on settling. Although it was only three leagues distant down the Guaire River, he did not wish to continue on that road, where there would be risk of exposure to ambush because the cane fields on its banks afforded protection for the natives. Thus, taking the right-hand route through the towns of Cacique Cuaricuao, he came out onto a fair and fertile valley. Bathed by the currents of the Turmero River, and abundant with food supplies, it offered comfortable accommodations in which to spend the remainder of Holy Week and the Easter season. For this reason, its name was changed to the Valley of La Pascua (Easter), instead of Cortés, by which it had been known since it was given in encomienda to Cortés Richo, a Portuguese, who had accompanied Losada on all the expeditions of his fatal conquest.

# CHAPTER IV

*The Indians kill Diego Paradas; Losada arrives at the Valley of San Francisco; he tries to avoid war, seeking peace by every means, but he does not attain it.*

THE Easter season passed without the Indians attempting to attack, contenting themselves with simply wandering about in groups through the hills near the camp, making frequent threats against the Spaniards. On Wednesday, April 3, 1567, Losada lifted camp to travel to the Valley of San Francisco, only a league away. Before leaving, however, he gave orders to Diego de Paradas to take ambush with twenty chosen men in a nearby canebrake, and from there to seize some Indians through whom to establish peace with the caciques. Losada earnestly desired this solution, for he knew how costly the subjugation of so indomitable a multitude would be.

About an hour after Losada had departed, eighty Indians of the Teques tribe entered the canebrake without being heard by Paradas's men until they arrived at the very spot that hid the ambush. There, the soldiers trying to seize some of the barbarians, and they to defend themselves, engaged in a skirmish that might even pass as a battle, with desperation on one side pitted against military art on the other. Diego de Paradas, answering a need for corporal evacuation, was at that time somewhat apart from his men, but, on hearing the noise of the struggle, impelled by the urge always to be first, he hastily mounted his horse. He threw his tunic over his shoulders without taking time to fasten it at the chest, a negligence that was to cost him his life, for one of the barbarians fired an arrow with such skill that he left Paradas with a mortal wound to the side. With his last bit of strength, however, he held his lance at a slant across his arm, rode at full speed and furiously attacked his assailant, striking him dead with the first blow. He attempted to persevere in his vengeance, but, greatly weakened now by the large amount of blood he had shed and overcome by the intense pain of the wound, he dismounted and sat on the ground to regain strength in rest. Meanwhile, his companions, roaring with anger and grief, converted swords into bolts of lightning and cut those naked bodies to pieces, their wrath not assuaged until all had been put to the knife. Only one Indian, Guayauta, a youth of little more than twenty years, was spared his life after performing marvels in his own defense and joining in single combat with Gonzalo Rodríguez, who would have been killed if his companions had not come to his aid. Skillfully dodging Rodríguez's sword, Guayauta released three arrows that nailed themselves into the soldier's face and almost drove him mad with pain. The warrior was so daring that even with the Spaniards hastening to Rodriguez's defense, he attempted to face them, and they succeeded in overpowering him only with difficulty as, blind with rage, he begged them to kill him. He was afterward so deeply resentful at having surrendered alive that, although Losada had him treated for his wounds, presented him a few trinkets, and gave him leave to depart, he would not go for more than a year. He gave as reason the shame he would feel at appearing with life before his people when his companions had had the glory of losing theirs for liberty and their homeland.

## CHAPTER IV

The youth's vengeance having been requited with the wounding of the Spaniard, the soldiers hurried to Paradas as he succumbed to this violence. Prostrate from loss of blood, he was in the last stages of life as his men applied those preservatives which the ill-provided site offered. All shared in carrying him on their shoulders as they hastily departed to join Losada, not yet informed of the event, in the Valley of San Francisco. There, nothing sufficed to prevent Paradas's death on the sixth day, to the regret of all, especially of Losada because they had been companions of long standing. Paradas was a native of Almendralejo in Estremadura, a gentleman of illustrious blood, to whom this province owes a great part of its conquest. There was no military expedition in his time to which he did not contribute, meriting his companions' acclaim as first in whatever grave straits. He accompanied Felipe de Utre in the discovery of the Omeguas, being one of the thirty-nine immortals who defeated the vast army of fifteen thousand, who fought against that bellicose tribe. His hopes of rest as a reward for his brave deeds were shattered by death brought on by one fatal moment of carelessness.

Losada, after relaxing with his troops for ten days in the Valley of San Francisco, was impelled to make every possible effort to attain its conquest by means of peace before resorting to war. In this respect, this celebrated commander was unique, for he never unsheathed his sword unless in the final throes of an emergency. He sent Juan de Gámez with thirty men down into the valley in an attempt to capture several Indians through whom Losada could express his desires to the caciques. After going about a league from the camp, Gámez arrived at Cacique Chacao's town, later allotted in encomienda to Francisco Maldonado, and found it abandoned, but well supplied with food. While the Spaniards were engaged in gathering what they could to take to the army, they saw on the savanna close to the town some Indians who were hurriedly seeking protection in the bed of a quebrada. The soldiers, dividing for the pursuit, captured a few with only slight resistance, including Cacique Chacao himself, who, like a New World Hercules, demonstrated a valor that was an intrinsic quality of his soul.

A short distance from the quebrada they found a young Indian, eight or nine years of age, who, seeing among those taken one of his little sisters suffering the outrages of captivity, was impelled to action either by love or rash courage. He first rescued a brother, whom he held in his arms, and then went out with his bow and arrows to face our men, believing that he could set his sister free. Then, with tremendous courage and resolution, he shot all the arrows in his quiver, slightly wounding two soldiers. Juan de Gámez, amazed at an act so incongruous in one of the boy's age, ordered that he not be fired upon or harmed in any way;

but in order that he should not escape, Gámez told his soldiers to surround him and clasp him in their arms. The youth, however, displaying the spirit that had fired his anger, still tried to defend himself with his bow until, exhausted, he acknowledged himself conquered, more by fatigue than by lack of courage.

Juan de Gámez then brought Cacique Chacao and the other prisoners back to the camp. Informed of the boy's actions, Losada praised his bravery, feasted him, gave him presents, and tried to persuade him to remain in his company. The little Indian would not assent to this proposal, however, insisting on his sister's freedom and permission to return to his people. Since Losada's desire was to pacify the province and reduce it to vassalage through friendship without violence, this seemed a good occasion to show the Indians that his actions corresponded to his words. He therefore not only freed the little Indian and released his sister but returned to Cacique Chacao all his captured subjects. Then he bade the cacique farewell, asking as recompense for his freedom nothing more than true friendship. The barbarian promised to conform; but he retained the memory of Losada's benevolence only as long as it was needed to regain his lost liberty. As he withdrew with his vassals, he manifested his feelings by shooting arrows at the horses grazing in the field. From his town in the nearby sierras, at the slightest negligence on the part of our men, he seized the opportunity for treachery so that no Indian servant or ally would wander from the camp lest he lose his life to the traitor's shot.

# CHAPTER V

*Losada enters the province of the Mariches, but before undertaking its conquest he returns to the Valley of San Francisco to assist his troops.*

DISAPPOINTED at the lack of progress that peaceful means had achieved in the subjugation of the province, Losada decided to pursue its conquest through war. Leaving the rest of the troops in the charge of Francisco Maldonado, he set out with only eighty men in search of the Mariches, a tribe whose territory bordered on the Valley of San Francisco on the east and occupied ten leagues of high, rocky terrain. The region was densely populated at that time and encompassed several towns, all

## CHAPTER V

now so totally destroyed that only the name of the province remains to recall where it was once located.

Losada departed with his eighty men and, after traveling three leagues down the valley, arrived at the first town. The Indians had abandoned it, however, leaving there only one old woman, who, because she was either disabled or useless, could not participate in the withdrawal. This trivial circumstance gave that spot the name by which it is called today, the Quebrada de la Vieja (The Old Woman's Quebrada). Cristóbal Gil, its encomendero, moved from there to the little town of Petare, where he remains until this day.

As soon as the Indians saw our men in possession of their town, they angrily burst into threats and insults. Waving several white shirts from the heights, they shouted: "What are you doing here, scoundrels? Go back, go back! These are your companions' shirts which the Taramainas sent to us after they had killed them. If you do not leave our town, you will die at our hands in like manner."

Losada, with long service in the wars of the Indies and vast experience in the guile of Indians, paid no attention to this warning, but continued his expedition to the interior of the province. He left part of his soldiers hidden in the houses so that when the Indians returned to their town the Spaniards could punish their arrogant daring. This plan succeeded at once, for hardly had Losada left the town than ten Indian warriors returned and all lost their lives. Leaving the cadavers palpitating in their own blood as a lesson for others, the Spaniards set out in search of Losada. They overtook him in a short while, but then he could find no passage free of obstacles and dangers such as bones, bits of wood, and brush cuttings which the Indians had placed there to obstruct his path. Thus, three days were required to cover the four leagues to Cacique Aricabacuto's town on the other bank of a deep quebrada, where the cacique had fortified its two high-crested rock cliffs with one thousand of his most valiant Indians. They had hardly discovered our camp than they filled the air with arrows, some horn-tipped, so that our men would know the risks that crossing the quebrada held. Losada, however, pressed his horse forward and ordered the men to follow him in single file while firing their harquebuses without cease. Accompanied by Juan Ramos, one group climbed a small hill to the cliffs at the summit while others, proceeding along the same path, constantly discharged their harquebuses despite a rain of arrows. The barbarians wounded Losada slightly beneath his helmet, but then, frightened by artillery fire, they suddenly abandoned the cliffs and left the town to the will of the Spaniards. An unexpected event obliged them to withdraw, however, leaving the pacification incomplete at that time.

BOOK V

As Losada left the Valley of San Francisco, the Indians judged this a good opportunity to seize our divided men. Consequently, up to two thousand warriors assembled from the sierras and, with continuous assaults, besieged Francisco Maldonado in his camp. His valor and military art were insufficient to resist effectively, and his lack of supplies rendered him incapable of remedying the situation. Therefore, to prevent even the servants from running the danger of dying at the hands of the natives, he decided to send an Indian ally to notify Losada of his adversities. This news was received just as Losada, about to sing the victory, was advancing on the rugged crags of Aricabacuto. As it seemed to him more prudent to conserve that which was already accomplished than to pursue the doubtful, he quickly returned to the Valley of San Francisco to help his men. Losada was so widely feared that, only at the word of his coming, the Indians abandoned the site and withdrew to the neighboring mountains, leaving Maldonado free of the stress under which he had been suffering.

# CHAPTER VI

*Losada sends Don Rodrigo Ponce to seek food among the Tarmas; he wins the Battle of the Quebrada and withdraws.*

ALTHOUGH the Indians' withdrawal brought the Spaniards some relief from battle, they suffered a lack of food, more severe each day because the natives had razed all the surrounding fields to make the war more ruthless. Losada accordingly sent Don Rodrigo Ponce with forty foot soldiers, four cavalrymen and a substantial number of Indian servants to go through the towns of the Tarmas and Taramainas, on the western side of the sierras that tower above the sea, to collect all the food possible.

When Don Rodrigo arrived about halfway up a hill, he could see on the plains bordering a quebrada, fields abundant with maize, yucca and other roots. Since they seemed easily accessible, he ordered his soldiers to go down and gather what they could while he and the four cavalrymen remained on the crest to guard them from the rear. Just at this time, however, five Indians wearing feathered headdresses, painted with bixa (*vija*), armed with bows and arrows, and filled with a strong

## CHAPTER VI

resolve to combat the five on horseback, came up one side of the rugged mountain.

Among the Indians, a Taramaina named Carapaica considered it unworthy to fight with the advantages afforded by the hill, for the horses could not be used because of the risky terrain. To show his courage he went out to a level space on the hill and faced the five, an arrogant act that provoked Don Rodrigo to spur his horse in order to bring the savage within reach of his lance. At this, Carapaica drew back his right foot, fixed an arrow in his bow, and released so violent a shot that it was nailed into Don Rodrigo's helmet at the same time as the latter slashed the native's left wrist to the bone. The barbarian, roaring with rage, grabbed the lance and pulled at it with such fury that, although Don Rodrigo used all his strength to prevent it, Carapaica climbed up behind him and pulled him from his saddle. The Spaniard therefore considered it wiser to release the weapon into the hands of the pagan, who lifted it high in triumph.

Meanwhile, the Spaniards were beset on all sides by more than three hundred warriors, who had hastened to the skirmish and occupied the ridges. Finding themselves on a hill too slick for use of the horses, they decided to withdraw to the fields where the foot soldiers were still gathering food. Then they all joined in a body on the banks of the quebrada to discourage the Indians from gloating over having taken the lance from Don Rodrigo. To remain masters of the field, they went back up the hill, but Carapaica, astute and cautious, without waiting for combat, led the barbarians away from the hill, feigning a cowardly retreat. At this our men, content not to pursue him further, returned to the quebrada and, protecting the food that had been gathered, started the march to the Valley of San Francisco, pleased with the help they were bringing to the rest of the army. As Carapaica's withdrawal had been an operation of military stratagem and not of cowardice, however, he amassed more troops and slid down a hillside to the quebrada without being seen by our men until he set upon them suddenly from behind and threw the rear guard into confusion.

Don Rodrigo halted with his men to face the enemy; but they had hardly released their first charge of arrows when they separated into groups and occupied all parts of the quebrada and foothills. They caused such confusion that our men were obliged to fight divided in opposing the multitude that assailed them from different places.

Francisco Infante and two other cavalrymen were protecting the rear guard of the infantry when, discovering nearby a group of Indians coming down as reinforcements, they attacked and forced them back up the hill. While pursuing them, however, Infante was under stress and did not observe where he was going. When he returned to reality, he found himself cut off among steep barrancas that prevented passage, while some of the frightened soldiers, unable to bear the barbarians' rain of arrows, began to withdraw toward Infante's position. Distressed at not being able to go out to help his men, and seeing among those fleeing Alonso Ruiz Vallejo, later an encomendero of Barquisimeto, natural son of the accountant Diego Ruiz Vallejo and an Indian woman of the Caiquetíos of Coro, Infante was seized with rage. He shouted: "Ha! Indian, how is it that you are fleeing, dishonoring the blood of your fathers? Though you are a son of Diego Ruiz Vallejo, you did not inherit your cowardice from him."

Alonso Ruiz, on hearing himself defamed, recovered from his fear and, grasping his shield and sword, determined to die to restore his reputation. Blind with rage, he was searching for his enemies when he came upon Carapaica on the hillside with Don Rodrigo's lance in his hands, infusing courage into his warriors. As this appeared to Ruiz a good occasion to wash out with blood the stain that had discredited him, without taking time to use his sword he grappled with Carapaica to recover the lance by hand, while the barbarian fought to prevent this action. They seized one another and hurtled together down a barranca into the quebrada, where twenty Indians rushed up to help Carapaica; but Alonso Ruiz, without losing courage although in pain from the fall, defended himself valiantly. Since his shield was now broken to pieces by blows from macanas, and he was gravely wounded in three places, however, he would have been overcome had he not been aided by two Indian allies, one named Juan, servant of Diego de Montes, and the other Diego, a Caiquetío, both of whom had come from Barquisimeto without troops. While one wielded a dagger and the other a lance, they bore themselves with such courage that, leaving eight of the enemy dead, they forced the rest to withdraw. The camp now deserted by the barbarians on all sides, the Spaniards sang the victory as they returned to the Valley of San Francisco, carrying the food supplies that had cost them so dearly.

## CHAPTER VII

*Losada founds the city of Caracas; the extent of its growth is noted.*

ALTHOUGH Losada had always thought it better not to settle until the province had been brought to peace, on realizing how long the conquest might take he resolved to found a city in the Valley of San Francisco. To perpetuate the memory of the governor, the province and himself, he named it Santiago de León de Caracas,[2] and, after performing official acts dictated by custom, he designated a site for the church and distributed homesites among the citizens. Also, he named as regidores Lope de Benavides, Bartolomé de Almao, Martín Fernández de Antequera and Sancho del Villar, who, meeting later in the Cabildo, selected as first alcaldes Gonzalo Osorio, Losada's nephew; and Francisco Infante.

The day on which Losada performed these functions is now obscure, as there is no person or archive that reveals it. The books of the Cabildo are so sketchy and lacking in information of those first years that the oldest papers they contain are of the time in which Juan Pimentel governed,[3] a singular omission on so recent a founding. Maestro Gil González Dávila, in his *Teatro eclesiástico,* deceived by the name of the city, assures readers that it was founded on the feast day of Santiago. He also errs in the year of founding, placing it in 1530.[4]

Caracas lies in a beautiful and fertile valley that stretches from west to east for four leagues in length and a little more than half a league in width. Ten and one-half degrees north of the equator, it lies at the foot of high mountains that separate it from the sea for a distance of five leagues. It occupies an area that four rivers encircle without any danger of flooding, so that this spot has every detail to qualify it as a paradise. Its location brings such a heavenly climate that, without any contradiction, it is the best in America. Besides being very healthful, it appears that spring chose the city as its permanent abode. Moderate all year, it knows neither sultry summers nor severe winters. Its waters are many, clear and delicate; and the four rivers which encompass it are pure crystal. Without excessive heat in summer, during the harshest dog days, the streams remain cool and become more than cold in December. Its streets are broad, long and straight, with access and exit equally available; and since they slope and are paved with stones, they are not dusty or muddy. Most of its buildings, for safety during earthquakes, are low, some of brick but most commonly of adobe, and are well designed. The houses are extensive and almost all have spacious patios, gardens and orchards watered by irrigation canals channeled from the Catuche River across the city; and they produce a variety of flowers in amazing abundance during the entire year. Its beauty is heightened by four plazas, three of medium size and the principal one very large, shaped in a well-proportioned square.

Besides a multitude of blacks and mulattoes, one thousand Spaniards reside here, having among them two titles from Spain and many cavaliers of well-known ancestry. Its creoles are of keen and ready wit, courteous, affable and well-bred. They speak Castilian with perfection, without those bad habits which corrupt it in most ports of the Indies. Because of the benevolent climate, they have graceful bodies and charming dispositions without there being any deformed or exceptionally ugly ones. In general they are of lively spirit and magnanimous heart, and so inclined to all that is cultural that even the blacks scorn those who do not know how to read and write. Their hospitality to foreigners inclines newcomers to linger so that he who stays as long as two months in Caracas never succeeds in leaving. The women are beautiful, modest and stately, and they are treated with such propriety and so fiercely protected that it is a marvel if any white woman ever lives scandalously; and if she does, she is generally from some other place, and is shunned for her misconduct.

Its cathedral church, begun in 1637 when Bishop Juan López Aburto de la Mata moved the bishopric from Coro, is dedicated to the apostle Santiago (Saint James). Its five naves are covered by an arched roof resting on brick pillars; and although each nave in itself is somewhat narrow, as a whole they are beautifully symmetrical. The chancel dome in the transept forms a graceful cupola in the finest of modern architectural styles.

Besides the five naves, four chapels endowed by specific patrons adorn the edifice and, united on the epistle side, form a separate nave. One chapel, dedicated to the Holy Trinity, was built and endowed by the purveyor Pedro de Jaspe Montenegro, native of the kingdom of Galicia, and former regidor of this city. In another there is the image of the Portent of Miracles, San Nicolás de Bari, placed there by Doña Melchora Ana de Tovar, widow of Don Juan de Ascanio y Guerra, knight of the Order of Santiago. The chapel of Nuestra Señora del Pilar de Zaragoza was endowed and ordered built by the *bachiller* Don José Melero, former dean of this cathedral; and that of Nuestra Señora del Pópulo was built by the most illustrious Bishop Don Diego de Baños y Sotomayor, who endowed it with nine thousand three hundred pesos

## CHAPTER VII

and an annual income for a chaplain to serve it. In it, the ashes of this beloved prelate rest beneath his statue, which kneels on the gospel side. In vaulted shape, it was completed by the author of this history, his nephew, who succeeded to its patronage upon the death of the bishop.

On the north side of the principal door, which gives on to the plaza, there is a lofty tower that holds ten sonorous bells; and to the south, the chapel of the apostle San Pedro (Saint Peter) extends above the porch. Built at the expense of this saint's confraternity, it is so spacious that it could stand alone as a church in some places; and it also serves as a chapel for the priests who administer the parish.

The income of this bishopric is not less than ten thousand pesos, and usually reaches twelve or fourteen. The capitular is shared among four prebends and four canonries; the dean is paid two hundred pesos; archdean, precentor, and treasurer one hundred and fifty; and the canons one hundred and thirty, without counting the chaplaincies and choir fees, which are considerable. It has two curate-rectors for the administration of the sacraments, and, to serve the church, a head sacristan, two lesser ones, and eight acolytes, ten choir chaplaincies, six instituted at the erection of the church, two added later, and two endowed with an income of two hundred and twenty-six pesos each by the ensign Pedro de Paredes, mayordomo for many years of the building; a subchanter, chapel master, organist, secretary of the Cabildo, a verger, prompter, and other officials. The divine offices are celebrated regularly with pomp and ritual; and rich damask and silver jewelry are used. Among many valuable ornaments, two opulent monstrances of precious stones are outstanding and cannot be matched by any other church in the Indies.

Elsewhere in the city, there are three chapels for the administration of the parish. One, dedicated to Nuestra Señora de Altagracia, is the seat of a pious society of mulattoes, who attend to its appearance and comfort with exceptional dedication, taking pains to celebrate its feasts with splendor. Another, devoted to San Pablo (Saint Paul), protohermit, also serves as a hospital in which all illnesses are treated. It enjoys an adequate income for assistance to the sick from revenue prescribed for this purpose on the founding of the bishopric. This church was built in 1580 when the city was afflicted by an epidemic of smallpox and measles that destroyed more than half the Indians of the province, and the protohermit was chosen as patron when the contagion ceased through his intercession. In gratitude, the people dedicated this temple to their benefactor; and in memory of his patronage, every year the Cabildo attends the celebration of his feast on January 15. Later, the general treasurer Domingo de Vera and his brother, Diego de Adame, great-grandsons of the conquistador Sebastián Díaz and his wife, Mariana Rodríguez de Ortega, rebuilt it, making it more spacious and adding a beautiful tower. In this church there is a miraculous image of Nuestra Señora de Copacabana, whose benevolence has brought singular marvels to this city. She is particularly effective in inducing rains, nothing more being needed to release floods of water than an appeal to her.

The chapel of Nuestra Señora de la Candelaria, outside the city proper, is a modern building that natives of the Canary Islands built in 1708. They were aided by Licentiate Pedro de Vicuña, a venerable priest; and there they profess their devotion for the one revered on the island of Tenerife.

The Hospital of Charity, where sick women are treated, serves also as a sanctuary for licentious ones whose conduct has been the subject of scandal. It was founded by Doña María Marín de Narváez, a rich and virtuous lady who never married and devoted all her possessions to this pious work.

The Order of Santo Domingo, the first supported by this city, is a part of the province of Santa Cruz de la Española, the oldest in the Indies, and maintains a convent that ordinarily houses forty occupants. The miraculous image of Nuestra Señora del Rosario, a gift from His Majesty, Philip II, is venerated in this church, where she is recognized by all as an efficacious patroness against earthquakes.

The Order of San Francisco consists of fifty religious who clean the temple, participate in the choir and serve as edification for the parishioners. In their convent they preserve as their most precious treasures a piece of the Lignum Crucis (Wood of the Cross), a gift of Governor Martín de Robles Villafañate; and an image of Nuestra Señora de la Soledad, a sculpture of artistry equal to that of the Victoria, so venerated in Madrid. Its tenderness steals the heart and moves one to compassion just to look at it.

The Order of Nuestra Señora de las Mercedes was founded in the year 1638 at a spot remote from the center of the city. General Ruy Fernández de Fuenmayor, governor of the province, whose honored title his grandson, Ruy Fernández de Fuenmayor y Tovar, enjoys today, was its patron. Its isolation brought with it many inconveniences for the religious, however, and they were obliged in the year 1681 to abandon its first site. They moved closer to the city, where its paltry income has caused them to lack conveniences. Nevertheless, sixteen religious maintain it, along with an allied temple, as the best in the city for elegant structure and solid foundation.

For the education of the young, the city has a seminary under the patronage of Santa Rosa de Lima, which the most illustrious Friar Antonio González de Acuña started building on the main plaza in 1664.

## CHAPTER VII

This edifice, finished and perfected later by the most illustrious Bishop Diego de Baños, uncle of the author, is large and has ample living quarters and spacious classrooms for the five professors who teach there. With their two courses in theology, one in philosophy, and two in grammar they cultivate keen minds and nurture the complete individual in both the scholastic and moral sense.

This city's most precious jewel is the convent of nuns of the Concepción. In 1617, Doña Juana de Villela, native of Palos, in the county of Niebla, widow of Captain Lorenzo Martínez, native of Villa-Castín, deceased encomendero of this city; and Doña Mariana de Villela, her daughter, widow of the Regidor Bartolomé de Masabel, applied their entire possessions to building and furnishing it, but because of unexpected events, its founding was delayed until 1637. In that year, Doña Isabel de Tiedra, its first abbess, came from the convent of Santa Clara of the city of Santo Domingo as teacher and administrator of this new institution. Then, on the eve of the Day of Concepción, Bishop Juan López Aburto de la Mata officially cloistered it and gave the habit to the first residents of this house of retreat. They were Doña Mariana de Villela, its founder, and six of her nieces, Doña Francisca Villela, Doña Ana Villela, Doña María Villela, Doña María de Ponte, Doña Juana de Ponte, and Doña Luisa de Ponte; also Doña María de Uruquijo, Doña Inés de Villavicencio, and Doña Elvira de Villavicencio. At present, sixty-two black-veiled nuns are cloistered there and, in continuous vigils, live close to God. At any hour of the night one may hear, on passing by their doors, the sounds of their harsh penitences and tender entreaties.

Besides the temples mentioned, this city has two hermitages. The one commonly called San Mauricio, although its advocation is to San Sebastián, was built by Losada as soon as he founded this city. In fulfillment of a vow he had made while in Villa Rica, he had chosen the Holy Martyr, San Sebastián, as patron against the venom of Indian arrows. Later, in 1574, this city, while suffering a plague of locusts, chose San Mauricio as advocate against them and built a church to him, which through carelessness was burned in 1579. While the temple was being repaired, San Mauricio was placed in the church of San Sebastián, and thus it lost its legitimate advocation, as from then on it was erroneously called San Mauricio. In the Cabildo held on June 13, 1608, the city voted to donate this church to the Order of Santo Domingo, at the request of its provincial, Friar Jacinto de Saona, so that he might move to it the convent of his order, but because of differences of opinion among the clergy, the donation never materialized. Later, in the Cabildo of March 14, 1667, it was conceded to the black brothers of the confraternity of San Juan Bautista, who still care for it with great devotion. The city reserves to itself its patronage, with the stipulation that it retain the advocations of both San Sebastián and San Mauricio, and that both their statues remain on the high altar as patrons of the church. The Cabildo attends services every year on September 22 to celebrate the feast of San Mauricio.

The hermitage of Santa Rosalia de Palermo was built by Bishop Don Diego de Baños y Sotomayor, who designated her as patron and set her day of veneration in 1696. In this way the city expressed its gratitude for her intercession, which freed it from a siege of black vomit from which it had suffered for sixteen continuous months. The illustrious founder of the hermitage left funds to endow the celebration of her feast day each year on the fourth of September in the cathedral. Responsibility for this and other pious works instituted by that venerable prelate lie now with the author of this history who, as his nephew, is its present patron.

# CHAPTER VIII

*A continuation of matters treated in previous chapters; Juan de Salas comes from Margarita to aid Losada; the English sack Coro.*

THE city of Caracas, as well as the entire province, is under the administration of a governor and captain general named by the king for a period of five years. His duties are to dispense royal patronage, present ecclesiastical benefices of the bishopric, and exercise complete authority over income for all governmental functions. For the ordinary distribution of justice, there are two alcaldes, elected by the Cabildo every year. By order of His Majesty Charles II, issued on September 18, 1676, they enjoy the singular privilege of governing the entire province and captaincy general whenever there is a vacancy until His Majesty fills it.[5] Neither the Audiencia nor the president of Santo Domingo may name an interim governor under any pretext. Its Cabildo is composed of twelve councilmen in addition to the four principal officials: chief ensign, head alguacil, provincial of the brotherhood, and general treasurer. These posts are always occupied by the most illustrious gentlemen of the land, who lend authority with their eminence to the public acts essential for a city. Caracas's coat of arms shows a brown bear rampant on a field of silver,

## CHAPTER VIII

holding between its paws a golden shell with the red cross of Santiago; and its seal is a crown with five golden points. His Majesty Philip II conceded these insignia by royal cedula issued in San Lorenzo on September 4, 1591, at the request of Simón de Bolívar, procurator general of this city at Court and its first perpetual regidor.[6]

Throughout the year the fertile soil around the city bears excellent vegetables of all varieties, all fruits native to America and many brought from Europe. It grows delicious pomegranates, quinces, apples, figs, grapes, limes, lemons, cantaloupes and watermelons, all perfect in taste, for the soil favors them as if they had not been transplanted.

Much sugar of good quality is produced, from which exquisite conserves are made, and the pasturage of the area nurtures livestock by the thousands. Added to these advantages is its brisk trade with Nueva España, the Canary Islands, the Windward Islands, and various places where exchanges are made for large quantities of cacao, dried tobacco, brazilwood, and other merchandise.

A few days after Losada had founded the city, Captain Juan de Salas arrived from Margarita in fulfillment of an agreement the two had reached in El Tocuyo. Although several unforeseen events had prevented his coming in time to participate in the first expedition, he wished to honor his promise. His help consisted of four pirogues loaded with urgently needed food, fifteen Spaniards, among whom were Andrés Machado, Melchor López, and Lázaro Vázquez, the latter a veteran of Fajardo's expeditions; and fifteen Guaiqueríes, who served with courage and loyalty in whatever way needed.

As Salas left Margarita, it happened that Melchor López, in charge of one pirogue, captured a coastal cacique, Guaipata, who feigned to be coming in search of items for barter. After his deception had been exposed, the cacique offered everything he owned for his freedom, but Melchor López would not accept, because he wanted to deliver him to Losada for whatever use he might make of him. From this decision originated the first moves toward pacification after this cacique, being treated with Losada's innate affability, was placed at liberty. The governor asked him to try to influence other caciques to accept him as a friend and not to proceed with a war which would force them to concede to arms what they refused to grant peacefully. The grateful Guaipata returned at the end of eight days with two other coastal caciques whom he had persuaded to proffer obedience to Losada and to pledge peace, which they maintained thereafter without any disloyalty.

At the time this accord was reached in the conquest of Caracas, Governor Pedro Ponce de León and Bishop Pedro de Agreda were in Coro. On the night of September 7, a ship of English corsairs anchored in the port and the men, landing at dawn the following day, attacked the city. Finding themselves unprepared for this sudden assault, its residents fled in such haste that they were obliged to hide the bishop in the brush so that he would not be exposed to the disrespect of that infidel rabble. After subduing the city, the corsairs committed heretical sacrileges on the sacred vessels and images of the cathedral. Then, planning to set fire to the buildings, they were deterred only when the residents collected three thousand pesos from those who had escaped. After four days on land, their greed satisfied in part, the corsairs lifted sail and left the city in such destruction that for many years afterward it did not regain its former state.

# CHAPTER IX

*Indians attack the city of Caracas and are easily defeated by Losada.*

GUAICAIPURO, disheartened by his experiences with Losada, awaited an occasion for revenge. Seeing him preoccupied with the town he had just founded, the barbarian determined to shake off his bonds before they could be drawn tighter, and undertook to incite other caciques and their tribes to do the same. Since it was a decision to be made by many, however, it was impossible to convene before the beginning of 1568, at which time it was agreed to resort to force. It was decided that on a certain day, with the largest number of troops each cacique could provide, all would attack Losada, trusting the outcome to this one battle in a siege on Maracapana, a high plain at the foot of the nearby mountains.

When the set day arrived, the caciques Naiguatá, Uripatá, Guaicamacuto, Anarigua, and Mamacuri, later the first to offer obedience to Losada; Querequemare, lord of Torrequemada; Prepocunate, Araguaire, and Guarauguta, who in Catia killed Diego García de Paredes, came from the coast and surrounding sierras and brought with them a total of seven thousand warriors. Aricabacuto and Aramaipuro, with three thousand archers, came from the land of the Mariches, as did the caciques Chacao and Baruta with troops from their towns. Guaicaipuro, captain general in command of the entire army, led two thousand warriors chosen from the most valiant of his Teques, to whom, on the way, two thousand Tarmas under the command of Caciques Paramaconi,

## CHAPTER IX

Urimaure and Parnamacay were added. These two tribes, however, were unable to meet the others at the appointed place because of an unexpected incident, and thus saved the city from a formidable tempest.

Losada, with no hint of what Guaicaipuro was plotting, early that morning had dispatched Pedro Alonso Galeas with sixty men to search the hills and quebradas of the Tarmas' land and bring back to the city all the food they could find. Pedro Alonso and his men were marching diligently to carry out this assignment when, at eight o'clock in the morning, the Teques and Tarmas came upon them unexpectedly. Since the natives surmised that their coalition had been discovered, for our men had come out armed when the Indians had expected to find them off guard in the city, they separated into groups and dispersed in terror throughout the hills.

Pedro Alonso, not knowing the barbarians' purpose in marching, could not decide for a short while whether to attack or wait for them. Finally, though, using experience he had acquired in the conquests of Peru, he led forays without openly declaring battle, seeking out situations in which he would hold the advantage. As if aware of how important it was to divert the troops, he kept them occupied the entire day without permitting them to take a step forward. Then, in fear of what might have happened to the other conspirators, the Indians retired in confusion to their towns.

The other tribes were in Maracapana awaiting the coming of the Teques and Tarmas to assault the city. Seeing that midday had passed and their allies had not yet arrived, however, they began to lose courage and to doubt the success of the venture because Guaicaipuro was not with them. Holding his absence as a presage of disaster, some of the caciques began to wander off with their troops without daring to pursue the enterprise, which they now viewed with distrust. Others considered that it would be demeaning to desist in the conflict, however, and started moving their squadrons toward the city.

Losada, slightly indisposed, was in bed when informed of the horde of barbarians marching toward the city. Without losing his natural calm or altering his conduct in any way, he started to dress and ordered that a horse be saddled for him. When it seemed time to him, he left the city, taking with him the cavalrymen Gabriel de Avila, Francisco Maldonado, Antonio Pérez, an old soldier of the African wars who had been with the emperor at the storming of Tunis; Francisco Sánchez de Córdoba, Sebastián Díaz, Alonso Andrea de Ledesma and Juan de Gámez. Foot soldiers accompanying him were Miguel de Santacruz, Juan Gallegos, Juan de San Juan, Alonso Ruiz Vallejo, Gaspar Pinto and others, up to the number of thirty, leaving the rest to guard the houses so that the Indians could not burn them. Then, calling on Santiago, he attacked the enemy on the plain by opening a path with lances that did not spare a life. Next the foot soldiers, grasping their shields and wielding their steel weapons, began to slice those naked bodies to pieces. The natives, thrown into disorder by their own great number, started a retreat, trampling on one another in an effort to save their lives. Thus, after a short while there remained on the field only one Indian, Tiuna, a native of Curucutí who, carrying a half-sword topped by a shaft of *guaica* cane, repeatedly shouted challenges to Losada.

Francisco Maldonado, unable to bear the Indian's insolence, lowered his lance and pressed his horse forward; but as he started to strike, Tiuna moved his body so skillfully that Maldonado rode the entire length of the field without being able to touch him. Not giving the Spaniard time to reverse his horse, Tiuna thrust at him so violently with the half-sword that it passed through his armor and penetrated his thigh. He then knocked Maldonado from his horse and, repeating the blow before he could rise, wounded him again in the arm. Juan Gallegos, Gaspar Pinto and Juan de San Juan, seeing Maldonado's precarious position and fearing that the barbarian would kill him, rushed to his aid. Tiuna, however, faced the three and began to play the *guaica* with such agility, range and movement that he wounded Juan Gallegos in the forehead, rendering him senseless. Then he made a move to attack Gaspar Pinto, but the blow landed on Juan de San Juan instead, cut through his arm and forced him to release his sword. Tiuna would have gone on to abuse his enemies even more if one of the Indian allies, a servant of Francisco de Madrid, had not hurled an arrow at Tiuna from behind, which passed through his shoulder and pierced his heart. As a slight recompense for their wounds, he left the three soldiers a little golden idol that he had been wearing about his neck, and some bracelets of the same metal. Taking these mementos back as proof of the restraint of the barbarian, the Spaniards accompanied Losada to the city. He did not continue in pursuit of the defeated Indians but consoled himself with the ease with which he had dissolved that powerful conspiracy without putting himself in serious danger.

# CHAPTER X

*The city of Borburata is abandoned; Losada founds Caraballeda and goes out to examine the land.*

THE discomforts that Borburata's residents experienced from unhealthful living conditions and continuous corsair invasions, aggravated by the inadequate defense of its port, made them so eager to move that Governor Pedro Ponce had forbidden such action under threats of severe penalties. Nevertheless, they did abandon the city in mid-1568, some going to live in Valencia but most coming in pirogues and canoes to Caracas to join Losada. He realized that, for the progress of Caracas, it was imperative to establish a port town on the coast in order to stimulate trade and the growth of the new city. Therefore, with the reinforcement of the newcomers and the men whom Juan de Salas had brought from Margarita, Losada took sixty men down to the coast to seek the best place for its founding. There, he established peace with the caciques Mamacuri, Guaicamacuto and others who, having learned a lesson from defeat, offered their services voluntarily. Since the best choice seemed to be the spot where Fajardo had founded El Collado, seven leagues from the city of Caracas, Losada, on September 8, 1568, established a settlement which he named Nuestra Señora de Caraballeda. Selecting thirty of his companions to remain there, he named as regidores Gaspar Pinto, Duarte de Acosta, Alonso de Valenzuela, and Lázaro Vázquez; and they, in turn, chose as first general alcaldes Andrés Machado and Agustín de Acona. This city was soon abandoned, however, because of violent and illogical attempts by Governor Luis de Rojas to mortify its occupants. Thus, the foundations on which it had started ultimately were destroyed as its inhabitants withdrew to escape the rigors of an absolute power.

After Losada returned from Caraballeda to Caracas, he considered it time to remunerate those who had accompanied him on his conquest by distributing encomiendas through authority he held from Governor Pedro Ponce. Since the matter was of such great consequence, he needed specific knowledge of the caciques and their tribes with the number of vassals in each so that the allotments would correspond to the merits of individual recipients. To determine these details, he went with seventy men throughout the land, observing as much as possible in the time set. Beginning with the province of the Teques, he halted on a hill later to be called Loma de los Caballos (Hill of the Horses) because of the large number of horses killed there by the Indians.

Cacique Anequemocane, who lived in that region, feigning to be distressed by war, sent vassals every day with gifts of food for Losada. With this pretext they entered the camp freely, leaving their arms hidden. On departing, however, if they found the Spaniards unobservant, they shot arrows at the horses in the field, hiding their actions so skillfully that six days passed without their treachery being suspected. As Losada stumbled by accident onto the evidence and did not wish to leave the evil deed unpunished, he prepared an ambush near the feed storage bin.

The next day, Cacique Anequemocane himself, in disguise, accompanied by eight companions, came bearing hens, avocados and yams; and, after the presentation ceremonies, they all confidently left the camp. As no one was in sight when they came to the field where the horses grazed, they began shooting the animals. At this, the Spaniards came out of ambush attacking, and Anequemocane fled with such speed that, although Juan Catalán split the cacique's helmet with a knife blow, it did not prevent his escape. During his entire life, however, he never forgot this event, for, deprived of rank and helmet, he was assigned in encomienda by Losada to Lázaro Vázquez, whom he abjectly served for many years.

His eight companions, following the example of their cacique, ran for the woods hoping to hide by climbing into the trees. Discovered by our men, however, the natives' obstinance was such that, unwilling to surrender, although assured of their lives, they resorted to arrows, shooting the entire supply in their quivers from above. When all had been used, in desperation they pulled out from their own bodies those the Spaniards' Indian allies had fired from below. They placed them in their bows with pieces of flesh still clinging to the tips and fired them again on their original owners. The Spaniards, appalled at such barbarity, at length brought them down with bullets, impaled them and left their corpses on the hill as a lesson in terror for others.

## CHAPTER XI

*Losada continues his exploration and arrives at Salamanca; after crossing the province of the Mariches, he returns to the city.*

LOSADA, after spending eight days on Loma de los Caballos, lifted camp to explore the entire province of the Teques, and arrived at nightfall at another high, clean hill. It was dotted by several abandoned villages, one of which was the town of Guayauta, who had been captured by the Spaniards in the skirmish in which Diego de Paredes was killed. He had remained with Losada for more than a year, but now with the governor's permission had returned to his own land, carrying a deep-rooted hatred against our people in his heart. In spite of the kindness received from the Spaniards, as soon as he learned that Losada was coming to his town, he decided to make use of military tricks which, like a house thief, he had observed among our men. Knowing that the first supply an army looks for is water, he hid the Indians in an ambush which he had established on the banks of an arroyo that ran alongside a hill. Since our soldiers had arrived thirsty from the extreme heat, Alonso Quintano, Pedro Serrato, and Diego Méndez rushed for the arroyo. Disaster struck quickly as Serrato, pierced through the chest, and Méndez through the entrails by poisoned arrows, both fell dead, raging from the strength of the venom. Alonso Quintano quickly knelt to the ground, compressed his body as much as possible, and covered himself with his shield against the rain of arrows until the other Spaniards arrived, whereupon the Indians retreated.

Losada, grieving for the death of his soldiers, sought revenge by ordering Jerónimo de Tovar with forty men to take ambush that same night at a crossing formed by two roads. There, Tovar arranged his men skillfully so that, by occupying the entrance to all four paths, they could block passage by whichever one the Indians attempted to make their attack. At dawn the following day, the Spaniards discovered that five hundred warriors had halted at the ambush. Our men, hidden as well as possible, allowed the natives to persist so they could be captured easily. Then, seeing that up to fifty were already in a spot from which they could not escape, Tovar gave the signal to attack. The Spaniards assaulted so suddenly that only by his exceptional speed did one cacique, Popuere, escape with his life; and even so, he had one shoulder split by a knife blow from Miguel de Santacruz. In order to frighten the main body of warriors, the forty-nine remaining Indians of the small group were slashed to pieces. Then all the others, although they had at first so boldly tried to defend themselves, retreated in terror.

Losada, satisfied with this demonstration in punishment, moved on through that territory which Juan Rodríguez had named Salamanca. He entered the Valley of Los Locos (Madmen) and arrived at some deserted towns that he called Estaqueros, because of the many poison-tipped stakes with which the roads had been laced. The natives had withdrawn hurriedly without taking time to put their scant treasures in a safe place, leaving their houses open to the free will of the invaders. Eight of our men entered a hut to pillage, and there on the fire they found a pot of yams and chunks of meat. In order not to miss the banquet they had found prepared, they enthusiastically seated themselves and were savoring the contents of the pot as if it had been the best of stews when one of them pulled out some fingers with nails, and a piece of skin from which one ear dangled. Knowing by this evidence that what they had eaten was human flesh, so great was their revulsion that, nauseated and sweating, they vomited what they had just enjoyed.

Among Losada's soldiers was Francisco Guerrero, a native of Baeza in Andalusia who, at the age of more than sixty, was renowned for the unusual events of his varied life. He had been a captive in Constantinople for twenty-three years, where, oppressed by his slavery and hoping to find a way out, he had denied his faith. Later, however, he sought alleviation for his tormented conscience by taking his leave on a galley of Turks off the shores of Calcedonia in the company of other Christians. Using his skill in speaking the Arabic language and feigning that he was going on a journey to Navarino, he passed through the Dardanelles to Rome, where he, deeply repentant, was reconciled with the Church. He had been in the assault at Rhodes and the formidable siege of Vienna as a mercenary in the armies of Soliman, the Turk, where he never used any defensive arms other than an old satin tunic. Although he took part in many battles and encounters in Asia, Europe and America, he was never wounded except when his captain, Diego de Montes, compelled him to wear an armored tunic, and on that day he was crippled forever by an arrow which struck him in the leg.

After Losada left the Estaqueros and entered the province of the Mariches, this same Francisco Guerrero, on passing through the town of Cacique Tapiaracay, abandoned like the rest, saw some chickens in a house. Accompanied only by a Spanish-speaking Indian servant, he remained there leisurely trying to catch the fowls and pillaging the house as his companions, not noting his absence, passed on to the Valley of

Noroguto. The Indians of Estaqueros, having retired to the brush from which they could watch, saw that one Spaniard remained alone in the town, and at once considered the prey as assured. More than two hundred went out determined to capture him alive, but Guerrero, who carried a musket and a small pocket pistol, faced them with the two firearms. As he was shooting one, his Indian servant loaded the other, in which manner, without allowing the barbarians to draw near, he killed five and was able to reach safety. He arrived that night at Noroguto to the amazement of all, who, on learning that he was missing, had judged him dead. Losada left this valley without any other incident of note, crossed the province of the Mariches, and returned to the city after thirty-two days spent on expedition.

# CHAPTER XII

*Losada decides to seize Guaicaipuro; he sends Francisco Infante to execute the order; the barbarian withdraws and loses his life fighting.*

LOSADA was disconsolate after he returned to the city, for he had recognized from the fractious nature of the Indians that his conquest was still in its initial stages, even after a year and a half of constant effort. If he sought peace with the caciques, past events had taught him that they were no longer consistently steadfast; and if he resorted to bellicose means, he found that these operations were so impractical as to make the outcome unpredictable. The Indians, favored by the rugged land, could not be subdued because of the ease with which they fled to the woods and avoided facing the enemy except when they knew the advantage was theirs.

Cacique Guaicaipuro gloried in the fact that his bravery had been sufficient to oblige Francisco Fajardo to abandon the two cities he had founded in the province. He also prized highly the tenacity with which he had resisted, and in the end killed, a captain of such renown as Juan Rodríguez Suárez. In addition, he could boast of the rout inflicted on Luis de Narváez and his men when, on the Hill of Terepaima, they were subjected to the blades of the Indians' macanas. The unbroken course of his success had raised this cacique to so high a level of esteem that all the neighboring tribes were obedient to his will. He inspired them to persevere in their defense and offered his protection in maintaining their freedom against Spanish dominion and gaining credence as being invincible.

Losada, aware of these designs, considered that so long as Guaicaipuro lived, the conquest would be extremely difficult. He determined to seize him, dead or alive, but in order better to justify his actions, he proceeded against him by a juridical route, bringing suit for his crimes and rebellions, if such names may be given to natural attempts at defense. Issuing an order for his capture, Losada entrusted to Alcalde Francisco Infante the task of going with faithful guides to the place where Guaicaipuro was hiding. Infante left the city with eighty men one afternoon at sunset and traveled until midnight to Guaicaipuro's village, five miles distant, and there he occupied the height of a sierra on whose foothills lay the town which served as Guaicaipuro's retreat. Since Infante felt that a means of withdrawal was needed against any unforeseen event, he remained with twenty-five men in reserve, and turned the rest over to Sancho del Villar to carry out the seizure.

The rumor of the many riches that Guaicaipuro had hidden was widespread, and each Spaniard was determined to be first in the pillage. Fernando de la Cerda, Francisco Sánchez de Córdova, Melchor Gallegos, Bartolomé Rodríguez and Juan de Gámez pushed to the forefront and reached Guaicaipuro's dwelling, but hearing noise and turmoil within, they did not dare enter. To assure the catch, they waited until the other soldiers arrived so that some might surround the dwelling while the rest attempted to occupy it. However, Guaicaipuro brandished a sword seven handbreadths long that had belonged to Juan Rodríguez and, aided by twenty-two archers, defended the entrance so effectively that all those who tried to storm it fell back badly wounded.

At the noise of the fighting, the whole town rushed to their cacique's aid, wielding their macanas and risking their lives. As most of them perished, there was much lamenting and confusion until our soldiers, weary of the barbarian's defense, threw a fire bomb into his house. While it began to spread, Guaicaipuro saw that by remaining inside he might perish in the voracious flames, and held it preferable to die among his enemies. He therefore went to the door with his estoc in hand,[7] and assailed Juan de Gámez by piercing him through the arm and shoulder. Flashing sparks of anger, Guaicaipuro shouted: "Ay, Spanish cowards! Because you lack courage to force me to surrender, you use fire to defeat me. I am the one you seek, Guaicaipuro, who never feared your haughty race. Since I am now in this position, though, kill me and through my death be free of the terror I inspire in you." He then threw himself into the midst of our men, desperately stabbing with his estoc, and there he and twenty-two other warriors lost their lives from Spanish swords.

This was the end of Cacique Guaicaipuro, whose victories rose to the heights but his joy in them was lost in his supreme moment when he thought the wheel of fortune was under his control. He was a barbarian of truly warlike spirit in whom the qualities of a famous leader were united, and it seemed that he should have been able to dictate a happy conclusion. His name was so formidable that even after death his presence instilled fear; and our men, in spite of having won the victory, were thrown into disorder on seeing his cold cadaver. They retired hastily to join Francisco Infante on the summit of the hill, and from there, after recovering from their fright, they turned back toward the city.

# CHAPTER XIII

*The Mariches attempt, under the guise of feigned peace, to assault the city of Caracas; their treachery is discovered and those implicated are impaled for the crime.*

SEVERAL days after the death of Cacique Guaicaipuro at the beginning of 1569, the Mariches learned that Losada had made allotments of Indians, designating the encomendero whom each individual was to serve and imposing work stints in the mines. Using the pretext of recognizing vassalage to their new masters, up to five hundred warriors, divided into groups so as not to look suspect, went to the city under cover of a feigned peace. They entered houses with offerings to palliate betrayal, and manifested their desire to be free of war in order to enjoy the peace they so much loved. This, they explained, was each one's motive in asking whom he was to serve so he could begin at once to treat him as master.

It was the desire of these barbarians, according to evidence from legal action later instigated against them, to make our men feel secure in the familiarity of their presence. Then, seeing them off guard, they would try by night to hide from them their arms and horses' bridles so they would offer no resistance to the attack. Either because this plan, being the decision of many, could not remain hidden, however, or because the conspiracy never had a strong foundation, the residents became suspicious at seeing so many people gathered together at once. The rumor of the risk that threatened took on such body that in even the most casual action of the Indians the Spaniards found circumstances to confirm it as certain. Wishing to stop the harm before it occurred, they hastened to Losada for him to punish the treason they judged evident. He recognized, though, how little justification the matter had, since it was founded only on the weakness engendered by fear. Governed by prudence born of experience, he commissioned the alcaldes ordinarios to initiate an investigation by juridical means.

Pedro Ponce de León and Martín Fernández de Antequera, those officials at that time, examined the witnesses, took depositions, and reached an indictment, whether with or without justification. The crime, they considered, warranted placing the twenty-three caciques and captains who appeared to be most culpable in prison and, without more charges, defense, or discussion, they were condemned to death at once. The Spaniards, forgetting both their obligations as Catholics and their human feelings, turned the prisoners over to the Indian allies and servants for execution. The method of death was so atrocious that only barbarians could have devised it. It consisted of thrusting into the lower part of the victims' torsos sharply-pointed wooden stakes which split the intestines and then came out through the brain. The caciques and captains suffered this martyrdom without any show of weakness, calling on their heaven to judge them innocent and undeserving of such appalling torture.

On this occasion there occurred an example worthy of being engraved in marble in the archives of time as a norm of the extent to which loyalty can reach. When Cuaricurián, a vassal of Cacique Chicuramay, learned that his master was one of the twenty-three destined for death and that he was even then being led to the scaffold, he wished to make a demonstration of his devotion. Going out toward the executioners, he said: "Wait a moment so that you will not through error take the life of an innocent person. You have been ordered to kill Chicuramay; but since I committed the crime, as you call it, and confess to it openly, give me death and set at liberty one who has not given any reason to be executed." Thus, sacrificing his own life to save that of his prince, he submitted to the torture; and the executioners, thinking that what he said was true, impaled him like the others, leaving Chicuramay free to withdraw to the mountains with the rest of his vassals. There his penalty would be tolerable, for in his retreat he might never again hear mention of the Spaniards.

## CHAPTER XIV

*On complaints of Francisco Infante, the governor revokes the powers he had given Losada; the latter abandons the conquest of Caracas; he dies in El Tocuyo.*

THE belief among officials that the art of governing is extremely difficult is lent credence by the history of Diego de Losada. Although his actions, in accord with his natural prudence, never exceeded the limits of justified moderation, they still spawned envy in some, principally Francisco Infante. With him, from the beginning of the conquest, disagreeable aspects had arisen, at first in secret complaints; but later, gossip and irresponsible stories were added until the point of openly declared resentment was reached. Since in the distribution of encomiendas each conquistador considered that his merits deserved the most substantial reward, the judgments that Losada made did not satisfy everyone, and many felt slighted by the recompense. This vexation was further fomented by Francisco Infante until it broke out in public demonstrations of dissatisfaction, the colonists being divided into factions by enmity and discord.

Francisco Infante knew well that his following could not prevail while Losada held his position as superior, and that to defy him openly would be to expose himself and his men to continued rebuff. Thus, he resolved to present before the governor a detailed list of Losada's actions; but to do so, he had to cross the Hill of Terepaima by night, accompanied only by the curate Baltasar García, Domingo Jiral and Francisco Román Coscorrilla. He left the city at nightfall and, proceeding with much secrecy, reached Las Lagunillas Mountain; but he lost his sense of direction in the darkness and found himself unable to locate the road. The danger to their lives being evident if dawn should come before they succeeded in crossing the hill, Infante asked Heaven's favor and commended himself to the Holy Virgin. Then, aided either by a miracle or by chance, he saw at something like fifteen paces before him a bird with the build and appearance of a large duck; and from it a resplendent light, sparkling like a torch, showed him the path and guided him out of danger. This miracle, accredited by tradition and Indian tales of there being at that place a nocturnal bird endowed by nature with the property of emitting rays of light, occurred on what is today a road so heavily traveled that no one has ever seen it. The same attribute may be observed in *cocuyos* (fireflies), as they are called in the Indies. Also, about twenty years ago there was seen in this city a piece of wood that the river Guaire had cast onto its banks during a flood and which by night, or even on a dark day, shone radiantly as if it were in flames. Since Providence gave this quality to a vegetal product, it might also be expected in a living, sentient being.

Francisco Infante and his companions, at the first rays of the sun, reached the banks of the Tuy, where up to sixty Arbacos warriors came down from the hill in pursuit. It seemed to them that, since the Spaniards were only four, they could easily be taken alive; but Infante, in order not to reveal any sign of weakness, turned to face the enemy. He and Francisco Román stopped their horses, waiting for the Indians to come close enough to assault; but Domingo Jiral, wishing to be unencumbered and master of his actions, dismounted to fight on foot. In this formation, the three Spaniards on horseback went at the Arbacos with such skill and speed that in a brief time they left seventeen dead and forced the rest to withdraw to the canebrakes on the banks of the river. Although Domingo Jiral, still on foot, wanted to follow them, he desisted after the first step because he struck a bog where, in order to extricate himself, he had to leave his alpargatas. In addition, he was called by his companions to help them, as they had been cut off by another group of barbarians attacking from the rear.

After Francisco Infante realized that an outstanding warrior, his head adorned by a crown of feathers, was their commander, he struck him through the chest with a lance. As he fell dead, the other Indians, uttering confused cries, retrieved the body and fled, leaving the field free to the Spaniards. From there they went on to the plains of Guaracarima, and without hindrance continued to Barquisimeto to set forth their complaints to Governor Pedro Ponce. As these allegations were dictated by Francisco Infante's enmity against Losada, the calumnies mounted so high that even the most justifiable actions were represented as enormous crimes. Also, since this report was effectively exaggerated by Francisco Infante and supported by the curate Baltasar García's ill will, the governor made a decision so inopportune and rash as to place the future of Caracas in jeopardy. With no more basis than that inflamed account, he revoked the powers he had given Losada, deprived him of his post as lieutenant governor and ordered that his own son, Francisco Ponce, govern in Losada's place and continue the conquest.

Losada was shocked to receive this news, for he could never have persuaded himself that his long services and illustrious blood would be so little regarded by the governor that he would allow his lieutenant governor's rivals to injure him in the sensitive matter of credence and honor. Taking whatever time he could to recover from his distress,

## CHAPTER XIV

however, Losada obeyed the order and turned over the staff of office to Francisco Ponce. He then left Caracas, accompanied by the most proficient of his adherents who, unwilling to serve under any other hand or accept the grievance done their general, abandoned the conquest, retiring to live in other cities of the province. This action left the two new cities of Caracas and Caraballeda so debilitated that they would have been deserted if help had not reached them.

Losada did not wish at that time to see the governor, so as not to risk being disrespectful to his superior. Thus, without entering Barquisimeto he passed on to El Tocuyo, where he hoped to assuage his disappointment; but he did not foresee that his official rebuff could affect his spirits so greatly that he would soon expire. At this outcome, even his adversaries felt remorse.

Losada was a native of the kingdom of Galicia, an illustrious knight, second son of the lord of Río Negro, of noble and affable conduct, circumspect in actions and conversation, and a natural courtier. When he crossed to America, he gave first hints of his valor in the conquests of Paria and Maracapana, where he was campmaster for Governor Sedeño. After the latter's death by poison administered on an expedition to explore the Meta River, Losada was unanimously selected by the soldiers to govern along with Pedro de Reinoso, son of the lord of Autillo, both trustworthy in matters of consequence. After his return to Maracapana he came to this province, where he held the esteem that his signal services merited, for there was no post in which at some time he did not serve. With Alonso Pérez de Tolosa he took part as campmaster in the discovery of the Sierras Nevadas and the Lomas del Viento. Against the rebellion of the black Miguel he was named general by the Cabildos, and the rout of the rebel army and death of that tyrant were credited to Losada. In the conquest of Caracas and the founding of its cities, he attained what other captains of great renown had been unable to gain. Almost at the same time as the death of Losada in El Tocuyo, Pedro Ponce de León died of dysentery in Barquisimeto,[8] leaving the government to each alcalde ordinario in his own district until such time as the Audiencia de Santo Domingo should make a more suitable arrangement.

# BOOK VI

## CHAPTER I

*Pedro de Silva contracts for the conquest of El Dorado; he arrives with his armada at the port of Borburata, and starts his exploration of the Llanos.*

In 1566 Captain Martín de Proveda and his troops left Chachapoyas in the kingdom of Peru to explore and conquer new lands. He crossed the cordillera of the Andes and entered the immense open sea of the Llanos, traveling always toward the north, where they suffered so severely from hunger, illness and other travails that most of them died. So that all would not perish, he turned west toward the sierras and came out through San Juan de los Llanos to the city of Bogotá. This journey bore no fruits other than information from some Llanos savages that by traveling more to the north by the same route, he would find densely populated provinces, so rich that the houses were decorated with gold and a thousand magnificent adornments. Their reports were replete with other lies designed to induce the Spaniards to pass out of their lands as soon as possible.

On reaching Bogotá, Proveda spread stories in such extravagant praise of these provinces that they created a considerable stir, everyone feeling certain that the hour of the discovery of El Dorado was at hand. Adelantado Gonzalo Jiménez de Quesada, ambitious for more fame than he had already acquired in the Nuevo Reino, immediately contracted with the Audiencia de Santa Fe de Bogotá for the conquest and settlement of that opulent land. He suffered imponderable difficulties there, however, with no outcome other than his own destruction.

One of the soldiers accompanying Proveda was Pedro Malaver de Silva, a man of vast wealth and noble spirit, a knight of Estremadura and native of Jerez who had married in Chachapoyas. Don Pedro imagined from information acquired in the Llanos that he already held in his hands those great riches for which the Spaniards were led to their ruin by the alluring name of El Dorado. He consequently decided in 1568 to go to Castile to solicit from the king this conquest to which his evil star led him, with no result other than the loss of his life.

## CHAPTER I

The king readily appointed Don Pedro adelantado of the lands of the Omeguas and Quinacos for a distance of three hundred leagues, the territory to be called Nueva Estremadura. He was granted in Aranjuez on May 15, 1568, the governorship for two lives of all that he might settle within an area of twenty-five square leagues, including its Indian inhabitants, with free choice of site. The post of alguacil mayor of the chancery, in case one should be founded, perpetual to his house, and many other favors, both honorary and practical, were also conferred. On that same day orders were given to Diego Fernández de Serpa for the conquest of Guayana and Guara, with three hundred additional leagues of jurisdiction, the territory to be named Nueva Andalucía. To avoid differences between those two generals over the limits of their grants, the Council declared that the three hundred leagues conceded to Diego de Serpa should begin at Boca de los Dragos and go south along the Orinoco River, and that where these lands ended those of Pedro de Silva should begin.

The two then started to raise men for their explorations, Serpa in Castile, and Silva in Estremadura and La Mancha. Among the six hundred men whom Don Pedro recruited within a few days were many who were noble and outstanding, especially two brothers from Alcántara, Diego and Alonso Bravo Hidalgo. The latter, brought up by Prince Ruy Gómez, was at once named campmaster by Don Pedro. Both were well-to-do young men who saw that Don Pedro lacked means for equipping the expedition and lent him one thousand ducats, to be repaid with better fortune. With this and funds gathered from the soldiers, the adelantado was able to provide the essential supplies.

Now ready for departure, the two commanders were in Seville when first news of the Moorish uprising in Granada reached that city. Don Pedro, fearing that his men might be conscripted for the pressing needs of the king, hastily embarked with them and sailed down to San Lúcar de Barrameda. Serpa, however, not having been forewarned, had to return to Court because his men had been withheld, and he was delayed for more than three months, presenting petitions that they be released to him. Don Pedro, in two ships that he had held ready in San Lúcar, lifted sail without any difficulties on March 19, 1569, and arrived with good weather soon afterward at the island of Tenerife. There he had to buy another ship in the port of Santa Cruz because the first two were too narrow for comfort. They left Tenerife in mid-April and anchored at Margarita with no mishaps at the end of May. There, the captains and principal leaders of the armada met in council in the ceiba-shaded plaza with the most responsible residents of the island, who had come at Don Pedro's invitation. After expounding his reasons for making preparations for war, he asked them to advise him on the best place in which to begin his conquest. All held that it should be Maracapana, where there was a small settlement of Spaniards which could serve as a safe refuge for the women they had brought and provide at little cost the cattle and beasts of burden needed to transport equipment.

Don Pedro was tenacious in his desire to begin exploration by way of Borburata and the plains of that province, and was not pleased with the advice of the men of Margarita. Rising to his feet, his disapproval manifest, he said: "You advise this, not because it is beneficial to me, but to have the opportunity to sell me your cattle and supplies." To this a man named Salas, more than seventy years old, said: "We only sought your advantage. Wealth will not come to us from the transaction. Without it we have sustained our families honorably from the time we first conquered these lands, and though you may not believe me, time will prove this truth very costly for you." Fingering his venerable beard, he turned toward Don Pedro's captains and said: "By these gray hairs, you will all lose if you follow your general's opinion." The Margarita residents then left Don Pedro alone with his campmaster and captains, who earnestly tried to convince him to take the counsel offered. It was acknowledged to be founded on reason, for by leaving the women and children in Maracapana they could begin the conquest at their convenience. Don Pedro was so inflexible in his resolution to enter by Borburata, however, that the campmaster, in exasperation, said: "I question whether these officers and men will place their lives in such evident risk solely to please Your Lordship." To this, Don Pedro shouted in rage: "If you fear it so much, I give you and all other cowards leave to remain here."

This permission was accepted by the campmaster and one hundred and fifty soldiers who foresaw the fatal end that such obstinacy promised. While they remained in Margarita, Don Pedro set sail the following day and with favorable weather arrived at Borburata, from where he sent the ships back to Spain. He went on with the men to Valencia, and in that brief transit of seven leagues they had a foretaste of future adversities. Discontented with both the expedition and Don Pedro's harsh nature, they began to break away, some drifting toward Barquisimeto and El Tocuyo, others hiding on the estates of residents of Valencia. The ones who remained in that city were primarily those with wives and children, whom the settlers gladly received and concealed, moved to compassion at seeing them exposed to hunger and need.

Six days after Don Pedro had left for Borburata, the campmaster Alonso Bravo and his brother Diego, who had remained in Margarita, embarked on a ship for Cartagena, accompanied by the soldiers who wished to follow them. Touching Borburata on the way, they found a quantity of clothing from Castile and jars of wine which Don Pedro had left with thirty soldiers to guard it. So as not to lose this opportunity to be repaid the thousand ducats they had lent him in Spain, they seized enough wine to satisfy the debt, and took with them some of the soldiers who had remained to watch over it, as they continued their journey to Cartagena.

Those who were still in the port at once sent word to Don Pedro of his loss and he, angered by the hoax Alonso Bravo had played on him, returned to Borburata. There he made a juridical report of the case and sentenced the two brothers to death for rebellion, thus compensating for the indignity suffered. He had the remaining merchandise transported to Valencia, and, seeing that his troops were diminishing by the minute, made every effort to depart as quickly as possible. Although he had brought six hundred men from Spain, he now had only one hundred and forty, but he left Valencia with them on July 2, 1569, and entered the Llanos.

## CHAPTER II

*Garci-González comes with eighty men to aid the city of Caracas; the Caribs descend upon Caraballeda but, after losses owing to resistance there, they withdraw.*

At the time of Pedro de Silva's arrival at Borburata with his armada, the residents of the two cities of Caracas and Caraballeda were experiencing serious dissensions. All of Diego de Losada's faction, irate at the governor for revoking their leader's powers because of Francisco Infante's complaints, left the province with Losada when he abandoned his conquest. So few remained that they could scarcely stay in their towns because of Indian terrorism. The alcaldes ordinarios heard of Losada's group from Pedro de Silva's armada, who had scattered throughout Valencia and its neighboring area, and they learned that Don Pedro's nephew, Captain Garci-González de Silva, was among them. Displeased with his uncle for his insufferably harsh nature, he would not follow him although he had come originally as his ensign. He received a letter describing the extreme necessity of the residents and stressing the great service that Garci-González would be doing if, mustering as many as possible of his uncle's former troops, he would come to help them. They added that they now had reached such pressing straits that they would have to abandon that which had already been conquered if they were not aided.

Garci-González had longed for an occasion to display his invincible nature, and decided at once to undertake the mission. He was confident of being able to provide help because of the respect and love with which his uncle's soldiers would look upon him. He was not disappointed in this concept, for after his intention was announced, eighty men, all from Estremadura and most of them sons of Mérida, his home city, offered to follow him. With them he marched to the Valley of Mariara, where he found Gabriel de Avila with fifteen horsemen waiting to escort him into the city, which they soon reached without incident.

During the interval of Avila's journey to convoy this help, the coast to the windward of Caraballeda was inundated by fourteen pirogues of Carib Indians from the island of Grenada. With their accustomed ferocity they went destroying with blood and fire everything before them, satiating their bestial appetite with the flesh of the Indians they were able to capture in the ports. Their primary aim was to assault Caraballeda, and although the few Spaniards residing there at that time were informed by some Indian allies of the Caribs' proximity, they gave scant credence to the warning, doing nothing more than station a sentinel.

The Caribs had disembarked three hundred warriors that night so they could assault the city at daybreak at the same time as the pirogues attacked the port. Marching to carry out their plan, they were heard by the sentinel but were already so close that he could only utter a few frightened cries. He rushed into the city and sounded the alarm as the rumble of the skirmish reverberated from all directions, causing the Spaniards, who finally recognized their negligence, to grasp their arms and face the danger. Taking advantage of the confusion with which the barbarians were diverted to pillage and capture servants, the Spaniards were able to unite the twenty men of the city in an attack on the Caribs, slashing all within reach with their swords. This assault was reinforced by the more than manly strength of a woman named Leonor de Cáceres, who, reviving memories of Tomyris and Zenobia,[1] grasped a shield and brandished a macana wrested from the hands of a Carib, with which she performed marvels.

The Indians considered themselves lost at the sight of such bold opposition, and, realizing that their most valiant warriors were now dead, they began to retire toward the shore to seek the protection of their pirogues. In the confusion of the flight, Gaspar Tomás saw Duarte de Acosta's wife being held captive in the arms of a barbarian as she begged the favor of Heaven. With no more aim than chance afforded, he braced his harquebus against his chest and fired with such luck that he split the native's head, thus sparing the innocent prey her life. The death of this Indian, one of the principal caciques, brought complete victory to the Spaniards as the Caribs rowed their pirogues rapidly out to sea. Later they restored their injured pride by killing the wretched slaves along the beaches during their festivals and drinking bouts, and eating them. This diversion gave a Spaniard, Benito Calvo, captured seven years earlier on the island of Dominica from a fortress built by Pedro Méndez on its coasts, the opportunity to flee during their drunkenness to the city, where he lived several more years.

# CHAPTER III

*Diego de Serpa arrives at the land of the Cumanagotos; he founds the town of Santiago de los Caballeros and attempts to start his conquest, but he and most of his men die at the hands of the Indians.*

AFTER Diego de Serpa had waited three months in Madrid for the restitution of his men who had been commandeered in Seville to help crush the uprising of the Moors of Granada, they were ordered returned to him. With them he marched down to Andalusia, where he hastily reassembled his other soldiers and set sail on three ships waiting in the port of San Lúcar. At the end of 1569, he anchored on the coast of the land of the Cumanagotos, a bellicose and populous tribe whose territory, within the limits of his grant, he had chosen for his first armed engagement. He thus avoided the risks to which his armada would have been exposed if he had entered by Boca de los Dragos.

Don Diego brought with him four hundred chosen men, among them many who had fought in Europe in famous engagements of that time. Since he was accompanied also by a large number of women and children, he founded at the mouth of the Salado River a city which he named Santiago de los Caballeros, and left them there with the necessary settlers to maintain and defend it. He then went out on a campaign with the rest of his men, intending to cross the province toward the south until he discovered the waters of the Orinoco.

The Indians had been observing the Spaniards' movements on the beach ever since Don Diego had dropped anchor, to discover the purpose of their manipulations. After the invaders had established a town and some were trying to go farther inland, the Indians considered the occasion propitious to rout them, since they were divided. They called to their aid the Chacopata tribe, and, having assembled more than ten thousand combatants, they allowed Don Diego to cross the pass of a low mountain until he came out at Comorocuao, three days' journey from the coast. There they confronted him, fatigued by the ordeals of the march, the burning heat, and a raging thirst, for there was a complete lack of water in that entire area. Attacked from all sides and striving to bring credit to himself, Don Diego's bad luck caused his horse to stumble during the first stages of the fight and throw him to the ground. His sergeant major, Martín de Ayala, who had served also in the wars of Lombardy and Piedmont, rushed up at once to help him, but his efforts only brought greater misfortune, as both were slain by the Indians. The warriors, emboldened by seeing our men's distress at this unexpected tragedy, in less than half an hour sent one hundred and eighty-six Spaniards to accompany their general in death.

Four days after Don Diego was killed and his army routed, the few who had been able to escape reached the city of Santiago de los Caballeros, but they were so badly wounded that most of them died soon afterward. Guillermo Loreto, who had been left in charge by Don Diego, surmising that the Indians would next attack the city, made plans to prepare a resistance to the assault. They did not allow him this opportunity, however, but the following day at dawn appeared at the edge of the city.

Although Loreto lacked food and all other essentials, he felt committed to continue the offensive. Not content with resisting the barbarians' attacks for fourteen days, he led his men out of the palisades in search of the enemy throughout the countryside. At this time, Captain Francisco de Cáceres arrived from Margarita with several pirogues full of soldiers. With their aid Loreto terrorized the Indians into becoming somewhat slack in combat, but, recognizing that with Don Diego's death it was impossible either to carry the conquest forward or maintain the city, he resolved to abandon it voluntarily before being obliged to do so with discredit. Embarking the women, children and servants on Cáceres's pirogues, Loreto and a group of soldiers escorted them down the Salado River to the beach. He then withdrew and, with his remaining men, started the march to Cumaná.

This was the end of Diego Fernández de Serpa's expedition. His desire to immortalize his name had led him, a rich citizen of Cartagena, to exchange the conveniences of his retirement there for the anxieties and financial losses with which he destroyed his estate and gained a pitiable death. He left his son, Don García, tied by heritage to his misfortune. Wishing to fulfill the obligations of his father's contract, he spent without profit the vast tributes that were rendered to him as encomendero of the great towns of Turuaco and Cipacua. And in the end he, too, lost his life in the struggle.

# CHAPTER IV

*Garci-González goes out in search of Paramaconi; the Audiencia names Juan de Chaves interim governor;[2] and the Indians of Mamo kill Don Julián de Mendoza.*

THE inhabitants of the city of Caracas, now free of the terrors in which the Indians had held them, and heartened by the assistance that Garci-González de Silva had brought, started at once to exact satisfaction for the distress they had suffered. Since it was Paramaconi, cacique of the Taramainas, from whom they had received the most damage, they decided that he should be the first to experience their revenge. An expedition of thirty men, under command of Garci-González and guided by a Taramainan boy of eleven or twelve years, went out quickly from the city at sunset and traveled until a little after midnight to the towns of Guaremaisen, Parnamacay and Prepocunate, all close neighbors. There, the Indians, in a general gathering of the caciques, were dancing and feasting as well as consulting a demon through the mediation of their wizards, asking advice on what conduct to follow with the Spaniards. Garci-González, however, wishing only to seize the cacique, dead or alive, ordered his men to march forward without stopping to cause any hostility in the towns, even though they could easily have done so, in view of the natives' carefree celebrations.

The cacique had retired in the most rugged part of that wild mountain to a house with two doors, one facing the summit and the other looking out to the valley over some crags, so as always to provide an exit by one side or the other. Garci-González and his men finally arrived halfway up the hill, although with much difficulty because of the jagged rocks and heavily-wooded cliffs. They discovered the house just as Paramaconi was rushing with macana in hand to the door on the cliffside to lead the four wives he had with him to safety. Meanwhile, six warriors armed with bows and arrows faced the intruders at the other door to repel them.

    Garci-González left his men battling the warriors and went around the house to close off the exit to the hillside just as the cacique was coming out of the house. He slashed at the Indian with his sword, but the barbarian, parrying the thrust with his macana at the last moment, struck the Spaniard a heavy blow to the chest. He tumbled backward to the ground, and Paramaconi took advantage of that mishap to lead his wives out to safety and hide them in the brush. Without waiting for his adversary to regain his feet, he hurled himself down over the crags to the valley below. Then Garci-González, either ignorant of the depth of the ravine or incited by his flaming anger, rose swiftly and plunged with sword in hand down the hillside in pursuit of the native. Sorely buffeted by rolling over the stones, he reached level ground, only to find Paramaconi, armed with his macana, awaiting him. Without delaying even to take a breath, they engaged in combat, at times both using weapons and at others their hands. They fought stubbornly until Garci-González wounded the cacique in the right side with a skillful thrust of his sword, at which Paramaconi, bellowing from the pain of the wound, dropped the macana to the ground. Grasping Garci-González in his arms, he attempted to crush him to death; but he soon recognized that he lacked the strength to succeed because of the blood gushing from his side. He therefore turned back toward the mountain in an attempt not to die in sight of the enemy; but before he could withdraw, he was struck by Garci-González with such force that the sword split his left shoulder and ripped his back open down to his waist. At this, the cacique fell to the ground as if dead, and Garci-González, judging this to be true, left him lying there while he tried to find a way back up the hill.

    The precipice was so steep that it would have been almost impossible for Garci-González to ascend had he not been helped by his soldiers. They had missed him after they had killed the six warriors who had been guarding the entrance to the house, and, locating him by his shouts for help, they had come to rescue him from the ravine. Since the only purpose of the expedition had been to punish Paramaconi, they started their return to the city without delay, for they regarded the cacique as dead. This general opinion was strengthened by the deception of the Indians, as the cacique remained hidden during his convalescence. The rumor of his death was so certain that no one doubted it until more than a year had passed, after which the cacique, accompanied by some of the leaders of the Taramaina tribe, entered Caracas seeking peace and offering obedience, which he maintained thereafter until his death. He felt so much devotion and friendship for Garci-González that every time he came to the city he stayed at the Spaniard's house; but as a reminder of his defiance, he carried signs of his wounds, and an arm could have fitted easily into the hole in his back.

At about this time Juan de Chaves, a native of Trujillo in Estremadura, now a resident of Santo Domingo on the island of Hispaniola, arrived in the city, sent there by the Royal Audiencia as interim governor in place of Pedro Ponce de León. Since Coro was designated as his residence, he named Bartolomé García as his representative in the city of Caracas. A few days later, Julián de Mendoza was killed as a result of the resentment felt by caciques Parnamacay, Prepocunate, and the others of the Valley of Mamo (or Huayabas) when Don Julián, as their encomendero, summoned them to work in his fields.

This order was so unfavorably received by those who by nature were accustomed to command, not to serve, that they determined to take his life for the offense. Dissimulating their intention with servile submission, they sent a few Indians to the city to offer obedience to Don Julián in the name of all, and to present to him, in addition to fruits and other edible delicacies of the land, some intricately woven hammocks. Don Julián considered this demonstration an indication of a sincere goodwill and was deeply affected by their deceptive mien. He then asked Bartolomé García's permission to explore the towns and take possession of his encomienda.

He left the city so confident of the Indians' friendship that he carried with him only two soldiers, more for their company than for their assistance.[3] On his arrival at the mouth of the Mamo River, where it empties into the sea, he found all the caciques and principal natives of the valley waiting for him with a display of false peace. Their purpose, however, was not what the exterior revealed, and the festivities with which Don Julián was received gave Prepocunate a chance to seize him by the shoulders. He then struck him such a heavy machete blow from behind that his head was split open down to his eyes and he fell lifeless.

The two companions, seeing Don Julián dead, and belatedly recognizing the Indians' perfidy, took shelter in a house on the banks of the river to delay death a while longer. This move only brought them to an even more piteous end, however, as the Indians set fire to the house, where the Spaniards perished between raging flames and stifling smoke.

The following day, news of this tragedy reached the city from the Indians themselves, and Bartolomé García at once sent Sancho del Villar with forty men to inflict punishment. The Indians, however, had withdrawn to the Anaocopón Mountain at the upper end of the valley and fortified themselves there in such a way that, although Sancho del Villar tried to take it by storm, the site was impregnable. Since the barbarians had the advantage of the rugged land, they were able to kill five Spaniards and gravely wound Pablo Bernáldez, Pedro Vázquez and Diego Vizcaino. Villar was obliged to return to the city with no more advantage than having been able to give burial to Don Julián's cadaver, which he found on the banks of the river, his genitals severed from his body and stuffed into his mouth.

The Indians were so proud of their success that they spurned the shelter of the woods and dared to leave the Valley of San Francisco to kill several servants they found in the fields. Bartolomé García, earnestly desiring to halt such damage before it spread, prepared a second expedition, and named as its commander Francisco de Vides. He experienced the same setbacks as Sancho del Villar, however, and was obliged to return to the city, leaving behind equipment that Parnamacay had won from him. The Indians remained free of Spanish subjection almost at the very gates of Caracas until early in 1570, they acknowledged that their strength was insufficient to oppose Garci-González de Silva. Entrusted by Governor Juan de Chaves with the pacification of that valley, he never took sword in hand that he did not come out victorious, for all that was necessary was for him to appear for the Indians to submit their necks to the yoke of obedience. They had learned from their first resistance, when Prepocunate and more than three hundred warriors had been killed in battle, that the only way to gain peace was to surrender.

# CHAPTER V

*Don Pedro de Silva continues his exploration but, deserted by his troops, he retires to Barquisimeto; he goes to Peru and then to Spain; after his return he is killed by Carib Indians.*

PEDRO Malaver de Silva, exploring the Llanos, traveled southward from Valencia without veering from the cordillera on his right, because the land along this route was drier and freer of mires than others. As the towns along it were few and sparsely populated, however, he immediately began to lack food. At first, he and his men had had hopes of finding improvement farther on, but as they penetrated that fathomless sea of the Llanos, their miseries multiplied; and as they shifted to a lower level

## CHAPTER V

the land, full of quaking bogs and flood-prone flatlands, became uninhabitable. The waters were made foul by excessive heat, and the swarms of mosquitoes and poisonous vermin were incalculable. They had to cross fields where the hay was so coarse that it cut their clothing to pieces, and they were left naked, obliged to cover their bodies to below their knees with deerskins.

These tribulations, added to the aridity of the terrain and the dour disposition of Don Pedro, made the soldiers so dissatisfied that not one followed him willingly. He was aware of their reluctance, but instead of placating them he aggravated them still more by his brusqueness, and refused communication with even his closest friends, observing a strange and intractable seclusion.

They had been traveling five months when Don Pedro, seeking relief from their afflictions, sent Captain Céspedes ahead with thirty men for forty or fifty leagues to determine whether the land promised any hope. They examined the entire region thoroughly, but found nothing except stronger prospects of more severe reverses. After twenty-six days of tribulations, his passage was blocked in all directions by a broad lake, but, recognizing that its depth was not so great as to present difficulty, he forded it in water at times neck-deep. On arriving at the other side, some of the soldiers noticed that the lake, breaking through a fissure in the cordillera, disembogued to the west. This circumstance, examined more carefully by a mestizo who had been added to the troops in Valencia because of his familiarity with the land, gave them reason to believe that those waters would come out quite close to Barquisimeto. Since they all desired to abandon so painful a conquest, and the mestizo offered to lead them to safety, they clamored for Céspedes to protect their lives, which they were risking solely to gratify Don Pedro's obduracy.

Céspedes offered no opposition to the proposal, but before they began the journey across the sierra, they informed Don Pedro of their plan so he would not waste time waiting for them. This letter, written on a piece of majagua bark, said: "Señor governor, weary of traveling without hope of finding better land or more riches than what we have seen until now, we have decided to proceed so as to die among Christians. If Your Lordship wishes to do the same, he is welcome to follow us as we open the way."

They sent this letter by one of Céspedes's Spanish-speaking Indian servants, who, because his wife had remained in the camp, gladly accepted the assignment. The soldiers, even more pleased, pursued their route although severely lacking food, for they had nothing except the wild fruits which the mestizo guide identified as safe. After they crossed the summit of the sierra, they went down barren hills into deep valleys, and in one they foraged at length because they found an arroyo with an abundance of fish, easily caught in their hands.

Don Pedro's anger was extreme when he received the letter. Bursting with rage and avid to punish their daring, he at once sent in pursuit of them one of his captains, Luis de Leiva, a youth of few years but much prudence. He ordered Leiva to hang Céspedes wherever he might find him, persuade the others to obedience, and bring them back. The measure with which Don Pedro attempted to ward off harm, however, only served to hasten his own downfall; for to Don Luis, Céspedes's judgment appeared more acceptable than that of his governor. Consequently, as soon as he felt free, he sent an Indian to inform Don Pedro of his decision to follow Céspedes, advising the governor not to wait for him because he had no thought of ever seeing him again.

Far from expecting such an outcome, Céspedes was casually fishing from the banks of the arroyo when he saw Don Luis and his men coming down the hill. Since at first it was not easy to determine who they were, he hastily called his soldiers to arms. Without paying any heed to the military display, however, Don Luis entered the camp with his men unarmed so that Céspedes might know that their motives were identical. They were so overjoyed to see each other again that past differences were forgotten, and they congratulated each other on their resolve to abandon Don Pedro and free themselves of his surly nature and hapless conquest.

After Don Luis's men had rested beside the arroyo for five days, enjoying the abundance of fish, the two captains decided not to delay their journey any longer. Their mestizo guide, however, confused by having turned a little to the left when he should have kept to the west, lost his sense of direction. After crossing the summit of a high sierra and descending to some vast plains, he had to confess that he did not know the way. He did recognize certain signs, which assured him that Barquisimeto could not be far away, and if they had traveled two leagues more in that direction, they would have come out onto the Royal Highway that runs from that city to Valencia. As the mestizo had now begun to lack confidence in the path they were following, however, he turned a bit farther to the left, which led them after a few days to the banks of a little river. They continued traveling without food other than roots and the hearts of bihai plants, until one afternoon an Italian soldier, going upstream to fish, found some radish leaves and lettuce hanging from a stick that extended across the running stream. Since those greens were of a kind never found among the Indians, he conjectured at once that there was a Spanish town somewhere nearby from which those leaves had come.

## CHAPTER V

With this good news the soldier quickly returned to his companions, who judged at first that Juan Bautista was playing one of his frequent jokes on them, but after examining the leaves in his hands, they were convinced. So as not to delay the discovery of the town any longer, they separated into two groups and started to march up the river within the hour, carefully scrutinizing everything on its banks. They must have traveled a little more than two leagues in this manner when those on the right came across a broad, well-worn path, and on entering it, came out in a brief time onto a plain where they found a cattle ranch belonging to Pedro Velázquez, a resident of Barquisimeto. Hospitably received by its owner, they lingered a while to recover from the calamities that had befallen them, then hastened on their way, unrepentant at having abandoned Don Pedro. He recognized belatedly the state to which his bitter temperament had led on receiving confirmation from Don Luis of his intention to join Céspedes. He realized that the men remaining with him were too few for him to persist in his conquest, and thus, in March of 1570, he decided to return to Barquisimeto before a way out became impossible.

This was the end of Pedro de Silva's expedition in search of El Dorado, this the conclusion of such strenuous effort and waste of money. If he had desisted, he could have avoided the miseries that his destiny was to entail. Still, he had so firmly rooted in his heart the yearning to attain fame, equal to that of Cortés and Pizarro, with the conquest of El Dorado that the ordeals of the first expedition did not deter him. Consequently, a few days after his arrival at Barquisimeto, he departed for Chachapoyas, of which he was a resident, and, selling all he possessed, returned to Spain with the thought that his conquest might succeed along a more moderate route. Fortune misled him in this respect, however, as, supplied anew in San Lúcar with a well-equipped ship and one hundred and sixty men, he undertook an exploration in 1574 along the coast that runs between the Marañón and the Orinoco. There, all perished, some from illness caused by the severe weather, and others, including Don Pedro and two of his young daughters, at the hands of Carib Indians. Only one soldier, Juan Martín de Albújar, was spared their ferocity, to relate the circumstances later. After being a captive for ten years, he came out at the mouth of the Esquino River in the province of the Arbacos, peaceful Indians who had relations with the Spaniards of Margarita. Through them, he succeeded in crossing to that island and later to the mainland, where he resided for several years, leaving branches of his descendancy in the city of Carora.

BOOK VI

# CHAPTER VI

*Alonso Pacheco founds the city of Maracaibo; Cristóbal Cobos and Gaspar Pinto go out to subdue the Chagaragatos; but one dies and the other, having had no success, withdraws.*

IN 1568, Governor Pedro Ponce de León commissioned Captain Alonso Pacheco, a resident of Trujillo, to found a city on Lake Maracaibo. Pacheco accordingly equipped two brigantines that he had had built on the site of Moporo, and circled the shores of the lake; but such was the opposition of the Saparas, Quiriquires, Aliles and Toas that he was unable to gain a hand's span of ground. After waging continuous war for three years to reduce these Indians to obedience, he finally attained his goal by founding on January 20, 1571, the city of Nueva Zamora. It is on the site where Ambrosio de Alfinger had had his camp on the shores of the lake, six leagues from the sandbar where its waters mix with the sea. Generally called Maracaibo, the ancient name for all that area, it is situated barely eleven degrees north of the equator. Its climate is extremely hot, but healthful because so dry; in fact, within twenty leagues going toward the sierra, there is no water other than that laboriously caught in large handmade clay basins. This is used for the livestock that grazes on those barren plains, suitable only for raising beef cattle, sheep and goats. Although the region abounds in all essentials, the lake is so conducive to free trade that the city receives any items that its own terrain fails to produce from Gibraltar, Mérida, Trujillo, Barinas, La Grita, and other nearby towns.

Rich from extensive commerce maintained with Nueva España, Santo Domingo, Cartagena, the Canary Islands, and other overseas provinces, the city has a safe port suitable for shipbuilding, with an abundance of excellent wood in its constantly crowded shipyards. If the Spaniards had known how to make use of the lake, its banks would have been a solid garden, and a kingdom might have been founded on its shores; and if it had not suffered repeated invasions from pirates, it would be one of the finest cities of America. These attacks impeded its growth, but even so, it boasts today more than five hundred inhabitants. Its buildings, all of stone, are light, spacious, and well designed; the parochial church, of modern workmanship, is elegantly built, and its plan well proportioned.

## CHAPTER VI

Here there is a devoutly venerated crucifix brought from Gibraltar when, after the Quiriquires rebelled against the Spaniards in 1600, they sacked and burned that city. With sacrilegious impiety the savages used the cross as a target for their arrows, hitting it six times and leaving blemishes that are still visible. There is an established and widespread tradition that the figure's head, previously lifted, when struck by an arrow above one brow, fell to its chest, the position it retains until this day.

The city maintains a convent of religious of the Order of San Francisco, a hospital under the protection of Santa Ana, and a hermitage, dedicated to San Juan de Dios, which the pious Captain Juan de Andrade built in 1686. In temporal matters the city was subject to the governor of this province until 1678, at which time, at the request of its residents, it was added to the jurisdiction of Mérida. Since it is a seaport and offers better possibilities for progress, governors have resided there from then on. For this reason it was designated as the seat of government and, as such, is the location of the tribunal of accountancy. The ease with which pirates sacked it because the sandbars of the lake were undefended brought about the construction of three forts supplied with artillery and manned by military forces, after which it ranked among the most esteemed cities of the Indies.

While Alonso Pacheco was occupied with settling Nueva Zamora de Maracaibo, the residents of the city of Caracas did not rest, wishing always to perfect their conquest, which they found increasingly difficult because of the Indians' obstinate resistance. They were encouraged, however, by now having subdued the two tribes of Tarmas and Taramainas through the actions of Garci-González. After he obliged Caciques Paramaconi and Parnamacay to render obedience, the Spaniards decided to direct their strength to subjecting the Chagaragatos and the Caracas, who inhabited the sierras halfway between the city and the sea, so that all of the province facing the coast would be subservient. For this purpose, the Cabildos of Caraballeda and Caracas convened, as both were concerned with the feasibility of working toward the total security of their commerce and trade. It was agreed that each should advance at the same time and attack individually, assuring that the corresponding diversion of enemy forces would facilitate the Spaniards' victory.

Gaspar Pinto, in command of the forces from Caraballeda, and Cristóbal Cobos of those from Caracas, gained a degree of success at their initial step, due to the Indians' negligence. The natives, however, recovering from their first fright, harried our troops so greatly that they despaired of effecting pacification while divided, and considered it preferable to form one body of the two camps. Then, with united forces, they could attack Cacique Guaimacuare, who had withdrawn from the coast with four hundred warriors to the most rugged part of the sierra from which he fomented the Indians' resistance.

Our men's decision did not remain hidden from the cacique, either because the Indian allies in our camp informed him or because he was able to surmise it. Thus, although the two captains planned the advance so that by traveling in darkness they might seize the barbarians unaware, they found him so alert that they had not yet penetrated the heart of the mountains when the conch horns sounded the call to arms from all directions. Then Gaspar Pinto, who commanded the vanguard that night, seeing the attack fail because of Guaimacuare's extreme vigilance, hastened the pace of his troops, followed by Cobos and his men. Directed by the low rumbling noise of the horde of Indians, they penetrated farther into the mountains until they came out at a village that served the cacique as a retreat. There, calling on Santiago and firing their harquebuses, they began a heated skirmish; but the obscurity of the night and the shouts and confusion of the struggle did not permit them to determine which side was winning. At the first light of day, however, the Indians began to retreat, but with such recognized advantages that they could claim the victory; for although our men retained possession of the village, it was only at the cost of ten soldiers killed. An added casualty was that Gaspar Pinto received a wound to one leg that appeared slight at first, but the poison-tipped arrow was so effective that his anguish increased and he died within six hours, raging in pain, his flesh falling off in pieces. This fatality cut the cord of the conquest, for Cobos, frightened by the death of his companion, returned to Caracas; and the troops from Caraballeda, seeing themselves alone and without a captain to lead them, likewise withdrew. The natives maintained the same state of rebellion; but later, trade and communication domesticated them, and, as time passed, they were annihilated so that now only a memory of them all and not any single individual survives.

# CHAPTER VII

*Governor Diego de Mazariego arrives in Coro; Captain Salamanca founds the city of Carora; and Pedro Alonso Galeas enters the territory of the Mariches.*

AFTER the death of Pedro Ponce de León, the king sent as governor Diego de Mazariego, who, despite many splendid qualities, because of his advanced age was more suited to relaxing at home than assuming such a post. Nevertheless, he embarked from San Lúcar and in February of 1572 arrived in Coro, where he soon realized that his years would prevent him from efficiently directing alone the affairs of the province. He therefore named as his lieutenant general Diego de Montes, resident of El Tocuyo, who in turn commissioned Captain Juan de Salamanca to settle the provinces of Curarigua and Carora. They lie to the north, between El Tocuyo and Lake Maracaibo, and were at that time inhabited by numerous misguided persons who had come from the Llanos with Pedro de Silva or had been with Diego Fernández de Serpa in the conquest of the Cumanagotos. After announcing the expedition, Salamanca easily enlisted seventy men, among them Alonso Gordon, Juan de Gámez, Benito Domínguez, Alonso Márquez, Domingo Muñoz, Pedro Francisco, Hernando Martín, Garci-López, Juan Pérez, Juan González Franco, Juan Esteban, and others with whom he had left El Tocuyo. He crossed part of the province of Curarigua and arrived at Baraquigua, where, on June 19, 1572, he founded on a hot but healthful plain a city which he named San Juan Bautista del Portillo de Carora. The new town lacked water, however, because the Morere River at times had a weak flow or none at all if the dry season lasted long.

In this region all species of livestock are raised, but goats are most abundant because the many thorns and thistles of the plains make the land suitable for their growth. It also boasts grain as fine as that of Mixteca, balsams so fragrant that those of Arabia do not surpass them, and other aromatic resins that have been proved to be admirable antidotes for treating wounds or preventing convulsions. Though small, its territory supports a parochial church with two priest-rectors and a sacristan. It has a convent of the Order of San Francisco with two or three religious, and a hermitage dedicated to Saint Dionysius Areopagiticus, which was endowed by the women of the town and provided adequate income and substantial chaplaincies.

## BOOK VI

As soon as Governor Mazariego arrived in Coro, he was given a report on the status of the conquest of Caracas. Since he ardently wished to see the struggle concluded quickly, he named as his lieutenant there Francisco Calderón, resident of Santo Domingo, who already had been acting in this capacity. Calderón tried to bring force at once to subdue the Mariches but they, having retired into the brush, had scorned communication with the Spaniards since Pedro Ponce and Martín Fernández de Antequera had committed the atrocity of impaling their caciques.

To lead the expedition, Calderón named Pedro Alonso Galeas, a practical soldier experienced in the wars of the Indies. This same task had been proposed to him in 1570 by Lieutenant Bartolomé García, but Pedro Alonso, having offered his services to Garci-González that year in the Valley of the Huayabas, could not accept the assignment at that time. Now, however, inspired by the new mission, he left Caracas around the end of 1572 with eighty Spaniards, Cacique Aricabacuto and some of his vassals. This cacique urgently desired to see the Mariches accept Spanish domination for, as a friend of ours with his town immediately adjoining the land of the offending tribe, he sought the protection of Spanish arms.

For this purpose, having voluntarily offered not only to follow Pedro Alonso but to serve as his guide, Aricabacuto led him to the center of the province; but as the local Indians had been terrified, the invaders found every town deserted. Finally, however, Garci-González de Silva went out one night with thirty men on Pedro Alonso's order to reconnoiter a quebrada, and came across almost two hundred women and children whom the men of Guayana had hidden in a thicket for security. The Spaniards tried to seize the natives but were so hampered by the confusion that some escaped. These, in turn, warned others who had gathered not far from the quebrada and, before our men had time to complete the capture, they were attacked in the valley by more than three hundred warriors commanded by Cacique Tamanaco. Incensed at seeing their women taken prisoner, they strove to preserve their honor, and cared little for their lives in comparison to the offense done them.

The night was dark, and the site, because of its depth and the thickets surrounding it, was inconvenient and difficult. Since the reputation of both sides was at stake, both Spaniards and Indians fought so diligently that the encounter continued for three hours. At dawn, however, after retrieving some of their women, the Indians retired up the hillside, although with a loss of ninety-six warriors who lay dead on the battlefield. The Spaniards were so exhausted that they were unable to follow, although Garci-González attempted it. Fierce opposition obliged him to retreat, however, because of the many wounded. Even so, their

## CHAPTER VII

wounds aggravated, that same day five men of Estremadura, Juan Rodríguez, Martín Sánchez, Juan de Viedma, Alonso Palomeque, and Luis Martínez, all died.

Pedro Alonso's grief at their death was so intense that, to temper his pain, he wished to reengage Tamanaco. He therefore proceeded with his troops until he sighted the town of Cacique Tapiaracay, whose vassals, offended by Cacique Aricabacuto's loyalty to our side, planned to kill him. Pedro Alonso, who had camped at the foot of a saddle-shaped ridge, went up to the town at its summit, where Cacique Tapiaracay came out into the open accompanied by six to eight of his warriors. Concealing the poison in his heart, the chieftain humbly expressed his desires to render obedience to the Spaniards and to free himself from the inescapable ravages of war. He was compelled, he said, to solicit peace in person, but he did not dare come to our camp without the support of someone known to both sides. Thus, he asked that Cacique Aricabacuto be sent to him so that, under his protection, he might put into effect without fear what he so ardently desired.

Pedro Alonso readily believed the barbarian, an error inexcusable in so experienced a captain. Aricabacuto was not in the camp at that time because he had tarried along the road with some of his vassals to hunt cashew birds. The captain consequently sent orders that one of the cacique's sons, a son-in-law, and two brothers-in-law should go in his name so that, reassured by their presence, Tapiaracay would come forth without fear. As the native's sole intention was to exact vengeance, he had scarcely caught sight of Aricabacuto's relatives than on signal his hidden warriors released their arrows. They shot so rapidly that, before our men could rush to help those attacked, they were pierced in a thousand places and expired in misery.

When Aricabacuto arrived at the camp and learned of the death of his kin, he felt such extreme grief that his pain and wrath could not be placated. Raging in anger, he attempted to kill with a broadsword the innocent women and children whom Garci-González had captured in Tamanaco's town, and he would have committed this cruelty if Tomé de Ledesma, on horseback and with lance in hand, had not prevented it. Ledesma's intervention started a clash that could have thrown the entire camp into turmoil as Aricabacuto grasped the broadsword to throw it at Ledesma, and the latter, holding his lance aslant over his arm, spurred his horse forward to kill the cacique. Just at that time, however, Garci-González arrived to calm their passions and keep the breach from widening. Ledesma was so upset by the cacique's rash actions that, turning to his soldiers, he said: "Gentlemen, since this expedition can no longer have a favorable outcome, it would be better to abandon it and return to our homes." This proposal dismayed Pedro Alonso so much that, putting hand to sword and turning toward Ledesma, he said: "If anyone dares attempt to return to the city without my leave, I will take his life with this sword or by garrote." His anger would have become even harsher if Garci-González had not intervened to quiet the disturbance.

Thus, they were free to pursue their march in peace to Patima from where, guided by the currents of the Guaire, they came out with no difficulty on the banks of the Tuy. Its waters served as a boundary for the Mariches, and were shared at that time with the Quiriquires, but everywhere Pedro Alonso found only signs of recent fires that had reduced all the towns to ashes. These fires manifested the obstinate rebellion of those barbarians, who were determined to defend the liberty they enjoyed now that their families were safely hidden in retreats. Thus, they followed Pedro Alonso's trail in single file, confidently expecting time and good fortune to bring victory.

Leery of the news of a general Indian retreat, Pedro Alonso resumed the march along the banks of the Guaire River back to Patima because he doubted that for the present he could accomplish the pacification he was attempting. A soldier named Tapia, meanwhile, walking with the advance guard along the river, saw a baby girl eight to ten months of age, lying on the sand. Her mother undoubtedly had abandoned her, either because the baby was a deterrent to flight or because fear was stronger than love. Forgetting the morality of a human being and his obligations as a Catholic, Tapia seized the infant by one foot, and shouting: "I baptize you in the name of the Father, the Son, and the Holy Spirit," he threw her into the river where she was submerged in its waters. Pedro Alonso, to punish this iniquity, ordered Tapia's hand cut off, but several soldiers intervened and the sentence was suspended. Divine Justice took account of this event, however, and not twenty-four hours passed before Tapia paid for this sin with his life. The following day, as our men crossed the canebrake beside the river, Tamanaco rushed out of hiding with the strongest of his warriors to obstruct Pedro Alonso's passage. Both sides battled fiercely with swords flashing and arrows whistling, and there was not a shot or blow that did not bring death and devastation. Tapia was killed at once, his heart split open by an arrow. This fatality put fear into the Spaniards that all might share the same penalty. They, urged on by Pedro Alonso, and the Indians by Tamanaco, attained true valor in desperation, though the Indians had the advantage of being protected by the canebrake. Pedro Alonso, seeking a better position, ordered Garci-González, accompanied by Fernando de la Cerda, Andrés Domínguez, Cristóbal Rodríguez Chanizo, Sandoval, and six others, to form an ambush, and when it seemed to him that Garci-

## CHAPTER VII

González would have had time to fulfill this order, he sounded the signal to regroup and began a rapid march, giving the appearance of retreating in fear.

The Indians, convinced that the simulation was real, hailed their victory with conch horns, and charged our men forcefully. When Pedro Alonso saw them approaching the ambush, he turned suddenly to face them, thus giving Garci-González and his men an opportunity to attack from the side. The upset at being assaulted when they had considered themselves victorious changed their bravery to dismay, confusion, and dejection. Only Tamanaco, gathering new inspiration from his men's unexpected disorder, provided gallant resolve and, with macana in hand, maintained the combat against that large number solely through his vindictiveness. As the adversaries were many, however, his perseverance could not match his spirit; and, his strength spent from his having killed Cerda and two other soldiers with his own hands, he fell prostrate to the ground. Thus he lost his freedom and, soon after, his life. After the cacique was sentenced to death by Pedro Alonso, the Spaniards planned the execution to offer a diversion by testing the level of that cacique's courage. They enclosed an amphitheater within palisades, and in it placed Tamanaco to fight in single combat with Amigo, a war dog of singular bravery which belonged to Garci-González de Silva.[4] Tamanaco was then offered liberty and life if, through the death of the dog, he came out of the arena victorious.

The barbarian gladly accepted the match, for it seemed to him as he stood in the circle with his macana in hand waiting for the dog to be released on him that his strong arm would bring a quick triumph. Seeing the animal come out to attack him, Tamanaco considered his victory so certain that, raising his macana, he cried out in his Mariche language: "Today you will die at my hands, and Spaniards will learn that there is no danger in the world that can make a coward of Tamanaco." His vain confidence was misplaced, however, for Amigo, fleeing the blow of the macana, did not give the Indian a second chance, but turned on him with extreme ferocity and, pawing at his chest, threw him to the ground. There, the bloodstained dog ripped the barbarian's head from his body, his claws serving as the instrument of decapitation. News of this gory spectacle, which caused horror even among those who had conceived it, spread so quickly among the Indians that, in order not to expose themselves to a similar fate, they pledged obedience to Pedro Alonso, and the rebellion of that obstinate tribe was thus suppressed.

BOOK VI

# CHAPTER VIII

*Gabriel de Avila enters the territory of the Teques and settles the mining town of Nuestra Señora; Garci-González makes various forays through which he subdues the Indians of that district.*

AFTER Pedro Alonso had subjugated the Mariches, there remained for the orderly growth of the city of Caracas only the pacification of the Teques. This arrogant tribe, guarding the ancient maxims of Cacique Guaicaipuro, not only remained rebellious against obedience to Spain but incited other tribes to make their conquest difficult in every respect. To overcome this obstacle, as well as to reap the profits of the gold mines that Francisco Fajardo had discovered on a site later settled by Juan Rodríguez, the residents decided in 1573 to bring the natives to peace by force of arms. The mission was committed to the alcalde ordinario, Gabriel de Avila, who soon set out with a troop of seventy illustrious colonists, whose common interest in the outcome led the most distinguished to vie to enlist. Without opposition from the natives, he reached the old mining town of Nuestra Señora, where he decided to settle, since the metals tested were found to be excellent, in order to devote himself to the development of the mines on that site. Rendered cautious by the seclusion and silence of the Indians, however, he wished to be well informed as to their attitude, so as to determine his course of action with them. He entrusted Garci-González de Silva with taking an exploratory turn with thirty men through the nearby towns, traveling by night, first to that of Cacique Conopoima, situated in a gulch at the foot of a prominent rock called the Crag of Los Teques. At the top of a hill he left Martín Fernández de Antequera and Augustín de Ancona, cavalrymen, with six foot soldiers, as a rear guard to make their withdrawal safe. With the rest of the men, he went into the town, which he found deserted because its inhabitants, advised by Indians who worked in the mines that the Spaniards were coming in search of them, had moved with their women and children to more distant places. All the men capable of bearing arms had then retired to separate villages in the valley below, some three gunshots' distance away, leaving hidden in the town only two Indians to advise them when they heard the enemy approaching.

Seeing the sentinels go out the false door of a hut, Garci-González, accompanied by Araujo, a mestizo from El Tocuyo, ran after them, stabbed one to death, and chased the second as he shouted to the other Indians. Overtaking him in a field of yucca, Garci-González threw a knife at the sentinel's head, and at this his brains spewed forth from his skull, now split completely in half. Francisco Sánchez de Córdova then rushed to join Garci-González, and the two took a path downward just as the Indians, hearing the shouts of their guard, were going up to defend their town. As the night was somewhat dark, however, and the field quite large, they did not catch sight of each other until they met face-to-face.

The Spaniards attacked where the path was so narrow that it did not permit more than two to fight at a time. With their keen swords they killed the foremost Indians at once, after which the others went trampling all over each other. Then, at Garci-González's shouts and the noise of battle, the rest of our men, who had remained in the town amusing themselves, rushed out to help. Finding the Indians in disorder, though, they easily put them to flight after forty-two more natives lost their lives on the hillside. Continuing the pursuit to the houses that had served the Indians as retreats, our men entered them and found coats of mail, swords, iron bars, pieces of wrought silver, rings, and other jewels of those which the natives had stolen when they killed Luis de Narváez. Among them, Pedro García Camacho at once recognized some gold buttons set with diamonds that he had lost in that rout, from which he alone had escaped with his life.

These spoils were gathered up quickly, and four Indians found in the house were taken prisoner. Then, before dawn, Garci-González again went with his men to the top of the hill where he had left Martín Fernández de Antequera with Augustín de Ancona. He was followed by Cacique Conopoima, who, having regrouped his disordered squadrons, was seeking satisfaction for the rout he had suffered that night. Before arriving at the summit, Garci-González was attacked from the rear by a dense cloud of arrows from the Indians. Although the damage was slight, he ordered Sorocaima, leader of the prisoners, to tell those following them not to shoot again because if they wounded a single soldier he would have them all impaled. As the gratification of his vengeance meant more to Sorocaima than his appreciation for life, however, he scorned the threat. Instead of doing as he had been ordered, he shouted encouragement to Cacique Conopoima to persist in battle and assured him that our men were so few that he could be sure of victory if he persevered.

This reaction stirred Garci-González to such anger that he ordered that Sorocaima's hand be cut off, and he released so that he might advise Conopoima from closer range. The barbarian, without altering his expression on hearing this sentence, extended his arm with complete courage. Garci-González, impressed by his proud bearing, revoked the punishment and ordered him set free. This generosity did not have general acceptance among his soldiers, and two of the most distinguished, not content with muttering about it, seized Sorocaima without Garci-González's knowledge. Then, as if operating on a dumb brute, they cut a circle of skin from around his wrist, and next, seeking out the joint with a knife, they separated the hand from the arm. In this torture, Sorocaima showed such courage that he remained motionless, not uttering a sigh. With singular ease he asked them to give him his hand and, without another word, clasping it in his remaining one, he went very deliberately toward Conopoima's retreat. There he revealed the mutilation, expecting the cacique to avenge the offense. The inhumanity of that punishment so terrorized the cacique, however, that, without daring to make any demonstration, he led the Indians as they withdrew in confusion. At the same time, Garci-González headed toward the mines, where Gabriel de Avila had remained with the rest of the men, engaged in extracting metals whose yield was becoming more substantial each day.

This abundance caused the Spaniards to seek more avidly the total subjugation of the Indians of this region for work stints in the mines as well as obligatory help in all tasks. Otherwise, the invaders would be constrained always to be on guard and never without their arms, constantly expecting attacks. To this end, they reconnoitered the terrain frequently, and harassed the natives to see if damage done to their towns and fields might be a means of compelling them to accept peace. The Indians' hatred for the invaders was so deeply rooted in their hearts, however, that even with the fires and deaths, they grew progressively more obdurate. Finally, one night, Garci-González went out suddenly to Cacique Acaprapocón's town with thirty men and succeeded in seizing houses and capturing many women and children. Hearing a noise from a hut, he entered to determine if there were any Indians hidden there. At this, a barbarian of gigantic proportions and corresponding strength came out to face him. Hoisting a macana aloft, he struck Garci-González such a savage blow on the head that, in spite of a steel shield covering his helmet, it was broken to pieces and he was left senseless from the violence of the blow. With the assistance of Juan Riveros, Ambrosio Hernández and Andrés Domínquez y Malpartida, however, he was able to recover while the barbarian tried to defend himself from the four. By underestimating the pagan's skill in wielding the macana, they allowed him to escape, thus leaving Garci-González badly slashed and in great pain.

That night, when the Spaniards gathered in the mining town, Garci-González's wrath was mitigated by the capture of some Indian women, for among them were Conopoima's principal wife, and two of Cacique

Acaprapocón's daughters, so beloved by their father that they were the sole object of his adoration. This circumstance brought about the end of the war and the absolute subjugation of that faction; for the two caciques, slaves to love, were more moved by affection than by rebellion. They consequently hastened to the town asking for peace with surrender; and as they consistently received good treatment, they maintained the truce faithfully. Most of them were consumed by a scourge of smallpox, however, with only a few families remaining alive. Those who survived that tragedy abandoned their own land, some going to the town in the Valley of La Pascua, but most went to live in the Valleys of Aragua. There, during the term of Governor Francisco de la Hoz Berrio, Lieutenant General Pedro Gutiérrez de Lugo, in 1617, gave them refuge in a sizable town on the site of the victory, where they still live today.

# CHAPTER IX

*Francisco Infante brings peace to the towns of Salamanca; Francisco Calderón enters the Valley of Tácata, but because of dissatisfaction among his soldiers the governor deprives him of his command.*

THE difficulty the first conquistadors had in pacifying the province of Caracas was due in large measure to the fact that it was inhabited by different tribes, each subject to individual caciques. Since the invaders were obliged to do battle with them separately, conquering the land span by span, eight years of continuous war were required for their total subjugation.

After the surrender of the Teques, the Spaniards undertook the conquest of the neighboring Quiriquires, who shared a common border on the southeast. Their towns extended along the banks of the Tuy for more than twenty-five leagues, up to the western boundary with the Tumusa tribe. In an attempt to dominate them, at the beginning of 1574 Francisco Infante marched with sixty Spaniards and one thousand Indian allies, eager to offer military service under Spanish banners. After overcoming some opposition, Infante succeeded at little cost in subjecting various towns that, separated by short distances, formed a district which Juan Rodríguez had named the province of Salamanca. There, the principal caciques submitted peacefully, but just as Infante thought this favorable beginning would quickly bring a glorious end to his conquest, he was obliged to abandon the project because he fell ill of a malignant fever. Spreading to his soldiers, the disease killed seven within three days and soon became epidemic. He did not dare to trust the recent friendship of those barbarians in so grave a situation, for if they saw the conquest faltering, they might attempt some rash action. Leaving the peace of those towns assured as best he could, he retired with his men to the city, where the benign climate helped them regain their health; but Francisco Infante was so weakened by the attack that his convalescence required many months.

Since Infante was incapacitated, Lieutenant Francisco Calderón assumed direction of the project and, with eighty Spanish soldiers and more than six hundred Indian allies, that same year he entered the towns of Salamanca. As he found them in the state of peace in which Francisco Infante had left them, he crossed the Valley of Tácata and proceeded along the banks of the Tuy until he came out at Súcata without meeting any opposition, for the Indians had taken advantage of the rough terrain and retired to the brush for the duration of the foray. On studying the situation, Calderón became convinced that until a city was founded in the center of the region from which to mount invasions, whatever efforts he might make to subjugate that race could be in vain. It was clear that as long as the expeditions originated in the city of Caracas, the protection of the mountains and the caution of the Indians would make a mockery of whatever preparations might be devised.

On the strength of that judgment, Calderón decided to found a city on the plains of Ocumare, bordering the Tuy River, on what appeared to him the most suitable site for the purpose. He found strong opposition in most of his soldiers, however, because they considered that under the circumstances disadvantages might originate from the forces being divided and unable to help one another. They added that, since the Spaniards in the province were so few, Caracas and Caraballeda would be weakened by a new town, lacking the settlers necessary to sustain them. It therefore seemed to them more prudent to postpone the establishment of the town than to endanger those already founded, since it could be left for a more opportune time.

Calderón knew how solid those reasons were, but since the proposal had assumed the aspect of a commitment, he insisted on carrying it out. At this, discord broke out which later brought the project to a halt when the soldiers, resolved not to settle in Ocumare, presented Calderón a juridical protest instructing him to desist in his intentions. Although he did suspend operation, he was bitter at the rebuff. He became intemperate in his speech concerning some of the leaders of the revolt, and went so far as to imprison Juan Riveros, Sebastián Díaz, Juan de Gámez, and four others, intending to bring suit against them.

All the aggrieved were noblemen who knew how to exact satisfaction. As soon as they returned to the city after the expedition, they sent a representative to Coro to express to Governor Mazariego their reasons for resentment and to stipulate terms for Calderón's conduct in office. The governor also considered his lieutenant's actions unwise, and attempted to pacify the colonists before the situation became more grave. As soon as he had heard the report, he deprived Calderón of his charge and sent power to the alcaldes of the city of Caracas, Francisco Maldonado de Almendáriz and Francisco Carrizo, to govern in his name. A short while later, before the year ended, however, he issued title to Carrizo alone to continue in office, without the need for joint jurisdiction. This readjustment made clear to Calderón the change in conditions as, repeatedly snubbed for his imprudent actions, he experienced the misery of being hated.

# CHAPTER X

*The Indians of Tácata kill Juan Pascual and Diego Sánchez; Lieutenant Carrizo enters the valley and leaves it in even greater tumult through his severe actions.*

WHILE discords continued between Calderón and the residents of Caracas, two soldiers, Juan Pascual and Diego Sánchez, went out from the city to barter. Alone except for four Teques as interpreters, they passed through the towns of Salamanca to the Valley of Tácata, where, after only a brief period of friendliness, the Indians decided to kill them. Assaulted unexpectedly, Pascual and Sánchez defended themselves with such spirit that they almost escaped, but the multitude's aggression exceeded that of the traders. They desperately tried by every means to die fighting, but finally, exhausted by the effort, with every part of their bodies pierced by arrows, they fell dead, bathed more in the blood of their enemies than in their own.

Meanwhile, the four Teques interpreters, not without apprehension that they might suffer the same fate as Pascual and Sánchez, fled back to the city. There, they informed Francisco Carrizo of what had happened, whereupon he, with ninety men and some Indian allies, entered

Tácata at the beginning of the year 1575. When he arrived at a point above the valley, he pretended that his expedition was moving toward another place by shifting the march to the right. He then entered the Valley of the Pao, and at length reached the banks of the Guárico. From there he hurriedly turned back to attack the Tácatas from the rear, but found them on the alert. Furthermore, Garci-González de Silva, leading the front ranks, sighted a squadron of up to five hundred archers withdrawing from a hayfield to establish a safer ambush on a mountain.

Garci-González, wishing to attack them on level ground, sounded the alarm and spurred his horse to overtake them before they could seek shelter in the brush, but the natives had already reached the thicket and established the ambush. He found in the field only one Indian, Yoraco, who, overestimating his own strength, awaited Garci-González with an arrow set firmly in his bow. The Spaniard on his horse quickly reached the native and struck him such a fierce blow with his lance that, lifting him above ground, he held him for a brief time suspended in the air. At length, Garci-González passed on to the road, thinking that he was leaving Yoraco dead, but glancing back later he saw him fighting with Juan de la Parra and Diego Méndez. Finally, several stabs having passed through his entire body, the Indian fell dead, but no blood flowed from the wounds even though most of them were deep. The Spaniards, trying to fathom the secret, by chance removed from Yoraco's neck a pouch filled with colored stones, at which all the blood in that inert cadaver instantly spurted forth. This experiment, demonstrating the natural characteristic of those stones to stanch the flow of blood, was repeated on various occasions by Garci-González, who always found the method efficacious, even with minimal application. From these results he developed an appreciation for that treasure, but some years later, having been informed of the properties of the stones, Governor Diego de Osorio took them from him under the pretext of sending them as a singular gift to King Philip II.[5]

Yoraco now dead and the Indians calm at last, Carrizo made camp that night among the barrancas formed by a quebrada. There, the sentinels captured five Indians who, when put to torture, confessed that they had come to examine the arrangement of our camp in order to attack safely before the next day dawned. Since Carrizo found this declaration sufficient reason to inflict punishment, he ordered four of them garroted immediately, but left the fifth one, Manarcima, alive because he was the brother of one of the principal caciques of that valley. Carrizo wanted to see if Manarcima might intervene to assure peace with those rebellious tribes, but later the treachery in that plan became evident. Carrizo dispatched Manarcima with a message to the caciques that if they would

## CHAPTER X

deliver those guilty of the deaths of Juan Pascual and Diego Sánchez, they could come without fear to discuss the establishment of new peace pacts. Camaco and Araguaire, the most important caciques of the area, believed the proposal and, accompanied by one hundred Indians bearing the products of their land, went out to meet Carrizo with no apprehension. Emphasizing their eagerness for peace, they continued to exonerate themselves in the deaths of the two Spaniards, claiming that they had not had a part in the crime but that some individual Indians had committed it without the sanction of the caciques. Since they had feared punishment, Camaco and Araguaire had fled to the brush. There they could not comply with the order to relinquish those they had accused but said that, as soon as they found them, they would bring them to the city to confirm their own innocence.

Carrizo might have accepted these excuses, although without quite believing them, because of the confidence with which those caciques put themselves into his hands. Carried away by a desire for vengeance, however, he dishonored his pledge of safe-conduct and at once placed the caciques in prison. He then proceeded with the investigation and, as a result, learned that most of the Indians present, although they had not taken part in the deaths of the Spaniards, had attended the feast at which their bodies were eaten. He consequently ordered the ears and nose of Cacique Camaco cut off, and the garrote given to the thirty-six who appeared most culpable. Although Cacique Araguaire cursed the duplicity with which Carrizo had acted, he also was sentenced and, after being subjected to torture, surrendered his life to the noose. So that Manarcima, who had served as interlocutor at the trials, should not remain unnoticed, his right hand was cut off, this unwarranted inhumanity being his payment for good intentions.

Carrizo's cruelty so infuriated the Indians that they determined to die with valor in war rather than perish with deception in peace. Taking up arms in desperate resolve, they thus made clear to Carrizo the lengths to which their wrath extended by pursuing him with constant assaults. Carrizo, desperate at the intensity of the continuous hostility, abandoned the valley and returned to the city. His senseless temerity had had no results other than discrediting his name and rendering impossible at that time the pacification of those peoples, now even more rebellious because of his atrocities.

BOOK VI

# CHAPTER XI

*Garci-González enters the Valley of Tácata; with magnanimous treatment, he subdues the Indians there.*

CARRIZO'S failure to subdue the Indians of Tácata was of greatest concern to Garci-González because those towns were in his repartimiento. Pondering the most effective means of pacifying them, Garci-González entered the valley with sixty men the following year of 1576, resolved to rectify through clemency a situation in which severity had failed. The Indians did not dare trust him, however, and would not face him to accept his proposals. Determined to carry the war forward, they named as their general Cacique Parayauta, who had been responsible for the deaths of Juan Pascual and Diego Sánchez. After recruiting troops and preparing provisions, he stood each morning on a rocky peak and mocked Garci-González and his men. Raising the sword he had taken from Diego Sánchez, he shouted: "I, Parayauta, killed your companions and if you do not return quickly to the city, I will do the same to you. Go back, poor hapless men. Misled by your pride, you are asking for the death awaiting you in my macana."

Garci-González wished to punish the barbarous arrogance of the cacique at once, but between them at the foot of the peak there was a quebrada so deep that he could not cross to the other side. During the first few days this obstacle to his desires was effective, but, seeing how openly the Indian continued to proclaim his threats, Garci-González determined to seek some way to raise an ambush against him. He set out one night with thirty men and, although they had to walk more than two leagues and break through a considerable stretch of mountain to cross the quebrada, before dawn he succeeded in placing them on the other side, at the back of the peak. He ordered a Tarma Indian to climb a tree to serve as lookout and advise him when the cacique approached. Shortly after dawn, the sentry gave a signal that Parayauta was coming with more than three hundred armed Indians. Walking arrogantly, and enjoying the situation, the barbarian stepped ahead of his warriors and alone fell into the ambush, where Garci-González slashed his face with his sword. Parayauta took two or three steps backward to allow space to shoot an arrow, but before he could adjust the bow cord, Garci-González had cut it also with his blade. Then, with another blow, he gave the cacique a sizable wound to the head upon which he, after staggering around a bit, sought protection among his warriors.

Seeing their cacique in torment, the Indians rushed to his defense, but they were quickly thrown into confusion, and Parayauta was taken prisoner by the rest of the Spaniards who came out of the ambush attacking. Then, for the first time, he experienced the magnanimity of Garci-González, as the Spaniard set Parayauta free after having his head wound treated. This action brought the greatest triumph that could have been hoped for from that war, as the cacique, thankful for this gentlemanly conduct, convoked the principal leaders of the valley and persuaded them to relinquish their arms. He obligated them through their respect for him to surrender and go out voluntarily to solicit peace and offer obedience to Garci-González. In this manner the conquest was easily effected though the pacification of those towns only a short time earlier held as doubtful. Thus let it be recognized that there is no race, no matter how barbarous, that they may not be coerced through gentleness while severity, on the other hand, infuriates.

# CHAPTER XII

*The Indians of Salamanca attempt to kill Francisco Infante and Garci-González; the latter defends himself and valiantly saves his companion from death.*

GARCI-GONZÁLEZ de Silva retired to Caracas after the pacification of the Valley of Tácata but had nothing on which to expend his valor at the time because all the tribes of the province of Caracas had been conquered. In the following year of 1577, he consequently decided to take a turn through the towns of Salamanca, which he held in repartimiento on halves with his brother-in-law Francisco Infante. He also invited two other Spanish soldiers to go, and all four undertook the journey without fear of the barbarians.

They were received in Salamanca with a singular display of friendship, for the benevolent treatment the Indians had always received from their two encomenderos deserved nothing less. Since no servitude is bearable to one who remembers that he once was free, however, it was enough to recall that the Spaniards were masters for the relationship gradually to become noxious. On several occasions the caciques met together to communicate with one another, and they were heartened by these conversations to seek to restore their lost liberty.

Although consideration of the inherent difficulties somewhat intimidated the caciques, the persuasions of an elderly sorceress and herbalist, Apacuana, mother of Cacique Guásema, were so efficacious that her hearers disregarded all foreseeable risks. She was set on revolt, beginning with the deaths of the four Spaniards; but, to achieve this outcome, it seemed desirable to delay action until they were almost ready to return to the city.

Garci-González and his companions were lodged in a house that he had had built on top of a steep incline a short distance from the town. On the night before they were to begin their journey, as many as two hundred of the most valiant warriors went up to the house, leaving below two thousand others ready to rush forward at the first signal. Hiding their treachery with servility, they told Garci-González that they were going to sleep there in order to accompany him back to the city, a courtesy that he gladly accepted.

The Indians appeared to be without arms because they did not carry them openly; but all, provided with firewood and bundles of straw to make their beds, carried their macanas hidden for later use. As none of the four Spaniards perceived the sly malice of their guests, they went confidently to their hammocks; but as soon as the Indians saw them asleep, they took their swords and all other arms into the house. Then, they attacked Francisco Infante and the two soldiers who were closer at hand and wounded them cruelly. At the same time, Garci-González, awakened by the noise of the barbarous mob, ran to look for his sword, but, not finding it anywhere, he had recourse to the only defense that haste permitted, a blanket that had served him that night as cover in the hammock. He wrapped it around his arm and, grasping a piece of wood from the fire, attacked his adversaries. His valor now converted into fury, he burned more angrily than the flaming wood, and did not strike a blow without bringing death, or make a threat that did not result in a wound. The Indians were unable to bear his repeated attacks and preferred to seize him with their hands rather than to take his life by force of arms. Their overconfidence misled them, however, for Garci-González saw that pressure was creating greater dangers, and his defense moved toward desperation. As the Indians lifted him into the air, carrying him on their shoulders, he succeeded in reaching a Moorish spur which he had hung from a nail on the wall the previous day. Gathering new courage from that feeble implement, he inflicted such blows by swinging the spur from side to side that they were obliged to release him. They left the house so hurriedly and with such violent trampling that some, unable to fit through the door in the rush, knocked down a reed and mud partition that had served as a wall.

## CHAPTER XII

Then Garci-González hurriedly untied a war dog that only that night he had ordered chained to a post so that it would not harm the Indians whom he then considered his friends. As if he had acquired strength to subject the world, armed with the blanket, the spur, and the dog, he went out to look for the Indians who had stopped a short distance from the house. Breaking through the squadron more ferociously than a bull, without awe of the macanas, he wounded some severely while the dog tore others to pieces. Garci-González left on all sides vestiges of his rage marked with blood until, having received a macana blow to his shoulder, he was brought to his knees on the ground. Now prostrate and without the help of his dog, which had already been killed,[6] he resorted to ingenuity. He shouted as if he had soldiers ready to come to his aid: "Friends, now is the time to attack these dogs so they will not go unpunished." At these words the Indians, in panic and without knowing from whom they were fleeing, uttered confused cries and hurled themselves down a hillside.

Garci-González then returned to the house seeking his companions. He had not seen them until then, nor did he know whether they were dead or alive, but he soon found them lying on the ground and realized that they were dying from their injuries. Francisco Infante alone had twelve wounds, some critical and all serious because of their abundant flow of blood. Nevertheless, he did not despair, but removed his white trousers and shirt and, tearing them into strips, bound the wounds of the three as best he could. He wished to see whether, with their blood contained by these bandages, they might recover enough strength to walk for there appeared to be no hope other than flight. The four left the house that same night, trusting darkness for protection, but Francisco Infante was so weakened by loss of blood and the vehement pain of his injuries that he had gone barely half a league when he recognized the impossibility of continuing. As he felt death to be imminent, he begged his companions to try to assure their own lives by proceeding without him. He felt that his demise could not in any way be avoided by all perishing simply to remain with him when, by using the strength they still had, they might escape.

BOOK VI

# CHAPTER XIII

*Garci-González lifts Francisco Infante to his shoulders; he walks with him all night until he arrives at the land of the Teques where, protected by the Indians, their lives are safe.*

FRANCISCO Infante was a brother-in-law of Garci-González, one being married to Beatriz and the other to Francisca de Rojas, daughters of Pedro Gómez de Ampuero and Ana de Rojas, whom the tyrant Aguirre, solely for his own entertainment, had had hanged in Margarita.[7] The other companions had died of exhaustion and their wounds, but Garci-González was determined not to abandon Infante. Seeing that the latter was too faint to walk, he placed him on his shoulders and started on the rugged road across the sierras. After walking vigorously for more than three leagues, he arrived at dawn at the quebrada of Los Paracotos, which marks the boundary between the Quiriquire tribe and the Teques.

The four injured Spaniards had hardly left the house at Salamanca when the Indians, to finish the slaughter, returned to look for them once more. Finding by chance the body of Cacique Guacicuana, whose life Garci-González had taken with blows of his spur, however, they were so amazed by the manner in which he had been killed that they stopped for discussion and to vent their feelings. They decided to follow the Spaniards to avenge the death of the cacique, but the delay occasioned by these deliberations had given the wounded Garci-González and Francisco Infante the time needed to reach Paracotos. Thus, when the Indians arrived at the summit of the hill over the quebrada, the two Spaniards were already safe on the other bank. The Teques, staunch enemies of the Quiriquires, seeing squadrons of their adversaries coming down the slope, surmised that they were invading because of ancient enmity. They hurriedly assembled at the call to arms from their flutes, and rushing to the quebrada to obstruct the enemy's passage, they found there those two Spaniards, wounded, bleeding and dying. Informed of the betrayal, the Teques assumed the responsibility of protecting the Spaniards. Thus, with courageous opposition and recognized advantage, they obliged the Quiriquires to retire in haste. The Teques' herb doctor then applied active simples and efficacious antidotes to Francisco Infante and Garci-González who, with the agitation and humidity, were covered with ulcerated and foul abscesses. They were soon out of danger, and regained

CHAPTER I

enough strength during a four-day rest to be transported in hammocks to Caracas, where they were received with amazement. This is the incident of the Moorish spur, which is still celebrated today as one of the most glorious deeds that Garci-González performed, among the many that make his name immortal.

# BOOK VII

## CHAPTER I

*Sancho García imposes punishment on the towns of Salamanca; Garci-González goes in search of the Caribs who have been threatening Valencia; and Don Juan Pimentel arrives to govern the province.*

EVEN as Garci-González was being extolled in Caracas for having saved the lives of two persons so much beloved as himself and Francisco Infante, distress arose from the recognition that tribes previously considered subdued retained hidden enmity.

Governing the city at that time were the alcaldes ordinarios, Juan de Guevara and Francisco Maldonado, because the previous official in charge, Francisco Carrizo, had been moved to Coro. They decided to punish the Indians quickly before other tribes followed their example, and Garci-González de Silva, though not yet recovered from his wounds, asked to be placed in charge of the expedition. The alcaldes did not consent to this request, however, because they did not want to jeopardize one who still had not completely convalesced. Instead they sent Sancho García, who left the city with fifty Spanish soldiers and a few Teques, cautiously trying to conceal their march. The Indians, however, having foreseen that their offense would provoke the Spaniards to seek revenge, had closed the roads with heavy wooden boards and branches, cutting off Sancho García in every direction. Exhausted by the exertion, he finally arrived at the town where the treason against Garci-González had been contrived, and found it abandoned because the Indians had retired to the most secluded part of the mountains. Sancho García therefore vented his wrath on impersonal targets, razing the fields and setting fire to towns. One morning, his scouts brought to him an Indian whom they had found placing poisoned stakes in trenches along the road so that our men would have been wounded if they had stepped on them. Under torture, the captive revealed that the Indians, encouraged at learning that the number of Spaniards destroying the region was small, had decided to attack, and to develop this plan, the caciques and commanders were to meet that night in a quebrada hidden in the mountains four leagues away.

Sancho García, pleased to have this information, marched with his men as soon as night fell, toward the place where the meeting was to be held. He took the Indian with him as guide and promised to restore his freedom for directing him to the quebrada where he might seize the caciques off guard. The barbarian guided Sancho García through shortcuts and roundabout ways until, a little after midnight, they arrived within sight of the quebrada. There they found about five hundred persons already assembled, whom Sancho García, pausing only to call on Santiago, attacked from all sides, so confusing them that their sole hope lay in flight. They retired hastily to the crest of a mountain, and there, after recovering from their first fright, they attempted to defend themselves. Repeated discharges of arrows from our friends, the Teques, however, caused them to dash away from the site in disorder without heeding the shouted threats of Cacique Acuareyapa, who was trying to inspire them to die fighting. Seeing what little effect his efforts were having, he had an arrogant desire to make the Spaniards understand that his valor alone was sufficient to oppose them. He therefore faced them at dawn and furiously assaulted Antonio de Villegas with a macana. Warding off the blows with his shield, however, Villegas responded by striking the cacique's head with his sword, from which the Indian fell stunned to the ground. Rising to his feet undaunted, he then sought his enemy a second time, and the two joined in obstinate battle until a soldier named Figueredo killed the cacique by slashing him from behind, thus splitting his heart in two.

Sancho García, exhausted from this assault, gathered with his men at the quebrada, where among several prisoners captured that night, one was immediately recognized as Apacuana, Cacique Guásema's mother. She had been the primary instigator of the uprising, and as a result of her efficacious counsel the Indians had conceived their daring treachery. As punishment, Sancho García ordered her to be hanged and left hanging

## CHAPTER I

for all to see, so that her cadaver would move the other Indians to horror. This action brought complete pacification of that rebellious tribe, as the natives, in terror at Apacuana's torture, and broken by the loss of more than two hundred warriors, at first retired to the sierras on the other side of the Tuy but soon returned to solicit peace.

While this was taking place in the city of Caracas, the residents of Valencia were under extreme duress from continuous invasions by the Caribs. With their bestial appetite for human flesh, they had left their villages on the banks of the Orinoco and, crossing the Llanos to the vicinity of Valencia, had not spared a town or village from their fury. Since this city was afraid of similar harm, and because its small population did not have the strength to oppose such power, officials sent a message to Governor Mazariego in Coro to ask for help; and he, judging that Caracas could most promptly come to Valencia's aid, ordered Garci-González to do so with all speed.

As soon as Garci-González received the dispatch from the governor, he raised thirty horsemen and some of the most valiant Indians allies, and left the city in search of the Caribs, having been informed that they were encamped beside Lake Tacarigua. When the Spaniards arrived on the banks of the Tiznados River, where evidence indicated that the Caribs had camped a short time previously, they came upon a spectacle that impelled them to seek even more urgently the punishment that those barbarians deserved. For, placed on grills in neat order, they found almost two hundred heads of Indians whom the Caribs had held prisoner and in their drunken festivals had sacrificed to satiate their inclination to gorge on human flesh. This sight enraged Garci-González to such an extent that, without stopping, he followed their tracks for eight days until he overtook them on the banks of the Guárico just as they had converted a beautiful town to ashes. Some of the inhabitants had been quartered, other roasted, and finally a formidable slaughter made of all. Because of Garci-González's speed in attacking, most of the Caribs considered it expedient to rush downstream in their canoes to the Orinoco, leaving our men defrauded by their sudden flight. To alleviate their anger, the Spaniards seized twenty-six Indians in the confusion of embarking, and Garci-González ordered them impaled. Then, with the hope of attaining other fruits from the thwarted expedition, he and his men withdrew to the city.

Named by the king at about this time to succeed Diego de Mazariego as governor and captain general of the province, Juan Pimentel embarked at Cádiz for Cartagena. Since his family was descended from the counts of Benavente, Pimentel was privileged to wear on his breast the vermilion insignia of Santiago. This cavalier, who came to port at

Caraballeda toward the end of 1577, was the first governor to establish his residence in Caracas. Following this example, all of his successors, motivated either by the benign climate or the advantages of its abundant trade, have resided there. Caracas acquired by this means all prerogatives as head of the province, much to the disappointment of Coro, which, deprived of this honor, which its priority deserved, still suffers abuse and scorn.

## CHAPTER II

*The governor sends Garci-González to conquer the Cumanagotos; he fights and defeats them at Chacopata and Unare, but they do not remain subdued.*

JUAN Pimentel, after assuming his post as governor, devoted his entire attention during 1578 to political and civil affairs that Caracas, as a new settlement, had held for his disposition. Now, at the beginning of 1579, to ensure communication on all sides and to reap common benefits for its residents, he undertook to found a city on a site from which he might subject the Quiriquires. He entrusted this task to Garci-González, and provided him a hundred Spaniards, more than four hundred Indians, and all the equipment needed for that mission, but it was ultimately judged more urgent to apply these armaments to an expedition against the Cumanagotos. These Indians were exultant over the woeful rout they had inflicted on General Diego Fernández de Serpa, in which they had slain him along with the flower of his troops. Since the Cumanagotos still were not content with defending their liberty and making their subjugation impracticable, however, they set out to sea to disrupt navigation in their pirogues. Soon coming across ships from Caraballeda en route to Margarita to barter for pearls, they robbed and killed all aboard with inhuman cruelty.

The province of Margarita was at that time under the jurisdiction of Venezuela because it was located in the district between Maracapana and Cabo de la Vela, the limits designated by Emperor Charles V in his lease to the Welsers. For this reason, as well as to protect trade with Margarita, Juan Pimentel, on learning of the rout of the ships, held it more urgent to remedy that damage than to divert his forces in a less pressing operation. Thus, he ordered Garci-González to proceed at once

## CHAPTER II

to conquer the Cumanagotos with the men he had prepared to settle the land of the Quiriquires.

The enterprise was risky, but as Garci-González's militant spirit always aspired to the most difficult, he considered it a splendid opportunity and gladly accepted the assignment. Thirty more Spanish soldiers having been recruited above the hundred he already had raised, he began his expedition on April 6, 1579. He followed the road that he deemed safest, although less direct, for, trying to prevent the Cumanagotos from learning of his campaign, he left the better-known coastal path and traveled along a semicircle toward the Valleys of Aragua. He then chose the road that today runs from San Sebastián to Nueva Barcelona, and at the end of twenty days came in sight of the towns of Cacique Querecrepe, where he made camp on the shores of a lake.

That cacique, whose friendship the Spaniards had always valued greatly, had been dead only a few days when his three sons were notified of Garci-González's arrival. They went to visit him the next day, bearing an abundance of local foods, a courtesy repeated a short while later by the caciques of the Palenques, of Barutaima, and of the lake of Cariamaná, as well as by Juan Caballo, head of the Píritu tribes, an old favorite of the Spaniards. After friendship had been reaffirmed among all, in order to assure the conquest Garci-González continued toward the coast, hoping to settle a town on the same site where Diego de Serpa had founded Santiago de los Caballeros on the banks of the Guatapanare (Salado) River. Since he came out onto the shore much to the leeward, however, he had to travel several leagues along the coast in search of the place best suited for his town. One afternoon, the Spaniards, camping on a site called Chacopata Hills, saw arriving in port about eighteen pirogues of Cumanagotos, who had been committing further acts of piracy at sea. It was believed at first that they were canoes of Cacique Juan Caballo, in which part of our equipment that had been left behind was being transported. Garci-González recognized them later, however, as enemy craft, and ordered some of his soldiers to occupy a nearby salt marsh and sandbank covered with prickly pear and tuna plants, so that the Cumanagotos would be unable to escape. With the rest of his men, he took possession of the pirogues, since the Indians had abandoned them after deciding to continue the struggle on land. The battle was waged with extreme intensity, the field covered with blood. The Indians, prostrate more from fatigue than weakness, after the loss of eighty-three warriors killed on the shore, retreated at length to the protection of the prickly pear and tuna thickets.

After burning the Cumanagotos' pirogues, Garci-González advanced to the Salado River; but not finding in all that area a suitable place to establish a town, he decided to found it in Querecrepe, so as to have a safe fort from which to continue the conquest. The Indians, however, still incensed by the prior rout and seeking revenge, one morning found Garci-González's camp on the banks of the Unare. Shooting their arrows and rending the air with shouts, the roll of drums and the shrill sound of conch horns, they rapidly provoked our men to battle.

Garci-González was at that time hearing Mass in his campaign tent and, without allowing this development to alter his actions, he continued to be attentive to this devout exercise until the priest concluded. He then mounted his horse and, accompanied by Lázaro Vázquez, Martín Alfonso, Duarte Fernández and others, hurried to the banks of the river whence the noise originated. As the Indians were on the other side, the adversaries were separated by a body of water that, flooded at that season, did not provide any place to ford. Because of this obstacle, the Spaniards for a brief time did nothing more than respond to the Indians' arrows with their harquebuses; but soon a greyhound, enraged by the clamor of battle, plunged into the river and swam across to the attack. Carefully noting this action, Garci-González said to his soldiers: "Friends, this animal is showing us what we should do in this case." At that, he spurred his horse, which entered the current to swim across. The rest followed his example, and all soon reached the opposite bank safely. There they plied their lances while the Indians wielded their macanas, and the battle raged for three hours without a winner being clearly indicated.

Garci-González and the forty-seven horsemen who had followed him into the river sustained the conflict against more than three thousand Cumanagotos (the Battle of the Unare), because the infantry had been unable to cross the swollen river. Inflamed with a desire to emulate their companions and assist their captain, however, these foot soldiers searched the riverbank until they found a place that offered the possibility of fording it. Finally on the other side, they desperately bloodied their swords on those naked bodies as the natives began to lose courage. At the same time, the cavalry, aided by the infantry, flashing their lances like lightning, threw the enemy into such disorder that they acknowledged their defeat in flight, leaving our men masters of the field.

## CHAPTER III

*Garci-González founds the city of Espíritu Santo in Querecrepe; he goes out again in search of the Cumanagotos, but after several unsuccessful attempts, he withdraws.*

As soon as several soldiers wounded in the battle were healed, Garci-González lifted camp from the banks of the Unare. On arrival at Querecrepe, he established a city that he named Espíritu Santo because it was founded during the octave of Pentecost. The new settlement had more the aspect of a fort than a town, but to observe formalities, he named alcaldes and regidores to administer it. After hastily building a wooden stockade, he left thirty soldiers there under command of Juan Fernández de León, and with the rest of the men went out again to complete the conquest of the Cumanagotos.

These Indians, aware that Garci-González would return to make an intensive search for them, observed his movements carefully from every direction, for they remembered the two previous defeats suffered at his hands with more fury than fear. Our men, returning to the Unare River through the region of the Palenques, entered the mountain area and found the road so well cleared that they realized that the Indians had done this deliberately, to show how little fear they felt. The soldiers marched cautiously with their weapons in hand, and at length came out onto a small plain. They had barely occupied it when from all sides the Indians began to discharge clouds of arrows, to which our men responded with fire from their harquebuses. Without spending more time in that dangerous place, the Spaniards continued their march through the woods, still fighting the Indians, whose intent had been to encircle them in that enclosure. From there on, they had blocked off the paths so that the Spaniards had to clear them and fight at the same time, but, all obstacles finally overcome, the invaders arrived in the late afternoon at Utuguane. They found this town in flames, the Indians having set fire to it to prevent our men from making camp there.

Utuguane occupied a spacious site on cleared ground, but it lacked water because the Indians had retained possession of the large pool that supplied the town. Nevertheless, Garci-González decided to camp there that night because his men were exhausted from the heat of the day. The soldiers, tormented by thirst and unable to tolerate it any longer when relief was so close at hand, resorted to arms. Unmindful of the disadvantages that darkness might occasion, during the first watch of the night they fell on the Indians guarding the pool and succeeded against strong resistance in taking possession of the water, but at the cost of some blood. They also captured several prisoners, from whom they learned that the Cumanagotos, supported by their auxiliary neighbors, the Chacopatas, Cores, and Chaymas, were only a short distance from the town and were determined to maintain their liberty.

Garci-González wished to restrict the encounter to one battle, as he sought only to break the tribe's arrogant spirit. Judging that it was possible to attain that end, he marched the following morning, guided by the prisoners, and met the foe a little more than a league and a half down the road on a beautiful plain, the site of Cacique Cayaurima's town. Garci-González, seeing that the enemy troops were many, divided his men into two squadrons; to the one under his own command, he named Juan de Gámez, Jerónimo Baquedaño, Rodrigo de León, Alonso Camacho, Antonio de Lima, Juan García Carrasco and others; and the second, composed of Martín Alfonso, Tomás Díaz, Juan Sánchez, Hernando Marcelo, Hernando Gutiérrez; and the rest of the soldiers, he assigned to Lázaro Vázquez to lead.

At ten o'clock in the morning, before the Indians had had time to form their squadrons, Garci-González attacked them on both sides, trapping most of them in the middle; but they formed two fronts to receive the assault of our men equally (the Battle of Cayaurima). Some rent the air with arrows while others, hurling stones in crackling slings, filled the land with tumult. Without allowing the rush of the horses, the blows of the lances or the discharge of the harquebuses to force them to discard their plan, after more than two hours they started marching off slowly, withdrawing to the protection of Cayaurima's village. This was a stratagem that, even with all his military experience, Garci-González did not comprehend. He approached the town without misgivings, but the Indians had hardly seen him enter than they set fire to the houses on all sides. Then, going out again onto the plains, they left him in the confusion caused by the fire, in which six soldiers and several servants were burned, Garci-González's full efforts being necessary to prevent the destruction of all.

This tragedy began to engender some doubts as to the favorable outcome of the expedition; but Garci-González, determined to persist, continued the march until they arrived at the huts of Píritu. The Cumanagotos did not lose any occasion to plague the Spaniards, but attacked from ambush wherever possible. Added to this torment were the extreme

## CHAPTER III

heat and arid land, for the Indians had filled all the wells that they thought the Spaniards might discover.

This ruse obliged Garci-González to continue without delay to Chacopata in search of a pool called Arará or Macaron; and although he found it unpolluted, since the natives used it themselves, he did suffer a severe loss. As they crossed a field thick with brambles near the shore, an Indian struck one of his best soldiers, Juan Fernández Morrillo, with an arrow from which he died. On leaving Querecrepe he had told friends that he had had a premonition several times that he would be killed in Chacopata. At his comrades' insistence that he ask his captain's leave to remain behind, he had responded: "God grant that I not desert my companions or fail in my duty through fear of death."

As soon as the Spaniards had set up camp at Chacopata, Garci-González called his men together for counsel as to what he should do in the present situation. Although their lack of supplies had been foreseen, the sterility of the land, the difficult marches, and their small number against so powerful an enemy convinced them that it would be wise to retreat to Querecrepe until a more opportune occasion.

Garci-González, however, rejected their proposal and decided, much to their displeasure, to go forward with the conquest. There was even one who said irritably that if Garci-González was so eager to place his own preference before what reason dictated, he need not have bothered to ask for counsel. Nevertheless, even while he was trying persistently to persuade the soldiers to his opinion, the Indians who had accompanied them as allies or servants fled one night either through exhaustion or fear of the Cumanagotos. Thus left without guides, he was obliged to abandon the project and return to Querecrepe.

BOOK VII

# CHAPTER IV

*Garci-González abandons the city of Espíritu Santo; he reestablishes it in the land of the Quiriquires, but it does not endure; he returns to Caracas, and the province suffers a great plague of smallpox.*

WHEN Garci-González returned to Espíritu Santo, he found a message from Governor Juan Pimentel telling him to terminate the effort to pacify the Cumanagotos if it could not be accomplished in a short while. He wanted him to discontinue it and abandon the city he had founded in order to proceed with the conquest of the Quiriquires. Weighing the results of each expedition, those promised by an early subjugation of the Quiriquires were more appreciable than the ones that might be expected from the lengthy conquest of the Cumanagotos. Since this evaluation corresponded to the soldiers' wishes, they willingly carried out the governor's order. After crossing the land of the Tumusas and the Valley of Caucagua, they emerged in the province of the Quiriquires, who received them docilely, so that without the use of arms, Garci-González was able to reestablish Espíritu Santo on a hilly site that sloped down to the Itecuao River. Nevertheless, when the Indians later realized that the Spaniards intended to live among them permanently, their friendship changed to hatred, and the previously amicable relationship ended in openly declared war. They inflicted all the hostilities deemed effective to rid themselves of their guests, including assaults and ambushes, and razed their fields so that the Spaniards could not profit from their yield.

This rebellion obliged Garci-González to take up arms for a turn throughout the quebradas and retreats where the Indians might be hiding in order to make his indignation clear and to resort to severity, since gentleness had failed. His adherence to this plan succeeded, as the Quiriquires were thrown into consternation at the tortures executed on the most culpable, some being subjected to the noose and others to the knife. They surrendered, asking for pardon and offering perpetual vassalage and constant obedience. Garci-González, satisfied with these promises, selected alcaldes and regidores to attend to the town's affairs and named as deputy-in-charge his chief ensign, Pedro González. Then, more quickly than was justified, he returned to Caracas accompanied only by his servants, to relate to Governor Juan Pimentel what he had done and to ask authority to allot Indians in repartimiento among the set-

## CHAPTER IV

tlers. Garci-González felt that it would be more reasonable for one who had witnessed the services of all to be in charge of distribution of the encomiendas so that rewards bestowed would give no occasion for complaint.

Because Garci-González was not on the scene at this crucial moment, however, the total ruin of the new city resulted. Since Pedro González's authority was not sufficient to stifle at their inception movements of discord that soon grew into serious dissensions, Garci-González lost the respect and veneration of the natives that he had won in peace. The Spaniards, disgruntled with one another, little by little abandoned the city, some to live in Valencia and others in Caracas; and at length, the few who had remained left it deserted out of fear of the Indians. Both the governor and Garci-González deeply regretted this misfortune, but, determined to restore what had been lost, they tried once again to reestablish the ill-fated city. About that time, however, a new situation developed in the province that obliged the two to set the matter aside until a more propitious time.

It happened just then, in the year 1580, that a Portuguese ship arrived from the coast of Guinea and brought an infestation of smallpox. At first this disease was not recognized, and when at length it was identified, it was beyond remedy. Since it was an illness that had never before attacked these parts, it spread with such violence among the Indians that it depopulated the province, consuming entire tribes without leaving more than a name to recall their memory. This fatality, among the gravest this nation has ever suffered since its discovery, left dead bodies by the dozen along the roads and quebradas. As a crowning desolation, the death of Bishop Pedro de Agreda, beloved prelate, occurred in Coro at the same time. During the twenty years that he governed this diocese, he was able through his integrity, gentleness, and prudence to hold the general benevolence of his parishioners, and his agreeable nature was a magnet that attracted the hearts of all. His death was even more deplorable since it came just when the province needed him to alleviate the increasing adversities that beset it.

Finally, at the beginning of 1581, the deaths not having ceased or the contagion lessened, Caracas had recourse to divine favor. The citizens made vows to their patron, San Pablo, protohermit, whose intervention was so efficacious that from that moment on the city miraculously began to experience improvement. In gratitude, as a perpetual memorial of benefits received, a church was built in his honor, and until today the custom of celebrating his feast day to render thanks to him in his church is observed every year on January 15.

BOOK VII

# CHAPTER V

*The Caribs menace the city of Valencia; Garci-González locates and defeats them near the Guárico River.*

AFTER the violence of the epidemic abated, the province started to recuperate, but the scarcity of Indians in the region is still apparent to the present day. In October of 1583, Luis de Rojas, a Madrilenian named to succeed Juan Pimentel as governor and captain general of the province, arrived at the port of Caraballeda accompanied by Friar Juan de Manzanillo, a religious of the Dominican Order, whom His Majesty had presented as bishop the preceding year in place of Pedro de Agreda.[1] Manzanillo was the first prelate to establish residence in Caracas, thus instituting a precedent. He initiated a plan that fifty-five years later was put into effect by a succeeding bishop, Juan López Aburto de la Mata, when the cathedral was moved from Coro to Caracas.[2]

Garci-González's desire to restore his lost city took on new life when the recently-arrived governor, apprised of its importance, decided to facilitate it. Events that occurred at this time gave a different aspect to the circumstances, however, for the Caribs of the Orinoco had gone back out onto the Llanos to hunt men, and had destroyed several Indian towns on the marshes near the river channels. When they had reached the vicinity of Valencia with their fires and cruelties, the residents asked for Governor Luis de Rojas's help, and he called upon Garci-González to rectify the situation. He valued the governor's confidence so highly that he felt obligated to think no more for the moment of rebuilding the city in the land of the Quiriquires.

Garci-González, having decided to make the expedition against the Caribs and pledged his reputation on the outcome, left the city with sixty foot soldiers, twenty cavalry, and one hundred Arbaco Indians under the command of Cacique Querepana. He marched through the plains in search of the Guárico River, whose banks served the Caribs as a campsite from which to start their invasions. As he did not know exactly where to find them, however, he took the lead with the sixteen cavalry and sixty Arbacos, leaving Pedro Alvarez Franco with orders to follow him with the rest of the men. At midnight of the next day he arrived on the banks of the Guárico, and by the light of a bonfire burning on the beach, he found four Indians calmly sleeping. He promptly captured them, and

## CHAPTER V

without coercion they told him that four leagues from there the Caribs, numbering up to six hundred, had their principal camp.

On learning this, some of the soldiers insisted that they attack that night, but Garci-González rejected the proposal as being dictated by fear, and decided to wait there until the troops he had left behind arrived. The entire body reassembled the next day under the command of Pedro Alvarez, and guided by Indian prisoners, departed at a rapid pace as soon as night fell in search of the Caribs. Not knowing that there might be Spaniards about, they were so carefree that the cacique, who was also principal military leader, went out early that morning to hunt on the riverbanks. Suddenly coming across our men, he was astounded for a moment by their unexpected appearance, and he quickly shot three or four arrows at Garci-González. One of them passed through his armored cloak and pierced his thigh, luckily at a slant. Then, in turn, he spurred his horse and hurled a lance blow at the cacique's chest that left him dead on the ground.

The main body of our men arrived at the Caribs' little town a short time later, and there the Indians saw hoisted high on a lance their cacique's head, borne by a soldier as a trophy. The Indians began to defend themselves in a dispirited way while one of the dead man's sons tried to animate them to avenge his father's death; but total ruin was soon to come to the natives (the Battle of Guárico). Garci-González was pursuing an Indian when his horse ran into a hole at such high speed that it stumbled and threw him from his saddle. As he lost control of the reins and could not restrain the steed, it broke through the squadron of Caribs, neighing and bucking. This threw them into such disorder that Damián del Barrio, Alonso Camacho, Alonso Ruiz, Juan García Carrasco, Andrés González, Alonso Pérez de Valenzuela, Tomás González, Francisco de Nava, Flores Rondón, and the other men on horseback were able to bring destruction to the confused barbarians with their lances. Further slashed to bits by the foot soldiers, the Indians' cadavers were left strewn on the field. The Spaniards then took away the canoes of those lucky enough to have reached them, and the rest suffered either death or perpetual slavery.

BOOK VII

## CHAPTER VI

*Sebastián Díaz founds the city of San Juan de la Paz in the land of the Quiriquires; he then crosses a mountain range and founds San Sebastián de los Reyes on the Llanos.*

ELATED at the defeat of the Caribs, Garci-González returned to Caracas to enjoy his reward. Governor Luis de Rojas gave him permission to return immediately to reestablish his lost town; but in truth, Garci-González either was tired of such repeated forays or he now looked with misgivings at that expedition on which he had had such bad luck. At any rate, he no longer wished to be involved, and gave any pretext that might serve as a legitimate excuse. Others previously had been inhibited by respect for him from aspiring to the mission, but many, seeing that he now desisted, began earnestly to solicit it. The principal one was Sebastián Díaz de Alfaro, native of San Lúcar de Barrameda, and the governor conceded the assignment to him because of his widely recognized merits as one of General Diego de Losada's former captains.

In the year 1584, Sebastián Díaz, accompanied by his son, Mateo Díaz de Alfaro, Melchor de San Juan, Juan Fernández Trujillo, Mateo de Laya, Melchor de León, Hernando Gómez, Alonso García Pineda, Diego de Ledesma, Juan Rodríguez Espejo, Bartolomé Sánchez, Frutos Díaz, Gaspar Hernández, Cristóbal Suárez, Vicente Galeas, Cristóbal Quintero, and up to eighty other well-known persons, including as chaplain Alonso López de San Martín, native of Badajoz, entered the land of the Quiriquires. He found the province calm, under the subjugation in which Garci-González had left it; he did not experience any activity that might suggest disobedience, and was received with flattering attention by the caciques. On the banks of the Tuy, four leagues below where its waters join the Guaire, he founded the city of San Juan de la Paz, wishing to suggest in this name that the attempt had succeeded without a sword being unsheathed.

The city began to flourish at once, and from the beginning promised prosperity, but the outcome was very different. After the mines of Apa and Carapa produced during their first two months of operation forty thousand castellanos of twenty-three–carat gold, it seemed clear that the population would vastly increase. That hope was extinguished, however, just as it was beginning to glow, for the intensely humid climate was

## CHAPTER VI

extremely unhealthful. The surrounding mountains did not permit the winds to blow across the land, and a continuous downpour frequently hid the sun for an entire month. The residents at length put health before potential profits, and abandoned the city so hastily that within two years it was completely deserted, even the memory of where the gold was extracted being lost with the passing of time. Again, in the year 1606, Governor Sancho de Alquiza made an attempt to acquire that unclaimed wealth, but he experienced the same reverses as his predecessors and abandoned the project completely. In later years, others consumed much time and money trying to rediscover the spot, but could never find it. Finally, in 1698, Francisco de Berrotarán, governor of the province, later marquis of the Valley of Santiago, sought it so persistently that, guided by clues found in old documents, he came across houses and other vestiges of the period during which the gold was extracted. Eventually, however, ever-increasing opposition and fiercely-contested lawsuits relating to ownership of the land so exasperated him that he left the matter suspended and the work unaccomplished.

San Juan de la Paz having enjoyed such initially favorable circumstances, Sebastián Díaz left the residents needed to administer it. With the rest of his men, he crossed the mountain to the south and came out onto the immense sea of the Llanos, which run for more than four hundred leagues along the border of the opulent provinces of Peru. Because of their extensive pasturage and the quality of their waters, these lands are very suitable for raising cattle. This benefit, added to the many that the fertility and beauty of the area offered, induced Sebastián Díaz to consider remaining there. He petitioned to settle, and with the approbation of all, founded the city of San Sebastián de los Reyes in the year 1584. Its first regidores were Bartolomé Sánchez, Frutos Díaz, Gaspar Hernández, and Mateo de Laya; the scribe of the Cabildo was Cristóbal Suárez, and its first alcaldes ordinarios were Hernando Gámez and Diego de Ledesma.

This city, which lies fifty leagues south of Caracas, and conserves in its name the memory of its founder, is sparsely populated because its site has been changed several times, as its inhabitants have fled the inconveniences that have hindered its growth. Nevertheless, the celebrated cacao of Orituco that persons of discerning taste so much enjoy, and which is traded along with tobacco and cattle, provides an assured, though meager, income for its citizens.

BOOK VII

# CHAPTER VII

*Cristóbal Cobos begins the conquest of the land of the Cumanagotos; he settles the city of San Cristóbal; and, offended by Don Luis de Rojas, he renders obedience to the governor of Cumaná.*

THE Cumanagoto Indians, vainglorious at having obliged Garci-González to abandon Espíritu Santo and withdraw from the province, were led by their pride to multiply their insults, confident that their continued victories had raised them to the highest rank. Since this presumptuous attitude constantly induced lamentable results, Governor Luis de Rojas was obliged to direct his endeavors toward finding a solution.

The Audiencia de Santo Domingo had condemned Cristóbal Cobos to serve at his own expense in whatever conquests might arise, to satisfy the penalty decreed for the death that his father had inflicted on Francisco Fajardo. Since the governor found in him a combination of all qualities needed for his purpose, he used the pretext of the verdict set by the Audiencia. He ordered Cobos to take as his own commitment the subjugation and punishment of the Cumanagotos, offering, however, to help with the expenses of the enterprise.

Cobos accepted the proposal at once, and, taking one hundred and seventy Spaniards and three hundred coastal Indians, he arrived on the borders of that land in March of 1585. When he reached the Salado River, he was met by Cacique Cayaurima, who led two thousand warriors under his banners. The battle broke out immediately without allowing our men to choose the most advantageous location; and the cacique would have defeated the Spaniards if Cobos had not made supreme efforts that day, commanding like a captain but fighting like a soldier. He succeeded after more than three hours of combat in forcing the Indians to retreat, leaving him unobstructed access to Macarón Pond, but at the cost of Juan Ortiz's life, and that of five or six other foot soldiers.

Cayaurima called other caciques to his aid and added his troops to the eight thousand who had already arrived. He found Cobos entrenched in his camp, provided with four small bronze culverins that, loaded with light ammunition, were aimed at the spot where he expected the enemy to attack. The Spaniards, firing their weapons as the Indians advanced on the fortress, did much damage, since the disordered multitude offered

## CHAPTER VII

an easy target for their shots. Finally, Cayaurima withdrew to a place where the culverins could not reach their mark, and from there he urged the Spaniards to leave their defensive shelter and come forth to show their courage on the open field.

Cobos did not refuse the challenge. Dividing his men into two squadrons, he threw the infantry on one side while he, with forty cavalrymen, attacked the other, thereby obliging the Indians to rush between the two sides to form opposing fronts (Battle of Macarón). Close to Cobos in the vanguard, Cristóbal Mejía de Avila and Hernando Tello plied their lances with such dexterity that the Indians recognized their own ruin as being evident. Thus, they turned as one body against the Spaniards and marked them as their fixed target. The two horsemen who, since their tunics could not resist the sharp penetration of so many arrows, fell dead to the ground at the first encounter, accompanied in disaster by their horses. The Indians considered this feat a certain indication of the victory they might expect, and gained more courage to press the battle.

Cobos, inspiring his men more by example than words, then broke through the barbarians' squadron, slitting with his lance all who tried to hinder him. Since Cayaurima's multitude was so vast, however, it exceeded the strength of our men. Cobos began to doubt the outcome as he observed the barbarians' disregard for life, and their intrepidity in offering their naked bodies to our slashing steel.

The foot soldiers were in no less confusion as, surrounded by an enormous horde of Indians, they did not even have space to wield their swords. Since courage pressed in such a manner often results in rashness, Juan de Campos and Alonso de Grados dashed through the enemy lines in search of Cayaurima. After they found him, they locked him in their arms and carried him off captive; and, supported by some of the cavalry, they took the captured cacique to the camp, where he was bound securely.

The Indians, afraid of risking the life of their cacique if they persisted, hastily deserted the field. Since they needed time to set Cayaurima free, they went to the camp the following day and offered obedience; but Cobos readily recognized that with their sudden surrender they sought only to liberate their cacique. Cobos professed to accept the deception, for he, too, wished to improve his position and to negotiate with that multitude through friendship, even though feigned. After placing a more secure guard on Cayaurima, Cobos assented to peace and moved his camp to the Salado River, a short distance from where it runs into the sea, and there he founded the city of San Cristóbal.

At this time, Rodrigo Núñez Lobo arrived in Cumaná to assume the post of governor and captain general of the province, and, on learning of the town that Cobos had founded and the successful progress of his conquest, he went to San Cristóbal to see him. After the two had communicated in strict secrecy, Cobos, moved either by the offers to share benefits that Rodrigo Núñez set forth or his wish to take revenge for Luis de Rojas's failure to provide the help promised for his conquest, repudiated his vows of loyalty to his legitimate governor. He then offered obedience to Rodrigo Núñez, and subjected his new town and all his followers to the jurisdiction of Cumaná. This action, regarded with contempt by Luis de Rojas, who ignored it, formed the basis on which that province from then on remained separated from this nation and subject to Cumaná.

# CHAPTER VIII

*The city of Caraballeda is abandoned; the residents of Caracas bring charges against Don Luis de Rojas; and Don Diego de Osorio comes to govern the province.*

By the beginning of 1586, all military expeditions necessary for the conquest and pacification of the province having been concluded, the settlers should have been enjoying the fruits of peace. Instead, they began to experience outrageous and irrational conduct that bred an enmity which endured for years.

At that time the cities of the province were governed by four regidores, whose duty it was to name alcaldes for the administration of justice. When Governor Luis de Rojas arrived in 1586, however, he ordered the regidores of Caraballeda not to make the customary selections, as he himself wished to appoint the officials. Thus dispossessed of a privilege inherent to their office, the regidores respectfully questioned the governor's mandate. Unwilling to accept those chosen, they met in Cabildo on January 1, and selected their own alcaldes. When his order was not followed, the governor indignantly declared the action an infringement of his rights, and ordered that the four regidores be taken as prisoners to Caracas.

Most of the residents of Caraballeda considered this rebuff of their regidores to be a common grievance. They consequently abandoned the city in favor of Valencia, a change easily made at that time, since the houses were no more than straw huts, and their owners were unconcerned with the small cost of losing them. This decision inflamed the governor even more, and branding the move open rebellion, he endeavored to substantiate that charge by introducing as accomplices various residents of Caracas, attributing to them the guilt of having had a part in the counsel. The principal person charged was Captain Juan de Guevara, who, because of his nobility, merits and wealth, was a leader in the province. Feeling himself unjustly slandered and abused by the harsh imprisonment imposed on him, he sought means to justify and avenge himself. Since relief could come only from a higher tribunal, however, he gave his power of attorney to a mestizo, Juan de Urquijo, whom he esteemed for his energy and intelligence, and sent him to Court to present his complaint and bring charges against Luis de Rojas.

On his arrival in Spain, Urquijo learned that the term of office for Luis de Rojas was almost over, and that the king had named Diego de Osorio, general of the galleys that guarded the coast of Santo Domingo, to fill that post. Urquijo submitted the charges to the Council, which ordered their verification through a residencia entrusted to Diego de Osorio himself. He, not yet informed of his promotion, was on the island of Hispaniola commanding his galleys when Urquijo arrived in Santo Domingo at the close of 1587, and delivered the dispatches by hand authorizing Osorio to take office immediately. After the residencia was announced, Luis de Rojas began to experience changes in his fortune. Besieged as a criminal, he learned belatedly the difference between being revered as a superior, and submissive as a subject. As the aggrieved were many and the rivals powerful, complaints increased and charges solidified. Subsequently, all his goods were attached, and he was placed in prison, where he was obliged to endure rebuffs that he did not deserve. He was even reduced to begging alms to support himself, but Juan de Guevara, who had brought the charges against him, was moved now to pity. He assisted him with whatever he needed and, after the litigation was concluded, he gave Don Luis five hundred doubloons for a voyage to Spain.

Licentiate Diego de Leguisamón brought additional discontent to the factions that had approved of Luis de Rojas's course of action when he was sent by the Audiencia de Santo Domingo in 1588 to investigate reports of mistreatment of the Indians, and to verify the manner in which they had been subjugated. Since most citizens were involved in these actions, those pronounced guilty were distressed by the excessive number of convictions and fines that the judge imposed so that his work would appear to have been productive. When the time limit of Leguisamón's activities was extended, the city, fearing its destruction, sent Juan Riveros, former lieutenant general of the province, to Santo

Domingo as their advocate. There he disclosed to the Audiencia Leguisamón's excesses and the prejudicial treatment which the citizenry suffered, their wealth being consumed by his vastly increased commissions. In view of documentary evidence presented to Riveros to justify their complaint, the Audiencia ordered Leguisamón to cease the practice and make restitution of taxes collected above the authorized amount. The city so greatly esteemed this benefit that, to show its gratitude for Riveros's solicitude, it made him a donation from the ejidos, or common lands, in the section called Tierras del Rincón (Corner Lands).

## CHAPTER IX

*The province sends Simón de Bolívar to Spain as its procurator; Don Diego de Osorio undertakes to put the affairs of government in order; and Juan Fernández de León settles the town of Guanare.*

Diego de Osorio, free at last of Luis de Rojas's residencia, now undertook to revive the deserted city of Caraballeda as a safe port for loading and unloading ships. The residents were so filled with rancor over their previous experience, however, that Osorio was unable to induce them to resettle it because a lack of security on that site left them exposed to attack by pirates.

Since it was imperative to select another port after Caraballeda was abandoned, Osorio chose La Guaira, a little more than a league to the leeward, because it was only five leagues from Caracas, and thus more convenient for trade and communication. At that time it contained nothing more than a few warehouses, but afterward dwellings gradually were built and people settled there, so that it has become a town of moderate size. It is provided with artillery units and one hundred and thirty garrisons, and it has a warden. In addition to being military commander of its forces, he is chief justice of the port, having been named to that post by the governor and accepted by the Cabildo of Caracas. The town owes its growth to Osorio's original plans and to his special gift for governing. This province recognizes that he protected it in every way, corrected abuses and defects, and established the economy it enjoys today.

For certain aspects of this reformation, Osorio first had to secure

## CHAPTER IX

orders from the king since he, as governor, could not arbitrate them. Then, as soon as the Cabildo of Caracas became aware of his desires, it readily found means to facilitate them. Osorio's pressing need for a coadjutor was met when in 1589 he named Simón de Bolívar to that vital post. As procurator general of the province, he was authorized to go to Spain to bring to the king's attention matters that required redress. Early in 1590, Bolívar attained without any difficulty not only his principal petitions but also other favors of consequence to the province. Counted as first among them should be permission to register those liable for sales taxes assessed in favor of the cities, in exchange for a small amount to be contributed to the king for a period of ten years. Almost equally valued concessions were the authority to admit one hundred shiploads of blacks without paying royal duties, and the extension of a privilege, previously granted at the request of Sancho Briceño, for the city of Caracas annually to name a person to bring at his own cost a registered merchant ship to the port of La Guaira.[3]

Simón de Bolívar spent the entire year of 1591 in making these petitions, and returned to the province in mid-1592. With the king's authorization, Osorio now began to put into action previously formulated plans to establish order. He allotted repartimientos, designated ejidos, assigned private lands, established archives, issued ordinances, congregated the Indians into towns and converted a shapeless embryo into a formal political entity. On reflection that from El Tocuyo and Barquisimeto southward to the boundary between this province and the Nuevo Reino there was much space without any town to secure possession of the region, he ordered Juan Fernández de León to settle the place that appeared most suitable. In fulfillment of this order, Espíritu Santo, now called Ciudad de Guanare, was founded in 1593 at an extremely hot but healthful site on the banks of the Guanare River. It abounds in fish, easily caught in the rivers that encompass it, and in cattle, because the extensive plains offer great advantage for raising them. This small town has in its church an image of Nuestra Señora de Coromoto, in dedication to whom devout pilgrims come from all the surrounding provinces, some to seek relief and others to fulfill vows.

To avert several disadvantages, Osorio next eliminated the Cabildos' annual election of regidores and established them on a perpetual basis. His Majesty already had appointed two in this category: Garci-González de Silva to the office of general treasurer for life, and Simón de Bolívar to that of royal official of the province, both bearing the privileges of regidor with voice and vote in the Cabildo of Caracas. Following these appointments, in 1594 Osorio announced the remaining officers: chief ensign, Diego de los Ríos; chief justice, Juan Tostado de

BOOK VII

la Peña; and regidores ordinarios, Nicolás de Peñalosa, Antonio Rodríguez, Martín de Gámez, Diego Díaz Bezerril, Mateo Díaz de Alfaro, Bartolomé de Masabel, and Rodrigo de León, the first to have received exclusive rights in perpetuity to these offices.

# CHAPTER X

*Sir Frances Drake (Francisco Draque, El Draque) sacks the city of Caracas; an account of all that happened in the province until the year 1600.*

IN 1594, the province began to suffer adversities. The first was severe hunger that originated from a plague of worms so voracious that they stripped the fields bare and reduced the plants to dust, not leaving enough seed to resow. This privation was common to all, and the affliction increased by the moment as the plague grew more extensive. Since no human remedy was found to eradicate it, the settlers finally sought the divine intercession of the glorious martyr, San Jorge (Saint George), whom they had chosen as patron, to serve as their intermediary. The plague was then controlled, and in gratitude the farmers vowed to build a chapel to the saint. Also, each promised to donate annually up to fifty fanegas of whatever grain he had sown and, through its sale, to adorn the chapel. As their fervor soon grew tepid and the circumstances for their having made the vow were forgotten, the farmers contented themselves with celebrating his feast day in the cathedral on April 23, a tradition that has continued until the present time.

The death of Bishop Juan de Manzanillo, a prelate venerated by this province more as a father than as a bishop, brought the tribulations of the year 1594 to a close. His Majesty appointed Friar Diego de Salinas,[4] of the Dominican Order, a native of Medina del Campo and product of the convent of San Andrés of the same town, to succeed him in this see. As procurator general, he was at Court on business for his order at that time and did not arrive in this bishopric until 1598, having been delayed in Spain by several negotiations.

Now, to pass on to events of the year 1595, Diego de Osorio, wishing to visit all the cities of the province so that, out of respect for his presence, they would be more firmly established, went first to Maracaibo. His absence was partially responsible for the disaster that

CHAPTER X

occurred to Caracas a short time later, for without his vigilance, it remained exposed to catastrophe. The scourge began early in June when the notorious corsair Sir Francis Drake sighted land at the port of Guaicamacuto, half a league to the windward of La Guaira. He disembarked five hundred men and occupied the shore without resistance, because the Indians who might have opposed him had deserted their town earlier and sought serenity in the mountains. Governing Caracas during Don Diego's absence, Garci-González de Silva and Francisco Rebolledo, as alcaldes ordinarios for that year, learned of the corsair's landing. They hastily gathered as many men of arms as they could and went out to meet him on the road from the port to Caracas, resolved to obstruct his entrance with force in case he should attempt to come into the city. This anticipation was well conceived, for they, occupying the narrow passes of the mountains in ambush, would have made it impossible for the corsair to transport his troops without suffering severe damage; but the plan was subverted by an infamous old man. On taking possession of Guaicamacuto, Drake found living there with the Indians a Spaniard named Villalpando, who was either unable or unwilling to withdraw when the natives did. Trying to gain information from this man, the corsair hoped to terrify him by ordering a rope placed around his neck and threatening him with death if he did not answer all questions truthfully. Villalpando was so suffocated by fear that he offered to conduct the pirate along a path so secret that he would come upon the city without being heard.

It was a hidden trail that rose from the town of Guaicamacuto to the summit of the mountain, and from there it descended to the Valley of San Francisco, a route so rugged and intractable that it appeared inconceivable that a human might walk along it. Guided by Villalpando, Drake pursued the march so cautiously that before he could be suspected he arrived with his five hundred men at a spot at the top of the hill from which they could see the city. There, affronted by Villalpando's evil conduct in betraying his own nation, Drake left him hanged from a branch so that the world might know that there still remain elderberry trees in the forests for the punishment of iscariotism.

The city was found to be unprotected because most of the residents had gone with the alcaldes by the Royal Highway to the coast, thinking that the enemy would attempt to march from that direction. Attacked suddenly, a few fled to the woods, but the rest remained exposed to the whim of the corsair and subject to pillage. Deeming it unworthy to turn his back on the enemy without a display of courage, Alonso Andrea de Ledesma, although of advanced age, rode out with his lance and shield to meet the corsair. Drake admired the gallantry of that lone challenger and gave express orders to his soldiers not to kill him, but they, seeing him spur his horse and flash his lance, fired several harquebus shots, from which he immediately fell dead. His demise brought pity and regret even to the corsairs, who carried his body to the city and gave it sepulcher with all the ceremony customarily observed by the military to enhance the obsequies of their leaders.

Garci-González de Silva and Francisco Rebolledo were very remote from all this, awaiting the enemy on the highway from the coast, when they received the news that Drake was already in the city. Seeing their plans countervailed by this unanticipated maneuver, they returned to the valley determined to venture everything on the outcome of one battle in an attempt to dislodge the enemy from the city. Drake, however, suspecting the measure that the alcaldes were preparing, had fortified his forces in the parochial church and palaces, a fact that, when reported to the alcaldes by spies, convinced them that any attempt to reach him would be indefensibly rash.

Since the Spaniards were unable to dislodge Drake, they separated into ambushes from which to hinder his leaving the city to rob the surrounding estates and farmsteads. They safeguarded the families and treasures that had been withdrawn to the country so effectively that the corsair was reduced to conducting himself as if under siege. At the end of eight days, not having dared to take a step outside of his confined space, he demolished many houses and set the rest on fire. Then, with the plunder that he could gather quickly, he returned to his ships, but even with the excellent order of his retreat, he was not spared deterrents to his march and embarcation.

Governor Diego de Osorio was in Trujillo undergoing a residencia when he learned of Drake's invasion. Hastening as much as possible to bring relief with his presence, he expedited the most urgent negotiations at hand and returned to Caracas at the beginning of 1596. There he found Licentiate Pedro de Liaño, recently arrived from Spain, who with terse orders from the king had come to verify certain frauds involving ransoms and the docking of unregistered ships. As anyone making such inquiries induces general anxiety in the public, even though Liaño did not exceed the limits of justified moderation, the citizens felt vulnerable. To relieve the situation and report to the king on the shortages being suffered in the provinces, they sent Nicolás de Peñalosa to Spain as their procurator general to petition that the inquiry be suspended. Their diligence had little effect, however, for the appeal was so much delayed that when the ruling did come from the Council, Liaño, his commission finished and the convictions and fines assessed, had already returned to Spain.

## CHAPTER X

The province was in this state when in 1597 the king promoted Diego de Osorio to the presidency of Santo Domingo in recompense for his services. Gonzalo Piña Lidueña, having founded the city of Gibraltar on the shores of Lake Maracaibo, was living in retirement in Mérida when he was notified that he had been named governor in Osorio's place. Piña Lidueña went at once to Caracas to assume his post, and carried out his duties until April 15, 1600, when, attacked by acute apoplexy, he died. That year, the alcaldes ordinarios, Diego Vázquez de Escobedo and Juan Martínez de Videla, by virtue of the royal cedula obtained in 1570 by Sancho Briceño, were declared alcaldes-governors that same day, and those of the rest of the cities, each in his own district, later received the same double title. They served only a short time, however, because on the death of Gonzalo Piña Lidueña, the Royal Audiencia named as interim governor Alonso Arias Baca, citizen of Coro and son of the learned Licentiate Bernáldez. Adding only Bishop Pedro de Salinas's death in El Tocuyo that same year, 1600, this first part ends, leaving the events of the following century for the second volume.[5]

THE END
O.S.C.S.M.E.C.
(Omnia Sub Correctione Sanctae Matris
Ecclesiae Catholicae—All subject to the censor-
ship of the Holy Mother, Catholic Church.)

# ANNOTATIONS

### INTRODUCTION

1. For clarity of meaning and economy of words, frequently used titles and personal and geographical names have been shortened after their first mention in the introduction, text and annotations to their more commonly recognized forms (for example, Quesada, Piedrahita, Caracas, Bogotá, instead of Jiménez de Quesada, Fernández de Piedrahita, Santiago de León de Caracas, Santa Fe de Bogotá). The index lists both with variants and appropriate cross-references.
2. Guillermo Morón says that Lope de Aguirre's daughter, Elvira, was eighteen years old at the time her father killed her, and that her murder was the last crime committed by this neurotic madman. Academia Nacional de la Historia edition of Aguado, *Historia de Venezuela*, n. 1, vol. 63, p. 365; see also, Archivo General de Indias, Santo Domingo file, 207.

## BOOK I

CHAPTER I

1. For the boundaries of sixteenth-century Venezuela, see Introduction.
2. Gonzalo Jiménez de Quesada gave the name Nuevo Reino de Granada to the central highland region around Santa Fe de Bogotá in 1538 to honor his home province of Granada, Spain. During the colonial period its limits were extended to approximately those of the present-day country. Its name was changed to Colombia in 1861. Larousse, *Diccionario; Century Dictionary and Cyclopedia*.
3. Variants used by chroniclers for the Orinoco River are so numerous and dissimilar as to warrant mention. They include Huyapari, Yuriapari, Yupapari, Vispari, Uriaparia, Uyapare, Arnacay, Urinoco, Urinococo, Uniraco, and Orinucu. Cesáreo Fernández Duro, n. 86, vol. 2 of Oviedo y Baños, *Historia* (1885 ed.)—subsequent references to this work will be abbreviated as Fernández Duro; Rodríguez, *Diccionario biográfico*.
4. Reference here is to the Mixteca Indians, a subdivision of the Timote tribe, which inhabited the upper Chama River region of Venezuela, and not to the Mixtecs of southern Mexico. Larousse, *Diccionario*; Steward, ed., *Handbook of South American Indians*.
5. The *león* of the New World is not of the African species but is the mountain lion (*Felix concolor*), also called puma or cougar; the *tigre* is not the Asiatic type but the jaguar. *Encyclopaedia Britannica; Webster's Third New International Dictionary*.

CHAPTER II

6. In addition to slashing branches from brazilwood trees and tossing tufts of grass to the wind, raising crosses, banners and flags, and reading proclamations were parts of the symbolic ritual observed in taking possession of a land for the kingdom of Spain. Morison says that Christopher Columbus mounted this performance only when a large audience of Indians was present

ANNOTATIONS

to be impressed. Samuel Eliot Morison, *Admiral of the Ocean Sea*, chap. XXXIX, pp. 541–543; Charles L. G. Anderson, *Old Panama and Castilla del Oro*, chap. X, p. 174; Manuel José Quintana, *Vidas de españoles célebres*, Pt. II, pp. 20–21; 39–40.

7. Río de la Hacha was named by the first Spaniards who settled on its banks in commemoration of their giving a hatchet to the Indians to induce them to reveal a source of fresh drinking water. Alcedo, *Diccionario geográfico-histórico*.

8. The mark (*marco*) is an old European measure of weight for gold, silver and precious stones, equivalent to eight ounces. Thus, the Spaniards had more than 1,200 ounces of pearls. *Webster's Third*.

CHAPTER III

9. Two persons of the name Rodrigo de Bastidas, father and son, are prominent in the history of the Indies, but Oviedo y Baños has recorded only the deeds of the bishop/governor son, since the explorer/conquistador father was active to the west of Venezuela in Santa Marta, Castilla del Oro and Cuba. Although Oviedo y Baños lists them as Rodrigo de las Bastidas, all other major chroniclers and historians list them as Rodrigo de Bastidas, the form followed in this translation. Aguado, *Historia de Venezuela*, bk. 2, chap. 21; Schäfer, ed., *Colección de documentos inéditos*.

10. Saint Nicholas, a noted bishop of Asia Minor, followed a busy schedule as patron saint of Russia, seafaring men, merchants, thieves, virgins, children and scholars. Upon his introduction to colonial America, his Dutch name, Sinterklass, was corrupted to Santa Claus. *Century Dictionary and Cyclopedia; Encyclopaedia Britannica*.

CHAPTER IV

11. Oviedo y Baños implies that only one island was granted to Juan de Ampués, but he was named lord of the Islas (plural) de Curazas. He was given the three off the coast from Coro; that is, Curaçao, Aruba and Bonaire. This group was also called Islas de los Gigantes (Islands of the Giants). Rodríguez, *Diccionario biográfico*; Fernández Duro, n. 6.

CHAPTER V

12. Because they found yams along its banks, the soldiers of Alonso Pérez de Tolosa in the Valley of Cúcuta called this stream the Río de las Batatas, a name that did not endure. Aguado, *Historia de Venezuela*, bk. 3, chap. 12; Fernández Duro, n. 55.

13. Oviedo y Baños corrected the names of three rivers which flow into Lake Maracaibo (the Chama, Catatumbo, and Sucui), misnamed Chaca, Cacatomo, and Socuy by Pedro Simón, *Noticias historiales*, notice 2, chap. 3.

14. At the juncture of the Catatumbo and Pamplona (Zulia) rivers, a phenomenon known as the Farol de Maracaibo (Lantern of Maracaibo) or the Relampago de Catatumbo (Lightning of Catatumbo) may be observed at night but is invisible at irregular intervals. It is believed that inflammable gases from Lake Maracaibo are the source of this extraordinary physical manifestation. Rodríguez, *Diccionario*.

15. In addition to Bartolomé Sailler's discovery of Lake Maracaibo, he may claim the distinction of having named the lake's Indian villages Venezuela

(Little Venice) because the houses were built on stilts over the water. This name later was extended to the entire province. Juan de Castellanos's line, "Y Venezuela de Venecia viene" (And Venezuela from Venice comes) corroborates this origin. Castellanos, *Elegías,* pt. 2, Introduction; Alcedo, *Diccionario.*

CHAPTER VI

16. *Alcojolado* is applied to an animal that has dark hair around its eyes. The Spaniards gave this name to a tribe of Indians that allowed a warrior to paint a stripe from the outer tip of his eyes to his ears after he had won a third victory. Those so marked were held in high esteem. Real Academia Española, *Diccionario.*

CHAPTER VII

17. The Index to Schäfer, ed., *Colección de documentos inéditos,* lists this captain as Vascuña. Additional variants include Vasconia, Gascunia, Gascuña and Bascuña. The most widely used and generally recognized form is Bascona.
18. Simón, *Noticias,* notice 2, chap. 5.

CHAPTER VIII

19. Although Gonzalo Jiménez de Quesada should be called Jiménez de Quesada in accordance with Spanish usage, Quesada, the name by which he is known to English-language readers, is used in this translation.
20. Miser or Misú (corruptions of the French *monsieur*) are still in general usage today in the language of the streets of Venezuela to indicate that the person referred to is a foreigner, that is, not a Venezuelan.

CHAPTER X

21. Jorge de Spira's surname is frequently spelled Espira in Spanish, occasionally Despira or Speyer, from the city of his birth. His name in Germany was Georg Formuth or Fermud; in royal cedulas he is called Jeorge Hohermut. Fernández Duro, n. 16; *Diccionario enciclopédico hispano-americano.*
22. Oviedo y Baños erroneously calls this encounter the Battle of Paria (a peninsula and gulf of Venezuela) instead of Pavia (a city of Italy). This battle was of special significance in military history as it demonstrated the superiority of the Spaniards' firearm, the harquebus, over the lance and pike of the French. *Century Dictionary and Cyclopedia; Encyclopaedia Britannica.*

CHAPTER XI

23. In present-day Venezuela there is a city named Acarigua in the state of Portuguesa. Its founding date was either 1641 or 1658, and its population in 1979 was 56,743. There is also a village named Aricagua in the state of Mérida whose population in 1979 was 239. It was founded in the mid-1540s. In a note to the 1885 edition, Fernández Duro states that there were variant spellings for the village, even before the city existed (vol. 1, p. 378). He cites Juan Pérez de Tolosa and Gonzalo Fernández de Oviedo as examples; and Fr. Pedro Simón added another syllable by calling it Acaricagua. It is understandable that this confusion should have existed both then and now, but in the context of Oviedo y Baños's narrative of Jorge de Espira's

expedition into the Andes, it is evident that Espira and his troops were in the village and not the city, since the latter did not exist during his lifetime.

## CHAPTER XIII

24. A note in the Academia Nacional de la Historia reprint of Simón's *Noticias* calls this reference to capes a "made up" or concocted phrase, the white capes designating those who still had to prove their merits while the black capes were troops who were already experienced. These terms, suggestive of a remote linguistic kinship with the black karate belt, may be taken as an expression of the tension and resentment felt among the Spaniards regarding their German superior officers. Simón, *Noticias*, notice 3, chap. 6; Oviedo y Baños, *Historia* (1723 ed.), bk. 1, chap. 13.
25. Sixteenth-century pharmacists mistook the jobo (hog plum or yellow mombin) for *Spondais lutea* and called it *mirobalanos* or *Hernandia Guianensis*. See Jerónimo Bécker's glossary in Aguado, *Historia*; Fernández Duro, n. 24.

# Book II

## CHAPTER I

1. See also Piedrahita, *Historia general*, bk. 3, chap. 4; Simón, *Noticias*, notice 3, chap. 13, for equally poetic accounts of this rare incident.

## CHAPTER III

2. In the language of the natives, *papamene* means "river of silver." Aguado, *Historia*, bk. 2, chap. 11.

## CHAPTER IV

3. Castellanos, Simón, and Aguado were equally critical of the Choques, calling them the dirtiest, most stupid and infamous of people. They ate their own wives and children as well as other kinsmen and the worst of filth; like dogs, they stuffed themselves voraciously on the Spaniards' Indian servants. Alcedo, *Diccionario*; Aguado, *Historia*, bk. 2, chap. 12; Fernández Duro, n. 29.

## CHAPTER VI

4. Poca-Vergüenza—a town near the Apure River and the city of San Fernando on the northern edge of the Llanos. Aguado also relates the origin of this unusual place-name, and finds it as surprising as Oviedo y Baños that Federmann should have spoken in a manner so completely contrary to his nature. Aguado, *Historia*, bk. 2, chap. 16.

## CHAPTER VIII

5. Oviedo y Baños's description of this creature follows that of Simón in almost every detail, except that Simón claimed that it had several heads, and that some of the soldiers called it by the broad generic name of serpent, while others specified that it was a snake. Simón, *Noticias*, notice 4, chap. 15.
6. The zipa who governed Bogotá was one of two principal hereditary chiefs of the Chibchas, Indians of the Nuevo Reino de Granada, the other being the cacique of Tunja. Each zipa was the son of his predecessor's sister, was cared for by a special guardian, and lived subject to singular rules; for

example, he could not look at the sun or eat salt. Alcedo, *Diccionario;* Larousse, *Diccionario.*

7. Accounts of Federmann's death vary widely. Licentiate Juan Pérez de Tolosa says that from Spain, Federmann went to Germany to solicit the governorship of Venezuela but was denied it by the Welsers, who confiscated all his belongings and threw him into prison, where he died. Fernández Duro, n. 32. Other authorities are certain that he left prison and, while sailing toward Spain, was drowned during a shipwreck. Another says he was imprisoned in Flanders for a while but returned to Madrid, where he was at liberty but subject to surveillance until his death in 1542. General uncertainty is expressed as to the time and place of both his birth and death. Rodríguez, *Diccionario.*

CHAPTER XI

8. Indians told the Spaniards the legend of a king, priest or great lord who on special occasions annointed his body with a balsam, covered it with gold dust and, like a resplendent ray of the sun, entered a lake to offer sacrifices. Simón writes that he held as certain that the scene of this ceremony was Lake Guatavita. The Land of the Gilded Man, El Dorado, quickly became the goal of all adventurers of the New World. Simón, *Noticias,* pt. 2, notice 3, chaps. 2 and 3; Fernández Duro, n. 37; *Century Dictionary.*

9. The nispero (medlar, sapodilla, naseberry) is a popular fruit. *Encyclopaedia Britannica* says that it is not fit to eat until it starts to decay, when it takes on a pleasing acid flavor and becomes somewhat astringent. To less critical tastes, medlar preserves are delicious. Its botanical name is *Achras Sapota.* See also *Webster's Third.*

CHAPTER XII

10. Doctor Don Miguel Jerónimo de Ballesteros was the second bishop of Venezuela. He arrived in Coro from Cartagena de Indias where he had been dean. He served in the Coro dioceses from 1550 until his death in 1558 (Rodríguez, Ramón Armando, *Diccionario biográfico).* After the Council of Trent initiated the Counter Reformation in 1554 to combat Protestantism, Spain became the leader of the Catholic world in this struggle. Ballesteros was a leader in this movement in America and in it consumed his energy (*Enciclopedia de Venezuela,* v. 6, p. 429).

CHAPTER XIII

11. The Omeguas occupied parts of eastern Venezuela. Some Omaguas lived on the banks of the Amazon in Brazil, and still others in Colombia and Venezuela. Close to these Omaguas were the Meguas, leading some etymologists to think that Omeguas may be a fusion of the two. The Omeguas became incorporated into the fable of El Dorado. Rodríguez, *Diccionario; Diccionario enciclopédico hispano-americano.*

# BOOK III

CHAPTER I

1. Piedrahita, *Historia general,* bk. 10, chap. 2.
2. Agustín de Zárate in his *Historia del descubrimiento y conquista de la provincia del Perú,* 1st ed. (Antwerp: Martin Nuncio, 1555), 2d ed. (rev.)

(Lima, Peru: Librería e Imprenta D. Miranda, 1944) (Edición revisada con anotaciones y concordances por Juan Kerminic y con prologo de Raúl Porras Barrenechea), bk. 1, chap. 2 used the term "sheep of the land" or "local sheep." Jan M. Kermenic, in an annotation to the 1944 edition of that work, observed that it was common among early chroniclers to call the llamas, alpacas, vicuñas, and guanacos of Peru, sheep. These animals are, however, more closely akin to camels, though they do not have humps; and they are highly valued as beasts of burden, being almost equal to mules in endurance. See also Pedro Cieza de León, *Crónica del Perú*, chap. 111; Santamaría, *Diccionario*; *Webster's Third*.

## CHAPTER II

3. Not only Utre but also Captain Martín de Arteaga was wounded in the same manner and treated by the same method on this occasion. Fernández Duro, n. 44; Castellanos, *Elegías*, pt. 2, elegía 3, canto 1.

4. Although Oviedo y Baños was able to identify only fourteen of Utre's companions, Castellanos named close to thirty. He also extolled a strong, unnamed Portuguese woman, not mentioned by Oviedo y Baños, who bravely wielded her lance alongside the other soldiers. Castellanos, *Elegías*, pt. 2, elegía 3, canto 1; Fernández Duro, n. 45.

5. La Canela was a vast land east of the Andes on tree-covered plains near the Napo River, discovered by Gonzalo Pizarro on his expedition of 1541. It was first settled in 1552, though sparsely, and still remains an uncultivated jungle. Pungent cinnamon (*canela*) gave its name to the region, now inhabited only by poverty-stricken Indians. Alcedo, *Diccionario*.

## CHAPTER III

6. Haman (Amán), minister and favorite of the Persian king Xerxes I, hated Mordecai the Jew because he would not kneel before him. Seeking vengeance, he persuaded Xerxes to order that Mordecai be hanged. When Esther, the condemned man's niece, told Xerxes of Haman's motives, however, the king had Haman hanged on the very gallows he had prepared for Mordecai. Holy Bible, Esther; Fernández Duro, n. 49.

## CHAPTER IV

7. Although Oviedo y Baños and Alcedo both say that Juan Pérez de Tolosa was a native of Segovia, a city of the region of Castile, his contemporaries called him a Biscayan or Basque. Alcedo, *Diccionario*; Rodríguez, *Diccionario*; Fernández Duro, n. 54.

8. Castellanos relates that Carvajal was dragged through the city from the tail of a nag to the place of his execution, and was hanged from a branch of a tree which some say then withered. Juan de Castellanos, *Elegías* (Introduccíon y anotaciones de Isaac J. Pardo, Caracas: pt. 2, elegía 3, canto 2. Academia Nacional de la Historia publicacion #57, 1962). In note 231, the annotator, Pardo, says that José Gil Fortoul wrote a novel of scant poetic value based on this legend, *El ceibo de Carvajal*, 1882.

## CHAPTER V

9. This river has been identified as the Uribante (Oribante), which, in the Venezuelan state of Táchira, flows into the Sarare to form the Apure. Larousse, *Diccionario*; Fernández Duro, n. 50.

## CHAPTER VI

10. Pliny the Elder (Caius Plinius Secundus), *Natural History,* bk. 2, chap. 27; Giovanni Benes Botero, *Relations of the World,* bk. 1.

## CHAPTER VIII

11. The original name, Nueva Segovia, soon fell into disuse, leaving the city with the same name as the province, Barquisimeto, now capital of the state of Lara. Rodríguez, *Diccionario*; Alcedo, *Diccionario.*

12. Diego García de Paredes, the father, served under El Gran Capitán (Gonzalo Fernández de Córdoba) in the sieges of Ronda, Málaga and Granada, and in the campaigns in Italy for which he was knighted by His Catholic Majesty Ferdinand V. Chronicles of Spain relate that while very young, this budding hero stopped with one hand the wheel of a mill turning at full speed. Aguado, *Historia,* bk. 3, chap. 18; Fernández Duro, n. 67. This heroic father is mentioned again in bk. 3, chap. 10, and in bk. 4, chap. 12.

## CHAPTER X

13. Castellanos calls Diego Ruiz Vallejo campmaster instead of accountant. *Elegías,* pt. 2, elegía 3, canto 3; see also Fernández Duro, n. 66.

14. *Yanacona (anacona, yanacón)* is a Quechua word meaning an Indian in the personal service of a Spaniard, although not a slave; especially one who carried burdens on his back along the roads (the equivalent of the Aztec *tlameme*). Santamaría, *Diccionario general*; Steward, ed., *Handbook,* vols. 2 and 5.

15. Escuque is the Indian name of a town that, when settled by the Spaniards in 1556, was named Trujillo, then Miravel in 1559, and finally, after a brief time, was renamed Trujillo. Guillermo Morón, note to Aguado, *Historia,* bk. 3, chap. 18; Rodríguez, *Diccionario.*

## CHAPTER XI

16. As to a possible second part, see Introduction.

17. The *Diccionario enciclopédico hispano-americano* gives this cacique's last name as Juan Cavare, and not Juan Caballo, as Oviedo y Baños called him.

18. Steward, ed., *Handbook* (vol. 4, p. 23), records that the Píritu Indians were known for their addiction to drinking the powdered hearts of their enemies in chicha.

19. González Dávila, *Teatro eclesiástico,* vol. 1, p. 299.

## CHAPTER XII

20. Miravel (Mirabel) was a temporary name for Trujillo. (See n. 15, bk. 3.)

## CHAPTER XIII

21. From this river, the Guaire, the town of La Guaira took its name. Simón spelled it Guairo. Sívoli G., *Diccionario geográfico de Venezuela*; Fernández Duro, n. 80.

22. In 1560 or 1562 (sources differ as to exact year), Francisco Fajardo founded a town which he named El Collado as a compliment to Governor and Captain General Pablo Collado, on the site of a community originally called Caraballeda. The town later was deserted, but in 1568 Diego de Losada established a city on the same site with its former name of Caraballeda.

ANNOTATIONS

When it, in turn, was abandoned, La Guaira, two leagues to its west, became the port for Caracas, as it is today. Rodríguez, *Diccionario*; Steward, ed., *Handbook,* vol. 4, p. 476.

CHAPTER XIV

23. This account of Juan Rodríguez Suárez's escape from prison in Bogotá and flight to Venezuela is repeated almost verbatim by Oviedo y Baños in bk. 4, chap. 6. He cites as his source Piedrahita (*Historia,* bk. 12, chap. 12), who gives his first name as Cristóbal, but it is Juan in the *Diccionario enciclopédico hispano-americano* and in the *Enciclopedia universal ilustrada europeo-americana.*

24. Here Oviedo y Baños gives the number of children murdered as three; on the next page, as two. The *Diccionario enciclopédico hispano-americano* says there were three.

# BOOK IV

CHAPTER I

1. Piedrahita, *Historia,* bk. 2, chaps. 5 and 8.
2. Bayano, king of the runaway black slaves of Los Palenques, Venezuela, fought against colonial power but was subdued by Pedro de Ursúa in 1560, in Panama, and sent as a prisoner to Spain, where he died in Seville. Conte Porras, *Diccionario biográfico de Panamá,* p. 27; Castellanos, *Elegías,* pt. 1, elegía 1, canto 1.
3. Simón says that Lope de Aguirre's men were called Marañones (conspirators, plotters) after the river Marañón because of the many entanglements and plots (*marañas*) in which they were constantly involved. Pedro Mártir de Anghiera and Yáñez Pinzón, among other explorers, had long before called the river the Marañón. Simón, *Noticias,* notice 6, chap. 23; Mártir de Anghiera, *Décadas del Nuevo Mundo,* decade 1, bk. 9, chap. 2.
4. In deference to chronology, this sentence has been shifted from its original position five pages earlier in the Spanish version to its logical place in the action.

CHAPTER III

5. Cecijunto, as it appears in Oviedo y Baños, is spelled *cexijunto* by Simón. It is descriptive of one whose eyebrows grow close together. Aguirre probably meant to suggest that Father Zúñiga was surly, as the tyrant was in no mood to be complimentary. Simón, *Noticias,* notice 6, chap. 36.

CHAPTER IV

6. Oviedo y Baños names this victim of Lope de Aguirre's wrath Diego Gómez de Ampuero here, and Pedro in bk. 6, chap. 13. He must be assumed to be the same person, however, as in both instances he is identified as the husband of Ana de Rojas, and was executed by order of the tyrant on the island of Margarita.
7. Although Oviedo y Baños states here that he was unable to identify the priest whom Lope de Aguirre had murdered, he speaks on the next page of the executions of Ana de Chaves and Simón de Sumorostro, as if this were the

## ANNOTATIONS

clergyman's name. Sumorostro is not listed in standard biographical sources of the Indies.

### CHAPTER V

8. Both the first (1723) and third (1885) editions of the *Historia* have "para pasar del Perú a Panamá" (to pass from Peru to Panama); but in the Fee de Erratas to the 1941 facsimile of the second edition (1824), that geographically impossible route, since the starting point was to have been Nombre de Dios, is corrected to "para pasar de Panamá al Perú" (to pass from Panama to Peru).
9. Practicing Catholics of this period commonly called less-devout persons Lutherans without inferring that they were actually followers of Martin Luther.

### CHAPTER VII

10. *Encyclopaedia Britannica* characterizes this letter as "extraordinary." A note on p. 188 of the William Bollaert translation for the Hakluyt Society of Simón's *Expedition of Pedro de Ursúa and Lope de Aguirre* (notice 6 of the *Noticias*) says that the Oviedo y Baños version of this "very curious" letter apparently was taken from a different manuscript from that used by Simón.
11. Since the action outlined here corresponds to that at Pucará, where large numbers of men deserted Francisco Hernández Girón to return to the royalist forces in October 1554, it is likely that the spelling of Pucaba is in error, even though it occurs in all editions of Oviedo y Baños's *Historia*. Philip Ainsworth Means, *Fall of the Inca Empire and the Spanish Rule in Peru: 1530–1780* (New York: Charles Scribner, 1932), chap. 4, p. 100.
12. William Bollaert in note 1, p. 191, to his translation of Simón's *Expedition of Ursúa and Aguirre*, notice 6 (p. 191), states that Monteverde was murdered long before he reached Margarita, but that since Aguirre killed so many, he could not keep track of the sequence.
13. Bollaert states that this is one of the lakes of Villa, near Chorillos, about fifteen miles from Lima. He suspects that Aguirre might still have been harboring feelings of resentment for having been punished for poaching there. Trans. of Simón, *Expedition of Ursúa and Aguirre*, n. 2, p. 192.
14. Beside the Yaracui River, Lope de Aguirre and his soldiers encountered beautiful female warriors of stately proportions with whom, according to Castellanos, the Spaniards did not lack amorous flames. To honor this memorable occasion, they gave the region the courtly name of Valle de las Damas (Valley of the Ladies). Castellanos, *Elegías*, pt. 2, elegía 1, canto 2.

### CHAPTER IX

15. For additional information and comments on this murder, see Introduction.

### CHAPTER X

16. Other historians place the number at sixty and say that it was Governor Bernáldez and not his predecessor, Collado, who dispatched the Narváez expedition. Aguado, *Historia*, bk. 3, chap. 21; Castellanos, *Elegías*, pt. 2, elegía 3, canto 4; Fernández Duro, n. 75.

## ANNOTATIONS

### CHAPTER XI

17. Licentiate Pablo Bernáldez was also called El Tuerto (The One-Eyed). Alcedo, *Diccionario*; Fernández Duro, n. 77.

### CHAPTER XII

18. Simón, *Noticias,* notice 7, chap. 1.
19. See bk. 3, chap. 8, n. 13.
20. Castellanos attributes Diego de Paredes's death to his desire to visit the fair Catalina de Miranda, said also to have granted favors to Juan de Carvajal and others, but Aguado conforms to the Oviedo y Baños account. Castellanos, *Elegías,* pt. 2, elegía 3, canto 4, and Pardo's note 251 of the Academia Nacional de la Historia edition; Aguado, *Historia,* pt. 2, bk. 3, chap. 21.

### CHAPTER XIII

21. This version does not conform to that of Castellanos. Fernández Duro believed that Oviedo y Baños's account is more credible, however, as he no doubt had access to documents of the families involved. Castellanos, *Elegías,* pt. 2, elegía 3, canto 4; Fernández Duro, n. 79.

# BOOK V

### CHAPTER I

1. Oviedo y Baños says there were one hundred and fifty conquistadors on the march with Losada, and the totals given for the three categories mentioned add up to that sum. His research produced only one hundred and twenty-nine individual names, however.

### CHAPTER VII

2. Santiago (San Diego), for Diego de Losada's baptismal name; León for Pedro Ponce de León, governor of Caracas; and Caracas, for the province and tribe of Indians who inhabited it.
3. Juan Pimentel, scion of the counts of Benavente and a knight of the Order of Santiago, was governor and captain general of Caracas from 1577 to 1583. Most reference sources list him as Juan de Pimentel, but Ernesto Schäfer's Index to the *Colección de documentos inéditos de Indias,* and all early editions of Oviedo y Baños's *Historia* omit the *de. Enciclopedia de Venezuela,* Index; *Diccionario enciclopédico hispano-americano.*
4. González Dávila states that Losada founded the city of Santiago de León de Caracas on the day of the apostle Santiago in 1530, thirty-seven years earlier than its actual founding date of 1567. *Teatro eclesiástico,* vol. 1, p. 287.

### CHAPTER VIII

5. For the contents of this cedula, see bk. 4, chap. 1.
6. First of his family to come to the Indies, Simón de Bolívar was the grandfather, four generations removed, of Simón Bolívar the Liberator. He was sent to Spain by the Cabildos of Venezuela to make various petitions at Court, and in 1592 was granted the favors asked.

### CHAPTER XII

7. The estoc or *estoque* was a thrusting weapon used between the thirteenth and seventeenth centuries. It had a long, narrow rectangular blade of which

only the point wounded. It was more slender than a regular sword (*espada*). Random House, *Dictionary of the English Language*; Real Academia Española, *Diccionario de la lengua castellana*.

CHAPTER XIV

8. Isaac A. Pardo says that Oviedo y Baños's statement that Losada and Ponce de León died almost simultaneously is inexact. This fact may be proved by the later efforts of Losada to obtain the governorship, which became vacant after the death of Ponce de León. Pardo, n. 253 to Academia Nacional de la Historia edition of Castellanos, *Elegías*, pt. 2, elegía 3, canto 4.

# BOOK VI

CHAPTER II

1. Both of these women warriors, Tomyris, queen of the Massagetae, and Zenobia, queen of Palmyra, have been the subjects of history, legend, poetry and fiction. *Oxford Companion to English Literature; Century Dictionary and Cyclopedia.*

CHAPTER IV

2. According to note 11 of the Academia Nacional de la Historia edition of Simón's *Noticias* (vol. 67, p. 512), this interim governor was called Juan de Chaves by Pedro Simón, but his correct name was Francisco Hernández de Chaves. Although the error was perpetuated by Aguado, Piedrahita, and Oviedo y Baños, Juan de Chaves has been retained in this translation for broader recognition, since all other sources consulted use this name.

3. The text reads "más para su asistencia que para su compañía" (more for their assistance than for their company), but the meaning of the sentence requires a shift of nouns. Oviedo y Baños, *Historia*, 1st ed., 1723.

CHAPTER VII

4. For a fuller account of this gladiatorial spectacle, see John Grier Varner and Jeannette Johnson Varner, *Dogs of the Conquest* (Norman: University of Oklahoma Press, 1983), pp. 170–171; see also *Enciclopedia de Venezuela*, Indice cronológico, vol. 6, p. 437; Rodríguez, *Diccionario*, s.v. "Tamanaco," p. 775.

CHAPTER X

5. For similar instances of the use of bone necklaces to stop blood flow, see Juan de Barrios, *Decades of Asia*, decade 2, bk. 6, chap. 2; and Damián de Gois, *Chronicles of King D. Manuel*, chap. 17, p. 3.

CHAPTER XII

6. Francisco Tosta García, in his chronicle-based *Leyendas de la conquista*, calls this animal Amigo, a favorite name for dogs among conquistadors. He mentions Oviedo y Baños's statement that the dog died at the country house, but Tosta García's story relates that Amigo lived and returned to Caracas with Garci-González. There, his master bade his wife, Doña Beatriz de Rojas, weeping for joy at her husband's safe return, to give the dog a fond embrace. (Francisco Tosta García, *Leyendas de la conquista* (Caracas: Tipograpía de Vapor Guttenberg, 1893), chap. 7.

## CHAPTER XIII

7. For the given name of Gómez de Ampuero, see note 6 to bk. 4, chap. 14.

# BOOK VII

## CHAPTER V

1. Friar Pedro de Agreda was appointed to succeed Friar Juan de Manzanillo in 1582. González Dávila, *Teatro eclesiástico*, vol. 1, p. 299; Aguado, *Historia*, bk. 3, chap. 22.
2. Juan López Aburto de la Mata assumed his post as eleventh bishop of Venezuela in 1634, when the cathedral was moved from Coro to Caracas for security reasons. Alcedo, *Diccionario*, vol. 1, p. 296; González Dávila, *Teatro eclesiástico*, vol. 1, pp. 302–303.

## CHAPTER IX

3. See bk. 4, chap. 1, for additional details of this royal cedula.

## CHAPTER X

4. In all three early editions of Oviedo's *Historia* (1723, 1824, 1885), this bishop, within the same chapter and only a few pages apart, is called both Diego de Salinas and Pedro de Salinas. Both the *Diccionario enciclopédico hispano-americano* and Rodríguez's *Diccionario* refer to him as Domingo. Reference apparently is to the same person, however, since details of his life are identical in all sources.
5. See Introduction as to the possibility of a second volume.

# GLOSSARY

Numerous words and phrases that would be suitable for either the Glossary or the Annotations have been placed in one or the other of these categories, but some are in both. Readers are urged to consult each of them in order to avoid an oversight. Spanish and Indian words commonly used in English are not italicized.

ADELANTADO  Military or civil official, leader of an expedition, governor of a province, captain general in time of war.

ALCALDE  Administrative and judicial officer in a village, town or district of Spain or region under Spanish dominion; magistrate, judge, justice of the peace.

*ALCOJOLADO*  Black-rimmed eyes; applied to animal that has dark hair around its eyes; Alcojolados, name of Indian tribe of Venezuela.

ALGUACIL (ALGUAZIL)  Officer of justice, formerly of high, now of inferior rank; sheriff or constable in Spain or regions under Spanish influence.

*ARCABUZ*  See HARQUEBUS.

ARROYO  Brook, creek, stream, watercourse, water-carved gulley or channel, dry wash, ravine, bed through which small stream flows.

AUDIENCIA  Royal tribunal, high court of justice, district under its jurisdiction, building in which it meets. In the Spanish colonies, a high court of justice frequently exercising military, judicial and political power.

AYUNTAMIENTO  Municipal council or governing body of a town or city of Spain or former Spanish colony; town hall, town, city or borough council, meeting, action and effect of meeting.

BACHILLER  Bachelor; one who has attained the equivalent of a bachelor's degree.

BALSA  Tree of Central America, South America and the West Indies; its wood is lighter than cork but is very strong; used especially for floats and rafts.

BARRANCA  Deep gulley or arroyo; water-carved ravine with sheer sides; a steep bank or bluff.

*BISAO*  See VIJAO.

BIXA (VIJA)  American genus of tree with cordate leaves and large pink or rose flowers from which red or yellowish-red dye is extracted; used especially for coloring oils, cheese and butter; paste also used by Indian warriors for disguise or to terrorize.

CABILDO  Town hall, town council, town council meeting; cathedral chapter house, chapter meeting, room where meeting takes place; body of ecclesiastics of a church.

CACAO  Tree native to South America and now extensively cultivated also in the West Indies, Mexico and Central America; chocolate (tree, powder and beverage).

CACICA  Feminine of CACIQUE, q.v.

CACIQUE  Native Indian chief, especially of West Indies, Central and South America (from Arawak, *kassequa*); king, prince.

## GLOSSARY

CANELA  Cinnamon spice and bark of aromatic smell and taste; used to perfume chocolate; monotypic genus of trees having alternate leathery dotted leaves and flowers with three sepals; produces berries. La Canela (Land of Cinnamon), region of Upper Peru.

CANEY  Antillean word meaning large hut or cabin with conical roof used to house Indian chiefs; later came to mean also peasant's hut.

CASHEW BIRD (GUAN, *PAUJÍ, PAUXÍ*)  Large tubercule, bluish and hard as a rock, protrudes above bird's beak; resembles cashew nut to such a remarkable degree that it has given origin to this evocative name; any of several large tropical American birds, highly valued for sport and food by hunters; similar to wild turkey in size; common in lowland forests.

CASSAVA  Of genus *manihot*, has fleshy root stock and yields nutritious starch; cultivated throughout tropics, where it provides a staple food; also called manioc and tapioca; used to make tapioca, cassava bread and starch.

CASTELLANO  Old Spanish gold coin bearing Castilian arms; ancient Spanish unit of weight equivalent to one-fiftieth of a mark.

CEDULA  In Spain or Latin America signifies official statement, such as a permit or order issued by the government; document or certificate; official writ acknowledging a debt; royal cedula is decree from king.

CEIBA  Large genus of tropical American trees with palmately compound leaves and bell-shaped flowers; silk-cotton tree; tree whose fruit contains cotton.

CHACHALACA  See GUACHACARACA.

CHAGUALA  Colombian word meaning metal ornament worn by Indians; nose ring; indigenous word for metal plaque, usually of gold, often in shape of eagle with outstretched wings, from which the Spaniards called it *águila* (eagle). Oviedo y Baños described it as a golden, eagle-shaped plaque worn around the neck, as a bracelet, or as earrings.

CHOQUES  A cannibalistic tribe of Indians of Venezuela; bellicose, filthy, belligerent.

CORDILLERA  Mountain ranges forming a system of parallel chains.

CULVERIN  Firearm, originally a rude musket, but in sixteenth and seventeenth centuries this word referred to a long cannon (such as an eighteen-pounder) with serpent-shaped handles; ancient artillery of small bore.

DEMORA  Forced labor; literally, delay. During the sixteenth century in the Indies this word designated an eight-month obligatory work period imposed on Indians in exchange for their exemption from annual taxes.

ENCOMIENDA  Colonial institution in America based on distribution of Indians among the conquistadors. The Indians were obliged to work or pay tribute to their masters, called encomenderos. For their part, the Spaniards had the obligation to teach the Indians the Christian religion and instruct them according to the Laws of the Indies. This system, initially in force in Hispaniola, spread to all the countries of Hispanoamerica.

ESCAUPIL  Quilted, cotton-padded jacket or tunic worn by the Indians as protective armor against arrows; quickly adopted by the Spaniards for themselves, their horses and dogs.

FALCON  Light piece of ordnance used from fifteenth to seventeenth century; ancient small cannon.

## GLOSSARY

FANEGA  Unit of capacity used in Spain and Spanish American countries, especially one of about 1.6 bushels; also unit of land measurement equal to 1.59 acres; measure of capacity for dry commodities (55.5 liters).

FISCAL  Agent of exchequer, public treasury; public officer (prosecutor or policeman) or colonial magistrate.

FOTUTO  In Cuba, claxon, horn or trumpet made of seashell; in Venezuela, Indian flute.

FRAGUA, LA  Forge, place where artisan works in hard materials; a smithy; place used to repair arms and tools.

GANDUL  In general, during conquest, this word meant fighting Indian, warrior; more specifically, it referred to a member of a tribe of Indians who inhabited the coast of Venezuela. In modern Spanish this word has the colloquial sense of vagrant, tramp.

GENTILHOMBRE DE BOCA  "Mouth gentleman"  Man of good family who served in royal dining hall; original functions were to serve the king at table and as a food taster to guard against poisoning; duties later broadened to accompany monarch when he rode outside palace grounds on horseback; followed mayordomo (majordomo, steward) in rank.

GUACHACARACA (CHACHALACA)  Texas guan or any bird of related species; name derives from Náhuatl, means the twittering of a bird; domestic fowl found in Venezuela and Colombia.

GUAICA  Genus of tropical American tree and shrub; has pinnate leaves, mostly blue flowers, and capsular fruit; yields hard greenish wood. In Venezuela, designates a kind of cane; javelin or dart that the Indians used in time of conquest; plant from which these darts were made.

HALBERD  Weapon used especially in fifteenth and sixteenth centuries; consisted typically of battle-ax and pike mounted on a handle about six feet long.

HANEGA  See FANEGA.

HARQUEBUS (ARCABUZ)  Portable matchlock gun invented in mid-fifteenth century; attached by fixed hook to support; wheel lock or flintlock modifications lightened weapon so that it could be fired from shoulder.

JAGUA  See YAGUA.

JAYO  See MALANGA.

JOBO (HOBO)  Hog plum or yellow mombin; tall, leafy tree with fragrant yellow flowers; flourishes in tropical countries, especially West Indies and Mexico.

KING'S FIFTH  See ROYAL FIFTH.

LA CANELA  See CANELA.

LEÓN, TIGRE  The lion of the New World is not the African species but is the mountain lion (*Felix concolor*), also called puma or cougar; the tiger is not the Asiatic type but is the jaguar.

LICENTIATE  One who has a license to practice a profession; authorized; one who holds university or college degree.

LLANOS  Region of Venezuela between cordilleras of the Andes and the Caribbean, between the Meta and Orinoco rivers; level, flat, extensive plain with few trees; branches occasionally into Colombia.

## GLOSSARY

MACANA   Wooden weapon or agricultural tool widely used by Indians of South America and Antilles; usually made like a flattened club or sword, sometimes edged or headed with stone; bruising weapon similar to machete; also a primitive hoe.

MAGAGUA (MAHAGUA)   Two malvaceous trees often considered variant forms of single species; shrubby, irregularly spreading tree, widely distributed along tropical shores; yields light, tough wood used especially for canoe outriggers and fibrous bast used for cordage or caulking; cultivated both for ornaments and its useful products.

MALANGA (JAYO)   Valued for its edible root, which may be cooked in variety of ways or used as fermented paste like the Hawaiian staple, poi.

MAR DEL NORTE   Sea of the North, Northern Sea. Commonly used name in sixteenth century for Caribbean.

MAR DEL SUR   Sea of the South, Southern Sea. Generally used of Pacific Ocean in sixteenth century to distinguish it from MAR DEL NORTE, q.v.

MARAVEDÍ   Moorish coin of Spain and Morocco dating from eleventh or twelfth century; of gold or copper worth one–thirty-fourth of a real.

MARCO Mark   European measure of weight for gold, silver or precious stones; equivalent to eight ounces; of German origin.

MOHÁN (MOJÁN)   *See* PIACHE.

NÍSPERO   Plants of genus *Achras* such as sapodilla, medlar, or naseberry; rosacious shrub with pink fruit and blossoms; thrives in Spanish America.

OIDOR   Judge, one who hears (from *oír*); magistrate who in Audiencias of Spain and Spanish America hears and passes sentence at trials.

PARAMO   High, bleak plateau; barren desert land.

PAVA DE MONTE   *See* UQUIRA.

PESO   Spanish and Spanish American monetary unit, formerly equal to eight reales; piece of eight, piaster; used in present-day Argentina, Colombia, Cuba, Dominican Republic, Mexico, Philippines and Uruguay.

PIACHE   Witch doctor, sorcerer, herbalist; pagans in pre-Columbian times made use of them to consult demons and to observe their auguries and superstitions; also called *mohán* or *moján*.

PIROGUE (PIRAGUA)   Dugout canoe, boat like a canoe, canoe made of hollowed tree trunk, navigated by oar or sail.

PITA   Fiber-yielding plants such as century plant, yucca, Central American wild pineapple; the fiber of a pita; thick, fleshy, pulpy leaves more than a meter in length. Oviedo y Baños mentions convent of Dominican nuns noted for their work with pita thread or string.

PROCURATOR   Proxy, agent, proctor, solicitor, one in charge of another's affairs.

PROVINCIAL   Monastic superior who directs all religious houses in a province of the same ecclesiastical order.

QUEBRADA   Ravine, gorge, break, split in earth caused by water, stream, rivulet.

QUINTO REAL   *See* ROYAL FIFTH.

REAL DE MINAS   Mining town. Term used in Indies for town that had silver or gold mines in vicinity.

## GLOSSARY

REGIDOR   Member of body of officers in charge of Spanish American municipality; corresponds to English alderman, councilman.

REPARTIMIENTO   Grant to Spanish colonists; concession of Indians for forced labor in mines, fields or construction; land on which they lived and worked, given in fief to conquerors of Spanish America as reward for services; similar to ENCOMIENDA, q.v.

RESIDENCIA   Obligatory inquiry or investigation held for seven months on retirement or reassignment of high official, such as viceroy, captain general, governor; directed by specially commissioned judge; comparable to *VISITA GENERAL*, q.v.

ROYAL FIFTH (KING'S FIFTH, QUINTO REAL).   Fifth part of proceeds from deposits of gold and silver mines owed to Crown by colonists of Spanish America; payment enforced by Mining Tribunal.

TACAMACA   Aromatic resin used in ointments, for incense and as efficacious relief of headaches; from Náhuatl, *tecomahiyac* (stinking pot tree).

TIERRA FIRME   Mainland of the Indies, term that designates northern coastal countries of South America from Gulf of Paria at mouth of Orinoco River, westward to Isthmus of Panama. Sometimes carelessly called Spanish Main by modern writers.

UQUIRA   Pheasant from eastern Venezuela and the Guayanas; dark bronze-colored with green reflections, has beautiful neck crest which it raises and lowers at will; neck and breast spotted with white. In Venezuela it is also called *pava de monte* (mountain turkey hen).

VARA   Spanish and Portuguese unit of length used in Latin America and southwestern United States; varies from 31 to 34 inches (33.33 inches in Texas).

VERA   Timber tree of northwestern South America; its very hard, brownish-yellow wood may be substituted for lignum vitae.

*VERSO*   *See* CULVERIN.

*VIJA*   *See* BIXA.

VIJAO   Tropical, banana-like plant with huge leaves and showy blooms; portions edible, but Juan de Castellanos describes it as bland, to be eaten only when nothing else available; its seeds are a source of black coloring matter. Also called *visao*.

VISITA GENERAL  General inspection.   Inspection or investigation intended to ensure honesty among officials, routinely conducted at end of term of governor or other dignitary of high rank; comparable to RESIDENCIA, q.v.

YAGUA (JAGUA)   Puerto Rican palm with thick woody sheathing leaf base, resembles royal palm; used as vegetable, to make huts, baskets, hats, and sisal or hemp rope; provides oil for lamps; has edible fruit, orange-sized, called genipap.

YANACONA (ANACONA, YANACÓN)   An Indian in personal service of a Spaniard.

ZIPA   Colombian-Antillean word meaning cacique.

# SELECT BIBLIOGRAPHY

For commentary on editions, reprints and facsimiles of José de Oviedo y Baños's *Historia de la conquista y población de la provincia de Venezuela*, see Introduction. The publisher, place of publication and date of each are:
1. Gregorio Hermosilla, Madrid, 1723.
2. Domingo Navas Spínola, Caracas, 1824.
3. Luis Navarro, Madrid, 1885.
4. Parra León Hermanos, Caracas, 1935.
5. Paul Adams (through Charles Scribner's Sons), New York, 1940 (deluxe edition); 1941 (trade edition).
6. Ediciones Atlas 19, Madrid, 1965.
7. Ediciones Ariel, S.A., Barcelona, Spain, 1967.
8. Fundación CADAFE, Caracas, 1982 (facsimile, 2 vols. Colección Caura: 2).

## Critical Works on José de Oviedo y Baños

GRASES, PEDRO. *De la imprenta en Venezuela y algunas obras de referencia.* Caracas: Universidad Central de Venezuela. Ediciones de la Facultad de Humanidades y Educación, Escuela de Bibliotecología y Archivología, 1979.

MIERES, ANTONIO. *Tres autores en la historia de Baralt.* Caracas: Instituto de Estudios Hispanoamericanos, Universidad Central de Venezuela, 1966.

MORÓN, GUILLERMO. *Los cronistas y la historia.* Caracas: Ministerio de Educación, Dirección de Cultura y Bellas Artes, 1957.

———. *José de Oviedo y Baños, 1671–1783.* Caracas: Fundación Eugenio Mendoza, 1958.

PARRA LEÓN, Caracciolo, comp. Part 1 of *Oviedo y Baños, "Historia de Venezuela." Analectas de historia patria.* Caracas: Parra León Hermanos, 1935.

PICÓN SALAS, MARIANO. *De la conquista a la independencia.* 2d ed. México, D.F.: Fondo de Cultura Económica, 1950.

PLANCHART, JULIO. *Discurso ante la Academia Nacional de la Historia, 15 de marzo, 1941.* (Tema: "Oviedo y Baños y su *Historia de Venezuela*"). Caracas: Tipografía Americana, 1941.

## Histories of the Caribbean Region During the Conquest Period

AGUADO, PEDRO DE. *Historia de Venezuela.* Part 2 of *Historia de Santa Marta y Nuevo Reino de Granada.* Madrid: Impr. J. Ratés, ca. 1581.

ANDERSON, CHARLES L. G. *Old Panama and Castilla del Oro,* New York: North River Press, 1911.

CASTELLANOS, JUAN DE. *Elegías de varones ilustres de Indias.* 4 parts. Madrid: M. Rivadeneyra, 1589 (part 1); 1847–1886 (parts 2–4).

GIL FORTOUL, JOSÉ. *Historia constitucional de Venezuela.* 4th ed. Caracas: Ministerio de Educación, Dirección de Cultura y Bellas Artes, 1954.

GONZÁLEZ DÁVILA, GIL. *Teatro eclesiástico de la primitiva iglesia de las Indias Occidentales.* Madrid: D. Díaz de la Carrera, 1649–1655.
HERRERA Y TORDESILLAS, ANTONIO DE. *Historia general de los hechos de los castellanos en las islas y Tierra Firme del mar océano.* Madrid: Impr. N. Rodríguez Franco, 1601–1615.
MÁRTIR DE ANGHIERA, PEDRO. *Décadas del Nuevo Mundo.* Alcalá de Henares: Miguel de Eguía, 1530.
MORISON, SAMUEL ELIOT. *Admiral of the Ocean Sea: A Life of Christopher Columbus.* Boston: Little, Brown & Company, 1944.
OVIEDO Y VALDÉS, GONZALO FERNÁNDEZ DE. *Historia general y natural de las Indias, islas y Tierra Firme del Mar Océano.* Sevilla: Juan Cromberger, 1535.
PIEDRAHITA, LUCAS FERNÁNDEZ DE. *Historia general de las conquistas del Nuevo Reino de Granada.* Antwerp: J. B. Verdussen, 1688.
SIMÓN, PEDRO. *Noticias historiales de las conquistas de Tierra Firme en las Indias Occidentales.* Cuenca: Domingo de las Iglesias, 1626–1627.

## ENCYCLOPEDIAS, HANDBOOKS AND BIBLIOGRAPHIES

*Century Dictionary and Cyclopedia.* Vol. 9, *Names.* New York: The Century Company, 1889.
*Enciclopedia de Venezuela.* Caracas: Andrés Bello, 1973–1975.
*Enciclopedia universal ilustrada europeo-americana.* Madrid: Espasa-Calpe, 1921.
*New Catholic Encyclopedia.* New York: McGraw-Hill, 1967.
STEWARD, JULIAN HAYNES, ed. *Handbook of South American Indians.* New York: Cooper Square Publishers, 1963.
WILGUS, ALVA CURTIS. *The Historiography of Latin America.* Metuchen, N.J.: Scarecrow Press, 1975.

## DICTIONARIES, GLOSSARIES AND INDEXES

ALVARADO, LISANDRO. *Glosario de voces indígenes de Venezuela.* Caracas: M. & R. Angel, 1921.
———. *Glosario del bajo español en Venezuela.* Caracas: Lito-Tip. Mercantil, 1929.
REAL ACADEMIA ESPAÑOLA. *Diccionario de la lengua castellana.* Madrid: Real Academia Española, 1726–1739 (also 19th ed., Buenos Aires: Espasa-Calpe, 1970).
SCHÄFER, ERNESTO, ed. *Colección de documentos inéditos de Indias.* Index. Madrid: Consejo Superior de Investigaciones Científicas, Instituto Gonzalo Fernández de Oviedo, 1946–.
SANTAMARÍA, FRANCISCO J. *Diccionario general de americanismos.* México, D.F.: Editorial Pedro Robredo, 1942.

## HISTORICAL, BIOGRAPHICAL AND GEOGRAPHICAL DICTIONARIES

ALCEDO, ANTONIO DE. *Diccionario geográfico-histórico de las Indias Occidentales o América.* Madrid: Impr. de B. Cano, 1786–1789.

## SELECT BIBLIOGRAPHY

CONTE PORRAS, J. *Diccionario biográfico de Panamá*. Ciudad de Panamá: Impr. de Panamá, 1975.

*Diccionario enciclopédico hispano-americano*. Barcelona: Montaner & Simón, 1887–1899.

LAROUSSE. *Diccionario enciclopédico*: Paris and Buenos Aires: Editorial Larousse, 1958.

RODRÍGUEZ, RAMÓN ARMANDO. *Diccionario biográfico, geográfico e histórico de Venezuela*. Madrid: Imprenta de los Talleres, Penitenciarios de Alcalá de Henares, 1957.

SÍVOLI G., ALBERTO. *Diccionario geográfico de Venezuela*. Caracas: Ediciones Eneva, 197?

VILA, MARCO AURELIO. *Diccionario de tierras y aguas de Venezuela*. Caracas: Ministerio de Obras Públicas, Dirección de Cartografía Nacional, 1976.

# INDEX

Aburto de la Mata, Juan López (bishop). *See* López Áburto de la Mata, Juan
Acaprapocón (cacique), 230–231
Achaguas (Indian tribe), 62
Acona, Agustín de (alcalde), 195
Acosta, Antonio de, 171
Acosta, Duarte de, 171, 195, 210
Acosta, Pedro de, 139
Acuareyapa (cacique), 241
Adame, Diego de, 187
Agorreta, Francisco, 171
Agreda, Pedro de (bishop), 107, 120–121, 191, 251–252
Agudo, Diego, 33
Aguilón (soldier), 58
Aguirre, Cristóbal de, 83
Aguirre, Juan de, 107, 139–140
Aguirre, Lope de (The Tyrant), 120, 122–141, 143–144, 147–157, 160, 164, 240
Alarcón, Diego de, 139, 143
Albornoz, Antón de, 116
Albújar, Juan Martín de, 219
Alcaraz, Diego de, 123
Alcojolados (Indian tribe), 19
Alderete, Jerónimo de (captain), 44–45, 58
Alemán, Jerónimo, 148
Alemán, Juan, 25–26
Alfinger, Ambrosio de (governor), 14–20, 23–26, 37, 40–41, 220
Alfinger, Enrique de, 14
Alfonso, Martín, 171, 246, 248
Aliles (Indian tribe), 220
Almao, Bartolomé de (alderman), 171, 185
Almarcha, Sebastián de, 83
Alonso, Hernando, 83, 90
Alonso, Juan, 158
Alonso, Rodrigo, 171
Alonso de los Hoyos, Pedro, 93–94, 148
Alquiza, Sancho de (governor), 255
Alvarado, Alonso de (marshal), 145, 158

Alvarez, Juan, 171
Alvarez, Pedro (inspector of royal treasury), 83, 89, 92, 253
Alvarez Franco, Pedro, 171, 252–253
Amazon River, 78, 123, 146. *See also* Marañón, Orellano
Ambrosio, Miser (valley). *See* Chinácota (valley)
Amescua, Sebastián de, 64
Amigo (Garci-González de Silva's dog), 227
Ampués, Juan de, 13–14, 16
Anaocopón (mountain), 215
Anarigua (cacique), 192
Ancona, Agustín de, 389, 529
Ancón de Refriegas (Bay of Skirmishes), 11
Andino, Andrés de (scribe), 68
Andrade, Juan de, 221
Andrea, Micer, 30
Anequemocane (cacique), 196
Angulo, Juan de, 171
Angulo, Pedro de, 130
Animals and Fowls (bears, cattle, chickens, deer, dogs, ducks, hogs, horses, goats, jaguars, mules, peccaries, rabbits, sheep, swine, tapirs, turkeys, unidentified rover animal), 7–8, 25, 35, 47, 73–75, 94, 109–110, 112, 155, 157, 170, 173, 223, 227, 239, 246, 255, 261
Antequera, Francisco de, 171
Antillano, Cristóbal de, 95
Antillano, Diego de, 171
Antillano, Juan de, 83
Apa (mines), 254
Apacuana (mother of cacique Guásema), 238, 242–243
Apure (river), 35, 54–55, 86–88
Aragua (river, valley), 159, 231, 245
Araguaire (cacique), 192, 235
Aramaipuro (cacique), 192
Araujo (mestizo), 228–229

# INDEX

Araya Point (peninsula), 10–12
Arbacos (Indian tribe, hill, province), 100, 112, 141, 158–159, 168, 175, 204, 219, 252
Arévalo (mountains), 25
Ariare (river), 47
Arias Baca, Alonso (interim governor), 265
Arias de Almesta, Pedro, 139, 143
Arias de Villacinda, Alonso (licentiate, governor), 98–99, 102–103, 108, 121, 131
Aricabacuto (cacique, town), 181–182, 192, 224–225
Aricagua (town, quebrada), 31, 34, 54
Arinas (river), 17. See also Unare (river)
Armacea, Sebastián de, 82
Arteaga, Martín de, 16, 64, 77, 131
Ascancio y Guerra, Juan de, 186
Astillero (river), 17
Atienza, Inés de, Doña, 123
Avellaneda, Juan de, 46
Aviamas (town), 88
Avila, Gabriel de (chief ensign), 170, 172, 193, 210, 228, 230
Ayala, Martín de (sergeant major), 212

Babur (Indian tribe), 91
Badillo, Juan de, 77
Baena, Juan de, 107
Ballesteros, Miguel Jerónimo (bishop), 67, 107, 120
Baltasar, Domingo, 171
Baños y Sotomayor, Diego de (bishop), 186, 189–190
Baquedaño, Jerónimo, 248
Baraquigua (town), 223
Baraure (province, river), 30, 35, 62
Barinas (city, province, river), 34, 94, 220
Barlovento (island). See Trinidad de Barlovento; Windward Islands
Barquisimeto (city, river, valley), 59–60, 65, 79–80, 94–100, 102, 158, 160, 184, 204, 261
Barrio, Antonio del, 83
Barrio, Damián del (of Coro), 171

Barrio, Damián del (of Granada), 29, 35, 38, 77, 83, 95, 150, 253
Barrio, Domingo del, 83
Barrio, Pedro del, 95–96
Baruta, (cacique), 192
Barutaima (town), 245
Bascona, Iñigo de, 20, 25–26
Bastida, Francisco de la, 107
Bastidas, Rodrigo de (bishop, governor), 14–15, 27–28, 56, 61–62, 64, 67, 82
Batatas, Río de las (River of Yams). See Pamplona (river)
Battles (Buría, Cayaurima, Guárico, Macarón, Pasos de Rodrigo, Quebrada, Unare), 11, 122, 182–183, 246–248, 250, 253, 256–257
Bautista, Juan (Italian soldier), 219
Bayano (black king), 122
Benalcázar, Sebastián de (captain), 56, 58, 64–65
Benavides, Lope de (alderman), 171, 185
Benítez, Juan, 107
Bernal, Maestro (Italian), 171
Bernáldez, Pablo (licentiate, governor, nicknamed Ojo de Plata, or Silver Eye), 109, 160–161, 163, 165, 167, 169, 265
Bernáldez, Pablo (soldier), 171, 216
Berrotarán, Francisco de (governor, later marqués del Valle de Santiago), 255
Beteta (captain), 45–52
Birds (cashew, chachalaca, dove, duck, mountain hen, partridge, peccary), 90
Boca de los Dragos (Estuary of the Dragons), 10, 207, 211
Boconó (river, valley), 102, 107–108
Bodebo, Miguel, 123
Bogotá, Santa Fe de (city), 27, 57–58, 87, 94, 108, 152, 206
Boiça, Diego de (governor, captain general), 66–67
Bolívar, Simón de (procurator general), 191, 260–161
Bonilla, Juan de, 68, 107

290

Borburata (port) (Puerto Cabello), 29–30, 32, 65, 68, 90, 92, 100, 105, 120–121, 126, 128, 163, 195, 206
Bordones (river, town), 165–167
Botero, Giovanni, 90
Boyacá (town, Colombia), 42
Bravo, Diego, 95
Bravo de Molina, Pedro, 137, 150–153, 155–157
Bravo Hidalgo, Alonso, 207–209
Bravo Hidalgo, Diego, 207–208
Brazos de Herina (bay). *See* Herina, Brazos de
Briceño, Sancho (captain), 15–16, 77, 89, 95, 107, 120–121, 261, 265
Bruno, Martín, 131
Burgos, Juan de, 104, 171, 173
Buría (mining town). *See* San Felipe de Buría
Buría (river), 95, 99

Caballero, Francisco, 154
Caballeros, Ciudad de los. *See* Santiago de los Caballeros
Caballo, Juan (cacique), 104–106, 134, 245
Caballos (Hill of the Horses), 196–197
Caballos, Antonio, 53
Cabo de Cordera (cape), 11, 101, 104
Cabo de la Vela (cape), 7, 10, 15, 32–33, 40, 58, 68, 90–91, 244
Cabrera, Pedro, 171
Cáceres (regidor), 128
Cáceres, Francisco de (captain), 36, 104, 212
Cáceres, Leonor de, 210
Caciques. *See under individual names of*: Acuareyapa, Anarigua, Anequemocane, Araguaire, Aramaipuro, Aricabacuto, Baruta, Caballo, Camaco, Cayaurima, Chacao, Charaima, Chicuramay, Conopoima, Coyegua, Cuarica, Cuaricuao, Guacicuana, Guaicaipuro, Guaicamacuto, Guaimacuare, Guaipata, Guarauguta, Guásema, Isabel Doña (cacica), Macarao, Mamacuri, Manaure, Naiguatá, Niscoto, Paisana, Paramaconi, Parayauta, Parnamacay, Popuere, Prepocunate, Querecrepe, Querepana, Sacama, Sunagoto, Tamalameque, Tamanaco, Tapiaracay, Terepaima, Urimaure, Uripatá
Caiquetía (Indian region, Caiquetíos Indian tribe), 13, 55, 60, 94, 184
Calderón, Francisco (lieutenant), 224, 231–233
Calvete, García, 43
Calvo, Benito, 211
Camacho, Alonso, 248, 253
Camaco (cacique), 235
Campos, Alonso de, 20, 28, 69, 184
Campos, Juan de, 37, 257
Canary Islands, 28, 41, 188, 191, 220
Canicamares (Indian tribe), 47
Cannibalism, 21–22, 48, 54, 198, 235, 243
Cantino, Francisco (count of Redondo), 148
Capacho (town), 89
Caracalleda (city, port), 112, 195, 205, 210, 221–222, 244, 252, 258, 260
Caracas (Indian tribe), 99, 100, 163, 167
Caracas (Santiago de León de) (city), 7, 10, 14, 75, 103–104, 111–112, 158, 165, 167–170, 172, 185–186, 190–192, 195, 201, 203–205, 216, 221, 250–252, 255, 258–265
Carapa (mines), 254
Carapaica (Indian warrior), 183–184
Carates (Indian tribe), 91
Cárdenas, Juan de (captain), 30
Cárdenas, Pedro de, 53
Cariaco (gulf of), 11
Cariamaná (lake), 245
Caribbean Sea (Mar del Norte), 78, 123
Caribs (Indian tribe), 209–211, 216,

219, 241, 252–254
Carmona, Jerónimo de, 107
Caroata (arroyo, stream), 118
Carora (city, province, plains, mountains), 7, 10, 29–30, 40, 42, 44, 59, 70, 102, 120, 219, 223
Carreño, Alonso, 101, 104
Carreño, Juan, 101, 104
Carrión, Francisco de (alguacil), 128, 144
Carrizo, Francisco (lieutenant) 233–236, 241
Cartagena (city, Colombia), 14, 58, 67, 209, 212, 220, 243
Caruao (city), 105, 111–112
Carvajal, Juan de (governor), 69–70, 79–86
Casanare (river), 35, 93
Castaldo, Bernabé, 171
Castaño, Rodrigo, 89, 107
Castilla, Sebastián de, 122, 158
Castillo (soldier), 116–117
Castillo, Francisco del, 18, 29
Castro, Luis de, 83, 107
Catalán, Juan, 171, 196
Cataño, Juan, 83, 171
Catatumbo (river), 17
Catia (city, port), 116–117, 163, 192. *See also* Maracapana
Catuche (river), 186
Caucagua (valley), 250
Cautino, Francisco (count of Redondo), 148
Cayaurima (cacique, Indian tribe, town, battle), 248, 256–257
Ceballos, Antonio, 53
Cerda, Fernando de la, 171, 200, 226–227
Ceruitá (paramos), 23, 37
Césare (river), 19
Céspedes (captain), 217–218
Chacao (cacique, town), 179–180, 192
Chacopata (Indian tribe, town, hills), 212, 244–245, 248–249
Chagaragatos (Indian tribe), 100, 112, 220–221
Chama (river), 17, 21
Charaima (cacique), 100–101
Charles I, king of Spain. *See* Charles V, emperor of the Holy Roman Empire and, as Charles I, king of Spain
Charles II, king of Spain, 96, 190
Charles V (emperor of the Holy Roman Empire and, as Charles I, king of Spain), 12, 14, 27, 244
Chaves (a young soldier), 129
Chaves, Ana de, 135
Chaves, Antonio de (captain), 32–33, 41
Chaves, Benito de (alcalde), 138–139, 143
Chaves, Cristóbal de, 122
Chaves, Juan de (interim governor), 213, 216
Chaves, Juan de (soldier), 157
Chaymas (Indian tribe), 248
Chicuramay (cacique), 202
Chimila (Indian tribe), 40
Chinácota (valley of Miser Ambrosio), 24–25
Chiscas (Indian tribe), 36
Chitareros (Indian tribe), 94, 122
Chitas (or Cocuyes) (Indian tribe), 93
Choques (Indian tribe), 48–49, 53, 56, 60
Chuspa (port, river), 101, 104, 111
Cipacua (town), 213
Cisneros, Juan de, 83
Clavijo, Gonzalo, 171
Cobos, Alonso (chief justice), 134, 165–167, 171
Cobos, Cristóbal, 171, 220–222, 256–258
Cochabamba (valley), 158
Cocinas (Indian tribe), 12, 33
Cocorote (copper mine site), 9
Col, Antonio, 16
Collado, Pablo (licentiate, governor), 107–109, 111–112, 137, 148, 151, 156–161, 164–165
Columbus, Christopher (The Admiral), 10–11
Comorocuao (town), 212
Conopoima (cacique, town), 228–230
Contreras, Pedro de (licentiate,

292

# INDEX

curate), 136, 144
Coquimbo (valley), 145
Cores (Indian tribe), 248
Coriana (province), 11, 13–14
Cornejo, Juan (lieutenant general), 39
Cornieles, Gaspar, 107, 110
Coro (city, district, mountains, province), 7, 10–12, 18, 20, 25–30, 32, 34, 41–42, 45, 67, 82, 98, 103, 106, 120, 184, 191, 251–252
Corsairs. See Pirates
Cortés (valley), 177
Cortés, Antonio, 89
Cortés, Baltasar, 123
Cortés, Hernán, 219
Cortés, Richo (a Portuguese), 104, 111–112, 177
Cosa, Juan de la (cartographer), 10
Coscorrila, Francisco Román, 171, 203
Coyegua, Alonso (cacique), 104, 134
Coyones (Indian tribe, province), 34
Cuaresma de Melo, Juan (regidor), 15–16, 37, 53
Cuarica (cacique), 74
Cuaricuao (cacique), 177
Cuaricurián (an Indian vassal), 202
Cubagua (island), 11, 33, 61, 67–70, 104, 126
Cubiro (valley), 86
Cucuizas (Indian tribe, coast, hill), 112, 173
Cúcuta (city, valley), 25, 86, 89, 91–93
Cuicas (Indian tribe, province), 100, 102, 107–109, 164
Cumaná (city, province), 7, 61, 67–68, 101, 128, 165, 212, 256–257
Cumanagoto (port, Indian tribe), 11, 134–135, 211, 245–249, 256
Curaçao (island), 16
Curarigua (province), 223
Curucutí (town), 194
Cuzco (city, Peru), 158

Díaz, Alonso, 98, 100, 145
Díaz, Andrés, 131

Díaz, Benito, 147
Díaz, Frutos, 255
Diaz, Gaspar (Portuguese), 154
Díaz, Miguel, 171
Díaz, Sebastián. See Díaz de Alfaro, Sebastián
Díaz, Tomás, 248
Díaz, Vicente, 89, 92, 171
Díaz Bezerril, Diego, 262
Díaz de Alfaro, Mateo (alcalde), 170, 262
Díaz de Alfaro, Sebastián, 170, 176, 186, 193, 233, 254–255
Díaz de Almendáriz, Martín, 132
Díaz Marillán, Juan, 89
Díaz Moreno, Alonso (commander and lieutenant governor), 92, 100, 170
Diego (Indian), 184
Ditaguas (Indian tribe), 70
Domínguez, Andrés, 226
Domínguez, Benito, 223
Domínguez, Francisco, 134
Domínguez, Juan, 89
Dominica (island), 211
Dragos, Boca de los. See Boca de los Dragos
Drake, Francis (Sir) (El Draque), 262–264
Duarte, Gonzalo, 123

El Collado (city, port, temporary name for Caraballedo), 111–117, 158–163, 195
El Dorado (mythical province), 64–66, 77–78, 82, 122, 206, 219
El Panecillo (port), 104, 111
El Tejar (city), 96
El Tocuyo (city, province, river, valley, Indian tribe), 7, 10, 29, 43–45, 59, 61, 70, 79–80, 82–87, 94, 97–100, 102–103, 105, 107–109, 112, 157, 191, 203, 205, 228, 261, 265
Encira, Lope de, 107
Eraso, Francisco de (scribe), 121
Escalante, Alonso de (inspector for royal treasury), 44
Escalante, Juan de, 89, 92
Escorcha, Diego de, 83, 89

## INDEX

Escoto, Bartolomé, 107
Escuque (Indian town), 102, 108.
  *See also* Miravel; Trujillo
Ese, Abrahán de (Flemish), 104
Española (island). *See* Hispaniola
  (island)
Espínola, Juan Jerónimo de, 156
Espira, Jorge de. *See* Spira, Jorge de
Espíritu Santo (city, Querecrepe),
  246–247, 249–250, 256, 261. *See
  also* Guanare
Esquino (river), 219
Estaqueros (Indian town), 198–199
Esteban, Juan, 223

Fajardo, Alonso, 111, 117, 142
Fajardo, Francisco, 100–101, 111–
  115, 117–118, 141, 158–161,
  163, 165–167, 170, 191, 228,
  256
Faria, Antonio de (Portuguese
  soldier), 137
Farol de Maracaibo. *See* Catatumbo
  (river)
Federmann (Fedreman), Nicolás de
  (lieutenant general), 28–30, 32–
  34, 37, 40–42, 45, 52–59, 65
Fernández. *See also* Hernández
Fernández, Baltasar, 171
Fernández, Duarte, 246
Fernández, Miguel, 171
Fernández, Pedro, 101, 104
Fernández de Antequera, Martín
  (alderman), 171, 176, 185, 202,
  224, 229
Fernández de Fuenmayor, Ruy
  (general, governor), 188
Fernández de Fuenmayor y Tovar,
  Ruy (grandson of governor), 188
Fernández de León, Juan, 171, 247,
  260–261
Fernández de Lugo, Pedro, 41, 57–
  58
Fernández de Piedrahita, Lucas. *See*
  Piedrahita, Lucas Fernández de
Fernández de Serpa, Diego, 207,
  211–212, 245
Fernández de Serpa, García (son of
  Diego Fernández de Serpa), 213
Fernández Morillo, Juan, 249

Fernández Trujillo, Juan, 171, 254
Figueredo (a soldier), 242
Flores Rondón, 253
Fonte, Lázaro (cacique), 58
Foods, 8–9, 21–22, 25, 34, 36, 53,
  66, 73, 94, 110, 198, 218. *See
  also* Animals and Fowl; Fruit
Fosca (valley), 57
Fowls. *See* Animals and Fowls
Fraga (a soldier), 116
Fragua (town). *See* Nuestra Señora
  de la Fragua
Fraile (corruption of proper name
  Freire), Leap of. *See* Freire's Leap
Francisco, Pedro, 223
Freire, Francisco, Freire's Leap, 15,
  159–160
Frías (licentiate, fiscal), 59, 66, 69,
  84–85
Fruits (apples, canteloupes, figs,
  grapes, lemons, limes, nisperos,
  papayas, pomegranates, quince,
  watermelons) 110, 143, 191. *See
  also* Foods
Frutos de Tudela, Juan (cantor), 28,
  77

Galeas, Pedro Alonso, 132–134,
  148, 153, 170–171, 173–174,
  176, 193, 224–228
Gallegos, Juan, 171, 193–194
Gallegos, Melchor, 171, 200
Gámez, Hernando (alcalde), 255
Gámez, Juan de, 171, 176, 179–
  180, 200, 223, 233, 248
Gámez, Martín de (regidor), 171,
  262
Gámez, Pedro de, 89, 92
García, Baltasar (friar, curate), 172,
  203–204
García, Bartolomé (lieutenant), 16,
  83, 216, 224
García, Cristóbal, 129, 153
García, Sancho, 241–242
García, Virgilio, 13, 16, 19
García Camacho, Pedro, 159, 172–
  173, 176, 229
García Carrasco, Juan, 248, 253
García Carrasco, Pedro, 107

# INDEX

García de Lerma. *See* Lerma, García de (governor)
García de Paredes, Diego (father) (Spanish hero), 95
García de Paredes, Diego (son) (campmaster, governor, captain general), 95, 100, 102–103, 107–109, 137, 149–150, 153–154, 156–157, 159, 163–164, 192, 197
García de Serpa. *See* Fernández de Serpa, García
Garci-Gonzalez de Silva (captain), 209–210, 213–214, 216, 221, 224–229, 234, 236–254, 256, 261
Gascón, Juan (commander), 43
Gayones (Indian tribe), 45
Germans, 14, 18, 58, 67, 82, 146
Gibraltar (city, Venezuela), 91, 110, 220–221, 265
Gil, Alonso, 171
Gil, Cristóbal, 171, 181
Gil, Gregorio, 171
Gómez, Cristóbal, 95, 171
Gómez de Ampuero, Diego (or Pedro), 134, 240
Gómez de Silva. *See* Silva, Gómez de
González, Andrés, 111, 171, 253
González, Martín (captain), 30
González, Pedro (chief engineer), 89, 95, 251
González Dávila, Gil (author), 185
González de Acuña, Antonio (friar), 188
González de Rivera, Luis, 89, 92
González de Silva, Garci. *See* Garci-González de Silva
Gramon, Monsieur (French pirate), 110
Granada, Nuevo Reino de. *See* Nuevo Reino de Granada (Colombia)
Graterol, Francisco, 29, 95, 107
Grenada (island, Lesser Antilles), 210
Grita, La. *See* La Grita
Guacara (valley), 170
Guacicuana (cacique), 240

Guaicaipuro (cacique), 118, 121, 141–142, 158, 160–163, 174–176, 192–193, 199–201, 228
Guaicamacuto, 161–162, 192, 195
Guaicamacuto (Macuto) (town, port, Indian tribe), 161, 172, 263
Guaimacuare (cacique), 101, 105–106, 111–112, 117, 222
Guaipata (cacique), 191
Guaiqueríes (Indian tribe), 100, 104–106, 133, 170, 191
Guaire (river, valley), 112, 176–177, 204, 226
Guajiros (Indian tribe), 33
Guanare (early names and variations: Espíritu Santo, q.v., Guanaguanare, Zazaribacoa) (city, river), 10, 87, 260–261
Guane (province, Colombia), 23, 37
Guaracarima (plains, valley), 112, 159, 165, 167–169, 204
Guaraguta, 163, 192
Guaremaisen (Indian town), 213
Guárico (river, battle), 252–253, 256–257
Guásema (cacique), 238–242
Guásema, 238, 242
Guatapanare (Salado) (river), 245
Guayana (province, town), 207, 224
Guayauta (Indian youth), 178, 197
Guayuare, 66, 71
Guayupes (Indian tribe), 47, 73
Guero (Indian tribe), 52
Guerra, Cristóbal, 10–12
Guerra, Diego, 106
Guerra, Luis (brother of Cristóbal Guerra), 11
Guerrero, Francisco, 153, 171, 198–199
Guevara, Iñigo de (licentiate, judge), 16
Guevara, Juan de (alcalde, captain), 16, 35, 77, 83, 241, 259
Guevara, Juan de (the Elder), 111
Guiomar (Negro Queen), 97–98
Gurbel (Grubel), Leonardo (son of Melchor Gurbel), 83
Gurbel (Grubel), Melchor (a German), 81, 83, 95
Gutiérrez, Rodrigo, 131, 140

# INDEX

Gutiérrez de la Peña. *See* Peña, Gutiérrez de la
Guzmán, Fernando de (prince of Peru), 122–123, 131, 147

Hacha, Río de la (River of the Axe), 12, 17
Henao, Alonso de (licentiate, chaplain), 123
Henares, Diego de, 171, 175
Herina, Brazos de (Arms, or Bay, of Herina), 41
Hernández. *See also* Fernández
Hernández, Andrés, 92, 171
Hernández, Gaspar, 124, 254–255
Hernández, Pedro, 83, 95
Hernández Girón, Francisco, 122, 145, 158
Hernández Trujillo, Juan, 111–112
Hinojosa, Pedro Alfredo de (general), 158
Hispaniola (Española) (island), 10, 12, 32–33, 64, 121, 126, 165, 259
Hoyos, Pedro Alonso de los. *See* Alonso de los Hoyos, Pedro
Hoz Berrio, Francisco de la (governor), 231
Huayabas (valley), 215, 224. *See also* Mamo Valley
Hurtado de Mendoza, Andrés (marquis of Cañete), 121, 145, 147
Hutten, Felipe de. *See* Utre, Felipe de

Indian customs, 9, 13, 22, 25, 48
Indian tribes. *See under individual names*: Achaguas, Alcojolados, Aliles, Abracos, Barburs, Caiquetíos, Caracas, Carates, Caribes, Cayaurimas, Chacopatas, Chagaragatos, Chaymas, Chimilas, Chiscas, Chitareros, Chitas, Choques, Cocinas, Cocuyes, Cores, Coyones, Cucuizas, Cuicas, Cumanagotas, Ditaguas, Gandules, Gayones, Guaicamacutos, Guaiquerís, Guajiros, Guayupes, Gueros, Jirajaras, Laches, Los Teques, Los Tocuyos, Macarros, Mariches, Mayas, Meregotas, Mixtecas, Motilones, Muzos, Olanchas, Omeguas, Palenques, Paracotos, Píritus, Pocabuces, Quinacos, Quiriquires, Ravichas, Saparas, Tácatas, Taironas, Taramainas, Tarmas, Timotes Tiznados, Toas, Tovoras, Tumusas
Industries: mining, 9, 94–96, 254; pearl fishing, 32–34, 40; shipbuilding, 220
Infante, Doctor (oidor, judge), 32
Infante, Francisco (alcalde), 29, 37, 54, 107, 148, 153, 170, 172–173, 176, 183, 199–201, 203–204, 231–232, 237
Insects (ants, bees, fireflies, locusts, mosquitoes, worms), 8, 42, 109, 189, 262
Isabel, Doña (cacica), 100–101, 104, 106
Itecuao (river), 250
Itotos (mountains), 19

Jaén, Martín de, 104, 111–112
Jaspe Montenegro, Pedro de (purveyor), 186
Jewels (beads, blue-veined crystals, bracelets, brooches, pearls, pendants), 9, 11–13, 32–34, 41, 71, 95, 101, 126, 194, 244
Jiménez de Quesada, Gonzalo, 23, 56–58, 206
Jiral, Domingo, 171, 203–204
Juan (Indian ally), 184
Juan Jorge (valley), 176
Juan Portugués (Negro), 173

Laches (Indian tribe), 94
La Grita (town), 220
La Guaira (city, port), 10, 112, 121, 260–261, 263
La Pascua (valley), 174–175, 177, 231
Las Almadranas (fortress), 169
Las Casas, Bartolomé de (friar, Defender of the Indians), 84
Las Charcas (early name of Sucre,

# INDEX

Bolivia) (city, province), 96, 158, 172
Las Damas, Valley of, 149
Las Lagunetas (mountains), 112, 141
Las Lagunillas (mountain), 175, 203
Las Palmas (city), 99. *See also* Nirgua; Nuestra Señora Victoria del Prado de Talavera; Villa Rica
La Torralva (a Spanish woman, companion of Elvira, Lope de Aguirre's daughter), 156
La Vieja, Quebrada de la (The Old Lady's quebrada), 181
Ledesma (a swordmaker), 156
Ledesma, Alonso Andrea de, 107, 171, 176, 193, 263
Ledesma, Diego de, 255
Ledesma, Tomé de, 83, 107, 171, 225–226
Leguisamón, Diego de (licentiate), 259–260
Leiva, Diego de, 83
Leiva, Luis de, 218–219
León, Luis de, 16, 77
León, Rodrigo de (regidor), 248, 262
Lerma, García de (governor), 15, 19, 32
Lezcano, Juan de (mestizo), 155
Liaño, Pedro de (licentiate), 264
Lima (Peru), 122, 146, 158
Limpias, Pedro de, 41, 57–58, 64, 72, 76–80, 82–83, 93
Llamoso, Antón de, 130, 156
Loma de los Caballos (Hill of the Horses), 196–197
Lomas del Viento (Hills of the Wind), 86, 91, 205
López, Cristóbal, 83, 89, 95
López, Hernando de (scribe), 166
López Aburto de la Mata, Juan (bishop), 14, 186, 189, 252
López de San Martín, Alonso (chaplain), 254
López de Triana, Francisco, 83, 95
Losada, Diego de (general), 59–60, 68–70, 75, 85–87, 94–95, 97, 169–170, 172–182, 185, 191–206

Los Llanos (del Orinoco, or de Venezuela), 35, 37, 54, 56, 59, 66, 68, 71, 87, 206, 252, 255
Los Locos (valley), 198
Los Palenques (Indian tribe, town), 122, 245, 247
Los Reyes, Ciudad de. *See* Lima (Peru)
Los Teques (Indian tribe, town, hill, region), 100, 112, 121, 141, 161–162, 175–176, 178, 192–193, 195, 197, 228, 231, 233, 240–241
Los Truenos (Thunder Plains), 109
Lugo, Alonso Luis de (adelantado), 60
Lugo, Lope Montalvo de. *See* Montalvo de Lugo, Lope
Luther, Martín, 138, 145

Macarao (cacique, Indian tribe), 176–177
Macarón (Arará) (pool, battle), 249, 256–257
Macatoa (city), 69–73, 77
Machado, Andrés (alcalde), 191, 195
Machífaro (province) (Colombia), 78, 122
Macomite (river, province), 32–33
Macuto. *See* Guaicamacuto
Madrid, Bernardo de, 83
Madrid, Francisco de, 29, 37, 83, 92, 168, 171, 194
Madrid, Hernando de, 95
Magdalena (river), 23, 40–41, 58
Malaver de Silva, Pedro, 2, 206–209, 216–219
Maldonado, Juan, 108–109
Maldonado de Almendáriz, Francisco, 148, 170, 173, 180, 193–194, 233, 241
Mal-País (Badland) (province), 37–38, 46
Mamacuri (cacique), 192, 195
Mamo (Huayabas) (valley, river), 213, 215. *See also* Huayabas (valley)
Manarcima (Indian), 234–235
Manaure (cacique), 13

297

# INDEX

Manzanedo, Alonso de (governor), 96, 163, 165
Manzanillo, Juan de (bishop), 252, 262
Mar del Norte (Sea of the North). See Caribbean Sea
Mar Septentrional. See North Sea
Maracaibo (Nueva Zamora) (city, lake, province), 7, 10, 12, 16–18, 20, 27, 32, 40–41, 60, 90, 102–110, 220–221, 262, 265
Maracapana (port, region), 10–11, 15, 44, 60, 66, 68, 104–105, 126, 128, 192–193, 205, 208, 244. See also Catia
Marañón (river, region), 122–123, 131–133, 146, 219. See also Amazon (river); Orellana (river)
Marañones (nickname of Lope de Aguirre's soldiers from the Marañón expedition), 123, 126, 129, 138, 140, 145, 149–151, 153–157, 159–160
Margarita (island, province), 11, 100–101, 104–107, 111, 120, 123–124, 126–127, 146, 158, 163, 167, 170, 190–191, 195, 207–208, 240
Mariara (valley), 169–170, 172, 210
Mariches (Indian tribe), 100, 113–115, 176, 180, 192, 197–198, 201, 224, 226–228
Marín de Narváez, María, 188
Márquez, Francisco, 171, 173
Márquez's Site, 172–174
Martel de Ayala, Gonzalo, 29, 37, 83, 95
Martín, Alonso, 32, 83
Martín, Esteban, 23–24, 48–52, 95, 171, 173
Martín, Francisco (companion of Aguirre), 137–138, 140
Martín, Francisco (companion of Alfinger), 21, 25–27
Martín, Hernando, 111, 223
Martín de Albújar, Juan. See Albujar, Juan Martín de
Martínez, Diego (captain), 42–45, 52–53

Martínez, Lorenzo (captain), 40, 189
Martínez de Videla, Juan (alcalde), 265
Maruachare (province), 65
Masabel, Bartolomé de (regidor), 189, 262
Mateos, Esteban, 13, 16, 83, 95
Mateos, Pedro, 95, 171
Maya (Indian tribe, valley), 100
Mazariego, Diego de (governor), 223–224, 233, 243
Medical Treatments (canafistula, Carora balsam, chinaroot, Cumaná oil, María oil, stones to stanch blood flow, tacamahac, tamarind), 8, 99, 234, 240
Medicine Men (Indian). See Witch Doctors
Melero, José (dean of cathedral), 186
Méndez, Diego, 171, 197, 234
Mendoza, Julián de, 114, 116–118, 138, 143, 171, 213, 215–216
Meneses y Padilla, Juan de (governor), 104
Meregotos (Indian tribe), 100, 159–160, 168
Mérida (city, province, mountains, paramo, Venezuela), 17, 21, 54, 87–88, 102, 108–109, 120, 157, 220–221, 265. See also Santiago de los Caballeros, early name for Mérida
Meta (river), 42, 59, 205
Metals (copper, gold, silver, tin), 19, 41, 74, 95, 126
Miedo Valley (Valley of Fear), 168, 172
Miguel (Negro King), 94, 96–98
Miranda, Pedro de, 111, 113–115
Miravel (city), 107–109. See also Escuque; Trujillo
Miser Ambrosio (valley). See Chinácota (valley)
Mixtecas (subdivision of Timote Indian tribe), 8, 223
Mompatare (port), 123, 128–130
Monguía, Pedro de (captain), 126, 128, 131, 137, 140

Montalvo (captain), 34
Montalvo de Lugo, Lope, 29, 59–60
Montero, Amador, 83, 138
Montes, Diego de (captain), 72, 75, 83, 99, 171, 198, 223
Montesinos, Antonio (friar, Order of Preachers), 15
Montesinos, Francisco de (Father, Your Paternity, the Provincial), 126, 128, 130–132, 137
Montoya, Alonso de, 122–123
Moporo (town, Venezuela), 17, 220
Morere (river), 223
Mosquera, Vasco de. *See* Vasco de Mosquera
Mostazas (hills), 159
Motatán (river), 17, 102, 109
Motilones (Indian tribe, river, province), 91, 122, 147
Muchacho (boy) (town), 54
Murcia (captain), 32
Muzos (Indian tribe), 122

Naiguatá (cacique), 101, 192
Narváez, Luis de, 83, 89, 95, 158–161, 163–164, 172, 174, 199, 229
Navarro (doctor), 56, 60–63
Navas, Alonso de, 61–62
Naveros, Antonio (accountant), 77
Neiva (valley, district), 58, 65
Nieto, Martín (captain), 44–45
Negroes, 94, 96–98, 122, 152, 171, 173–174, 186, 193, 205
Nirgua (city, river, province), 10, 95, 98–99, 103, 148. *See also* Las Palmas; Nuestra Señora Victoria del Prado de Talavera; Nueva Jerez; Villa Rica
Niscoto (cacique), 101
Nombre de Dios (port, city, Panama), 124, 126
Noroguto (valley), 198–199
North Sea (Mar Septentrional), 90
Northern Sea (Mar del Norte). *See* Caribbean Sea
Nuestra Señora (Real de Minas, mining town), 46, 67, 77–78, 228
Nuestra Señora de Altagracia (church), 187
Nuestra Señora de Candelaria (church), 188
Nuestra Señora de Chiquinquirá (hermitage), 110
Nuestra Señora de Copacabana, 188
Nuestra Señora de Coromoto (religious image), 261
Nuestra Señora de la Candelaria, 188
Nuestra Señora de la Concepción de la Borburata, 90
Nuestra Señora de la Concepción del Tocuyo, 83
Nuestra Señora de la Fragua (Forge; or San Juan de los Llanos), 57, 65
Nuestra Señora de la Paz, 109
Nuestra Señora de la Soledad (religious image), 188
Nuestra Señora de la Victoria del Prado de Talavera (town), 104. *See also* Las Palmas; Nirgua; Nueva Jerez; Villa Rica
Nuestra Señora de las Mercedes (church, religious order), 188
Nuestra Señora de Táriba (shrine), 88
Nuestra Señora del Pilar de Zaragoza (chapel), 186
Nuestra Señora del Pópulo (chapel), 186
Nuestra Señora del Rosario (religious image and organization), 188
Nueva Barcelona (town, Venezuela), 245
Nueva Jerez (city), 103
Nueva Segovia de Barquisimeto. *See* Barquisimeto
Nueva Valencia del Rey. *See* Valencia (city)
Nueva Zamora de Maracaibo. *See* Maracaibo (Nueva Zamora) (city)
Nuevo Reino de Granada (Colombia), 7, 23, 25, 27, 36–37, 41, 58, 87, 122, 206, 261
Nuevo Trujillo. *See* Trujillo (city, Venezuela)

## INDEX

Núñez, Pedro, 138–139
Núñez Lobo, Rodrigo (governor), 257–258

Ocaña (city, sierra), 17, 41, 91
Ocumare (plains), 232
Olachas (Indian tribe), 36
Omeguas (Indian tribe) (later called Ditaguas, q.v.), 70–80, 82, 94, 99, 122, 158, 179, 207
Opia (Upia) (river), 34, 36
Ordaz, Diego de (commander), 39, 44
Orellana, Enríquez de (captain), 126, 130
Orellana (river), 123. *See also* Amazon (river); Marañón (river)
Orinoco (Uriaparia) (river), 7, 44, 207, 211, 219, 243, 252,
Orituco (river), 255
Oro, Río del (River of Gold), 23, 93–94
Ortal, Jerónimo de (governor), 43–44, 52
Ortega, Diego de, 83, 95
Ortiz, Alonso (scribe), 171
Osorio, Diego de (governor), 234, 259–265
Osorio, Gonzalo (alcalde), 107, 170, 185

Pacheco, Alonso (captain), 29, 35, 46, 77, 92, 107, 220–221
Paisana (cacique), 105–106
Palencia (captain), 82
Palencia, Nicolás de, 35, 49–51
Palenques (Indian tribe), 122, 245, 247
Pallarés (soldier), 116–117
Pampán (valley), 109
Pamplona (city, Colombia), 24, 88, 122
Pamplona (Zulia, or Batatas River), 17, 91
Panama, 122, 136
Paniagua, Pedro de, 134–135
Pao (river, valley), 62, 234
Papamene (province, river), 46–48, 70

Paracotos (Indian tribe, quebrada), 240
Paradas, Diego de, 77, 99, 170, 173–174, 176–179
Paraguache (cove) (now called Puerto del Traidor, Traitor's Port), 123
Paraguaná (port), 69
Paramaconi (cacique), 116–119, 129, 213–214, 221
Parayauta (cacique), 236–237
Parados (peak), 66–67, 70
Paredes, Diego García de. *See* García de Parades, Diego (father and son)
Paredes, Pedro de (ensign), 187
Paria (peninsula, gulf), 11, 13, 44, 205
Parnamacay (cacique, town), 193, 213, 215–216, 221
Parra, Juan de la, 171, 174, 176, 234
Pasca (town), 58
Pascual, Juan, 233, 235–236
Pasos de Rodrigo (battle), 122
Pasto (city), 65
Paternity, Your. *See* Montesinos, Francisco de (Father, the Provincial)
Patima (town, Venezuela), 226
Pauto (river), 57
Peña, Gutierrez de la (general, governor), 103, 105, 107–108, 137, 148–153, 155, 157, 159, 163, 167
Peñalosa, Nicolás de (regidor), 262, 264
Pérez, Antonio (African from Orán), 171, 193
Pérez, Juan, 139, 223
Pérez, Martín (campmaster), 123–125, 127–130
Pérez de la Muela, Hernán (licentiate), 16, 19, 37–83
Pérez de Quesada, Gonzalo (brother of Hernán), 60, 65–66
Pérez de Quesada, Hernán (brother of Gonzalo), 60, 65–66, 82
Pérez de Tolosa, Alonso (brother of Juan), 86–89, 91–94, 205

# INDEX

Pérez de Tolosa, Juan (governor), 84–91, 93, 121
Peru, 102, 121–126, 130–131, 193
Petare (town, Venezuela), 181
Philip II (king), 39, 85, 96, 131–132, 144–145, 147, 157, 167, 191, 234
Piedrahita, Juan de (captain), 145, 151
Pimentel, Juan (governor, captain general), 185, 241, 244, 250, 252
Piña Lidueña, Gonzalo (governor), 265
Pinto, Gaspar, 171, 193–195, 220–222
Pirates (English, French), 93, 110, 172, 190–192, 245, 262, 264. *See also* Drake, Sir Francis; Gramon, Monsieur
Pírita (port, town, Indian tribe), 104–106, 245, 248
Pizarro, Francisco, 58, 219
Pizarro, Gonzalo, 78, 102, 122, 164
Pocabuces (Indian tribe), 19
Pocó (valley), 110
Poco-Vergüenza (Little Shame) (town), 52–53
Ponce de León, Francisco (son of Governor Pedro Ponce de León), 170, 173, 176, 205
Ponce de León, Pedro (governor), 93, 103, 109, 169–170, 191, 195, 202, 204–205, 220, 224
Ponce de León, Pedro (son of Governor Pedro Ponce de León), 170
Ponce de León, Rodrigo (son of Governor Pedro Ponce de León) 170, 182–184
Popayán (city, province, Colombia), 58, 65, 131, 163
Popuere (cacique), 197
Portugués, Juan (Negro), 174
Prepocunate (cacique), 192, 213, 215
Products (bixa, cacao, cotton, pita, salt, sugar, tobacco) 8, 110, 182, 191, 255. *See also* Foods; Fruits; Woods
Proveda, Martín de (captain), 206

Provincial, The. *See* Montesinos, Father Francisco de
Puente, Blas de la (priest), 172
Puerto Cabello. *See* Borburata
Puerto del Traidor (Traitor's Port, cove), 123
Puerto Rico, 56, 67
Punta de Araya. *See* Araya, Punta de (Araya Point)
Punta de Piedras (Rocky Point), 128–130

Quebrada, Battle of, 182–183
Quebrada de la Vieja (The Old Lady's Quebrada), 181
Querecrepe (cacique), 245
Querecrepe (town). *See* Espíritu Santo; Guanare
Querepana (cacique), 252
Querequemare (cacique, Lord of Torrequemada), 192
Quesada, Gonzalo Jiménez de. *See* Jiménez de Quesada, Gonzalo
Quibor (valley), 81
Quinacos (Indian tribe), 207
Quincozes de la Llana, Juan de (scribe), 83, 95
Quiñones, Juan Jorge de, 111, 118–119, 162
Quintano, Alonso, 171, 197

Ramada (town, Venezuela), 32
Ramos Barriga, Juan, 171, 181
Ravichás (Indian tribe), 24
Real de Minas de Nuestra Señora. *See* Nuestra Señora (Real de Minas de)
Real de Minas de San Felipe de Buría. *See* San Felipe de Buría (mining town)
Rebolledo, Francisco, 263–264
Redondo, count of. *See* Cantino, Francisco (count of Redondo)
Refriegas, Ancón de (cove, bay). *See* Ancón de Refriegas (cove, bay)
Reinoso, Pedro de (captain), 59–60, 205
Relámpago de Catatumbo. *See* Catatumbo (river)
Remboldt, Enrique (German)

(interim governor, captain general), 66–68
Reyes, Ciudad de los. *See* Lima (Peru)
Ríos, Diego de los (chief ensign), 261
Ríos, Gonzalo de los, 16, 77, 83, 89, 95
Rivera, Juan de (captain), 32–33, 40–41
Riveros, Juan (lieutenant governor), 232, 259–260
Robles Villafañate, Martín de (governor), 188
Rodríguez, Alonso, 135–136
Rodríguez, Antonio (regidor), 171, 262
Rodríguez, Bartolomé, 171, 200
Rodríguez, Cristóbal, 83, 87
Rodríguez, Gonzalo, 171, 178
Rodríguez, Juan, 118–119, 121, 128, 138, 143, 159, 169, 198, 200, 225, 228, 231
Rodríguez, Manuel (alcalde), 124, 128
Rodríguez de Robledo, Juan (dean of cathedral), 28
Rodríguez Suárez, Juan (lieutenant governor), 114–116, 121, 141–143, 199–200
Rojas, Ana de, 132, 134
Rojas, Beatriz de, 240
Rojas, Francisca de, 240
Rojas, Luis de (governor), 195, 252, 256, 258–260
Román, Francisco, 171, 204
Román Coscorilla, Francisco. *See* Coscorilla, Francisco Román
Romero, Diego (captain), 82, 87–88, 103
Rosario (town, Venezuela), 103, 105
Royal Fifth (Crown's Fifth, King's Fifth), 15, 126
Royal Highway (Camino Real), 218, 263
Ruiz, Francisco, 107–108, 171
Ruiz, Toribio (chaplain), 81, 83, 97
Ruiz Vallejo, Alonso, 171, 174, 184, 193

Ruiz Vallejo, Diego (accountant), 16, 68, 83, 102, 193
Ruy Gómez (Spanish prince), 207

Sacama (cacique), 101
Sailler, Bartolomé, (lieutenant), 15, 17
Salado (river), 211–212, 245, 256–257. *See also* Guatapanare (river)
Salamanca (Venezuela), 197–198, 231–233, 237, 240
Salamanca, Juan de (captain), 43, 83, 233
Salas, Juan de (captain), 169–170, 190–191, 195
Salduendo, Lorenzo de, 122–123
Salinas, Diego de or Pedro de (bishop), 262, 265
Salsillas (Venezuela), 38
Samaniego, Francisca de, 16
Samaniego, Luisa de, 16
San Cristóbal (city, river, Venezuela), 88, 256–258
San Felipe de Buría (mining town), 94–96, 103
San Francisco (town, valley), 112, 114, 118, 158–161, 177, 179–180, 183–184, 216, 263
San Francisco, Order of, 83, 96, 100, 110, 121, 188, 221, 223
San Gregorio de Valladolid (school), 107
San Jorge (Saint George Martyr), 262
San Juan, Andrés de, 107, 171
San Juan, Francisco de (scribe), 83, 89–90, 92
San Juan, Juan de (Biscayan), 104, 111, 171, 193–194
San Juan Bautista (confraternity), 189
San Juan Bautista del Portillo de Carora. *See* Carora
San Juan de Dios (hermitage), 221
San Juan de la Paz (city, Venezuela), 254–255
San Juan de los Llanos (later name of Nuestra Señora de la Fragua, q.v.), 46, 206
San Lúcar de Barrameda (city, port,

# INDEX

Spain), 11, 28, 170, 207
San Martín, Pedro de (general, factor), 16, 25–26, 82
San Nicolás (bishop, hermitage), 14
San Nicolás de Bari (religious image), 186
San Pablo (protohermit), 187, 251
San Pedro (Saint Peter) (apostle), 187
San Pedro (plains, river, battle of, early name of San Felipe de Buría, q.v.), 17, 91, 141, 175–176
San Sebastián (hermitage), 189–190
San Sebastián de los Reyes (city, feast day, hermitage), 10, 254–255. See also San Sebastián (hermitage)
Sánchez, Diego, 233, 235–236
Sánchez, Juan, 171, 248
Sánchez de Córdova, Francisco, 171, 173, 176, 193, 200, 229
Sánchez Moreno, Juan, 83, 89–90
Santa Ana (hospital), 221
Santa Ana de Coro. See Coro
Santa Clara (convent), 189
Santacruz, Miguel de, 171, 193, 198
Santa Cruz de la Española (province, Santo Domingo), 188
Santa Fe de Bogotá. See Bogotá, Santa Fe de (city)
Santa Marta (city, province, Venezuela), 7, 15, 32, 40–41, 58, 122
Santa Rosa de Lima (seminary), 188
Santa Rosalía de Palermo (hermitage), 190
Santiago, Marqués del Valle de. See Berrotarán, Francisco de
Santiago (Saint James) (apostle), 175, 185–186, 191, 194, 222, 242–243
Santiago (valley, Venezuela), 88–89, 93
Santiago de León de Caracas. See Caracas (Santiago de León de)
Santiago de los Caballeros (city, Venezuela), 211–212, 245. See also Mérida

Santo Domingo, Audiencia de, 12–13, 56, 59–60, 64, 67, 69–70, 81–82, 103, 108, 121, 161, 190, 205, 256, 259–260
Santo Domingo, Order of (convent), 83, 110, 121, 126, 134, 188
Santo Tomás, Domingo (bishop), 172
Saona, Jacinto de (friar), 189
Saparas (Indian tribe), 60–61, 220
Sarare (river, Venezuela, Colombia), 35, 54, 93
Sarmiento, Antonio, 89, 92
Sedeño, Antonio (governor), 44, 59–60, 169, 205
Seijas, Luis de, 111, 113–114
Serpa, Diego. See Fernández de Serpa, Diego
Serpa, García. See Fernández de Serpa, García
Serrano, Juan, 159, 171, 175–176
Serrato, Pedro, 171, 197
Sierra Nevadas, 86–87, 89, 108, 205
Silva, Gómez de (Portuguese), 148, 153
Silva, Pedro Malaver de. See Malaver de Silva, Pedro
Slavery, 9, 64, 96, 98, 121, 253
Sorocaima (an Indian), 229–230
Speier (Speyer), Georg von. See Spira, Jorge de (governor)
Spira, Jorge de (governor), 27–30, 41, 46–50, 53–57, 60–64, 82
Suárez, Cristóbal (scribe), 255
Suárez, Juan, 107
Suárez, Juan (the Clown), 171
Suárez, Pablo (chief constable) 89, 92
Suárez, Pedro, 89, 95
Suárez del Castillo, Pedro (general solicitor), 95
Sucre, Bolivia. See Las Charcas
Sucui (Socui) (river), 17
Súcuta (town, Venezuela), 232
Sunaguto (cacique), 114

Tacarigua (lake, province valley, early name of Lake Valencia,

303

q.v.) 40, 42, 89–90, 92, 95, 98, 100, 243
Tácata (Indian tribe, river valley), 231–234, 236, 237
Tairona (Indian tribe), 122
Tamalameque (cacique, province, lake), 18–20, 23, 26
Tamanaco (cacique, province), 224–227
Tapiaracay (cacique), 198, 225
Taramainas (Indian tribe), 100, 112, 114, 116, 118, 182–183, 213, 221
Tarmas (Indian tribe), 100, 176, 182, 192–193, 236
Tenerife (Canary Islands), 188, 207
Terepaima (cacique, hill), 112, 141, 158–159, 173, 199, 203
Tiedra, Isabel de (abbess), 189
Tierra Firme (mainland), 7, 10, 32, 101, 111
Timaná (mountain range), 65
Timotes (Indian tribe), 108
Tinajero, Martín, 42
Tiquire (river), 168
Tirado, Diego, 124, 154–155
Tiznados (Indian tribe, river), 59, 243
Toas (Indian tribe), 220
Tolosa, Alonso Pérez de. *See* Pérez de Tolosa, Alonso
Tolosa, Juan Pérez de. *See* Pérez de Tolosa, Juan
Tomás, Gaspar, 104, 111, 171, 210
Tomyris, 210
Torondoy (river, Venezuela), 17
Torralva, La (companion of Elvira, daughter of Lope de Aguirre). *See* La Torralva
Tostado de la Peña, Juan (chief justice), 261
Tovar, Jerónimo de, 171, 197
Tovar, Melchora Ana de, 186
Tovoros (Indian tribe), 88
Traidor, Puerto del. *See* Paraguache (cove)
Trinidad (de Barlovento) (island, province), 10. *See also* Windward Islands
Trujillo (city, Venezuela), 10, 100, 102, 108–110, 120, 220, 264. *See also* Escuque; Miravel
Trujillo, María de, 130
Tudela (city, Colombia), 122
Tumusas (Indian tribe), 231
Tunja (city, Colombia), 42, 94
Turmero (river), 177
Turriaga, Juan de, 127–128
Turuaco (town, Venezuela), 213
Tuy (river, town, Venezuela), 112, 160, 168, 204, 226, 232

Umúcaro (valley, Venezuela), 85
Unare (peak, region, river, battle, Venezuela) (also called Arinas River, q.v.), 7, 246–247
Upar (valley, Venezuela), 19, 40–41
Urimaure (cacique), 193
Uripatá (cacique), 192
Urquijo, Juan de (mestizo), 259
Urquijo, María de, 189
Ursúa, Pedro de, 24, 94, 122, 132–133, 147, 158
Utre (Urre, Hutten), Felipe de, 55, 64–67, 69–82, 94, 99, 122, 179
Utuguane (Indian town), 247

Váez, Alvaro, 83, 89
Valdespina (a soldier), 51–52
Valencia (city, lake, Venezuela), 10, 65, 98, 100, 111–112, 143, 160, 195, 251–252, 258. *See also* Tacarigua
Valenzuela, Alonso de, 171, 195
Vallejo, Alonso Ruiz. *See* Ruiz Vallejo, Alonso
Vasco de Mosquera, 83, 95
Vascona (Vascuña), Iñigo de. *See* Bascona, Iñigo de
Vázquez, Tomás, 145, 151
Vázquez de Escobeda, Diego (Alcalde), 265
Vázquez de Rojas, Lázaro, 111–112, 191, 195–196, 246, 248
Vela, Cabo de. *See* Cabo de la Vela
Vela León, Alonso, 89, 92
Velasco, Francisco de (lieutenant), 34–35
Vélez (city, Colombia), 23, 43

## INDEX

Venegas, Francisco (captain), 19, 25–26
Venezuela, 7, 10, 17, 100, 102, 121, 123
Vera, Domingo de (general treasurer), 187
Vicuña, Pedro de (licentiate, priest), 188
Vides, Francisco de, 171, 176, 216
Viedma, Pedro de (chief justice), 167
Viento, Lomas del (Hills of the Wind), 89, 93, 205
Villa Rica (city, Venezuela) 103, 170, 189. *See also* Las Palmas; Nirgua; Nuestra Señora de la Victoria del Prado de Talavera; Nueva Jerez
Villacinda. *See* Arias de Villalcinda, Alonso
Villafuerte (lieutenant general), 15
Villalpando (Spanish traitor), 263
Villandrando, Juan de (governor), 124, 128, 133
Villas, Sancho de (alderman), 83, 171, 185, 200, 215–216
Villarroel, Gaspar de (archbishop), 96
Villavicencio, Elvira de, 189
Villavicencio, Inés de, 189
Villegas, Francisco de, 83, 95
Villegas, Juan de (captain, alcalde, governor), 15, 19, 25, 31, 35, 37, 60–61, 63, 66–70, 83, 85, 89–92, 94–95
Villela, Ana, 189

Villela, Francisca, 189
Villela, Juana de, 189
Villela, María, 189
Villela, Mariana de, 189
Villena, Alonso de, 122, 134
Viltre, Pedro (German), 95
Viñas, Alonso, 171, 176

Welser (Belser), Bartolomé, 64, 76, 78, 81–82
Welsars (Belsars) (family, commercial agents), 14–16, 26, 28, 30, 55–56, 58, 60, 62, 64, 67, 82, 84–85, 244
Windward Islands (Barlovento), 9, 191. *See also* Trinidad (de Barlovento)
Witch Doctors, 9, 22, 240
Woods (brazilwood, cedar, ceiba, divi-divi, jacarandá, lignum vitae, mahogany), 8, 17, 82, 188, 191

Yaracui (river), 149
Yoraco (an Indian), 234

Zamora, Juan de, 89, 92, 95
Zamora, Nueva. *See* Maracaibo
Zaparas (Indian tribe). *See* Saparas (Indian tribe)
Zapatosa (lake). *See* Tamalameque
Zarare (river). *See* Sarare (river)
Zazaribacos (river). *See* Guanare (river)
Zenobia, 210
Zulia (river). *See* Pamplona (river)
Zuñiga, Gonzalo de, 127, 131

Designer: Linda M. Robertson
Compositor: Prestige Typography
Text: 10/12 Sabon
Display: Sabon

www.ingramcontent.com/pod-product-compliance
Lightning Source LLC
Chambersburg PA
CBHW031435230426
43668CB00007B/539